Cisco Networking Academy Program: Second-Year Companion Guide

Vito Amato, Ph.D.
Series Editor

CISCO SYSTEMS

CISCO PRESS

Cisco Press
201 West 103rd Street
Indianapolis, IN 46290

Cisco Networking Academy Program: Second-Year Companion Guide

Vito Amato, Ph.D., Series Editor

International Standard Book Number: 1-57870-169-4

Library of Congress Catalog Card Number: 99-61712

2002   01   00   4   3   2

Interpretation of the printing code: The rightmost double-digit number is the year of the book's printing; the rightmost single-digit, the number of the book's printing. For example, the printing code 99-1 shows that the first printing of the book occurred in 1999.

Trademark Acknowledgments

Warning and Disclaimer

Feedback Information

At Cisco Press, our goal is to create in-depth technical books of the highest quality and value. Each book is crafted with care and precision, undergoing rigorous development that involves the unique expertise of members from the professional technical community.

Readers' feedback is a natural continuation of this process. If you have any comments regarding how we could improve the quality of this book, or otherwise alter it to better suit your needs, you can contact us at ciscopress@mcp.com. Please make sure to include the book title and ISBN in your message.

We greatly appreciate your assistance.

Publisher	*John Wait*
Executive Editor	*Dave Dusthimer*
Cisco Systems Program Manager	*Jim LeValley*
Managing Editor	*Patrick Kanouse*
Development Editor	*Kitty Wilson Jarrett*
Project Editor	*Theresa Wehrle*
Technical Reviewers	*Denise Hoyt*
	Doug MacBeth
	Mark McGregor
Team Coordinator	*Amy Lewis*
Book Designer	*Gina Rexrode*
Cover Designer	*Karen Ruggles*
Production	*Steve Gifford*
	Gina Rexrode
	Argosy
Proofreader	*Sheri Replin*
Indexer	*Tim Wright*

About the Series Editor

Vito Amato is a senior technical writer at Cisco Systems for World Wide Education. Previously, he was the Information Technology Director at the Arizona Department of Education. Vito earned his Ph.D. at Arizona State University, specializing in curriculum and instruction with an emphasis on educational media and computers. In addition, Vito is currently teaching distance education theory and practice at ASU. During the last three years, Vito has been involved in the planning, writing, and implementation of the Cisco Networking Academy program. Lastly, his research, writing, and teaching focus is the integration of information technology into the teaching/learning environment.

About the Technical Reviewers

This book's technical reviewers contributed their considerable practical, hands-on expertise to the entire development process for *Cisco Networking Academy Program: Second-Year Companion Guide*. As the book was being written, these folks reviewed all the material for technical content, organization, and flow. Their feedback was critical to ensuring that *Cisco Networking Academy Program: Second-Year Companion Guide* fits our reader's need for the highest quality technical information.

Denise Hoyt has been a teacher for 16 years. She received her bachelor's degree from California State University, Chico, and her master's in administration from the University of Redlands. She received her Cisco Networking Academy Program Instructor certification in the summer of 1998. In the fall of 1998, she became the Cisco Systems Academy Regional Coordinator for San Bernardino County. She also serves as the technology coordinator and teaches the Cisco Networking Academy Program Curriculum courses at Yucaipa High School in Yucaipa, California.

Doug MacBeth is an IOS documentation manager at Cisco Systems, Inc. He has more than 15 years of experience in technical documentation and has worked for Cisco Systems, Inc., since 1993. While at Cisco, Doug has been an editor and a project leader for the Cisco IOS documentation set. Doug lives in San Jose, California, and holds a bachelor's degree in technical and business communications from San Jose State University.

Mark McGregor, CCNA, is a Cisco Networking Academy Program instructor at Los Medanos College and Antioch Adult School in Northern California. He holds a bachelor's degree in English from the University of California, Davis, and has taught in public schools for five years with a focus on at-risk youth and alternative education. In 1997, he began teaching the academy program, Novell NetWare, and UNIX to high school and adult students in Antioch, where he makes his home with his wife, Kelli.

Acknowledgments

This book would not have been possible without the vision and commitment of George Ward, Kevin Warner, Alex Belous, and David Alexander to the Cisco Networking Academy Program. Their support for the book has been tremendous, and I would like to acknowledge their support in not only making the book a reality, but also making the Cisco Networking Academy Program come alive. I would like to acknowledge Jai Gosine and Dennis Frezzo for sharing their subject matter expertise, which allowed me to organize the content of this book. Most importantly, I would like to thank my wife, Bonnie, and my kids, Tori, Michael, Matthew, and Laura, for their patience and support.

This book is a synthesis and integration of many Cisco educational publications. I would like to thank the WWE team at Cisco for its contribution, and especially Danielle Graser. Finally, I would like to thank the team at Cisco Press and the reviewers—Dave Dusthimer, Amy Lewis, Kitty Jarrett, Mark MacGregor, and Denise Hoyt—for guiding me through the publication of this book.

Overview

Table of Contents

Preface

With the full implementation of the Cisco Networking Academy Program over the past two years, Cisco has instituted an online learning system approach that integrates the multimedia delivery of a networking curriculum with testing, performance-based skills assessment, evaluation, and reporting through a Web interface. The Cisco Networking Academy Program curriculum goes beyond traditional computer-based instruction by helping students develop practical networking knowledge and skills in a hands-on environment. In a lab setting that closely corresponds to a real networking environment, students work with the architecture and infrastructure pieces of networking technology. As a result, students learn the principles and practices of networking technology.

The Cisco Networking Academy Program provides in-depth and meaningful networking content, which is being used by regional and local academies to teach students around the world by utilizing the curriculum to integrate networking instruction into the classroom. The focus of the Cisco Networking Academy Program is on the integration of a Web-based network curriculum into the learning environment. This element is addressed through intensive staff development for teachers and innovative classroom materials and approaches to instruction, which are provided by Cisco. The participating educators are provided with resources, the means of remote access to online support, and the knowledge base for the effective classroom integration of the Cisco Networking Academy Program curriculum into the classroom learning environment. As a result, the Cisco Networking Academy Program provides the means for the dynamic exchange of information by providing a suite of services that redefine the way instructional resources are disseminated, resulting in a many-to-many interactive and collaborative network of teachers and students functioning to meet diverse educational needs.

The Cisco Networking Academy Program curriculum is especially exciting to educators and students because the courseware is interactive. Because of the growing use of interactive technologies, the curriculum is an exciting new way to convey instruction with new interactive technologies that allow instructors and trainers to mix a number of media, including audio, video, text, numerical data, and graphics. Consequently, students can select different media from the computer screen and custom design their instructional content to meet their instructional needs, and educators have the option of either designing their own environment for assessment or selecting from the applicable assessments.

Finally, by developing a curriculum that recognizes the changing classroom and workforce demographics, the globalization of the economy, changing workforce knowledge and skill requirements, and the role of technology in education, the Cisco Networking Academy Program supports national educational goals for K–12 education. As support for the Cisco Network Academy Program, Cisco Press has published this book, *Cisco Networking Academy Program: Second-Year Companion Guide*, as a companion guide for the curriculum used in the Cisco Networking Academy Program.

Introduction

Cisco Networking Academy Program: Second-Year Companion Guide is designed to act as a supplement to your classroom and laboratory experience with the Cisco Networking Academy Program, whose curriculum is designed to empower you to enter employment or further education and training in the computer networking field.

The book is designed to further train you beyond the online training materials that you have already used in this program, along with the topics pertaining to the Cisco Certified Networking Associate (CCNA) exam. The book closely follows the style and format that Cisco has incorporated into the curriculum. In addition, the book follows the two-semester curriculum model that has already been developed for the Cisco Networking Academy Program. Finally, this book is complemented by a CD-ROM, which contains cross-referenced movies presented in an interactive multimedia format as learning reference materials.

This book introduces and extends your knowledge and practical experience with the design, configuration, and maintenance of switches, local-area networks (LANs), and virtual local-area networks (VLANs). The concepts covered in this book will enable you to develop practical experience in skills related to configuring LANs, wide-area networks (WANs), Novell networks, Internetwork Packet Exchange (IPX) routing, and Interior Gateway Routing Protocol (IGRP) protocols and network troubleshooting. In addition, this book extends your knowledge and practical experience with WANs, Integrated Services Data Network (ISDN), Point-to-Point Protocol (PPP), and Frame Relay design, configuration, and maintenance. Finally, the topics discussed in this book will enable you to develop practical experience in skills related to configuring WANs, ISDN, PPP, and Frame Relay protocols and network troubleshooting.

The Washington Project

Chapter 4 introduces the Washington Project. This project is designed to help you learn by allowing you to apply the knowledge that you have gained to a real-life example. The Washington Project is introduced in the first course of the curriculum. However, the actual project work is not done until Courses 3 and 4 of the curriculum, which are covered in this book. As concepts are introduced in this book, you'll learn to apply them. Each chapter contains content, concepts, and topics that will help you build the knowledge you need to complete the Washington Project.

A district in Phoenix, Arizona, is the field model for the Washington Project. You will be given architectural drawings (electronically) of the various schools in the district, along with the actual wiring drawings (also in electronic format). Your teacher will give you the completed design considerations, specifications, and technical requirements document as resources. You will be required to keep an engineering journal during the project, and you will be required to submit a final design document and make an oral presentation of your project design near the end of Course 4. Cisco Press also is publishing *Cisco Networking Academy Program: Engineering Journal and Workbook*, Volume II, which is a supplement that provides additional information to help you succeed with the Washington Project.

The Goal of This Book

The goal of this book is to educate you about Cisco-supported networking technologies and to help you understand how to design and build networks and to configure Cisco routers. It is designed for use in conjunction with the Cisco Networking Academy Program curriculum or as a standalone reference.

The Book's Audience

The book is written for anyone who wants to learn about networking technologies. The main target audience for this book is students in high schools, community colleges, and four-year institutions. Specifically, in an educational environment, this book could be used both in the classroom as a textbook companion and in computer labs as a lab manual.

The secondary target audience is corporate training faculty and staff members. In order for corporations and academic institutions to take advantage of the capabilities of networking, a large number of individuals have to be trained in the design and development of networks.

A third target audience is general users. The book's user-friendly and nontechnical approach should be appealing to readers who prefer to stay away from technical manuals.

This Book's Features

Many of this book's features help facilitate a full understanding of the networking and routing covered in this book:

- Chapter objectives—At the beginning of each chapter is a list of objectives to be mastered by the end of the chapter. In addition, the list provides a reference to the concepts covered in the chapter, which can be used as an advanced organizer.

- Figures, examples, and tables—This book contains figures, examples, and tables that help explain theories, concepts, commands, and setup sequences; they reinforce concepts and help you visualize the content covered in the chapter. In addition, examples and tables provide such things as command summaries with descriptions, examples of screen outputs, and practical and theoretical information.

■ Washington Project notes—Beginning in Chapter 4, each chapter includes Washington Project notes. These notes relate to the concepts introduced in the chapter and provide information that will help you apply the knowledge that you have gained to the Washington Project.

■ Engineering Journal notes—Starting in Chapter 4, each chapter includes engineering notes. These notes relate to the concepts introduced in the chapter and provide supplemental information above and beyond what you learn in the course that will help you apply what you're learning to real-world situations.

■ Chapter summaries—At the end of each chapter is a summary of the concepts covered in the chapter; it provides a synopsis of the chapter and serves as a study aid.

■ Washington School District Project task—Starting in Chapter 4, each chapter includes a School District project task. This task reinforces the concepts introduced in the chapter by allowing you to apply the knowledge that you have gained to the Washington Project.

■ Chapter review—The end of each chapter presents 10 review questions that serve as an end-of-chapter assessment. In addition, the questions reinforce the concepts introduced in the chapter and help you test your understanding before you move on to new concepts.

■ Key terms—After the review questions are key terms that provide a summary of the new terms covered in the chapter and that serve as a study aid. In addition, the key terms reinforce the concepts introduced in the chapter and help your understanding of the chapter material before you move on to new concepts. You can find the key terms highlighted in blue throughout the chapter where they are used in practice.

Conventions Used in This Book

In this book, the following conventions are used:

■ Important or new terms are *italicized*.

■ Key terms, defined at the end of each chapter and in the Glossary, appear in blue.

■ All code examples appear in monospace type, and parts of code use the following conventions:

— Commands and keywords are in **monospaced bold** type.

— Arguments, which are placeholders for values the user inputs, appear in *monospaced italics*.

— Square brackets ([ ]) indicate optional keywords or arguments.

— Braces ({ }) indicate required choices.

— Vertical bars (|) are used to separate required choices.

This Book's Organization

This book is divided into 12 chapters, 3 appendixes, and a Glossary.

Chapter 1 presents a review of the Open System Interconnection (OSI) reference model and an overview of network planning and design considerations related to routing.

Chapter 2 discusses problems in LANs and possible solutions that can improve LAN performance. In addition, this chapter covers the advantages and disadvantages of using bridges, switches, and routers for LAN segmentation and the effects of switching, bridging, and routing on network throughput. Finally, this chapter presents Ethernet, Fast Ethernet, and VLANs and the benefits of these technologies.

Chapter 3 provides an overview of VLANs and switched internetworking, compares traditional shared LAN configurations with switched LAN configurations, and discusses the benefits of using a switched VLAN architecture.

Chapter 4 presents an overview of the LAN design process. In addition, the chapter discusses LAN design goals, network design issues, network design methodology, and the development of LAN topologies.

Chapter 5 discusses how routers can be used to connect two or more networks and how they are used to pass data packets between networks based on network protocol information. This chapter presents how routers operate and what kinds of protocols they use. Finally, this chapter covers routing and IP routing protocols and discusses Cisco's proprietary protocol IGRP.

Chapter 6 presents standard and extended access control lists (ACLs), which you use to control network traffic, and describes how ACLs are used as part of a security solution. In addition, this chapter includes tips, considerations, recommendations, and general guidelines for how to use ACLs, and includes the commands and configurations needed to create ACLs. Finally, this chapter provides examples of standard and extended ACLs and how to apply ACLs to router interfaces.

Chapter 7 covers Novell's IPX protocols, operation, and configuration. In addition, this chapter explains how Cisco routers are used in NetWare networks and discusses how to verify IPX operation and connectivity between routers, along with troubleshooting in IPX operations.

Chapter 8 presents the various protocols and technologies used in WAN environments. This chapter describes the basics of WANs, including common WAN technologies, types of wide-area services, encapsulation formats, and link options. Finally, this chapter discusses point-to-point links, circuit switching, packet switching, virtual circuits, dialup services, and WAN devices.

Chapter 9 provides an overview of the methodologies used to design WANs. It includes a description of WAN communication and the process and considerations for designing a WAN. It all covers the process for gathering user requirements for WAN design, as well as the benefits of using a hierarchical design model.

Chapter 10 discusses the basic components, processes, and operations that define PPP communication. Additionally, this chapter describes how to configure and verify the configuration of PPP along with PPP authentication.

Chapter 11 presents the services, standards, components, operation, and configuration of ISDN communication.

Chapter 12 discusses Frame Relay services, standards, components, and operation. In addition, this chapter covers the configuration tasks for Frame Relay service, along with the commands for monitoring and maintaining a Frame Relay connection.

Appendix A provides the answers to the chapter review questions you'll find at the end of each chapter.

Appendix B describes and defines the commands related to configuring and using Cisco routers that are used throughout this book. It is arranged alphabetically so that you can easily find information on a given command, and each command is also cross-referenced to the chapters where it is used so you can easily find more information.

Appendix C contains cross-referenced information about each of the movies contained on the CD-ROM.

The Glossary defines the terms and abbreviations related to networking used in this book.

Objectives

After reading this chapter, you will be able to

- Describe the overall function of the OSI reference model and the problems it solves
- Describe the characteristics of the physical layer of the OSI reference model
- Describe the characteristics of the data link layer of the OSI reference model
- Describe the characteristics of the network layer of the OSI reference model
- Describe the characteristics of the transport layer of the OSI reference model
- Describe the function of routing in networks
- Understand the different classes of routing protocols

Chapter 1

Review: The OSI Reference Model and Routing

Introduction

Networks are complex environments involving multiple media, multiple protocols, and interconnections to networks outside an organization's central office. Well-designed and carefully installed networks can reduce the problems associated with growth as a networking environment evolves.

Designing, building, and maintaining a network can be a challenging task. Even a small network that consists of only 50 routing nodes can pose complex problems that lead to unpredictable results. Large networks that feature thousands of nodes can pose even more complex problems. Despite improvements in equipment performance and media capabilities, designing and building a network is difficult.

This chapter provides a review of the Open System Interconnection (OSI) reference model and an overview of network planning and design considerations related to routing. Using the OSI reference model as a reference for network design can facilitate changes. Using the OSI reference model as a hierarchical structure for network design allows you to design networks in layers. The OSI reference model is at the heart of building and designing networks, with every layer performing a specific task to promote data communications. In the world of networking, Layer 1 through Layer 4 are the focus. These four layers define the following:

- The type and speed of LAN and WAN media to be implemented
- How data is sent across the media
- The type of addressing schemes used
- How data will be reliably sent across the network and how flow control will be accomplished
- The type of routing protocol implemented

The Layered Network Model: The OSI Reference Model

Network models use layers to simplify the networking functions. The separation of networking functions is called layering. To understand the importance of layering, let's consider the OSI reference model, a layered model for understanding and implementing computer communications. By using layers, the OSI reference model simplifies the tasks required for two computers to communicate with each other. Each layer can be focused on specific functions, thereby allowing the networking designer to choose the right networking devices and functions for the layer. In the OSI reference model, seven numbered layers indicate distinct functions.

The reasons for this division of network functions include the following:

- Layers divide the aspects of network operation into less complex elements.
- Layers define standard interfaces for plug-and-play compatibility.
- Layers enable engineers to specialize design and development efforts on modular functions.
- Layers promote symmetry in the different network modular functions so that they work together.
- Layers prevent changes in one area from affecting other areas, so each area can evolve more quickly.
- Layers divide the complexity of networking into separate, more easily learned operations.

As shown in Figure 1-1, each layer of the OSI reference model serves a specific function:

- Application layer (Layer 7)—This layer provides network services to user applications. For example, a word processing application is serviced by file transfer services at this layer.
- Presentation layer (Layer 6)—This layer provides data representation and code formatting, along with the negotiation of data transfer syntax. It ensures that the data that arrive from the network can be used by the application, and it ensures that information sent by the application can be transmitted on the network.
- Session layer (Layer 5)—This layer establishes, maintains, and manages sessions between applications.
- Transport layer (Layer 4)—This layer segments and reassembles data into a data stream. The transport layer has the potential to guarantee a connection and offer reliable transport.
- Network layer (Layer 3)—This layer determines the best way to move data from one place to another. The router operates at this layer. This layer uses logical addressing schemes that can be managed by an administrator. This layer uses the Internet Protocol (IP) addressing scheme, along with Apple-Talk, DECnet, VINES, and IPX addressing schemes.

- Data link layer (Layer 2)—This layer provides physical transmission across the medium. It handles error notification, network topology, and flow control. This layer uses Media Access Control (MAC) addresses, which also are referred to as physical or hardware addresses.

- Physical layer (Layer 1)—This layer provides the electrical, mechanical, procedural, and functional means for activating and maintaining the physical link between systems. This layer uses such physical media as twisted-pair, coaxial, and fiber-optic cable.

FIGURE 1-1
The OSI reference model defines layer functions that can be used by any network products vendor to help guide the design and development of network products.

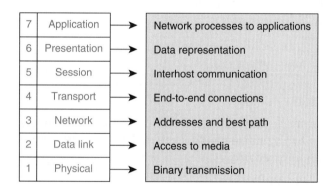

Peer-to-Peer Communication

The OSI reference model describes how information makes its way from application programs (such as spreadsheets) through a network medium (such as wires) to another application program in another computer. As the information to be sent descends through the layers of a given system, it looks less and less like a human language and more and more like the ones and zeros that a computer understands.

Each layer uses its own layer protocol to communicate with its peer layer in the other system. Each layer's protocol exchanges information, called protocol data units (PDUs), between peer layers.

Figure 1-2 shows an example of OSI-type communication. Host A has information to send to Host B. The application program in Host A communicates with Host A's application layer, which communicates with Host A's presentation layer, which communicates with Host A's session layer, and so on, until Host A's physical layer is reached. The physical layer puts information on (and takes information off) the physical network medium. After the information traverses the physical network medium and is absorbed into Host B, it ascends through Host B's layers in reverse order (first the physical layer, then the data link layer, and so on) until it finally reaches Host B's application layer.

FIGURE 1-2
In host-to-host peer-layer protocol communication, the layer below the current layer provides services to the current layer.

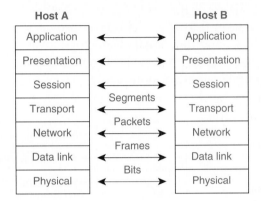

Although each Host A layer communicates with its adjacent layers, each layer in a host has a primary task it must perform. The primary task of each layer is to communicate with its peer layer in Host B. That is, the task of Layer 1 in Host A is to communicate with Layer 1 in Host B; Layer 2 in Host A communicates with Layer 2 in Host B; and so on.

The OSI reference model's layering prohibits direct communication between peer layers in different hosts. Each layer in Host A must therefore rely on services provided by adjacent Host A layers to help achieve communication with its Host B peer. Assume that Layer 4 in Host A must communicate with Layer 4 in Host B. To do this, Layer 4 in Host A must use the services of Layer 3 in Host A. Layer 4 is said to be the *service user,* and Layer 3 is the *service provider.* Layer 3 services are provided to Layer 4 at a service access point (SAP), which is a location at which Layer 4 can request Layer 3 services.

Thus, as shown in Figure 1-2, the TCP segments become part of the network-layer packets (also called datagrams) exchanged between IP peers. In turn, the IP packets must become part of the data-link frames exchanged between directly connected devices. Ultimately, these frames must become bits as the data is finally transmitted by the physical-layer protocol using hardware.

Data Encapsulation

How does Layer 4 in Host B know what Layer 4 in Host A wants? Layer 4's specific requests are stored as control information, which is passed between peer layers in a header block that is attached to the actual application information. Each layer depends on the service function of the OSI reference model layer below it. To provide this service, the lower layer uses encapsulation to put the PDU from the upper layer into its data field; then, it can add whatever headers and trailers the layer will use to perform its function.

The concept of a header and data is relative, depending on the layer currently analyzing the information unit. For example, to Layer 3, an information unit consists of a Layer 3 header and the data that follows. Layer 3's data, however, can potentially contain headers from Layers 4, 5, 6, and 7. Further, Layer 3's header is simply data to Layer 2. This concept is illustrated in Figure 1-3. Finally, not all layers need to append headers. Some layers simply perform a transformation on the actual data they receive to make the data readable to their adjacent layers.

FIGURE 1-3
The network layer has the task of moving data through the network by encapsulating the data within a header.

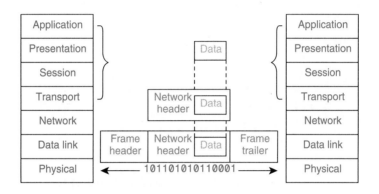

For example, the network layer provides a service to the transport layer, and the transport layer presents data to the network: It accomplishes this task by encapsulating the data within a header. This header contains information required to complete the transfer, such as source and destination logical addresses. The data link layer, in turn, provides a service to the network layer: It encapsulates the network-layer information in a frame. The frame header contains information required to complete the data-link functions. For example, the frame header contains physical addresses. The physical layer also provides a service to the data link layer: It encodes the data-link frame into a pattern of ones and zeros for transmission on the medium (usually a wire).

For example, let's assume that Host A wants to send the following e-mail to Host B:

```
The small gray cat ran up the wall to try to catch the red bird.
```

Five conversion steps occur during data encapsulation, which enables the transmission of the e-mail to the appropriate destination:

Step 1   As a user sends an e-mail message, its alphanumeric characters are converted to data, starting at Layer 7 down through Layer 5, and are sent over the network.

Step 2   By using segments at Layer 4, the transport function packages data for the network transport and ensures that the message hosts at both ends of the e-mail system can reliably communicate.

Step 3   The data is placed into a packet (or datagram) at Layer 3 that contains a network header with source and destination logical addresses. Then, the network devices send the packets across the network along a chosen path.

Step 4   Each network device must put the packet into a frame at Layer 2. The frame allows connection to the next directly connected network device on the link. Each device in the chosen network path requires framing to connect to the next device.

Step 5   The frame must be converted into a pattern of ones and zeros for transmission on the medium (usually a wire) at Layer 1. A clocking function enables the devices to distinguish these bits as they traverse the medium. The medium on the physical network can vary along the path used. For example, the e-mail message can originate on a LAN, cross a campus backbone, and go out a WAN link until it reaches its destination on another remote LAN.

The Physical Layer

Together, Ethernet and IEEE 802.3 currently maintain the share of any local-area network (LAN) protocol. Today, the term *Ethernet* is often used to refer to all carrier sense multiple access collision detect (CSMA/CD) LANs that generally conform to Ethernet specifications, including IEEE 802.3.

When it was developed, Ethernet was designed to fill the middle ground between long-distance, low-speed networks and specialized, computer-room networks carrying data at high speeds for very limited distances. Ethernet is good for applications where a local communication medium must carry sporadic, occasionally heavy traffic at high-peak data rates.

The term *Ethernet* refers to the family of LAN implementations that includes three principal categories:

■ Ethernet and IEEE 802.3—LAN specifications that operate at 10 Mbps over coaxial cable.

■ 100-Mbps Ethernet—A single LAN specification, also known as *Fast Ethernet*, that operates at 100 Mbps over twisted-pair cable.

■ 1000-Mbps Ethernet—A single LAN specification, also known as *Gigabit Ethernet*, that operates at 1000 Mbps (1 Gbps) over fiber and twisted-pair cables.

Ethernet has survived as an essential media technology because of its tremendous flexibility and because it is simple to implement and understand. Although other technologies have been promoted as likely replacements, network managers have turned to Ethernet and its derivatives as effective solutions for a range of campus implementation requirements. To resolve Ethernet's limitations, creative users (and standards bodies) have created bigger and bigger Ethernet pipes. Critics might dismiss Ethernet as a technology that cannot grow, but its underlying transmission scheme continues to be one of the principal means of transporting data for contemporary campus applications.

Ethernet/802.3 Physical Connections

The Ethernet and IEEE 802.3 wiring standards define a bus topology LAN that operates at 10 Mbps.

Figure 1-4 illustrates the three defined wiring standards:

■ 10Base2—Known as *thin Ethernet*, 10Base2 allows network segments up to 185 meters on coaxial cable.

■ 10Base5—Known as *thick Ethernet*, 10Base5 allows network segments up to 500 meters on coaxial cable.

■ 10BaseT—10BaseT carries Ethernet frames on inexpensive twisted-pair wiring.

Ethernet and IEEE 802.3 wiring standards specify a bus topology network with a connecting cable between the end stations and the actual network medium. In the case of Ethernet, that cable is called a *transceiver cable*. The transceiver cable connects to a transceiver device attached to the physical network medium. The IEEE 802.3 configuration is much the same, except that the connecting cable is referred to as an attachment unit interface (AUI), and the transceiver is called a media attachment unit (MAU). In both cases, the connecting cable attaches to an interface board (or interface circuitry) within the end station.

Stations are attached to the segment by a cable that runs from an AUI in the station to an MAU that is directly attached to the Ethernet coaxial cable. Because the 10BaseT standard provides access for a single station only, stations attached to an Ethernet LAN by 10BaseT are almost always connected to a hub or a LAN switch.

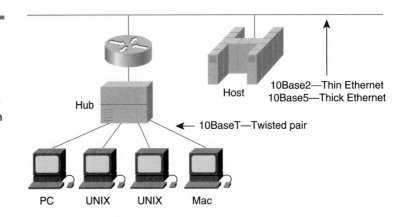

FIGURE 1-4
The 10Base2, 10Base5, and 10BaseT standards provide access for several stations on the same LAN segment.

The Data Link Layer

Access to the networking media occurs at the data link layer of the OSI reference model. The data link layer, Layer 2, where the MAC address is located, is adjacent to the physical layer. No two MAC addresses are ever alike. Thus, on a network, the network interface card (NIC) is where a device connects to the medium, and each NIC has a unique MAC address.

Before each NIC leaves the factory, the hardware manufacturer assigns it a MAC address. This address is programmed into a chip on the NIC. Because the MAC address is located on the NIC, if a computer's NIC is replaced, the physical address of the station changes to that of the new NIC's MAC address.

MAC addresses are written using base 16 (hexadecimal) numbers. There are two formats for MAC addresses: 0000.0c12.3456 and 00-00-0c-12-34-56.

Imagine that you operate a motel. Room 207 has a lock called Lock A. Key A will open the door to Room 207. Room 410 has a lock called Lock F. Key F will open the door to Room 410.

You decide to swap the locks on Rooms 207 and 410. After you switch the two locks, Key A opens the door of Room 410, and Key F opens the door to Room 207.

In this analogy, the locks are like NICs. When the NICs are swapped, the matching keys also must be changed. In this analogy, the keys are like the MAC addresses.

On an Ethernet network, when one device wants to send data to another device, it can open a communication pathway to the other device by using its MAC address. When data is sent out on a network by a source, it carries the MAC address of its intended destination. As this data travels along the network media, the NIC in each device on the network checks to see if its MAC address matches the physical destination address carried by the data packet. If no match is made, the NIC ignores the data packet, and the data packet continues along the network to the next station.

However, when a match is made, the NIC makes a copy of the data packet, which it places in the computer where it resides at the data link layer. Even though this copy has been made by the NIC and placed on the computer, the original data packet continues along the network, where other NICs will be able to look at it to determine whether a match can be made.

The Ethernet/802.3 Interface

The Ethernet and 802.3 data links provide data transport across the physical link joining two devices. For example, as Figure 1-5 shows, the three devices can be directly attached to each other over the Ethernet LAN. The Apple Macintosh on the left and the Intel-based PC in the middle show MAC addresses used by the data link layer. The router on the right also uses MAC addresses for each of its LAN-side interfaces.

FIGURE 1-5
To indicate the 802.3 interface on a router, you use the Cisco Internetwork Operating System (IOS) interface type abbreviation E, followed by an interface number (for example, 0).

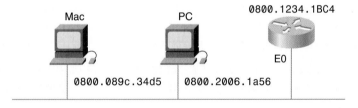

The Network Layer

Several protocols operate at the OSI reference model network layer:

- IP provides connectionless, best-effort delivery routing of datagrams. It is not concerned with the content of the datagrams; instead, it looks for a way to move the datagrams to their destinations.
- Internet Control Message Protocol (ICMP) provides control and messaging capabilities.
- Address Resolution Protocol (ARP) determines the data link layer addresses for known IP addresses.
- Reverse ARP (RARP) determines network addresses when data link layer addresses are known.

IP Addressing and Subnets

In a TCP/IP environment, end stations communicate with servers, hosts, or other end stations. This occurs because each node using the TCP/IP protocol suite has a unique 32-bit logical address, known as the IP address. In addition, within a TCP/IP environment, each network is seen as a single unique address. That address must be reached before an individual host within that network can be contacted. Each network has an address; the hosts that live on that network share that same network address, but each host has a unique address as well (see Figure 1-6).

FIGURE 1-6
Each network has an address and each host is identified by a unique address on that network.

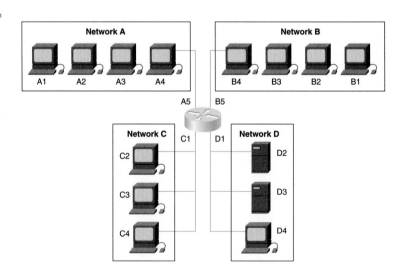

Networks can be segmented into a series of smaller networks called subnetworks. Thus, an IP address is broken up into the network number, the subnetwork number, and the host number. Subnets use unique 32-bit subnet addresses that are created by borrowing bits from the host field. Subnet addresses are visible to other devices on the same network, but they are not visible to outside networks. Subnetworks are not visible to outside networks because they use subnet masks.

With subnets, network address use is more efficient. There is no change to how the outside world sees the network, but within the organization, there is additional structure. In Figure 1-7, network 172.16.0.0 is subdivided into four subnets: 172.16.1.0, 172.16.2.0, 172.16.3.0, and 172.16.4.0.

FIGURE 1-7
Routers determine the destination network by using the subnet address, limiting the amount of traffic on the other network segments.

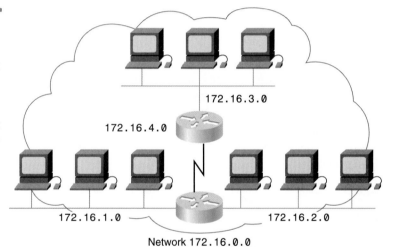

Path Determination

Path determination is the path traffic should take through the network cloud. As shown in Figure 1-8, routers evaluate the best path for traffic. Path determination occurs at Layer 3, the network layer. Routing services use network topology information when evaluating network paths. This information can be configured by the network administrator or collected through dynamic processes running in the network.

The network layer connects to networks and provides best-effort end-to-end packet delivery services to its user, the transport layer. The network layer sends packets from the source network to the destination network based on the IP routing table. After the router determines which path to use, it can proceed with switching the packet: taking the packet it accepted on one interface and forwarding it to another interface or port that reflects the best path to the packet's destination.

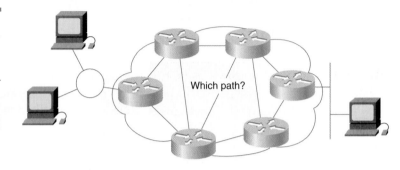

FIGURE 1-8
The path determination function enables a router to evaluate the available paths to a destination and to establish the preferred handling of a packet.

Which path?

Path Communication

For path communication to be truly practical, a network must consistently represent the paths available between routers. As Figure 1-9 shows, each line between the routers has a number that the routers use as a network address. These addresses must convey information that can be used by a routing process.

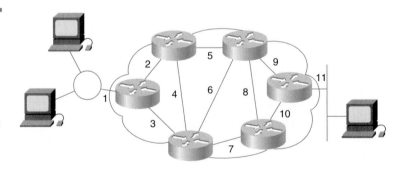

FIGURE 1-9
An address must have information about the path of media connections that are used by the routing process to pass packets from a source toward a destination.

The network address contains a path part and a host part. The path part identifies a path part used by the router within the network cloud; the host part identifies a specific port or device on the network. The router uses the network address to identify the source or destination network of a packet within a network. Figure 1-10 shows three network numbers coming from the router and three hosts sharing the network number 1. For some network-layer protocols, a network administrator establishes this relationship by assigning network addresses ahead of time according to a network-addressing plan. For other network-layer protocols, assigning addresses is partially or completely dynamic.

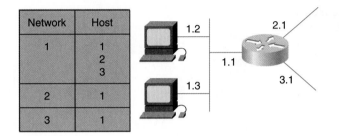

FIGURE 1-10
Most network-protocol addressing schemes use some form of a host or node address.

The consistency of Layer 3 addresses across the entire network also improves the use of bandwidth by preventing unnecessary broadcasts. Broadcasts cause unnecessary traffic and waste capacity on any devices or links that do not need to receive the broadcasts. By using consistent end-to-end addressing to represent the path of media connections, the network layer can find a path to the destination without unnecessary use of devices or links on the network.

ICMP

ICMP messages are carried in IP datagrams and are used to send error and control messages. ICMP uses the following types of defined messages; others exist, but are not included on this list:

- Destination unreachable
- Time exceeded
- Parameter problem
- Source quench
- Redirect
- Echo
- Echo reply
- Timestamp
- Timestamp reply
- Information request
- Information reply

- Address request
- Address reply

For example, Figure 1-11 shows a router receiving a packet that it is unable to deliver to its ultimate destination; the router sends an ICMP host unreachable message to the source. The message might be undeliverable because there is no known route to the destination. On the other hand, Figure 1-12 shows an echo reply that is a successful reply to a `ping` command.

FIGURE 1-11
The router issues a destination unreachable message, indicating that the host, the port, or the network is unreachable.

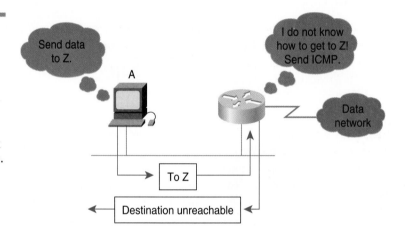

FIGURE 1-12
Results of a `ping` command also could include other ICMP messages, such as unreachable and timeout messages.

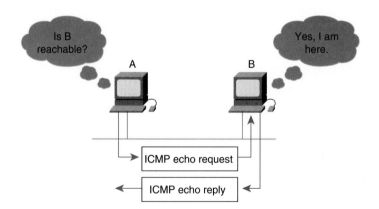

ARP

To communicate on an Ethernet network, the source station must know the destination station's IP and MAC addresses. When the source has determined the IP address for the destination, the source's Internet protocol looks into its ARP table to locate the MAC address for the destination. If the Internet protocol locates a mapping of destination IP address to destination MAC address in its table, it binds the IP address with the MAC address and uses them to encapsulate the data. The data packet is then sent out over the networking media to be picked up by the destination.

If the MAC address is not known, the source must send out an ARP request. To determine a destination address for a datagram, the ARP table on the router is checked. If the address is not in the table, ARP sends a broadcast looking for the destination station. Every station on the network receives the broadcast.

The term *local ARP* is used when both the requesting host and the destination host share the same medium, or wire. In the example in Figure 1-14, prior to issuing the ARP, the subnet mask was consulted. The mask determined that the nodes are on the same subnet.

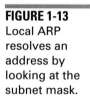

FIGURE 1-13
Local ARP resolves an address by looking at the subnet mask.

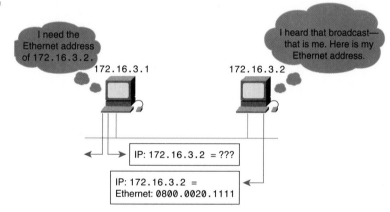

Routing

The network layer must relate to and interface with various lower layers. Routers must be capable of seamlessly handling packets encapsulated into different lower-level frames without changing the packets' Layer 3 addressing. Figure 1-14 shows an example of this with LAN-to-LAN routing. In this example, packet traffic from Host 4 on Ethernet Network 1 needs a path to Host 5 on Network 2.

When the router checks its routing table entries, it discovers that the best path to Network 2 uses outgoing Port To0, the interface to a Token Ring LAN. Although the lower-layer framing must change as the router switches packet traffic from the Ethernet on Network 1 to the Token Ring on Network 2, the Layer 3 addressing for source and destination remains the same. In

Figure 1-14, the destination address remains Network 2, Host 5, despite the different lower-layer encapsulations.

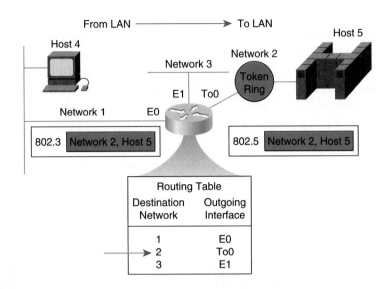

FIGURE 1-14
The LAN hosts depend on the router and its consistent network addressing to find the best path.

Router Operations

Routers generally relay a packet from one data link to another. To relay a packet, a router uses two basic functions: a path determination function and a switching function. Figure 1-15 illustrates how routers use addressing for routing and switching functions.

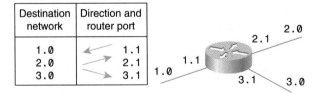

FIGURE 1-15
A router passes the packet to the next network along the path and uses the network portion of the address to make path selections.

The switching function allows a router to accept a packet on one interface and forward it on a second interface. The path determination function enables the router to select the most appropriate interface for forwarding a packet. The node portion of the address refers to a specific port on the router that leads to an adjacent router in that direction.

When a host application needs to send a packet to a destination on a different network, a data-link frame is received on one of a router's interfaces. The network-layer process examines the header to determine the destination network and then references the routing table that associates networks to outgoing interfaces. The original frame is stripped off and discarded. The packet is again encapsulated in the data-link frame for the selected interface and in a queue for delivery to the next hop in the path.

This process occurs each time the packet switches through another router. At the router connected to the network containing the destination host, the packet is again encapsulated in the destination LAN's data-link frame type and delivered to the destination host.

Static Versus Dynamic Routes

Static routing is administered manually: A network administrator enters it into the router's configuration. The administrator must manually update this static route entry whenever a network topology change requires an update. Static routing reduces overhead because routing updates are not sent (in the case of RIP, every 30 seconds).

Dynamic routing works differently. After the network administrator enters configuration commands to start dynamic routing, route knowledge is updated automatically by a routing process whenever new information is received from the network. Changes in dynamic knowledge are exchanged between routers as part of the update process.

Static routing has several useful applications. It allows a network administrator to specify what is advertised about restricted partitions. For security reasons, the administrator can hide parts of a network. Dynamic routing tends to reveal everything known about a network.

Additionally, when a network is accessible by only one path, a static route to the network can be sufficient. This type of partition is called a stub network. Configuring static routing to a stub network avoids the overhead of dynamic routing because routing updates are not sent.

A Default Route Example

Figure 1-16 shows a use for a default route—a routing table entry that is used to direct frames for which the next hop is not explicitly listed in the routing table. In this example, Company X routers possess specific knowledge of the topology of the Company X network, but not of other networks. Maintaining knowledge of every other network accessible by way of the Internet cloud is unnecessary and unreasonable, if not impossible.

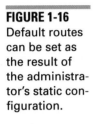

FIGURE 1-16
Default routes can be set as the result of the administrator's static configuration.

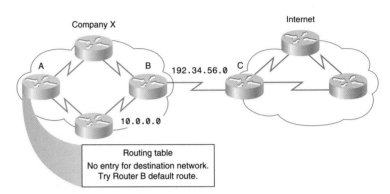

Instead of maintaining specific network knowledge, each router in Company X is informed by the default route that it can reach any unknown destination by directing the packet to the Internet.

Routed Versus Routing Protocols

Confusion often exists between the similar terms routed protocol and routing protocol:

- Routed protocol—Any network protocol that provides enough information in its network-layer address to allow a packet to be forwarded from host to host based on the addressing scheme. Routed protocols define the format and use of the fields within a packet. Packets generally are conveyed from end system to end system. IP is an example of a routed protocol.

- Routing protocol—A protocol that supports a routed protocol by providing mechanisms for sharing routing information. Routing protocol messages move between the routers. A routing protocol allows the routers to communicate with other routers to update and maintain tables. TCP/IP examples of routing protocols are Routing Information Protocol (RIP), Interior Gateway Routing Protocol (IGRP), Enhanced Interior Gateway Routing Protocol (Enhanced IGRP), and Open Shortest Path First (OSPF) protocol.

Routing Protocols

The success of dynamic routing depends on two basic router functions:

- Maintenance of a routing table
- Timely distribution of knowledge—in the form of routing updates—to other routers

Dynamic routing relies on a routing protocol to share knowledge. A routing protocol defines the set of rules used by a router when it communicates with neighboring routers. For example, a routing protocol describes

- How updates are sent
- What knowledge is contained in these updates
- When to send this knowledge
- How to locate recipients of the updates

Exterior routing protocols are used to communicate between autonomous systems. Interior routing protocols are used within a single autonomous system.

IP Routing Protocols

At the network layer (Layer 3) of the OSI reference model, a router can use IP routing protocols to accomplish routing through the implementation of a specific routing protocol. Examples of IP routing protocols include

- RIP—A distance-vector routing protocol
- IGRP—Cisco's distance-vector routing protocol
- OSPF—A link-state routing protocol
- EIGRP—A balanced-hybrid routing protocol

Classes of Routing Protocols

Most routing protocols can be classified as one of two basic types: distance vector or link state. The distance-vector routing protocol determines the direction (vector) and distance to any link in the network. The link-state routing protocol (also called the shortest path first [SPF] protocol) approach re-creates the exact topology of the entire network (or at least the partition in which the router is situated). A third type of protocol, the balanced-hybrid protocol, combines aspects of the link-state and distance-vector protocols.

Convergence

Routing protocols, which are used to determine the best route for traffic from a particular source to a particular destination, are fundamental to dynamic routing. Whenever the topology of the network changes because of growth, reconfiguration, or failure, the network knowledge base also must change. The knowledge needs to reflect an accurate, consistent view of the new topology. This accurate, consistent view is called convergence.

When all routers in a network are operating with the same knowledge, the network is said to have converged. Fast convergence is a desirable network feature because it reduces the period of time that routers have outdated knowledge for making routing decisions that could be incorrect, wasteful, or both.

Distance-Vector Routing

Distance-vector routing protocols pass periodic copies of a routing table from router to router. Each router receives a routing table from its direct neighbor. (See Figure 1-17.) For example, Router B receives information from Router A. Router B adds a distance-vector number (such as a number of hops), increases the distance vector, and then passes the routing table to its other neighbor, Router C. This same step-by-step process occurs in all directions between direct-neighbor routers.

FIGURE 1-17
Regular updates between routers communicate topology changes.

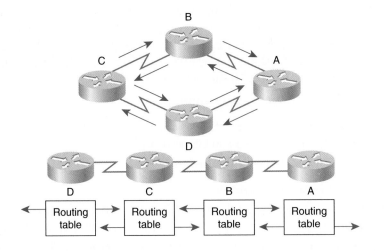

In this way, the protocol accumulates network distances so it can maintain a database of network topology information. Distance-vector protocols do not allow a router to know the exact topology of a network.

Link-State Routing

The second basic protocol used for routing is the link-state protocol. Link-state routing protocols maintain a complex database of topology information. Whereas the distance-vector protocol has nonspecific information about distant networks and no knowledge of distant routers, a link-state routing protocol maintains full knowledge of distant routers and how they interconnect.

Link-state routing uses link-state advertisements (LSAs), a topological database, the SPF protocol, the resulting SPF tree, and finally, a routing table of paths and ports to each network. Engineers have implemented this link-state concept in OSPF routing.

Distance-Vector Routing Versus Link-State Routing

You can compare distance-vector routing to link-state routing in several key areas:

- Distance-vector routing gets all topological data from the routing table information of its neighbors. Link-state routing obtains a wide view of the entire network topology by accumulating all necessary LSAs.

- Distance-vector routing determines the best path by adding to the metric value it receives as tables move from router to router. For link-state routing, each router works separately to calculate its own shortest path to destinations.

- With most distance-vector routing protocols, updates for topology changes come in periodic table updates. These tables pass from router to router, often resulting in slower convergence. With link-state routing protocols, updates usually are triggered by topology changes. Relatively small LSAs passed to all other routers usually result in faster time to converge on any network topology change.

IP Routing Configuration Tasks

The selection of IP as a routing protocol involves the setting of global parameters. Global parameters include selecting a routing protocol, such as RIP or IGRP, and assigning IP network numbers without specifying subnet values.

IP Address Configuration

You use the `ip address` command to establish the logical network address of the interface. You use the `term ip netmask-format` command to specify the format of network masks for the current session. Format options are bit count, dotted-decimal (the default), and hexadecimal.

Dynamic Routing Configuration

Dynamic routing occurs when routers send periodic routing update messages to each other. Each time such a message is received and it contains new information, the router recalculates the new best route and sends new update information to other routers. By using routing commands, routers can adjust to changing network conditions.

The following router commands start routing processes:

Router Command	Description
`protocol`	Defines an IP routing protocol, which can be either RIP, IGRP, OSPF, or EIGRP.
`network`	The `network` subcommand is a mandatory configuration command for each routing process.

The following `network` command is required because it allows the routing process to determine which interfaces will participate in the sending and receiving of routing updates:

network Command	Description
`network` *network-number*	Specifies a directly connected network.

RIP

Key characteristics of RIP include the following:

- It is a distance-vector routing protocol.
- Hop count is used as the metric for path selection.
- The maximum allowable hop count is 15.
- Routing updates are broadcast every 30 seconds by default.

The `router rip` command selects RIP as the routing protocol. The `network` command assigns a NIC-based address to which the router is directly connected. The routing process associates interfaces with the proper addresses and begins packet processing on the specified networks (see Figure 1-18).

- `router rip`—Selects RIP as the routing protocol.
- `network 1.0.0.0`—Specifies a directly connected network.
- `network 2.0.0.0`—Specifies a directly connected network.

The Cisco A router interfaces connected to networks 1.0.0.0 and 2.0.0.0 will send and receive RIP updates.

The Transport Layer

As the transport layer sends its data segments, it can ensure the integrity of the data. One method of doing this is called flow control. Flow control avoids the problem of a host at one side of the connection overflowing the buffers in the host at the other side. Overflows can present serious problems because they can result in the loss of data.

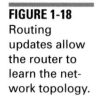

FIGURE 1-18
Routing updates allow the router to learn the network topology.

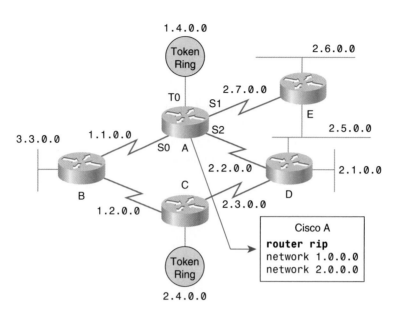

Transport-layer services also allow users to request reliable data transport between hosts and destinations. To obtain such reliable transport of data, a connection-oriented relationship is used between the communicating end systems. Reliable transport can accomplish the following:

- Segment upper-layer applications
- Establish a connection
- Transfer date
- Provide reliability with windowing
- Use acknowledgment techniques

Segmenting Upper-Layer Applications

One reason for using a layered network model is so that several applications can share the same transport connection. Transport functionality is accomplished segment by segment. This means that different applications can send data segments on a first-come, first-served basis. Such segments can be intended for the same destination or for many different destinations.

Establishing a Connection

To establish a connection, one machine places a call that must be accepted by the other. Protocol software modules in the two operating systems communicate by sending messages across the network to verify that the transfer is authorized and that both sides are ready. After all synchronization has occurred, a connection is established, and the transfer of data begins. During transfer, the two machines continue to communicate with their protocol software to verify that data is received correctly.

Figure 1-19 depicts a typical connection between sending and receiving systems. When you first meet someone, you often greet the person by shaking his or her hand. The act of shaking hands is understood by both parties as a signal for a friendly greeting. We speak of connections on the network in the same way. The first handshake, or greeting, requests synchronization. The second and third handshakes acknowledge the initial synchronization request, as well as synchronize connection parameters in the opposite direction. The final handshake segment is an acknowledgment used to inform the destination that both sides agree that a connection has been established. After the connection has been established, data transfer begins.

FIGURE 1-19
For data transfer to begin, both the sending and receiving application programs must inform their respective operating systems that a connection will be initiated.

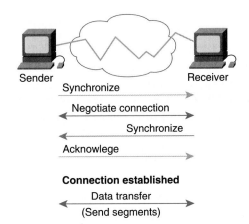

Data Transfer

When data transfer is in progress, congestion can arise for two different reasons. First, a high-speed computer might be able to generate traffic faster than a network can transfer it. Second, if many computers simultaneously need to send datagrams to a single destination, that destination can experience congestion, even though no single source caused the problem.

When datagrams arrive too quickly for a host or gateway to process, they are temporarily stored in memory. If the traffic continues, the host or gateway eventually exhausts its memory and must discard additional datagrams that arrive. Therefore, as shown in Figure 1-20, an indicator acts like a stoplight and signals the sender to stop sending data. When the receiver can handle additional data, the receiver sends a "ready" transport indicator, which is like a "go" signal. When it receives this indicator, the sender can resume segment transmission.

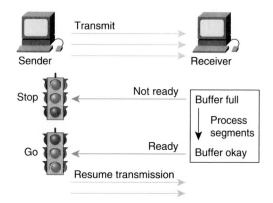

FIGURE 1-20
Instead of allowing data to be lost, the transport function can issue a "not ready" indicator to the sender.

Reliability with Windowing

In the most basic form of reliable connection-oriented data transfer, data packets must be delivered to the recipient in the same order in which they were transmitted. The protocol fails if any data packets are lost, damaged, duplicated, or received in a different order. The basic solution is to have a recipient acknowledge the receipt of every data segment.

If the sender has to wait for an acknowledgment after sending each segment, throughput is low. Because time is available after the sender finishes transmitting the data packet and before the sender finishes processing any received acknowledgment, the interval is used for transmitting more data. The number of data packets the sender is allowed to have outstanding—without yet receiving an acknowledgment—is known as the window.

Windowing is a method to control the amount of information transferred end-to-end. Some protocols measure information in terms of the number of packets; TCP/IP measures information in terms of the number of bytes.

Acknowledgment Techniques

Reliable delivery guarantees that a stream of data sent from one machine will be delivered through a data link to another machine without duplication or data loss. Positive acknowledgment with retransmission is one technique that guarantees reliable delivery of data streams. Positive acknowledgment requires a recipient to communicate with the source, sending back an acknowledgment message when it receives data. The sender keeps a record of each data packet it sends and waits for an acknowledgment before sending the next data packet. The sender also starts a timer when it sends a segment, and it retransmits a segment if the timer expires before an acknowledgment arrives.

Figure 1-21 shows the sender transmitting Data Packets 1, 2, and 3. The receiver acknowledges receipt of the packets by requesting Packet 4. Upon receiving the acknowledgment, the sender sends Packets 4, 5, and 6. If Packet 5 does not arrive at the destination, the receiver acknowledges with a request to resend Segment 5. The sender resends Packet 5 and must receive an acknowledgment to continue with the transmission of Packet 7.

FIGURE 1-21
Positive acknowledg-ment requires a recipient to communicate with the source, send-ing back an acknowledg-ment message when it receives data.

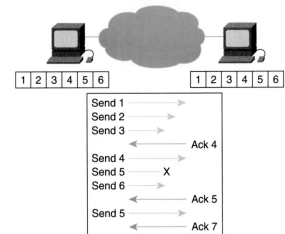

Summary

- By using layers, the OSI reference model simplifies the task required for two computers to communicate.

- Each layer's protocol exchanges information, called PDUs, between peer layers.

- Each layer depends on the service function of the OSI reference model layer below it. The lower layer uses encapsulation to put the PDU from the upper layer into its data field; then, it can add whatever headers and trailers the layer will use to perform its function.

- The term *Ethernet* is often used to refer to all CSMA/CD LANs that gener-ally conform to Ethernet specifications, including IEEE 802.3.

- The Ethernet and 802.3 data links provide data transport across the physi-cal link that joins two devices.

- IP provides connectionless, best-effort delivery routing of datagrams. It is not concerned with the content of the datagrams, but it looks for a way to move the datagrams to their destination.

- ICMP messages are carried in IP datagrams and are used to send error and control messages.

- ARP is used to map a known IP address to a MAC sublayer address to allow communication on a multiaccess medium, such as Ethernet.

- The switching function allows a router to accept a packet on one interface and forward it on a second interface.

- Routed protocols are network protocols that provide enough information in the network-layer address to allow a packet to be forwarded from host to host based on the addressing scheme.

- Routing protocol supports routed protocols by providing mechanisms for sharing routing information. Routing protocol messages move between the routers.

- Most routing protocols can be classified into one of two basic protocols: distance-vector or link-state.

- Routers must be capable of seamlessly handling packets encapsulated into different lower-level frames without changing the packets' Layer 3 addressing.

- Examples of IP routing protocols include RIP, IGRP, OSPF, and EIGRP.

- Transport-layer services allow users to request reliable data transport between hosts and destinations.

Chapter Review

Complete all the review questions to test your understanding of the topics and concepts covered in this chapter. Answers are listed in Appendix A, "Chapter Review Answer Key."

1. Which OSI reference model layer best describes 10BaseT standards?

   A. The data link layer

   B. The network layer

   C. The physical layer

   D. The transport layer

2. Which of the following best describes the function of the transport layer of the OSI reference model?

   A. It sends data by using flow control.

   B. It provides the best path for delivery.

   C. It determines network addresses.

   D. It allows for network segmentation.

3. Which of the following functions does a router use to relay data packets between networks?

   A. Application and media

   B. Path determination and switching

   C. Broadcast and collision detect

   D. None of the above

4. Which of the following are two basic types of dynamic routing?

   A. Static and default

   B. TCP and UDP exchange

   C. Distance vector and link state

   D. None of the above

5. When all the routers in a network are operating with the same knowledge, the network is said to have done which of the following?

   A. Converged

   B. Formalized

   C. Reconfigured

   D. None of the above

6. Describe the purpose of data encapsulation.

7. Describe the main function of the transport layer of the OSI reference model.

8. Describe the purpose of ICMP.

9. Describe windowing in a TCP/IP implementation.

10. Describe the main function of the network layer of the OSI reference model.

Key Terms

application layer   Layer 7 of the OSI reference model. This layer provides network services to user applications. For example, a word processing application is serviced by file transfer services at this layer.

ARP (Address Resolution Protocol)   An Internet protocol used to map an IP address to a MAC address. Defined in RFC 826.

AUI (attachment unit interface)   An IEEE 802.3 interface between a MAU and a network interface card. The term *AUI* also can refer to the rear panel port to which an AUI cable might attach, such as those found on a Cisco LightStream Ethernet access card. Also called a *transceiver cable*.

balanced-hybrid protocol   A protocol that combines aspects of the link-state and distance-vector protocols.

best-effort delivery   This delivery occurs when a network system does not use a sophisticated acknowledgment system to guarantee reliable delivery of information.

Cisco IOS (Internetwork Operating System) software   Cisco system software that provides common functionality, scalability, and security for all products under the CiscoFusion architecture. The Cisco IOS software allows centralized, integrated, and automated installation and management of internetworks, while ensuring support for a wide variety of protocols, media, services, and platforms.

convergence   The speed and capability of a group of internetworking devices running a specific routing protocol to agree on the topology of an internetwork after a change in that topology.

data link layer   Layer 2 of the *OSI reference model*. This layer provides reliable transit of data across a physical link. The data link layer is concerned with physical addressing, network topology, line discipline, error notification, ordered delivery of frames, and flow control. The IEEE divided this layer into two sublayers: the MAC sublayer and the LLC sublayer. Sometimes, this layer is called simply the link layer. This layer roughly corresponds to the data link control layer of the SNA model.

datagram   A logical grouping of information sent as a network-layer unit over a transmission medium without prior establishment of a virtual circuit. IP datagrams are the primary information units in the Internet. The terms *cell*, *frame*, *message*, *packet*, and *segment* also are used to describe logical information groupings at various layers of the OSI reference model and in various technology circles.

default route   A routing table entry that is used to direct frames for which a next hop is not explicitly listed in the routing table.

distance-vector routing protocol   A routing protocol that iterates on the number of hops in a route to find a shortest-path spanning tree. Distance-vector routing protocols call for each router to send its entire routing table in each update, but only to its neighbors. Distance-vector routing protocols can be prone to routing loops, but are computationally simpler than link-state routing protocols. Also called *Bellman-Ford routing algorithm*.

dynamic routing   Routing that adjusts automatically to network topology or traffic changes. Also called *adaptive routing*.

Enhanced IGRP (Enhanced Interior Gateway Routing Protocol)   An advanced version of IGRP developed by Cisco. Provides superior convergence properties and operating efficiency, and combines the advantages of link-state protocols with those of distance-vector protocols. Also called *EIGRP*.

flow control   A technique for ensuring that a transmitting entity does not overwhelm a receiving entity with data. When the buffers on the receiving device are full, a message is sent to the sending device to suspend the transmission until the data in the buffers has been processed. In IBM networks, this technique is called *pacing*.

header   Control information placed before data when encapsulating that data for network transmission.

hop   The passage of a data packet between two network nodes (for example, between two routers).

ICMP (Internet Control Message Protocol)   A network-layer Internet protocol that reports errors and provides other information relevant to IP packet processing. Documented in RFC 792.

IGRP (Interior Gateway Routing Protocol)   A protocol developed by Cisco to address the problems associated with routing in large, heterogeneous networks.

IP address   A 32-bit address assigned to hosts by using TCP/IP. An IP address belongs to one of five classes (A, B, C, D, or E) and is written as four octets separated by periods (that is, dotted-decimal format). Each address consists of a network number, an optional subnetwork number, and a host number. The network and subnetwork numbers together are used for routing, and the host number is used to address an individual host within the network or subnetwork. A subnet mask is used to extract network and subnetwork information from the IP address. Also called an *Internet address*.

layering   The separation of networking functions used by the OSI reference model, which simplifies the tasks required for two computers to communicate with each other.

link-state routing protocol   A routing protocol in which each router broadcasts or multicasts information regarding the cost of reaching each of its neighbors to all nodes in the internetwork. Link-state protocols create a consistent view of the network and are therefore not prone to routing loops, but they achieve this at the cost of relatively greater computational difficulty and more widespread traffic (compared with distance-vector routing protocols).

LSA (link-state advertisement)   A broadcast packet used by link-state protocols that contains information about neighbors and path costs. LSAs are used by the receiving routers to maintain their routing tables. Sometimes called *link-state packets (LSPs)*.

MAC (Media Access Control)   The part of the data link layer that includes the 6-byte(48-bit) address of the source and destination, and the method of getting permission to transmit.

MAU (media attachment unit)   A device used in Ethernet and IEEE 802.3 networks that provides the interface between the AUI port of a station and the common medium of the Ethernet. The MAU, which can be built into a station or can be a separate device, performs physical-layer functions including the conversion of digital data from the Ethernet interface, collision detection, and injection of bits onto the network. Sometimes referred to as a *media access unit* (also abbreviated MAU) or as a *transceiver*.

network   A collection of computers, printers, routers, switches, and other devices that are able to communicate with each other over some transmission medium.

network layer   Layer 3 of the *OSI reference model*. This layer provides connectivity and path selection between two end systems. The network layer is the layer at which routing occurs. Corresponds roughly with the path control layer of the SNA model.

NIC (network interface card)   A board that provides network communication capabilities to and from a computer system. Also called an *adapter*.

OSPF (Open Shortest Path First) protocol   A link-state, hierarchical routing protocol proposed as a successor to RIP in the Internet community. OSPF features include least-cost routing, multipath routing, and load balancing.

packet   A logical grouping of information that includes a header containing control information and (usually) user data. Packets are most often used to refer to network-layer units of data. The terms *datagram*, *frame*, *message*, and *segment* also are used to describe logical information groupings at various layers of the OSI reference model and in various technology circles.

path determination   The decision of which path traffic should take through the network cloud. Path determination occurs at the network layer of the OSI reference model.

PDU (protocol data unit)   The OSI term for a packet.

physical layer   Layer 1 of the OSI reference model. This layer defines the electrical, mechanical, procedural, and functional specifications for activating, maintaining, and deactivating the physical link between end systems. Corresponds with the physical control layer in the SNA model.

presentation layer   Layer 6 of the OSI reference model. This layer provides data representation and code formatting, along with the negotiation of data transfer syntax. It ensures that the data that arrives from the network can be used by the application, and it ensures that information sent by the application can be transmitted on the network.

queue   1. Generally, an ordered list of elements waiting to be processed. 2. In routing, a backlog of packets waiting to be forwarded over a router interface.

RARP (Reverse Address Resolution Protocol)   A protocol in the TCP/IP stack that provides a method for finding IP addresses based on MAC addresses.

RIP (Routing Information Protocol)   A protocol supplied with UNIX BSD systems. The most common Interior Gateway Protocol (IGP) in the Internet. RIP uses hop count as a routing metric.

routed protocol   A protocol that can be routed by a router. A router must be able to interpret the logical internetwork as specified by that routed protocol. Examples of routed protocols include AppleTalk, DECnet, and IP.

routing protocol   A protocol that accomplishes routing through the implementation of a specific routing protocol. Examples of routing protocols include IGRP, OSPF, and RIP.

session layer   Layer 5 of the OSI reference model. This layer establishes, maintains, and manages sessions between applications.

SPF (shortest path first) protocol   A routing protocol that iterates on length of path to determine a shortest-path spanning tree. Commonly used in link-state routing protocols. Sometimes called *Dijkstra's algorithm*.

static routing   Routing that is explicitly configured and entered into the routing table. Static routes take precedence over routes chosen by dynamic routing protocols.

stub network   A network that has only a single connection to a router.

subnet mask   A mask used to extract network and subnetwork information from the IP address.

subnetwork   A network that is segmented into a series of smaller networks.

transport layer   Layer 4 of the OSI reference model. This layer segments and reassembles data into a data stream. The transport layer has the potential to guarantee a connection and offer reliable transport.

window   The number of octets that the sender is willing to accept.

Objectives

After reading this chapter, you will be able to

- Describe the various LAN communication problems, such as
    - Collisions
    - CSMA/CD
    - Demands of multimedia applications on the network
    - Normal latency
    - Distances and repeaters
    - Excessive broadcasts
- Describe full-duplex transmitting and the Fast Ethernet standard as two methods to improve LAN performance
- Describe the effects of LAN segmentation with bridges, routers, and switches
- Describe switching
- Describe the operation and benefits of LAN switching
- Describe the Spanning-Tree Protocol
- Describe the benefits of VLANs

Chapter 2

LAN Switching

Introduction

Today, network designers are moving away from using bridges and hubs and are primarily using switches and routers to build networks. Chapter 1, "Review: The OSI Reference Model and Routing," provides a review of the OSI reference model and an overview of network planning and design considerations related to routing.

This chapter discusses problems in a local-area network (LAN) and possible solutions that can improve LAN performance. You will learn about LAN congestion and its effect on network performance and the advantages of LAN segmentation in a network. In addition, you will learn about the advantages and disadvantages of using bridges, switches, and routers for LAN segmentation and the effects of switching, bridging, and routing on network throughput. Finally, you will learn about Ethernet, Fast Ethernet, and VLANs, and the benefits of these technologies.

Network Demands

Today's LANs are becoming increasingly congested and overburdened. In addition to an ever-growing population of network users, several other factors have combined to expand the capabilities of traditional LANs:

- Faster CPUs—In the mid-1980s, the most common desktop workstation was a PC. At the time, most PCs could complete 1 million instructions per second (MIPS). Today, workstations with 50 to 75 MIPS of processing power are common, and input/output (I/O) speeds have increased accordingly. As a result, two workstations on the same LAN can easily saturate the network.

- Faster operating systems—With the three most common desktop operating systems (Windows, UNIX, and Mac) being able to multitask, users are able to initiate simultaneous network transactions. With the release of Windows 95, which reflected a redesign of DOS/Windows that includes multitasking, PC users are able to increase their demands for network resources.

- Network-intensive applications—Use of client/server applications such as the World Wide Web is increasing. Client/server applications allow administrators to centralize information, thus making it easy to maintain and protect. Client/server applications free users from the burden of maintaining information and the cost of providing enough hard disk space to store it. Given the cost benefit of client/server applications, such applications are likely to become even more widely used in the future.

The Ethernet/802.3 Interface

The most common LAN medium is Ethernet. Ethernet is used to transport data between devices on a network, such as computers, printers, and file servers. As shown in Figure 2-1, all the devices are connected to the same delivery medium. Ethernet media use a data frame broadcast method of transmitting and receiving data to all nodes on the shared media.

The performance of a shared-medium Ethernet/802.3 LAN can be negatively affected by several factors:

- The data frame broadcast delivery nature of Ethernet/802.3 LANs
- Carrier sense multiple access collision detect (CSMA/CD) access methods allowing only one station to transmit at a time
- Network congestion due to increased bandwidth demands from multimedia applications such as video and the Internet
- Normal latency (propagation delay) of frames as they travel across the LAN Layer 1 media and pass through Layer 1, 2, and 3 networking devices
- Extending the distances of the Ethernet/802.3 LANs by using Layer 1 repeaters

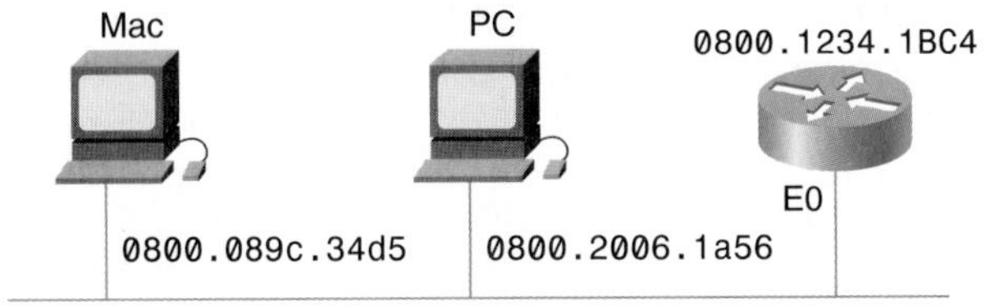

FIGURE 2-1
Ethernet is known as a shared-medium technology used to transport data between devices on a network.

Mac — 0800.089c.34d5
PC — 0800.2006.1a56
0800.1234.1BC4
E0

Ethernet using CSMA/CD and a shared medium can support data transmission rates of up to 10 Mbps. CSMA/CD is an access method that allows only one station to transmit at a time. The goal of Ethernet is to provide a best-effort delivery service and allow all devices on the shared medium to transmit on an equal basis. As shown in Figure 2-2, one of the inherent problems with CSMA/CD technology is collisions.

FIGURE 2-2
CSMA/CD is an access method that allows only one station to transmit at a time, thus reducing collisions

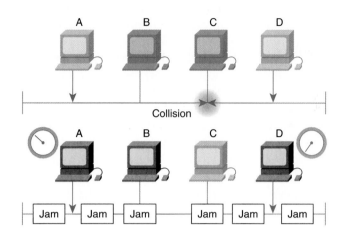

Half-Duplex Ethernet Design

Ethernet is a half-duplex technology. Each Ethernet host checks the network to see whether data is being transmitted before it transmits additional data; if this is the case, the transmission is delayed. Despite transmission deferral, two or more Ethernet hosts can transmit at the same time, which results in a collision. When a collision occurs, the hosts enter a backoff phase and retransmit later. As more hosts are added to the network and begin transmitting, collisions are more likely to occur.

Ethernet LANs become saturated because users run network-intensive software, such as client/server applications, which cause hosts to transmit more often and for longer periods of time. The physical connector used by devices on an Ethernet LAN provides several circuits so that communications between devices can occur.

Congestion and Bandwidth

Technology advances are producing faster and more intelligent desktop computers and workstations. The combination of more powerful computers/workstations and network-intensive applications has created a need for network capacity, or bandwidth, that is much greater than the 10 Mbps that is available on shared Ethernet/802.3 LANs.

Today's networks are experiencing an increase in the transmission of large graphics files, images, full-motion video, and multimedia applications, as well as an increase in the number of users on a network. All these factors place an even greater strain on Ethernet's 10-Mbps bandwidth capacity.

As more people utilize a network to share large files, access file servers, and connect to the Internet, network congestion occurs. This can result in slower response times, longer file transfers, and network users becoming less productive due to network delays. To relieve network congestion, more bandwidth is needed or the available bandwidth must be used more efficiently. The methods used to implement these solutions are discussed later in the chapter.

Latency

Latency, sometimes called propagation delay, is the time a frame, or packet, of data takes to travel from the source station or node to its final destination on the network. Because Ethernet LANs use CSMA/CD to provide best-effort delivery, there must be a certain amount of latency in the system to detect collisions and negotiate transmission rights on the network.

Latency does not depend solely on distance and number of devices. For example, if three switches separate two workstations, the workstations experience less latency than if two routers separated them. The intermediate devices, the switches, greatly enhance network performance.

Ethernet Transmission Times

Transmission time is the time it takes a frame or packet (the data being placed into a packet or frame) to move from the data link layer to the physical layer (onto the physical cabling of the network). Table 2-1 represents the transmission time for four different packet sizes.

TABLE 2-1   **Ethernet Transmission Times**

Packet Size in Bytes	Transmission Time in Microseconds
64	51.2
512	410
1000	800
1518	1214

Each Ethernet bit has a 100-ns window for transmission. A byte is equal to 8 bits. Therefore, 1 byte takes a minimum of 800 ns to transmit. A 64-byte frame takes 51,200 ns, or 51.2 microseconds, to transmit (64 bytes at 800 ns equals 51,200 ns, and 51,200 ns/1000 equals 51.2 microseconds). Transmission time of a 1000-byte packet from Workstation 1 to the server or to Workstation 2 requires 800 microseconds due to the latency of the devices in the network.

Extending Shared-Media LANs by Using Repeaters

The distance that a LAN can cover is limited due to attenuation; attenuation means that the signal weakens (that is, attenuates) as it travels through the network. Attenuation is caused by the resistance in the cable, or medium. An Ethernet repeater is a physical-layer device on the network that boosts or regenerates the signal on an Ethernet LAN. When you use an Ethernet repeater to extend the distance of a LAN, a single network can cover a greater distance and more users can share that same network, as shown in Figure 2-3. However, using repeaters also compounds the issue of broadcasts and collisions and has a negative effect on the overall performance of the shared-media LAN.

FIGURE 2-3
An Ethernet repeater allows for only one transmission at a time, connects all nodes to a single communication channel, and transmits the same data to all the repeater's ports.

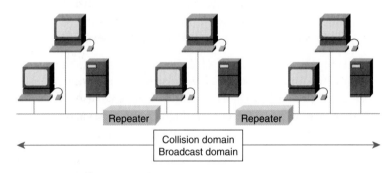

A multiport repeater is also known as a hub. In a shared-medium LAN that uses hubs, the broadcast and collision problems are compounded, and the total bandwidth of the LAN is 10 Mbps.

Improving LAN Performance

The performance of a shared-medium LAN can be improved by using one or more of the following solutions:

- Full-duplex Ethernet
- LAN segmentation

Full-Duplex Ethernet

Full-duplex Ethernet allows the transmission of a packet and the reception of a different packet at the same time. This simultaneous transmission and reception requires two pairs of cables and a switched connection between each node. This connection is considered point-to-point and is nearly collision free. Because both nodes can transmit and receive at the same time, there are no negotiations for bandwidth. Full-duplex Ethernet can use an existing shared medium as long as the medium meets minimum Ethernet standards:

Standard	Distance
10BaseT/10BaseTX	100 meters
10BaseFL	2 kilometers

To transmit and receive simultaneously, a dedicated port is required for each node. Full-duplex connections can use 10BaseT, 100BaseT, or 100BaseFL media to create point-to-point connections. The network interface cards (NICs) on both ends need to have full-duplex capabilities.

The full-duplex Ethernet switch takes advantage of the two pairs of required cables in this configuration by creating a direct connection between the transmit (TX) at one end of the circuit to the receive (RX) end of the other circuit. With these two stations connected this way, a collision-free domain is created because the transmission and receipt of data occurs on separate non-competitive circuits.

Ethernet usually can only use 50%–60% of the 10-Mbps available bandwidth because of collisions and latency. Full-duplex Ethernet offers 100% of the bandwidth in both directions. This produces a potential 20-Mbps throughput—10-Mbps TX and 10-Mbps RX.

LAN Segmentation

A network can be divided in smaller units called segments. Each segment uses the CSMA/CD access method and maintains traffic between users on the segment. Figure 2-4 shows an example of a segmented Ethernet network. The entire network has 15 computers (6 file severs and 9 PCs). By using segments in a network, fewer users/devices are sharing the same 10 Mbps when communicating to one another within the segment. Each segment is considered its own collision domain, as shown in Figure 2-5.

By dividing the network into three segments, a network manager can decrease network congestion within each segment. When transmitting data within a segment, the five devices within each segment are sharing the 10-Mbps bandwidth per segment. In a segmented Ethernet LAN, data passed between segments is transmitted on the backbone of the network using a bridge, router, or switch.

FIGURE 2-4
Without segmenting the network, all 15 devices would need to share the same 10-Mbps bandwidth and would reside in the same collision domain.

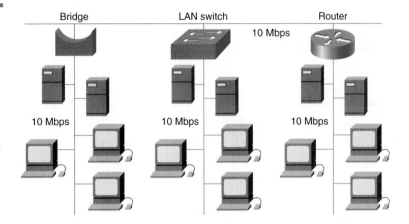

FIGURE 2-5
The backbone network is its own collision domain and uses CSMA/CD to provide best-effort delivery service between segments.

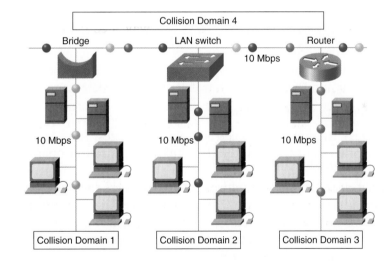

Segmentation with Bridges

Ethernet LANs that use a bridge to segment the LAN provide more bandwidth per user because there are fewer users on each segment. In contrast, LANs that do not use bridges for segmentation provide less bandwidth per user because there are more users on a nonsegmented LAN.

Bridges "learn" a network's segmentation by building address tables (see Figure 2-6) that contain the address of each network device and which segment to use to reach that device. Bridges are Layer 2 devices that forward data frames according to the frames' Media Access Control (MAC) addresses. In addition, bridges are transparent to the other devices on the network.

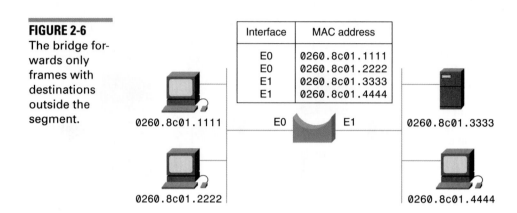

FIGURE 2-6
The bridge forwards only frames with destinations outside the segment.

Interface	MAC address
E0	0260.8c01.1111
E0	0260.8c01.2222
E1	0260.8c01.3333
E1	0260.8c01.4444

0260.8c01.1111

0260.8c01.2222

E0   E1

0260.8c01.3333

0260.8c01.4444

Bridges increase the latency in a network by 10%–30%. This latency is due to the decision making required of the bridge or bridges in transmitting data. A bridge is considered a store-and-forward device because it must examine the destination address field in the frame and then determine which interface to forward the frame to. The time it takes to perform these tasks, or make these decisions, slows the network transmissions, which causes latency.

Segmentation with Routers

Routers are more advanced than typical bridges. A bridge is passive on the network and operates at the data link layer. A router operates at the network layer and bases all its decisions about forwarding between segments on the network-layer protocol address. Routers create the highest level of segmentation, as shown in Figure 2-7, by forwarding data to the hub, to which workstations are connected. A router makes forwarding decisions to segments by examining the destination address on the data packet and looking in its routing table for forwarding instructions.

A router must examine a packet to determine the best path for forwarding that packet to its destination. This process takes time. Protocols that require an acknowledgement from the receiver to the sender for every packet as it is delivered (known as *acknowledgement-oriented protocols*) have a 30%–40% loss of throughput. Protocols that require minimal acknowledgements (sliding-window protocols) suffer a 20%–30% loss of throughput. This is due to the fact that there is less data traffic between the sender and receiver (that is, fewer acknowledgements).

FIGURE 2-7
Routers deter-
mine to which
hub and seg-
ment the data
packet should
be forwarded.

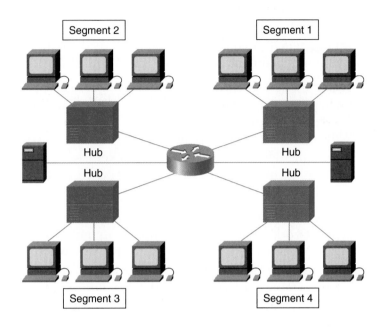

Segmentation with LAN Switches

LAN switching eases bandwidth shortages and network bottlenecks, such as
those between several PCs and a remote file server. As shown in Figure 2-8,
a switch segments a LAN into microsegments, which creates collision-free
domains from one larger collision domain. Although the LAN switch eliminates collision domains, all hosts connected to the switch are still in the same
broadcast domain. Therefore, all nodes connected through the LAN switch
can see a broadcast from just one node.

FIGURE 2-8
A LAN switch is
a very high-
speed multi-
port bridge
with one port
for each node
or segment of
the LAN.

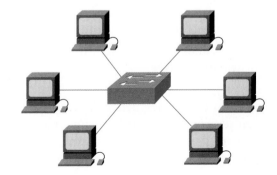

Switched Ethernet is based on Ethernet. Each node is directly connected to one of its ports or a segment that is connected to one of the switch's ports. This creates a 10-Mbps bandwidth connection between each node and each segment on the switch. A computer connected directly to an Ethernet switch is its own collision domain and accesses the full 10 Mbps.

A LAN that uses a Switched Ethernet topology creates a network that behaves as though it has only two nodes—the sending node and the receiving node. These two nodes share the 10-Mbps bandwidth between them, which means that nearly all the bandwidth is available for the transmission of data. Because a Switched Ethernet LAN uses bandwidth so efficiently, it can provide a faster LAN topology than Ethernet LANs. In a Switched Ethernet implementation, the available bandwidth can reach close to 100%.

Ethernet switching increases the bandwidth available on a network by creating dedicated network segments (that is, point-to-point connections) and connecting those segments in a virtual network within the switch. This virtual network circuit exists only when two nodes need to communicate. This is why it is called a virtual circuit—it exists only when needed and is established within the switch.

Switching and Bridging Overview

Switching is a technology that decreases congestion in Ethernet, Token Ring, and Fiber Distributed Data Interface (FDDI) LANs by reducing traffic and increasing bandwidth. LAN switches often replace shared hubs and are designed to work with existing cable infrastructures so that they can be installed without disrupting existing network traffic.

Today in data communications, all switching equipment perform two basic operations:

- Switching data frames—This happens when a frame arrives on an input media and is transmitted to an output medium.
- Maintaining switching operations—In this operation, switches build and maintain switching tables.

The term bridging refers to a technology in which a device known as a bridge connects two or more LAN segments. A bridge transmits datagrams from one segment to their destinations on other segments. When a bridge is powered on and begins to operate, it examines the MAC address of the incoming datagrams and builds a table of known destinations. If the bridge knows that the destination of a datagram is on the same segment as the source of the datagram, it drops the datagram because there is no need to transmit it. If the bridge knows that the destination is on another segment, it transmits the datagram on that segment only. If the bridge does not know the destination segment, the bridge transmits the datagram on all segments except the source segment (a technique known as flooding). The primary benefit of bridging is that it limits traffic to certain network segments.

Both bridges and switches connect LAN segments, use a table of MAC addresses to determine the segment on which a datagram needs to be transmitted, and reduce traffic. Switches are better than bridges because they operate at much higher speeds than bridges and can support new functionality, such as virtual LANs (VLANs).

LAN Switch Latency

Each switch used on an Ethernet LAN adds latency to the network. However, the type of switching used can help overcome the built-in latency of some switches.

A switch between a workstation and a server adds 21 microseconds to the transmission process. A 1000-byte packet has a transmission time of 800 microseconds. A packet sent from a workstation to a server has a total transmission time of 821 microseconds (800 + 21 = 821). Because of the switching employed, the MAC address of the destination device is read and the switch begins transmitting the packet before the packet arrives in the switch. This more than makes up for the inherent latency in the switch.

Layer 2 and Layer 3 Switching

There are two methods of switching data frames—Layer 2 and Layer 3 switching. Switching is the process of taking an incoming frame from one interface and delivering it out through another interface. Routers use Layer 3 switching to route a packet; switches (Layer 2 switches) use Layer 2 switching to forward frames.

The difference between Layer 2 and Layer 3 switching is the type of information inside the frame that is used to determine the correct output interface. With Layer 2 switching, frames are switched based on MAC address information. With Layer 3 switching, frames are switched based on network-layer information.

Layer 2 switching does not look inside a packet for network-layer information as does Layer 3 switching. Layer 2 switching looks at a destination MAC address within a frame. It sends the information to the appropriate interface if it knows the destination address location. Layer 2 switching builds and maintains a switching table that keeps track of which MAC addresses belong to each port or interface.

If the Layer 2 switch does not know where to send the frame, it broadcasts the frame out all its ports to the network to learn the correct destination. When the frame's reply is returned, the switch learns the location of the new address and adds the information to the switching table.

The manufacturer of the data communications equipment determines the Layer 2 addresses. They are unique addresses that are derived in two parts—the manufacturing (MFG) code and the unique identifier. The Institute of Electrical and Electronic Engineers (IEEE) assigns the MFG code to each vendor. The vendor assigns a unique identifier. Except in Systems Network Architecture (SNA) networks, users have little or no control over Layer 2 addressing because Layer 2 addresses are fixed with a device, whereas Layer 3 addresses can be changed. In addition, Layer 2 addresses assume a flat address space with universally unique addresses.

Layer 3 switching operates at the network layer. It examines packet information and forwards packets based on their network-layer destination addresses. Layer 3 switching also supports router functionality.

For the most part, the network administrator determines the Layer 3 addresses. Protocols such as IP, IPX, and AppleTalk use Layer 3 addressing. By creating Layer 3 addresses, a network administrator creates local areas that act as single addressing units (similar to streets, cities, states, and countries) and assigns a number to each local entity. If users move to another building, their end stations obtain new Layer 3 addresses, but their Layer 2 addresses remain the same.

Because routers operate at Layer 3 of the OSI reference model, they can adhere to and create a hierarchical addressing structure. Therefore, a routed network can tie a logical addressing structure to a physical infrastructure, for example, through TCP/IP subnets or IPX networks for each segment. Traffic flow in a switched (that is, flat) network is therefore inherently different from traffic flow in a routed (that is, hierarchical) network. Hierarchical networks offer more flexible traffic flow than flat networks because they can use the network hierarchy to determine optimal paths and contain broadcast domains.

Implications of Layer 2 and Layer 3 Switching

The increasing power of desktop processors and the requirements of client/server and multimedia applications have created an increased need for greater bandwidth in traditional shared-media environments. These requirements are prompting network designers to replace hubs in wiring closets with switches.

Layer 2 switches use microsegmentation to satisfy the demands for more bandwidth and increased performance, but network designers are now faced with increasing demands for intersubnet communication. For example, every time a user accesses servers and other resources that are located on different subnets, the traffic must go through a Layer 3 device. Potentially, there is a tremendous bottleneck, which can threaten network performance. To avoid this bottleneck, network designers can add Layer 3 capabilities throughout the network, which alleviates the burden on centralized routers. Therefore, a switch improves bandwidth by separating collision domains and selectively forwarding traffic to the appropriate segments of a network.

How a LAN Switch Learns Addresses

An Ethernet switch can learn the address of each device on the network by reading the source address of each packet transmitted and noting the port where the frame entered the switch. The switch then adds this information to its forwarding database. Addresses are learned dynamically. This means that as new addresses are read, they are learned and stored in content-addressable memory (CAM). When a source is read that is not found in CAM, it is learned and stored for future use.

Each time an address is stored, it is time stamped. This allows for addresses to be stored for a set period of time. Each time an address is referenced or found in CAM, it receives a new time stamp. Addresses that are not referenced during a set period of time are removed from the list. By removing aged or old addresses, CAM maintains an accurate and functional forwarding database.

The Benefits of Switching

Switches have many benefits. A LAN switch allows many users to communicate in parallel through the use of virtual circuits and dedicated network segments in a collision-free environment. This maximizes the bandwidth available on the shared medium. Also, moving to a switched LAN environment is very cost-effective because you can reuse existing hardware and cabling. Finally, the power of the switch combined with the software to configure LANs give network administrators great flexibility in managing the network.

Symmetric and Asymmetric Switching

Symmetric switching is one way to characterize a LAN switch according to the bandwidth allocated to each port on the switch. As shown in Figure 2-9, a symmetric switch provides switched connections between ports with the same bandwidth, such as all 10-Mbps ports or all 100-Mbps ports.

As shown in Figure 2-10, an asymmetric LAN switch provides switched connections between ports of unlike bandwidth, such as a combination of 10-Mbps and 100-Mbps ports.

Asymmetric switching makes the most of client/server network traffic flows where multiple clients are communicating with a server at the same time, requiring more bandwidth dedicated to the switch port that the server is connected to in order to prevent a bottleneck at that port.

FIGURE 2-9
Even distribution of network traffic across the entire network optimizes a symmetric switch.

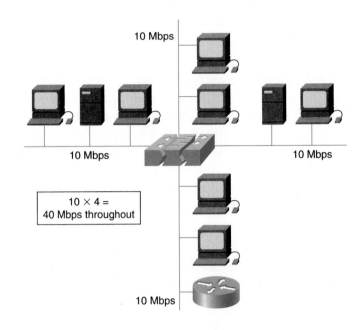

10 Mbps

10 Mbps

10 Mbps

$10 \times 4 =$
40 Mbps throughout

10 Mbps

FIGURE 2-10
Asymmetric provides switched connections between 10-Mbps ports and 100-Mbps ports.

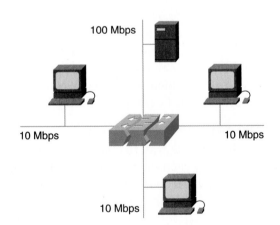

100 Mbps

10 Mbps

10 Mbps

10 Mbps

As you will learn in the next section, memory buffering in an asymmetric switch is required to allow traffic from the 100-Mbps port to be sent to a 10-Mbps port without causing too much congestion at the 10-Mbps port.

Memory Buffering

An Ethernet switch may use a buffering technique to store and forward packets to the correct port or ports. The area of memory where the switch stores the destination and transmission data is called the memory buffer. This memory buffer can use two methods for forwarding packets—port-based memory buffering and shared memory buffering.

In port-based memory buffering, packets are stored in queues that are linked to specific incoming ports. A packet is transmitted to the outgoing port only when all the packets ahead of it in the queue have been successfully transmitted. It is possible for a single packet to delay the transmission of all the packets in memory because of a busy destination port. This delay occurs even if the other packets can be transmitted to open destination ports.

Shared memory buffering deposits all packets into a common memory buffer that is shared by all the ports on the switch. The amount of memory allocated to a port is determined by how much is required by each port. This is called *dynamic allocation of buffer memory*. The packets in the buffer are then linked dynamically to the transmit port—the packet is linked to the memory allocation of that transmit port. This allows the packet to be received on one port and transmitted on another port, without moving it into a different queue.

The switch maintains a map of the ports that a packet needs to be transmitted to. The switch clears out this map of destination ports only after the packet has been successfully transmitted. Because the memory buffer is shared, the packet is restricted by the size of the entire memory buffer, not just the allocation to one port. This means that larger packets can be transmitted with fewer dropped packets. This is important to 10/100 switching, where a 100-Mbps port can forward a packet to a 10-Mbps port.

Two Switching Methods

Two switching modes can be used to forward a frame through a switch:

- *Store-and-forward*—The entire frame is received before any forwarding takes place. The destination and/or the source addresses are read and filters are applied before the frame is forwarded. Latency occurs while the frame is being received; the latency is greater with larger frames because the entire frame takes longer to read. Error detection is high because of the time available to the switch to check for errors while waiting for the entire frame to be received.

- *Cut-through*—The switch reads the destination address before receiving the entire frame. The frame is then forwarded before the entire frame arrives. This mode decreases the latency of the transmission and has poor error detection. Fast-forward and fragment-free are two forms of cut-through switching:

— *Fast-forward switching*—Fast-forward switching offers the lowest level of latency by immediately forwarding a packet after receiving the destination address. Because fast-forward switching starts forwarding before the entire packet is received, there may be times when packets are relayed with errors. Although this occurs infrequently and the destination network adapter discards the faulty packet upon receipt, the superfluous traffic may be deemed unacceptable in certain environments. Use the fragment-free option to reduce the number of packets forwarded with errors. In fast-forward mode, latency is measured from the first bit received to the first bit transmitted, or first in, first out (FIFO).

— *Fragment-free switching*—Fragment-free switching filters out collision fragments, which are the majority of packet errors, before forwarding begins. In a properly functioning network, collision fragments must be smaller than 64 bytes. Anything greater than 64 bytes is a valid packet and is usually received without error. Fragment-free switching waits until the received packet has been determined not to be a collision fragment before forwarding the packet. In fragment-free mode, latency is measured as FIFO.

The latency of each switching mode depends on how the switch forwards the frames. The faster the switching mode, the smaller the latency in the switch. To accomplish faster frame forwarding, the switch takes less time to check for errors. The tradeoff is less error checking, which can lead to a higher number of retransmissions.

VLANs

An Ethernet switch physically segments a LAN into individual collision domains. However, each segment is still part of one broadcast domain. The total number of segments on a switch equals one broadcast domain. This means that all nodes on all segments can see a broadcast from a node one segment.

A VLAN is a logical grouping of network devices or users that are not restricted to a physical switch segment. The devices or users in a VLAN can be grouped by function, department, application, and so on, regardless of their physical segment location. A VLAN creates a single broadcast domain that is not restricted to a physical segment and is treated like a subnet.

VLAN setup is done in the switch via software. VLANs are not standardized and require the use of proprietary software from the switch vendor.

Spanning-Tree Protocol

The main function of the Spanning-Tree Protocol is to allow duplicate switched/bridged paths without incurring the latency effects of loops in the network.

Bridges and switches make their forwarding decisions for unicast frames based on the destination MAC address in the frame. If the MAC address is unknown, the device floods the frame out all ports in an attempt to reach the desired destination. It also does this for all broadcast frames.

The Spanning-Tree Algorithm, implemented by the Spanning-Tree Protocol, prevents loops by calculating a stable spanning-tree network topology. When creating fault-tolerant networks, a loop-free path must exist between all Ethernet nodes in the network. The Spanning-Tree Algorithm is used to calculate a loop-free path. Spanning-tree frames called bridge protocol data units (BPDUs) are sent and received by all switches in the network at regular intervals and are used to determine the spanning-tree topology.

A switch uses Spanning-Tree Protocol on all Ethernet- and Fast Ethernet–based VLANs. Spanning-Tree Protocol detects and breaks loops by placing some connections in a standby mode, which are activated in the event of an active connection failure. A separate instance of Spanning-Tree Protocol runs within each configured VLAN, ensuring Ethernet topologies that conform to industry standards throughout the network.

Understanding Spanning-Tree Protocol States

The Spanning-Tree Protocol states are as follows:

- Blocking—No frames forwarded, BPDUs heard
- Listening—No frames forwarded, listening for frames
- Learning—No frames forwarded, learning addresses
- Forwarding—Frames forwarded, learning addresses
- Disabled—No frames forwarded, no BPDUs heard

The state for each VLAN is initially set by the configuration and later modified by the Spanning-Tree Protocol process. You can determine the status, cost, and priority of ports and VLANs by using the `show spantree` command. After the port-to-VLAN state is set, Spanning-Tree Protocol determines whether the port forwards or blocks frames. Ports can be configured to immediately enter Spanning-Tree Protocol forwarding mode when a connection is made, instead of following the usual sequence of blocking, learning, and then forwarding. The capability to quickly switch states from blocking to forwarding rather than going through the transitional port states is useful in situations where immediate access to a server is required.

Summary

- The combination of more powerful computers/workstations and network-intensive applications has created a need for bandwidth that is much greater than the 10 Mbps available on shared Ethernet/802.3 LANs.

- As more people utilize a network to share large files, access file servers, and connect to the Internet, network congestion occurs.

- A network can be divided in smaller units, called *segments*. Each segment is considered its own collision domain.

- In a segmented Ethernet LAN, data passed between segments is transmitted the network by a bridge, switch, or router.

- A LAN that uses a switched Ethernet topology creates a network that behaves like it only has two nodes—the sending node and the receiving node.

- A switch segments a LAN into microsegments, creating collision-free domains from one larger collision domain.

- Switches achieve high-speed transfer by reading the destination Layer 2 MAC address of the packet, much the way a bridge does. This leads to a high rate of speed for packet forwarding.

- Ethernet switching increases the bandwidth available on a network by creating dedicated network segments (point-to-point connections) and connecting those segments in a virtual network within the switch.

- Symmetric switching is one way of characterizing a LAN switch according to the bandwidth allocated to each port on the switch.

- An asymmetric LAN switch provides switched connections between ports of unlike bandwidth, such as a combination of 10-Mbps and 100-Mbps ports.

- Two switching modes can be used to forward frame through a switch: store-and-forward and cut-through.

- A VLAN is a grouping of network devices or users that is not restricted to a physical switch segment.

- The main function of the Spanning-Tree Protocol is to allow duplicate switched/bridged paths without suffering the latency effects of loops in the network.

Chapter Review

Complete all the review questions to test your understanding of the topics and concepts covered in this chapter. Answers are listed in Appendix A, "Chapter Review Answer Key."

1. Which of the following broadcast methods does an Ethernet medium use to transmit and receive data to all nodes on the network?

   A. A packet

   B. A data frame

   C. A segment

   D. A byte at a time

2. What is the minimum time it takes Ethernet to transmit 1 byte?

   A. 100 ns

   B. 800 ns

   C. 51,200 ns

   D. 800 microseconds

3. Characteristics of microsegmentation include which of the following?

   A. Dedicated paths between sender and receiver hosts

   B. Multiple traffic paths within the switch

   C. All traffic visible on network segment at once

   D. A and B

4. LAN switches are considered to be which of the following?

   A. Multiport repeaters operating at Layer 1

   B. Multiport hubs operating at Layer 2

   C. Multiport routers operating at Layer 3

   D. Multiport bridges operating at Layer 2

5. Asymmetric switching is optimized for which of the following?

   A. Client/server network traffic where the "fast" switch port is connected to the server

   B. An even distribution of network traffic

C. Switches without memory buffering

D. A and B

6. In _____ switching, the switch checks the destination address and immediately begins forwarding the frame, and in _____ switching, the switch receives the complete frame before forwarding it.

   A. store-and-forward; symmetric

   B. cut-through; store-and-forward

   C. store-and-forward; cut-through

   D. memory buffering; cut-through

7. The Spanning-Tree Protocol allows which of the following?

   A. Routers to communicate link states

   B. Switches to communicate hop counts

   C. Bridges to communicate Layer 3 information

   D. Redundant network paths without suffering the effects of loops in the network

8. Distinguish between cut-through and store-and-forward switching.

9. Describe full- and half-duplex Ethernet operation.

10. Describe the advantages of LAN segmentation that uses switches.

Key Terms

acknowledgment   A notification sent from one network device to another to acknowledge that some event (for example, receipt of a message) has occurred. Sometimes abbreviated ACK.

attenuation   Loss of communication signal energy.

backbone   The structural core of the network, which connects all the components of the network so that communication can occur.

bandwidth   The difference between the highest and lowest frequencies available for network signals. Also, the rated throughput capacity of a given network medium or protocol.

bit   A binary digit used in the binary numbering system. Can be zero or one.

BPDU (bridge protocol data unit)   A Spanning-Tree Protocol hello packet that is sent out at configurable intervals to exchange information among bridges in the network.

bridge   A device that connects and passes packets between two network segments that use the same communications protocol. Bridges operate at the data link layer (Layer 2) of the OSI reference model. In general, a bridge filters, forwards, or floods an incoming frame based on the MAC address of that frame.

bridging   A technology in which a bridge connects two or more LAN segments.

broadcast   A data packet that is sent to all nodes on a network. Broadcasts are identified by a broadcast address.

byte   A series of consecutive binary digits that are operated on as a unit (for example, an 8-bit byte).

CAM (content-addressable memory)   Memory that maintains an accurate and functional forwarding database.

client/server application   An application that is stored centrally on a server and accessed by workstations, thus making it easy to maintain and protect.

collision   In Ethernet, the result of two nodes transmitting simultaneously. The frames from each device collide and are damaged when they meet on the physical medium.

collision domain   In Ethernet, the network area within which frames that have collided are propagated. Repeaters and hubs propagate collisions; LAN switches, bridges, and routers do not.

congestion   Traffic in excess of network capacity.

CSMA/CD (carrier sense multiple access collision detect)   A media-access mechanism wherein devices ready to transmit data first check the channel for a carrier. If no carrier is sensed for a specific period of time, a device can transmit. If two devices transmit at once, a collision occurs and is detected by all colliding devices. This collision subsequently delays retransmissions from those devices for some random length of time. Ethernet and IEEE 802.3 use CSMA/CD access.

cut-through   A packet-switching approach that streams data through a switch so that the leading edge of a packet exits the switch at the output port before the packet finishes entering the input port. A device using cut-through packet switching reads, processes, and forwards packets as soon as the destination address is looked up and the outgoing port is determined. Also known as *on-the-fly packet switching*.

data link layer   Layer 2 of the *OSI reference model*. This layer provides reliable transit of data across a physical link. The data link layer is concerned with physical addressing, network topology, line discipline, error notification, ordered delivery of frames, and flow control. The IEEE has divided this layer into two sublayers: the MAC sublayer and the LLC sublayer. Sometimes simply called link layer. Roughly corresponds to the data link control layer of the SNA model.

Ethernet   A shared medium that can support data transmission rates of up to 10 Mbps and uses CSMA/CD.

Fast Ethernet   Any of a number of 100-Mbps Ethernet specifications. Fast Ethernet offers a speed increase ten times that of the 10BaseT Ethernet specification, while preserving such qualities as frame format, MAC mechanisms, and MTU. Such similarities allow the use of existing 10BaseT applications and network management tools on Fast Ethernet networks. Based on an extension to the IEEE 802.3 specification.

fast-forward switching   Switching that offers the lowest level of latency by immediately forwarding a packet after receiving the destination address.

flooding   When a bridge transmits the datagram on all segments except the source segment.

fragment-free switching   A switching technique that filters out collision fragments, which are the majority of packet errors, before forwarding begins.

full-duplex Ethernet   A capability for simultaneous data transmission between a sending station and a receiving station.

half-duplex Ethernet   A capability for data transmission in only one direction at a time between a sending station and a receiving station.

hub   Generally, a device that serves as the center of a star-topology network. Also called a *multiport repeater.*

interface   1. A connection between two systems or devices. 2. In routing terminology, a network connection.

latency   The delay between the time a device requests access to a network and the time it is granted permission to transmit.

memory buffer   The area of memory where the switch stores the destination and transmission data.

microsegmentation   The division of a network into smaller segments, usually with the intention of increasing aggregate bandwidth to network devices.

network layer   Layer 3 of the OSI reference model. This layer provides connectivity and path selection between two end systems. The network layer is the layer at which routing occurs. Corresponds roughly with the path control layer of the SNA model.

NIC (network interface card)   A board that provides network communication capabilities to and from a computer system. Also called an *adapter*.

node   An endpoint of a network connection or a junction common to two or more lines in a network. Nodes can be processors, controllers, or workstations. Nodes, which vary in routing and other functional capabilities, can be interconnected by links, and serve as control points in the network. *Node* is sometimes used generically to refer to any entity that can access a network, and is frequently used interchangeably with device.

physical layer   Layer 1 of the OSI reference model. This layer defines the electrical, mechanical, procedural, and functional specifications for activating, maintaining, and deactivating the physical link between end systems. Corresponds with the physical control layer in the SNA model.

port   An interface on an internetworking device (such as a router). A female plug on a patch panel that accepts the same size plug as an RJ-45 jack. Patch cords are used in these ports to cross connect computers wired to the patch panel. It is this cross-connection that allows the LAN to function.

propagation delay   The time required for data to travel over a network, from its source to its ultimate destination. Also called *latency*.

queue   1. Generally, an ordered list of elements waiting to be processed. 2. In routing, a backlog of packets waiting to be forwarded over a router interface.

repeater   A device that regenerates and propagates electrical signals between two network segments.

router   A network-layer device that uses one or more metrics to determine the optimal path along which network traffic should be forwarded. Routers forward packets from one network to another based on network layer information. Occasionally called a *gateway* (although this definition of gateway is becoming increasingly outdated).

routing table   A table stored in a router or some other internetworking device that keeps track of routes to particular network destinations and, in some cases, metrics associated with those routes.

segment   A section of a network that is bounded by bridges, routers, or switches.

sliding window   A window whose size is negotiated dynamically during the TCP session.

Spanning-Tree Protocol   A bridge protocol that utilizes the spanning-tree algorithm, enabling a learning bridge to dynamically work around loops in a network topology by creating a spanning tree. Bridges exchange BPDU messages with other bridges to detect loops, and then remove the loops by shutting down selected bridge interfaces. Refers to both the IEEE 802.1 Spanning-Tree Protocol standard and the earlier Digital Equipment Corporation Spanning-Tree Protocol on which it is based. The IEEE version supports bridge domains and allows the bridge to construct a loop-free topology across an extended LAN. The IEEE version is generally preferred over the Digital version.

store-and-forward   A packet-switching technique in which frames are completely processed before being forwarded out the appropriate port. This processing includes calculating the CRC and checking the destination address. In addition, frames must be temporarily stored until network resources (such as an unused link) are available to forward the message.

switch   A network device that filters, forwards, and floods frames based on the destination address of each frame. The switch operates at the data link layer of the OSI reference model.

switching   The process of taking an incoming frame from one interface and delivering it out through another interface.

topology   A physical arrangement of network nodes and media within an enterprise networking structure.

unicast   A message sent to a single network destination.

virtual circuit   A logical circuit created to ensure reliable communication between two network devices. A virtual circuit is defined by a VPI/VCI pair, and can be either permanent (a PVC) or switched (an SVC). Virtual circuits are used in Frame Relay and X.25. In ATM, a virtual circuit is called a *virtual channel*. Sometimes abbreviated VC.

VLAN (virtual LAN)   A group of devices on a LAN that are configured (using management software) so that they can communicate as if they were attached to the same wire, when in fact they are located on a number of different LAN segments. Because VLANs are based on logical instead of physical connections, they are extremely flexible.

Objectives

After reading this chapter, you will be able to

- Explain what VLANs are
- Name reasons to create VLANs and describe the benefits of VLANs
- Describe the role that switches play in the creation of VLANs
- Describe VLAN frame filtering, frame identification, and frame tagging
- Describe how switches can be used with hubs
- Name and describe the three methods of VLAN implementation

Chapter 3

VLANs

Introduction

Chapter 2, "LAN Switching," discusses problems inherent in a LAN and possible solutions to improve LAN performance. You learned about the advantages and disadvantages of using bridges, switches, and routers for LAN segmentation and the effects of switching, bridging, and routing on network throughput. Finally, you briefly learned about the benefits of Fast Ethernet and virtual local-area networks (VLANs). This chapter provides an introduction to VLANs and switched internetworking, compares traditional shared LAN configurations with switched LAN configurations, and discusses the benefits of using a switched VLAN architecture.

VLAN Overview

A VLAN is a logical grouping of devices or users, as shown in Figure 3-1. These devices or users can be grouped by function, department, application, and so on, regardless of their physical segment location. VLAN configuration is done at the switch via software. VLANs are not standardized and require the use of proprietary software from the switch vendor.

Existing Shared LAN Configurations

A typical LAN is configured according to the physical infrastructure it is connecting. Users are grouped based on their location in relation to the hub they are plugged in to and how the cable is run to the wiring closet. The router interconnecting each shared hub typically provides segmentation and can act as a broadcast firewall, whereas the segments created by switches do not. This type of segmentation does not group users according to their workgroup association or need for bandwidth. Therefore, they share the same segment and contend for the same bandwidth, although the bandwidth requirements may vary greatly by to workgroup or department.

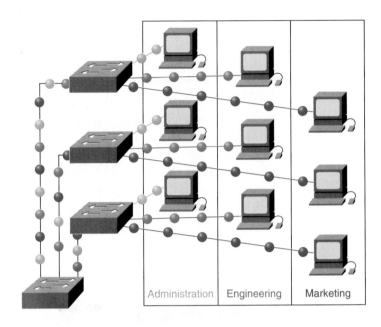

FIGURE 3-1
A VLAN is a group of network devices or users that is not restricted to a physical switch segment.

Administration | Engineering | Marketing

Segmenting with Switching Architectures

LANs are increasingly being divided into workgroups connected via common backbones to form VLAN topologies. VLANs logically segment the physical LAN infrastructure into different subnets (or broadcast domains, for Ethernet) so that broadcast frames are switched only between ports within the same VLAN.

Initial VLAN implementations offered a port-mapping capability that established a broadcast domain between a default group of devices. Current network requirements demand VLAN functionality that covers the entire network. This approach to VLANs allows you to group geographically separate users in networkwide virtual topologies. VLAN configurations group users by logical association rather than physical location.

The majority of the networks currently installed provides very limited logical segmentation. Users are commonly grouped based on connections to the shared hub and the router ports between the hubs. This topology provides segmentation only between the hubs, which are typically located on separate floors, and not between users connected to the same hub. This imposes physical constraints on the network and limits how users can be grouped. A few shared-hub architectures have some grouping capability, but they restrict how you configure logically defined workgroups.

VLANs and Physical Boundaries

In a LAN that utilizes LAN switching devices, VLAN technology is a cost-effective and efficient way of grouping network users into virtual workgroups regardless of their physical location on the network. Figure 3-2 shows the difference between LAN and VLAN segmentation. Some of the main differences are as follows:

- VLANs work at Layer 2 and Layer 3 of the OSI reference model.
- Communication between VLANs is provided by Layer 3 routing.
- VLANs provide a method of controlling network broadcast.
- The network administrator assigns users to a VLAN.
- VLANs can increase network security by defining which network nodes can communicate with each other.

FIGURE 3-2
Within a switched network, VLANs provide segmentation and organizational flexibility.

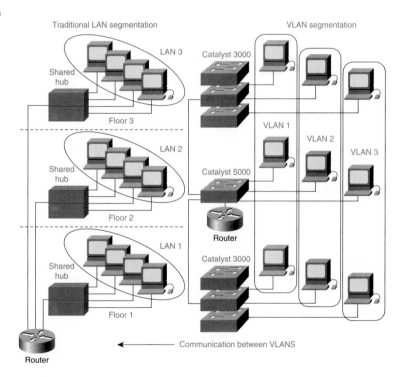

Using VLAN technology, you can group switch ports and their connected users into logically defined workgroups, such as the following:

- Coworkers in the same department
- A cross-functional product team
- Diverse user groups sharing the same network application or software

You can group these ports and users into workgroups in a single switch or on connected switches. By grouping ports and users together across multiple switches, VLANs can span single-building infrastructures, interconnected buildings, or even wide-area networks (WANs), as shown in Figure 3-3.

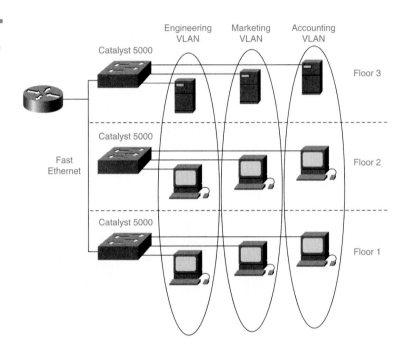

FIGURE 3-3
VLANs remove the physical constraints of workgroup communications.

Transporting VLANs Across Backbones

Important to any VLAN architecture is the ability to transport VLAN information between interconnected switches and routers that reside on the corporate backbone. The VLAN transport enables enterprisewide VLAN communications. These transport capabilities remove the physical boundaries between users, increase the configuration flexibility of a VLAN solution when users move, and provide mechanisms for interoperability between backbone system components.

The backbone commonly acts as the collection point for large volumes of traffic. It also carries end-user VLAN information and identification between switches, routers, and directly attached servers. Within the backbone, high-bandwidth, high-capacity links are typically chosen to carry the traffic throughout the enterprise.

Routers in VLANs

The role of the router in VLANs changes from the traditional LAN role of providing firewalls, broadcast management, and route processing and distribution. Routers remain vital for switched architectures configured as VLANs because they provide communication between logically defined workgroups. Routers provide VLAN access to shared resources such as servers and hosts. They also connect to other parts of the network that are either logically segmented with the more traditional subnet approach or require access to remote sites across wide-area links. Layer 3 communication, either embedded in the switch or provided externally, is an integral part of any high-performance switching architecture.

You can cost-effectively integrate external routers into the switching architecture by using one or more high-speed backbone connections. These are typically FDDI, Fast Ethernet, or ATM connections, and they provide benefits by

- Increasing the throughput between switches and routers
- Consolidating the overall number of physical router ports required for communication between VLANs

VLAN architecture not only provides logical segmentation, but it greatly enhances the efficiency of the network.

Switched Networking Configuration

The problems associated with shared LANs and the emergence of switches are causing traditional LAN configurations to be replaced with switched VLAN networking configurations. Switched VLAN configurations vary from traditional LAN configurations in the following ways:

- Switches remove the physical constraints imposed by a shared-hub architecture because they logically group users and ports across the enterprise. Switches replace hubs in the wiring closet. Switches are easily installed with little or no cabling changes, and can completely replace a shared hub with per-port service to each user.
- Switches can be used to create VLANs in order to provide the segmentation services traditionally provided by routers in LAN configurations.

Switches are one of the core components of VLAN communications. As shown in Figure 3-4, they perform critical VLAN functions by acting as the entry point for end-station devices into the switched fabric and for communication across the enterprise.

Each switch has the intelligence to make filtering and forwarding decisions by frame, based on VLAN metrics defined by network managers, and to communicate this information to other switches and routers within the network.

The most common approaches for logically grouping users into distinct VLANs are frame filtering and frame identification. Both of these techniques look at the frame when it is either received or forwarded by the switch. Based on the set of rules defined by the administrator, these techniques determine where the frame is to be sent, filtered, or broadcast. These control mechanisms can be centrally administered (with network management software) and are easily implemented throughout the network.

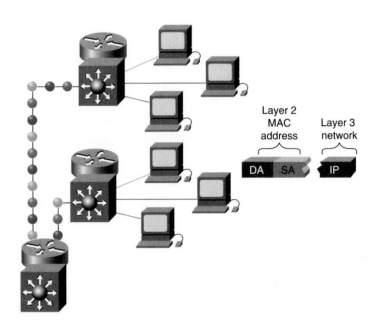

FIGURE 3-4
You can use switches to group users, ports, or logical addresses into common communities of interest.

Frame filtering examines particular information about each frame. A filtering table is developed for each switch; this provides a high level of administrative control because it can examine many attributes of each frame. Depending on the sophistication of the LAN switch, you can group users based on a station's Media Access Control (MAC) addresses or network-layer protocol type. The switch compares the frames it filters with table entries, and it takes the appropriate action based on the entries.

In their early days, VLANs were filter-based and they grouped users based on a filtering table. This model did not scale well because each frame had to be referenced to a filtering table.

Frame tagging uniquely assigns a user-defined ID to each frame. This technique was chosen by the Institute of Electrical and Electronic Engineers (IEEE) standards group because of its scalability. Frame tagging is gaining recognition as the standard trunking mechanism; in comparison to frame filtering, it can provide a more scalable solution to VLAN deployment that can be implemented campus-wide. IEEE 802.1q states that frame tagging is the way to implement VLANs.

VLAN frame tagging is an approach that has been specifically developed for switched communications. Frame tagging places a unique identifier in the header of each frame as it is forwarded throughout the network backbone. The identifier is understood and examined by each switch prior to any broadcasts or transmissions to other switches, routers, or end-station devices. When the frame exits the network backbone, the switch removes the identifier before the frame is transmitted to the target end station. Frame identification functions at Layer 2 require little processing or administrative overhead.

VLAN Implementations

A VLAN makes up a switched network that is logically segmented by functions, project teams, or applications, without regard to the physical location of users. Each switch port can be assigned to a VLAN. Ports assigned to the same VLAN share broadcasts. Ports that do not belong to that VLAN do not share these broadcasts. This improves the overall performance of the network. The following sections discuss three VLAN implementation methods—port-centric, static, and dynamic—that can be used to assign a switch port to a VLAN.

Port-Centric VLANs

In port-centric VLANs, all the nodes in the same VLAN are attached to the same router interface. Figure 3-5 shows VLAN membership by router port, which make an administrator's job easier and the network more efficient because

- Users are assigned by port.
- VLANs are easily administered.
- It provides increased security between VLANs.
- Packets do not "leak" into other domains.

Static VLANs

Static VLANs are ports on a switch that you statically assign to a VLAN. These ports maintain their assigned VLAN configurations until you change them. Although static VLANs require the administrator to make changes, they are secure, easy to configure, and straightforward to monitor. Static VLANs work well in networks in which moves are controlled and managed.

Dynamic VLANs

Dynamic VLANs are ports on a switch that can automatically determine their VLAN assignments. Dynamic VLAN functions are based on MAC addresses, logical addressing, or protocol type of the data packets. When a station is initially connected to an unassigned switch port, the appropriate switch checks the MAC address entry in the VLAN management database and dynamically configures the port with the corresponding VLAN configuration. The major benefits of this approach are less administration within the wiring closet when a user is added or moved and centralized notification when an unrecognized user is added to the network. Typically, more administration is required up front to set up the database within the VLAN management software and to maintain an accurate database of all network users.

FIGURE 3-5
In port-centric VLANs, membership is easily controlled across the network. Also, all nodes attached to the same port must be in the same VLAN.

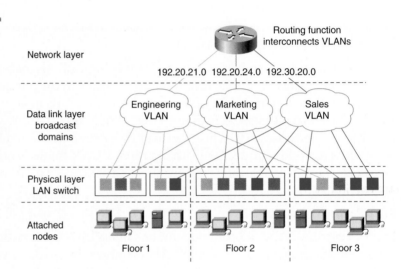

Benefits of VLANs

VLANs provide the following benefits:

- They reduce administration costs related to solving problems associated with moves, additions, and changes.
- They provide controlled broadcast activity.
- They provide workgroup and network security.
- They save money by using existing hubs.

Adding, Moving, or Changing User Locations

Companies are continuously reorganizing. On average, 20% to 40% of the workforce physically moves every year. These moves, additions, and changes are one of a network manager's biggest headaches and one of the largest expenses related to managing the network. Many moves require recabling, and almost all moves require new station addressing and hub and router reconfigurations.

VLANs provide an effective mechanism for controlling these changes and reducing much of the cost associated with hub and router reconfigurations. Users in a VLAN can share the same network address space (that is, the IP subnet), regardless of their location. When users in a VLAN are moved from one location to another, as long as they remain within the same VLAN and are connected to a switch port, their network addresses do not change. A location change can be as simple as plugging a user in to a port on a VLAN-capable switch and configuring the port on the switch to that VLAN, as shown in Figure 3-6.

FIGURE 3-6
VLAN-capable switches simplify the rewiring, configuration, moving of users, and debugging that are required to get a user back online.

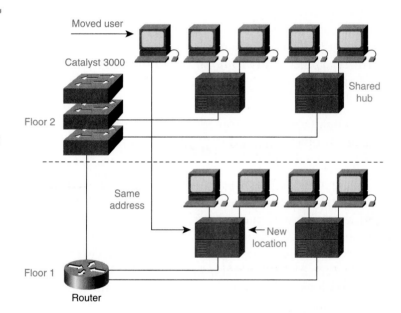

VLANs are a significant improvement over the typical LAN-based techniques used in wiring closets because they require less rewiring, configuration, and debugging. Router configuration is left intact; a simple move for a user from one location to another does not create any configuration modifications in the router if the user stays in the same VLAN.

Controlling Broadcast Activity

Broadcast traffic occurs in every network. Broadcast frequency depends on the types of applications, the types of servers, the amount of logical segmentation, and how these network resources are used. Although applications have been fine-tuned over the past few years to reduce the number of broadcasts they send out, new multimedia applications are being developed that are broadcast and multicast intensive.

You need to take preventive measures to ensure against broadcast-related problems. One of the most effective measures is to properly segment the network with protective firewalls that, as much as possible, prevent problems on one segment from damaging other parts of the network. Thus, although one segment may have excessive broadcast conditions, the rest of the network is protected with a firewall commonly provided by a router. Firewall segmentation provides reliability and minimizes the overhead of broadcast traffic, allowing for greater throughput of application traffic.

When no routers are placed between the switches, broadcasts (Layer 2 transmissions) are sent to every switched port. This is commonly referred to as a flat network, where there is one broadcast domain across the entire network. The advantage of a flat network is that it can provide both low-latency and high-throughput performance and it is easy to administer. The disadvantage is that it increases vulnerability to broadcast traffic across all switches, ports, backbone links, and users.

VLANs are an effective mechanism for extending firewalls from the routers to the switch fabric and protecting the network against potentially dangerous broadcast problems. Additionally, VLANs maintain all the performance benefits of switching.

You create firewalls by assigning switch ports or users to specific VLAN groups both within single switches and across multiple connected switches. Broadcast traffic within one VLAN is not transmitted outside the VLAN, as shown in Figure 3-7. Conversely, adjacent ports do not receive any of the broadcast traffic generated from other VLANs. This type of configuration substantially reduces the overall broadcast traffic, frees bandwidth for real user traffic, and lowers the overall vulnerability of the network to broadcast storms.

The smaller the VLAN group, the smaller the number of users affected by broadcast traffic activity within the VLAN group. You can also assign VLANs based on the application type and the number of applications broadcasts. You can place users sharing a broadcast-intensive application in the same VLAN group and distribute the application across the campus.

Providing Better Network Security

The use of LANs has increased at a very high rate over the past several years. As a result, LANs often have confidential, mission-critical data moving across them. Confidential data requires security through access restriction. One problem of shared LANs is that they are relatively easy to penetrate. By plugging in to a live port, an intrusive user has access to all traffic within the segment. The larger the group, the greater the potential access.

FIGURE 3-7
Restricting both the number of switch ports within a VLAN and the users residing on these ports can easily control the size of a broadcast domain.

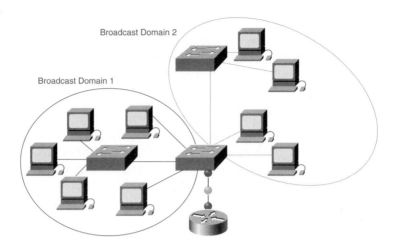

One cost-effective and easy administrative technique to increase security is to segment the network into multiple broadcast groups, as shown in Figure 3-8, which allows the network manager to

- Restrict the number of users in a VLAN group
- Disallow another user from joining without first receiving approval from the VLAN network management application
- Configure all unused ports to a default low-service VLAN

FIGURE 3-8
VLANs provide security firewalls, restrict individual user access, and flag any unwanted intrusion to a network manager.

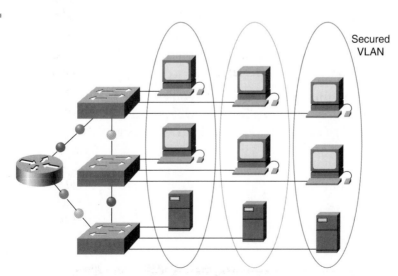

Implementing this type of segmentation is relatively straightforward. Switch ports are grouped together based on the type of applications and access privileges. Restricted applications and resources are commonly placed in a secured VLAN group. On the secured VLAN, the router restricts access into the group as configured on both the switches and the routers. Restrictions can be placed based on station addresses, application types, or protocol types.

You can add more security enhancements by using access control lists, which will be covered in Chapter 6, "Access Control Lists." These are especially useful when communicating between VLANs. On the secured VLAN, the router restricts access to the VLAN as configured on both switches and routers. You can place restrictions on station addresses, application types, protocol types, or even by time of day.

Saving Money by Using Existing Hubs

Over the past several years, network administrators have installed a significant number of hubs. Many of these devices are being replaced with newer switching technologies. Because network applications require more dedicated bandwidth and performance directly to the desktop, these hubs still perform useful functions in many existing installations. Network managers save money by connecting existing hubs to switches.

Each hub segment connected to a switch port can be assigned to only one VLAN, as shown in Figure 3-9. Stations that share a hub segment are all assigned to the same VLAN group. If an individual station needs to be reassigned to another VLAN, the station must be relocated to the corresponding hub. The interconnected switch fabric handles the communication between the switching ports and automatically determines the appropriate receiving segments. The more the shared hub can be broken into smaller groups, the greater the microsegmentation and the greater the VLAN flexibility for assigning individual users to VLAN groups.

By connecting hubs to switches, you can configure hubs as part of the VLAN architecture. You can also share traffic and network resources directly attached to switching ports with VLAN designations.

FIGURE 3-9
The connections between hubs and switches provide opportunities for VLAN segmentation.

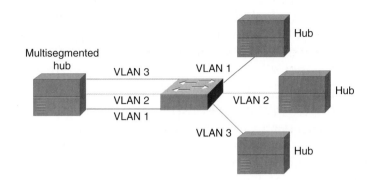

Summary

- An Ethernet switch is designed to physically segment a LAN into individual collision domains.

- A typical LAN is configured according to the physical infrastructure it connects.

- In a LAN that uses LAN switching devices, VLAN technology is a cost-effective and efficient way of grouping network users into virtual workgroups, regardless of their physical location on the network.

- VLANs work at Layer 2 and Layer 3 of the OSI reference model.

- Important to any VLAN architecture is the ability to transport VLAN information between interconnected switches and routers that reside on the corporate backbone.

- The problems associated with shared LANs and switches are causing traditional LAN configurations to be replaced with switched VLAN networking configurations.

- The most common approaches for logically grouping users into distinct VLANs are frame filtering, frame tagging, and frame identification.

- There are three main types of VLANs: port-centric VLANs, static VLANs, and dynamic VLANs.

- VLANs provide the following benefits:
  - They reduce administration costs related to solving problems associated with moves, additions, and changes.
  - They provide controlled broadcast activity.
  - They provide workgroup and network security.
  - They save money by using existing hubs.

Chapter Review

Complete all the review questions to test your understanding of the topics and concepts covered in this chapter. Answers are listed in Appendix A, "Chapter Review Answer Key."

1. Describe the benefits of VLANs.

2. What is the effect of VLANs on LAN broadcasts?

3. What are the three main VLAN implementations?

4. What is the purpose of VLAN frame tagging?

5. The phrase *microsegmentation with scalability* means which of the following?

   A. The ability to increase networks without creating collisions domains

   B. The ability to put a huge number of hosts on one switch

   C. The ability to broadcast to more nodes at once

   D. All of the above

6. Switches, as the core element of VLANs, provide the intelligence to do which of the following?

   A. They group users, ports, or logical addresses into a VLAN.

   B. They make filtering and forwarding decisions.

   C. They communicate with other switches and routers.

   D. All of the above.

7. Each _____ segment connected to a _____ port can be assigned to only one VLAN.

   A. switch; hub

   B. hub; router

   C. hub; switch

   D. LAN; hub

8. Which of the following is *not* an advantage of using static VLANS?

   A. They are secure.

   B. They are easy to configure.

C. They are easy to monitor.

D. They automatically configure ports when new stations are added.

9. Which of the following is *not* a criterion on which VLANs can be based?

   A. Port ID and MAC address

   B. Protocol

   C. Application

   D. All of the above are criteria on which VLANs can be based

10. Which of the following is a beneficial effect of adding a VLAN?

   A. Switches do not need to be configured.

   B. Broadcasts can be controlled.

   C. Confidential data can be protected.

   D. Physical boundaries that prevent user groupings can be removed.

Key Terms

ACL (access control list)   A list kept by a Cisco router to control access to or from the router for a number of services (for example, to prevent packets with a certain IP address from leaving a particular interface on the router).

broadcast   A data packet that is sent to all nodes on a network. Broadcasts are identified by a broadcast address.

broadcast domain   The set of all devices that will receive broadcast frames originating from any device within the set. Broadcast domains are typically bounded by routers because routers do not forward broadcast frames.

broadcast storm   An undesirable network event in which many broadcasts are sent simultaneously across all network segments. A broadcast storm uses substantial network bandwidth and, typically, causes network time-outs.

collision domain   In Ethernet, the network area within which frames that have collided are propagated. Repeaters and hubs propagate collisions; LAN switches, bridges, and routers do not.

dynamic VLAN   A VLAN that is based on the MAC addresses, the logical addresses, or the protocol type of the data packets.

firewall   A router or an access server, or several routers or access servers, designated as a buffer between any connected public networks and a private network. A firewall router uses access control lists and other methods to ensure the security of the private network.

flat network A network in which there are no routers placed between the switches, broadcasts and Layer 2 transmissions are sent to every switched port, and there is one broadcast domain across the entire network.

frame A logical grouping of information sent as a data link–layer unit over a transmission medium. Often refers to the header and trailer, used for synchronization and error control, that surround the user data contained in the unit. The terms *datagram, message, packet,* and *segment* are also used to describe logical information groupings at various layers of the OSI reference model and in various technology circles.

hub A hardware or software device that contains multiple independent but connected modules of network and internetwork equipment. Hubs can be active (where they repeat signals sent through them) or passive (where they do not repeat, but merely split, signals sent through them).

IEEE (Institute of Electrical and Electronic Engineers) A professional organization whose activities include the development of communications and network standards. IEEE LAN standards are the predominant LAN standards today.

LAN switch A high-speed switch that forwards packets between data-link segments. Most LAN switches forward traffic based on MAC addresses. LAN switches are often categorized according to the method they use to forward traffic: cut-through packet switching or store-and-forward packet switching. An example of a LAN switch is the Cisco Catalyst 5000.

MAC (Media Access Control) address A standardized data link–layer address that is required for every port or device that connects to a LAN. Other devices in the network use these addresses to locate specific ports in the network and to create and update routing tables and data structures. A MAC address is 6 bytes long. MAC addresses are controlled by the IEEE and are also known as hardware addresses, MAC-layer addresses, and physical addresses.

microsegmentation The division of a network into smaller segments, usually with the intention of increasing aggregate bandwidth to network devices.

multicast Single packets copied by a network and sent out to a set of network addresses. These addresses are specified in the destination address field.

port An interface on an internetworking device (such as a router).

port-centric VLAN   A VLAN in which all the nodes in the same VLAN are attached to the same switch port.

protocol   A formal description of a set of rules and conventions that govern how devices on a network exchange information.

router   A network-layer device that uses one or more metrics to determine the optimal path along which network traffic should be forwarded. Routers forward packets from one network to another based on network-layer information. Occasionally called a *gateway* (although this definition of gateway is becoming increasingly outdated).

scalability   The ability of a network to grow, without any major changes to the overall design.

segment   A section of a network that is bounded by bridges, routers, or switches.

static VLAN   A VLAN in which the ports on a switch are statically assigned.

switch   A network device that filters, forwards, and floods frames based on the destination address of each frame. The switch operates at the data link layer of the OSI reference model.

VLAN (virtual LAN)   A group of devices on a LAN that are configured (using management software) so that they can communicate as if they were attached to the same wire, when, in fact, they are located on a number of different LAN segments. Because VLANs are based on logical instead of physical connections, they are extremely flexible.

Objectives

After reading this chapter, you will be able to

- Explain LAN design goals
- Identify LAN design issues
- Explain network design methodology
- Describe how to gather and analyze network equipment
- Identify Layer 1 (media and topology) design issues
- Identify Layer 2 (LAN switching) design issues
- Identify Layer 3 (routing) design issues
- Describe the physical and logical network implementation documentation

Chapter 4

LAN Design

Introduction

Chapter 3, "VLANs," provided an introduction to virtual LANs (VLANs) and switched internetworking, compared traditional shared local-area network (LAN) configurations with switched LAN configurations, and discussed the benefits of using a switched VLAN architecture. Despite improvements in equipment performance and media capabilities, network design is becoming more difficult. The trend is toward increasingly complex environments involving multiple media and interconnection to networks outside any single organization's controlled LAN. Keeping all the many factors in mind is important because carefully designing networks can reduce the hardships associated with growth as a networking environment evolves.

One of the most critical steps to ensure a fast and stable network is the design of the network. If a network is not designed properly, many unforeseen problems can arise, and network growth can be jeopardized. This design process is truly an in-depth process. This chapter provides an overview of the LAN design process. In addition, LAN design goals, network design issues, network design methodology, and the development of LAN topologies are covered in this chapter.

Washington Project: Designing the Network

Throughout this book, you will be applying what you learn to the Washington School District Project. The fictional Washington School District is located in Phoenix, Arizona. The school district is in the process of designing and implementing an enterprisewide network, which will include LANs at each site and a wide-area network (WAN) to provide data connectivity between all school sites.

In this chapter, you will begin the process of designing the Washington School District LAN. As concepts and requirements are introduced, you will be able to apply them in your network design.

You will need to make sure to address the following requirements when designing the Washington School District network:

- The network is meant to serve different "workgroups" of staff members and students. This logical division will require the use of VLANs and will be a major design configuration. For example, VLANs should be used to secure the administrators' machines from the students' machines.

- Access to the Internet from any site in the school district is also an integral part of this implementation.

> ### Washington Project: Designing the Network (Continued)
>
> - A series of servers is needed to facilitate online automation of all the districts administrative functions and many of the curricular functions.
> - Because this network implementation will have to continue to be functional for a minimum of 7–10 years, all design considerations should include 100% growth in the LANs.
> - A minimum of 1.0 Mbps to any host computer in the network and 100 Mbps to any server host in the network is required.
> - Only two routed protocols will be allowed to be implemented in the network: TCP/IP and Novell's IPX.

LAN Design Goals

Designing a network can be a challenging task. Designing a network involves more than just connecting computers together. A network requires many features in order to be scalable and manageable. To design reliable, scalable networks, network designers must realize that each of the major components of a network has distinct design requirements. Even a network that consists of only 50 routing nodes can pose complex problems that lead to unpredictable results. Attempting to design and build networks that feature thousands of nodes can pose even more complex problems.

The first step in designing a LAN is to establish and document the goals of the design. These goals are particular to each organization or situation. However, the following requirements tend to show up in most network designs:

- Functionality—The network must work. That is, it must allow users to meet their job requirements. The network must provide user-to-user and user-to-application connectivity with reasonable speed and reliability.
- Scalability—The network must be able to grow. That is, the initial design should grow without any major changes to the overall design.
- Adaptability—The network must be designed with an eye toward future technologies, and it should include no element that would limit implementation of new technologies as they become available.
- Manageability—The network should be designed to facilitate network monitoring and management to ensure ongoing stability of operation.

These requirements are specific to certain types of networks and more general in other types of networks. This chapter discusses how to address these requirements.

Network Design Components

With the emergence of high-speed technologies such as Asynchronous Transfer Mode (ATM) and more complex LAN architectures that use LAN switching and VLANs over the past several years, many organizations have been upgrading existing LANs or planning, designing, and implementing new LANs.

To design LANs for high-speed technologies and multimedia-based applications, network designers should address the following critical components of the overall LAN design:

- The function and placement of servers
- Collision detection
- Segmentation
- Bandwidth versus broadcast domains

These components are discussed in the following sections.

Function and Placement of Servers

One of the keys to designing a successful network is to understand the function and placement of servers needed for the network. Servers provide file sharing, printing, communication, and application services, such as word processing. Servers typically do not functions as workstations; rather, they run specialized operating systems, such as NetWare, Windows NT, UNIX, and Linux. Today, each server usually is dedicated to one function, such as e-mail or file sharing.

Servers can be categorized into two distinct classes: enterprise servers and workgroup servers. An enterprise server supports all the users on the network by offering services, such as e-mail or Domain Name System (DNS), as shown in Figure 4-1. E-mail or DNS is a service that everyone in an organization (such as the Washington School District) would need because it is a centralized function. On the other hand, a workgroup server supports a specific set of users, offering services such as word processing and file sharing, which are services only a few groups of people would need.

Enterprise servers should be placed in the main distribution facility (MDF). This way, traffic to the enterprise servers has to travel only to the MDF and does not need to be transmitted across other networks. Ideally, workgroup servers should be placed in the intermediate distribution facilities (IDFs) closest to the users accessing the applications on these servers. You merely need to directly connect servers to the MDF or IDF. By placing, workgroup servers close to the users, traffic only has to travel the network infrastructure to that IDF, and does not affect other users on that network segment. Within the MDF and IDFs, the Layer 2 LAN switches should have 100 Mbps or more allocated for these servers.

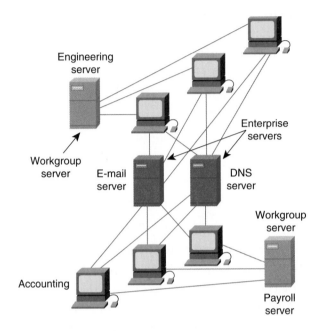

FIGURE 4-1
The differences between enterprise servers and workgroup servers involve the services needed.

Engineering server

Enterprise servers

Workgroup server

E-mail server

DNS server

Workgroup server

Accounting

Payroll server

Washington Project: Server Placement and Function

You should categorize all file servers for the Washington School District as enterprise or workgroup types, and then place servers in the network topology according to the anticipated traffic patterns of users and according to the functions described in here.

DNS and E-Mail Services

Each hub location should contain a DNS server to support the individual schools serviced out of that location. Each school should also contain a host for DNS and e-mail services (that is, a local post office) that will maintain a complete directory of the staff members and students for that location.

The Administrative Server

Each school location should have an administration server for the student tracking, attendance, grading, and other administrative functions. This server should run TCP/IP as its protocol suite and should be made available only to teachers and staff members.

The Library Server

The school district is implementing an automated library information and retrieval system for an online curricular research library. This server should run TCP/IP as its OSI Layer 3 and Layer 4 protocol and should be made available to anyone at the school site.

Washington Project: Server Placement and Function (Continued)
Application Server
All computer applications, such as word processing and spreadsheet software, should be housed in a central server at each school location.
Other Servers
Any other servers implemented at the school sites should be considered departmental (work-group) servers, and should be placed according to user group access needs. An example would be a server running an instructional application for a specific school site.

Intranets

One common configuration of a LAN is an intranet. Intranet Web servers differ from public Web servers in that, without the needed permissions and passwords, the public does not have access to an organization's intranet. Intranets are designed to be accessed by users who have access privileges to an organization's internal LAN. Within an intranet, Web servers are installed in the network, and browser technology is used as the common front end to access information, such as financial data or graphical, text-based data stored on those servers.

The addition of an intranet on a network is just one of many application and configuration features that can cause an increase in needed network bandwidth over current levels. Because bandwidth has to be added to the network backbone, network administrators should also consider acquiring robust desktops to get faster access into intranets. New desktops—and servers—should be outfitted with 10/100-Mbps Ethernet network interface cards (NICs) to provide the most configuration flexibility, thus enabling network administrators to dedicate bandwidth to individual end stations as needed.

Collision Detection

You should decide carefully on the selection and placement of networking devices to be used in the LAN in order to decrease the collision detection and media contention on a network. Contention refers to excessive collisions on Ethernet caused by too many devices, each with a great demand for the network segment. The number of broadcasts becomes excessive when there are too many client packets looking for services, too many server packets announcing services, too many routing table updates, and too many other broadcasts dependent on the protocols, such as Address Resolution Protocol (ARP).

An Ethernet node gets access to the wire by contending with other Ethernet nodes for the right to do so. When your network grows to include more nodes on the shared segment or wire, and these nodes have more and more messages to transmit, the chance that a node will contend successfully for its share of the wire gets much worse, and the network bogs down. The fact that this media access method—contention—does not scale or allow for growth, is Ethernet's main disadvantage.

As shown in Figure 4-2, as traffic increases on the shared media, the rate of collisions also increases. Although collisions are normal events in Ethernet, an excessive number of collisions further (sometimes dramatically) reduces available bandwidth. In most cases, the actual available bandwidth is reduced to a fraction (about 35% to 40%) of the full 10 Mbps. This reduction in bandwidth can be remedied by segmenting the network by using bridges, switches, or routers.

FIGURE 4-2
In a shared bus topology, collisions reduce the effective available bandwidth.

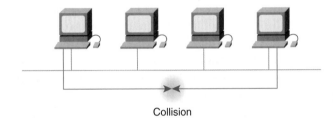

Collision

Segmentation

Segmentation is the process of splitting a single collision domain into two or more collision domains, as shown in Figure 4-3. Layer 2 (the data link layer) bridges or switches can be used to segment a logical bus topology and create separate collision domains, which results in more bandwidth being available to individual stations. Notice in Figure 4-3 that the entire bus topology still represents a single broadcast domain because, although bridges and switches do not forward collisions, they forward broadcast packets.

All broadcasts from any host in the same broadcast domain are visible to all other hosts in the same broadcast domain. Broadcasts must be visible to all hosts in the broadcast domain in order to establish connectivity. The scalability of the bandwidth domain depends on the total amount of traffic, and the scalability for a broadcast domain depends on the total broadcast of the traffic. It is important to remember that bridges and switches forward broadcast (FF-FF-FF-FF-FF) traffic, and that routers normally do not.

FIGURE 4-3
Routers and switches are used for segmentation.

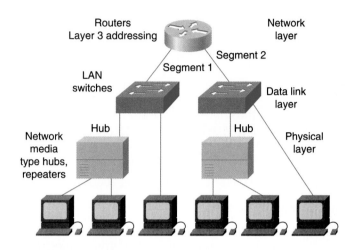

Bandwidth Versus Broadcast Domains

A *bandwidth domain* is everything associated with one port on a bridge or switch. In the case of an Ethernet switch, a bandwidth domain is also known as a *collision domain*. A switch can create one bandwidth domain per port. As shown in Figure 4-4, all workstations within one bandwidth domain compete for the same LAN bandwidth resource. All the traffic from any host in the bandwidth domain is visible to all the other hosts. In the case of an Ethernet collision domain, two stations can transmit at the same time, causing a collision.

FIGURE 4-4
A collision domain has shared bandwidth, and a broadcast domain is visible across a subnet.

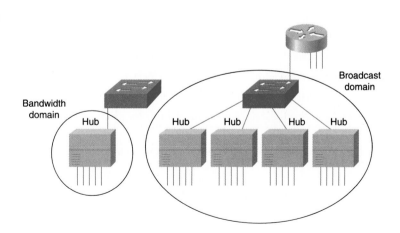

Network Design Methodology

For a LAN to be effective and serve the needs of its users, it should be designed and implemented according to a planned series of systematic steps, which include the following:

1. Gathering the users' requirements and expectations

2. Analyzing requirements

3. Designing the Layer 1, 2, and 3 LAN structure (that is, topology)

4. Documenting the logical and physical network implementation

These steps are described in the following sections.

Gathering Requirements

The first step in designing a network should be to gather data about the organizational structure. This information includes the organization's history and current status, projected growth, operating policies and management procedures, office systems and procedures, and the viewpoints of the people who will be using the LAN. You need to answer the following questions: Who are the people who will be using the network? What is their level of skill, and what are their attitudes toward computers and computer applications?

Answering these and similar questions will help determine how much training will be required and how many people will be needed to support the LAN.

Washington Project: Understanding the Customer

First and foremost, you must understand the customer. In the case of the Washington School District, you need to talk to major users of the network; find out their geographic location, their current applications, and their plans for the future; and determine who the major players will be in helping you design the network.

After you have gathered data on the districts organizational structure, you need to

- Determine where information flows in the district

- Find out where shared data resides and who uses it

- Determine whether data outside the district—for example, data on the Internet—is accessed

- Define the issues or problems that need to be addressed

Ideally, the information gathering process helps clarify and identify the problems. You also need to determine whether there are documented policies in place. Has some data been declared mission critical? Have some operations been declared mission critical? (*Mission-critical* data and operation are those that are considered key to businesses, and access to them is critical to the business running on a daily basis.) What protocols are allowed on the network? Are only certain desktop hosts supported?

Next, you should determine who in the organization has authority over addressing, naming, topology design, and configuration. Some companies have a central Management Information Systems (MIS) department that controls everything. Some companies have very small MIS departments and, therefore, must delegate authority to departments. Focus on identifying the resources and constraints of the organization. Organization resources that can affect the implementation of a new LAN system fall into two general categories: computer hardware and software resources and human resources. An organization's existing computer hardware and software must be documented, and projected hardware and software needs identified. How are these resources currently linked and shared? What financial resources does the organization have available? Documenting these types of things helps you estimate costs and develop a budget for the LAN. You should make sure you understand performance issues of any existing network.

Analyzing Requirements

The next step in designing a network is to analyze the requirements of the network and its users that were gathered in the last step. Network user needs constantly change. For example, as more voice- and video-based network applications become available, the pressure to increase network bandwidth will become intense.

Another component of the analysis phase is assessing the user requirements. A LAN that is incapable of supplying prompt and accurate information to its users is of little use. Therefore, you must take steps to ensure that the information requirements of the organization and its workers are met.

Washington Project: Availability

Find out what *availability* means to your customer. In the case of the Washington School District, you need to conduct a detailed analysis of current and projected needs in order to help meet this need. Analysis of network requirements includes analyzing the district's business and technical goals.

You need to answer the following questions:

- What applications will be implemented?
- What new networks will be accessed?
- What are the success criteria?
- How can you tell if the new design is successful?

Availability and Network Traffic

Availability measures the usefulness of the network. Many things affect availability, including the following:

- Throughput
- Response time
- Access to resources

Every customer has a different definition of *availability*. For example, there may be a need to transport voice and video over the network. However, these services require more bandwidth than is available on the network or backbone. You can increase availability by adding more resources. But resources drive up cost. Network design seeks to provide the greatest availability for the least cost.

Washington Project: Determining Network Traffic Load

You need to determine the network traffic load for the Washington School District before developing a network structure and acquiring hardware.

Additionally, when analyzing the district's technical requirements, you should estimate the traffic load caused by applications in packet size (for example, you need to estimate the size of files in bytes per second needed to be transmitted over the network).

Certain types of network use can generate large volumes of traffic and, therefore, can cause congestion, including congestion of the following:

- Internet access
- Computers loading software from a remote site
- Anything that transmits images or video
- Central database access
- Department file servers

You should estimate worst-case traffic load on the network during the busiest times for users and during regularly scheduled network services, such as file server backups.

Designing the Network Topology

After determining the overall requirements for the network, the next step is to decide on an overall LAN topology that will satisfy the user requirements. In this book, we concentrate on star topology and extended star topology. As you have seen, the star/extended star topology, which is illustrated in Figure 4-5, uses Ethernet 802.3 carrier sense multiple access collision detect (CSMA/CD) technology. The reason that this book focuses on a CSMA/CD star topology is that it is by far the dominant configuration in the industry.

FIGURE 4-5
The star and extended star topologies are the most widely used models in networking and are extremely stable.

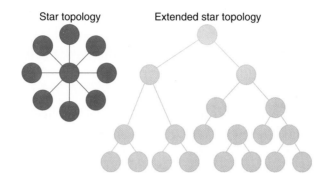

Star topology   Extended star topology

The major pieces of a LAN topology design can be broken into three unique categories of the OSI reference model—the network layer, the data link layer, and the physical layer—as shown in Figure 4-3. These components are discussed in the following sections.

Designing the Layer 1 Topology

In this section, we examine Layer 1 star and extended star topologies.

Washington Project: Speed and Expansion
For the Washington School District network, you need to build the Layer 1 components of the district network with speed and expansion capabilities. As you know, the physical layer controls the way data is transmitted between the source and a destination node. Therefore, the type of media and topology you select helps you determine how much data can travel across the network and how quickly.

Cabling. The physical cabling is one of the most important components to consider when designing a network. Design issues include the type of cabling to be used (typically copper or fiber) and the overall structure of the cabling. Layer 1 cabling media include types such as Category 5 unshielded twisted-pair (UTP) and fiber-optic cable, along with the EIA/TIA 568 standard for layout and connection of wiring schemes.

In addition to distance limitations, you should carefully evaluate the strengths and weaknesses of various wiring topologies because a network is only as effective as its underlying cable and is only as good as its cable because most problems that come up on a network are Layer 1 problems. If you are planning any significant changes for a network, you should do a complete cable audit to identify areas that require upgrades and rewiring.

Whether you are designing a new network or recabling an existing network
and high-speed technologies such as Fast Ethernet, ATM, and Gigabit Ethernet, the cable system, at a minimum, should have fiber-optic cable in the backbone and risers and Category 5 UTP cable in the horizontal runs. The cable
upgrade should take priority over any other needed changes, and enterprises
should ensure—without exception—that these systems conform to well-
defined industry standards, such as the TIA/EIA 568 specifications.

The EIA/TIA 568 standard specifies that every device connected to the network should be linked to a central location with horizontal cabling, as shown
in Figure 4-6. This is true if all the hosts that need to access the network are
within the 100-meter distance limitation for Category 5 UTP Ethernet, as
specified by EIA/TIA 568B standards. Table 4-1 lists cable types and their
characteristics.

FIGURE 4-6
Smaller net-
work imple-
mentations
may only
require one
wiring closet at
the center of
the star.

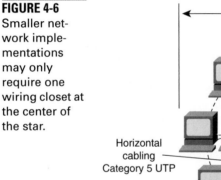
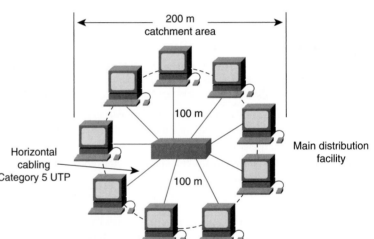

TABLE 4-1   Cable Type Characteristics and IEEE 802.3 Values

Characteristic	10BaseT	10BaseFL	100BaseTX	100BaseFX
Data rate	10 Mbps	10 Mbps	100 Mbps	100 Mbps
Signaling method	Baseband	Baseband	Baseband	Baseband

TABLE 4-1   Cable Type Characteristics and IEEE 802.3 Values (Continued)

Characteristic	10BaseT	10BaseFL	100BaseTX	100BaseFX
Medium type	Category 5 UTP	Fiber-optic	Category 5 UTP	Multi-mode fiber (two strands)
Maximum length	100 meters	2000 meters	100 meters	400 meters

Star Topology. In a simple star topology, as shown in Figure 4-7, with only one wiring closet, the MDF includes one or more horizontal cross-connect (HCC) patch panels. HCC patch cables are used to connect the Layer 1 horizontal cabling with the Layer 2 LAN switch ports. The uplink port of the LAN switch, which is unlike other ports because it does not cross over, is connected to the Ethernet port of the Layer 3 router using patch cable. At this point, the end host has a complete physical connection to the router port.

FIGURE 4-7
The number of horizontal cable runs and the size (that is, the number of ports) of the HCC patch panels should be determined by the user's requirements.

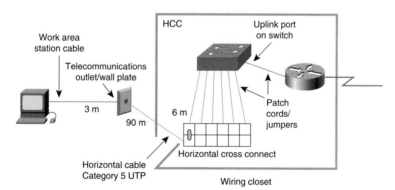

> **Washington Project: Catchment Areas**
>
> You should review the Washington School District's requirements to determine what the user expects for the number of horizontal cable runs to each room that the MDF or IDF will be servicing in its catchment area.

Extended Star Topology. In larger networks, it is not unusual to have more than one wiring closet if there are hosts that need network connectivity but are outside the 100-meter limitation for Category 5 UTP Ethernet. By creating multiple wiring closets, multiple catchment areas are created. The secondary wiring closets are referred to as IDFs (see Figure 4-8). EIA/TIA 568 standards specify that IDFs should be connected to the MDF by using vertical cabling, also called backbone cabling.

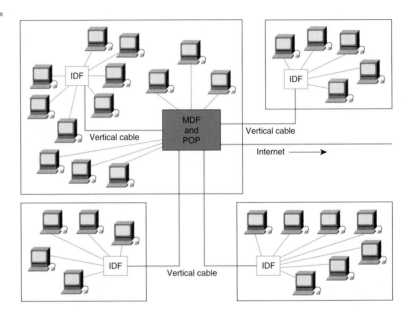

FIGURE 4-8
Extended star topology in a multibuilding campus.

As shown in Figure 4-9, a vertical cross-connect (VCC) is used to interconnect the various IDFs to the central MDF. Because the vertical cable lengths typically are longer than the 100-meter limit for Category 5 UTP cable, as shown in Figure 4-10, fiber-optic cabling normally is used.

Washington Project: Connection Speeds
In the Washington School District network, the vertical cabling should carry all data traffic between the IDFs and MDFs. Therefore, the speed of this connection should be designed to be the fast link in the network. All traffic across the district network backbone will traverse this link, so this link should be at least 100 Mbps.

Fast Ethernet—MDF-to-IDF Vertical Cabling. Fast Ethernet is Ethernet that has been upgraded to 100 Mbps. This type uses the standard Ethernet broadcast-oriented logical bus topology of 10BaseT, along with the familiar CSMA/CD method for Media Access Control (MAC). The Fast Ethernet standard is actually several different standards based on copper-pair wire (100BaseTX) and on fiber-optic cable (100BaseFX), and it is used to connect the MDF to the IDF, as shown in Figure 4-11.

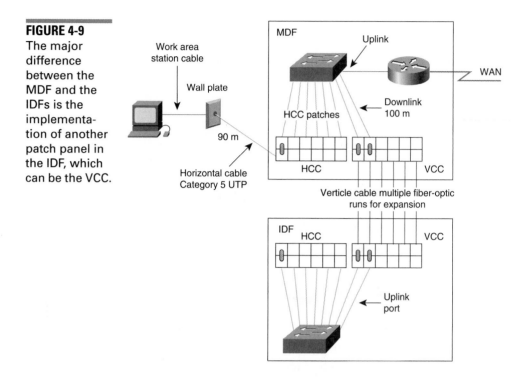

FIGURE 4-9
The major difference between the MDF and the IDFs is the implementation of another patch panel in the IDF, which can be the VCC.

Layer 1 Documentation. As shown in Figure 4-12, the logical diagram is the network topology model without all the detail of the exact installation path of the cabling. It is the basic road map of the LAN. Elements of the logical diagram include

- The exact locations of the MDF and IDF wiring closets.
- The type and quantity of cabling used to interconnect the IDFs with the MDF, along with how many spare cables are available for increasing the bandwidth between the wiring closets. For example, if the vertical cabling between IDF 1 and the MDF is running at 80% utilization, you can use two additional pairs to double the capacity.
- Detailed documentation, as shown in the cut sheet in Figure 4-13, of all cable runs, the identification numbers, and which port on the HCC or VCC the run is terminated on. For example, say Room 203 has lost connectivity to the network. By examining the cutsheet, you can see that Room 203 is running off cable run 203-1, which is terminated on HCC 1 port 13. You can now test that run by using a cable tester to determine whether the problem is a Layer 1 failure. If it is, you can simply use one of the other two runs to get the connectivity back and then troubleshoot run 203-1.

FIGURE 4-10
All vertical cabling is connected to the MDF to create a single LAN segment.

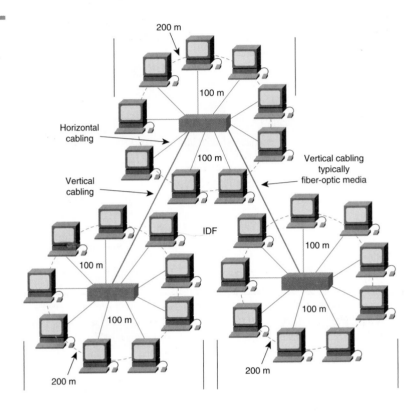

FIGURE 4-11
Fast Ethernet connects the MDF to the IDF by utilizing bandwidth at 100 Mbps using CSMA/CD technology.

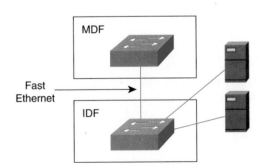

FIGURE 4-12
The logical diagram is a snapshot of the overall view of the LAN implementation and is useful in troubleshooting problems and implementing expansion in the future.

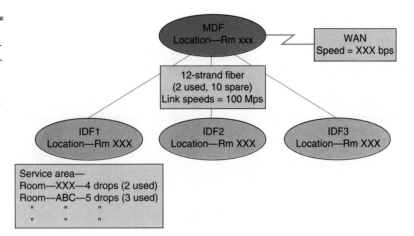

Washington Project: LAN Wiring Scheme Requirements

As you're planning the wiring for the Washington School District network, you need to take into account certain LAN requirements related to user access, segmentation, infrastructure, cabling, MDFs, and IDFs. Therefore, you should address the requirements described here when designing the network.

Requirement 1

Two LAN segments need to be implemented in each school and the district office. One LAN needs to be designated for student/curriculum usage and the other needs to be designated for administration usage.

Requirement 2

The LAN infrastructure needs to be based on Ethernet LAN switching, which will allow for a migration to faster speeds (that is, more bandwidth) to the individual computers and between MDFs and IDFs without revamping the physical wiring scheme to accommodate future applications. The transport speeds need be Ethernet 10BaseT, 100BaseT, and 100BaseFx.

Requirement 3

Horizontal cabling needs to be Category 5 UTP and needs to have the capacity to accommodate 100-Mbps. Vertical (backbone) cabling needs to be Category 5 UTP or fiber-optic multimode cable.

The cabling infrastructure needs to comply with EIA/TIA 568 standards.

Requirement 4

In each location, an MDF room needs to be established as the central point to which all LAN cabling will be terminated. This will also be the point of presence (POP) for the WAN connection. The IDF should service its geographical area, and the IDF should be connected directly to the MDF in a star or extended star topology.

FIGURE 4-13
The cutsheet becomes a valuable tool in troubleshooting any Layer 1 network problems.

IDF1
Location—Rm XXX

Connection	Cable ID	Cross Connection Paired#/Port#	Type of Cable	Status
IDF1 to Rm 203	203-1	HCC1/Port 13	Category 5 UTP	Used
IDF1 to Rm 203	203-2	HCC1/Port 14	Category 5 UTP	Not used
IDF1 to Rm 203	203-3	HCC2/Port 3	Category 5 UTP	Not used
IDF1 to MDF	IDF1-1	VCC1/Port 1	Multimode fiber	Used
IDF1 to MDF	IDF1-2	VCC1/Port 2	Multimode fiber	Used

Designing the Layer 2 LAN Topology

As you learned in Chapter 2, "LAN Switching," and Chapter 3, "VLANs," the purpose of Layer 2 devices in the network is to provide flow control, error detection, error correction, and to reduce congestion in the network. The two most common Layer 2 devices (other than the NIC, which every host on the network must have) are bridges and LAN switches. Devices at this layer determine the size of the collision domains and broadcast domains. This section concentrates on the implementation of LAN switching at Layer 2.

Washington Project: Layer 2 Design Goals
The following are Layer 2 LAN topology design goals for the Washington School District network: • You should install LAN switching devices that use microsegmentation in order to reduce the collision domain size. • You should create VLANs and unique broadcast domains based on user workgroups.

Collisions and collision domain size are two factors that negatively effect the performance of a network. By using LAN switching, you can microsegment the network, thus eliminating collisions and reducing the size of collision domains. As shown in Figure 4-14, another important characteristic of a LAN switch is how it can allocate bandwidth on a per-port basis, thus allowing more bandwidth to vertical cabling, uplinks, and servers. This type of switching is referred to as asymmetric switching, and it provides switched connections between ports of unlike bandwidth, such as a combination of 10-Mbps and 100-Mbps ports.

FIGURE 4-14
An example of asymmetric switching.

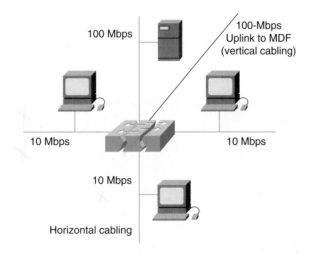

As you have learned, microsegmentation means using bridges and switches to boost performance for a workgroup or a backbone. Typically, boosting performance in this manner involves Ethernet switching. As shown in Figure 4-15, switches can be used with hubs to provide the appropriate level of performance for different users and servers.

FIGURE 4-15
You can avoid congestion on a LAN by using microsegmentation to eliminate collision domains.

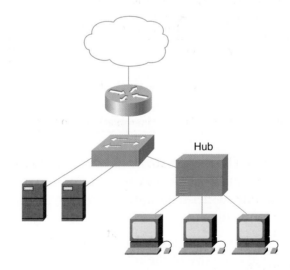

By installing LAN switching at the MDF and IDFs and vertical cable between the MDF and the IDFs, the vertical cable is carrying all the data traffic between the MDF and the IDFs; therefore, the capacity of this run must be larger than that of the runs between the IDFs and workstations.

Horizontal cable runs use Category 5 UTP, and no cable drop should be longer than 100 meters, which allows links at 10 Mbps or 100 Mbps. In a normal environment, 10 Mbps is adequate for the horizontal cable drop. Because asymmetric LAN switches allow for mixing 10-Mbps and 100-Mbps ports on a single switch, the next task is to determine the number of 10-Mbps and 100-Mbps ports needed in the MDF and every IDF. This can be determined by going back to the user requirements for the number of horizontal cable drops per room and the number of drops total in any catchment area, along with the number of vertical cable runs.

For example, say user requirements dictate that 4 horizontal cable runs be installed to each room. The IDF that services a catchment area covers 18 rooms. Therefore, 4 drops × 18 rooms = 72 LAN switch ports.

Washington Project: LAN Topology Requirements
As you're planning the LAN topology for the Washington School District network, you need to keep in mind certain requirements for rooms that need access to the network and the room's wiring POPs.
Requirement 1
Each room requiring connection to the network needs to be able to support 24 workstations and be supplied with four Category 5 UTP runs for data, with one run terminated at the teacher's workstation. These cable runs should be terminated in the closest MDF or IDF. All Category 5 UTP cable runs need be tested end-to-end for 100-Mbps bandwidth capacity.
Requirement 2
A single location in each room needs be designated as the wiring POP for that room. It needs to consist of a lockable cabinet containing all cable terminations and electronic components (that is, data hubs). From this location, data services need to be distributed within the room via decorative wire molding. Network 1 needs to be allocated for general curriculum use, and Network 2 needs to be allocated for administrative use.

Layer 2 Switch Collision Domains. To determine the size of a collision domain, you must determine how many hosts are physically connected to any single port on the switch. This also affects how much network bandwidth is available to any host.

In an ideal situation, there is only one host connected on a LAN switch port. This would make the size of the collision domain 2 (the source host and destination host). Because of this small collision domain, there should be almost no collisions when any two hosts are communicating with each other.

Another way to implement LAN switching is to install shared LAN hubs on the switch ports and connect multiple hosts to a single switch port, as shown in Figure 4-16. All hosts connected to the shared LAN hub share the same collision domain and bandwidth, as shown in Figure 4-17.

FIGURE 4-16
When you're using hubs, the size of the collision domain increases and bandwidth is shared.

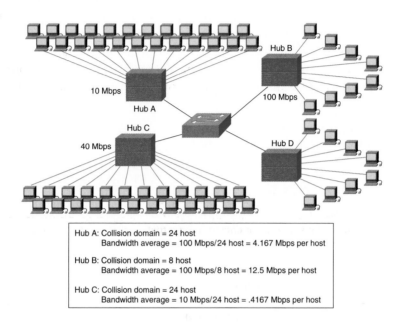

Hub A: Collision domain = 24 host
       Bandwidth average = 100 Mbps/24 host = 4.167 Mbps per host

Hub B: Collision domain = 8 host
       Bandwidth average = 100 Mbps/8 host = 12.5 Mbps per host

Hub C: Collision domain = 24 host
       Bandwidth average = 10 Mbps/24 host = .4167 Mbps per host

FIGURE 4-17
In a pure LAN switched environment, the size of the collision domain is 2 hosts, and in a LAN that uses hubs, the collision domain is much larger.

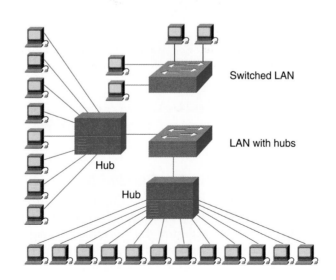

Note that some older switches, such as the Catalyst 1700, don't truly support sharing the same collision domain and bandwidth because they don't maintain multiple MAC addresses mapped to each port. In that case, there are many broadcasts and ARP requests.

Using a Layer 2 Switch with Hubs. Shared-media hubs generally are used in a LAN switch environment to create more connection points at the end of the horizontal cable runs, as shown in Figure 4-18. This is an acceptable solution, but you must ensure that collision domains are kept small and bandwidth requirements to the host are accomplished according to specifications gathered in the requirements phase of the network design process.

FIGURE 4-18
You can use hubs to supply more connection points for a host.

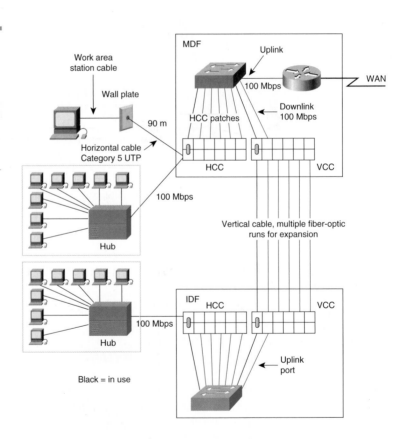

Layer 2 Migration to Higher Bandwidth. As the network grows, the need for more bandwidth increases. In the vertical cabling between MDF and IDFs, unused fiber optics can be connected from the VCC to 100-MB ports on the switch. The network in Figure 4-19 doubles the capacity of the vertical cabling in the network in Figure 4-18 by bringing up another link.

FIGURE 4-19
Migration to higher bandwidth is as simple as patching to a higher-speed port or adding more higher-speed ports.

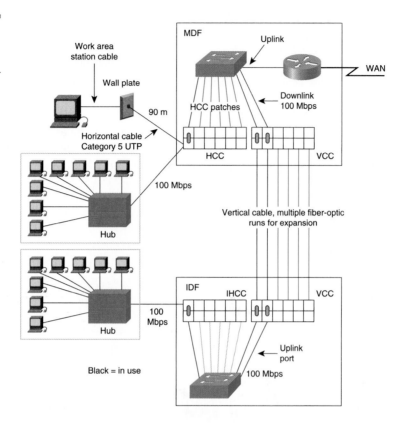

In the horizontal cabling, you can increase the bandwidth by a factor of 10 by repatching from the HCC to a 100-MB port on the switch and changing from a 10-MB hub to 100-MB hub. When sizing the Layer 2 LAN switch, it is important to make sure there are enough 100-MB ports to allow for this migration to higher bandwidth. It is important to document the speed at which each active cable drop is running.

Designing the Layer 3 LAN Topology

Layer 3 (the network layer) devices, such as routers, can be used to create unique LAN segments and allow communication between segments based on Layer 3 addressing, such as IP addressing. Implementation of Layer 3 devices, such as routers, allows for segmentation of the LAN into unique physical and logical networks. Routers also allow for connectivity to wide-area networks (WANs), such as the Internet.

Layer 3 Router Implementation. As shown in Figure 4-20, Layer 3 routing determines traffic flow between unique physical network segments based on Layer 3 addressing, such as IP network and subnet. The router is one of the most powerful devices in the network topology.

FIGURE 4-20
Layer 3 routing addresses issues such as the need for physically separate subnets.

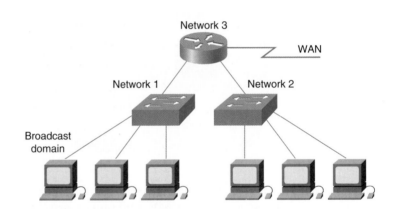

As you have learned, a router forwards data packets based on destination addresses. A router does not forward LAN-based broadcasts such as ARP requests. Therefore, the router interface is considered the entry and exit point of a broadcast domain and stops broadcasts from reaching other LAN segments.

VLAN Implementation. One important issue in a network is the total number of broadcasts, such as ARP requests. By using VLANs, you can limit broadcast traffic to within a VLAN and thus create smaller broadcast domains, as shown in Figure 4-21. VLANs can also be used to provide security by creating the VLAN groups according to function, as shown in Figure 4-22.

FIGURE 4-21
Routers provide communication between VLANs.

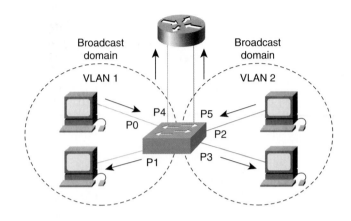

FIGURE 4-22
VLANs provide broadcast containment and security.

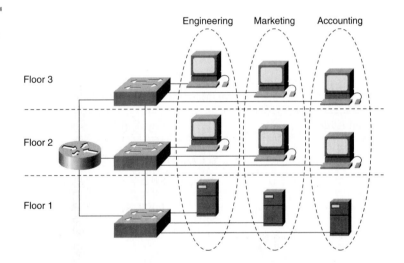

In Figure 4-21, a physical port association is used to implement VLAN assignment. Ports P0, P1, and P4 have been assigned to VLAN 1. VLAN 2 has ports P2, P3, and P5. Communication between VLAN 1 and VLAN 2 can occur only through the router. This limits the size of the broadcast domains and uses the router to determine whether VLAN 1 can talk to VLAN 2. This means you can create a security scheme based on VLAN assignment.

Using Routers to Create Scalable Networks. Routers provide scalability because they can serve as firewalls for broadcasts, as shown in Figure 4-20. In addition, because Layer 3 addresses typically have structure, routers can provide greater scalability by dividing networks and subnets, as shown in

Figure 4-23, therefore, adding structure to Layer 3 addresses. The ways in which greater scalability in networks can occur are shown in Table 4-2. When the networks are divided into subnets, the final step is to develop and document the IP addressing scheme to be used in the network.

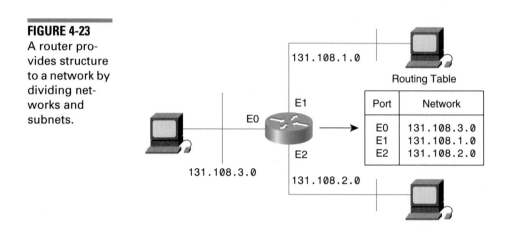

FIGURE 4-23
A router provides structure to a network by dividing networks and subnets.

TABLE 4-2   **Logical Addressing, Mapped to the Physical Network**

Logical Address	Physical Network Devices
x.x.x.1–x.x.x.10	Router, LAN, and WAN ports
x.x.x.11–x.x.x.20	LAN switches
x.x.x.21–x.x.x.30	Enterprise servers
x.x.x.31–x.x.x.80	Workgroup servers
x.x.x.81–x.x.x.254	Hosts

Routing technology filters data-link broadcasts and multicasts. By adding router ports with additional subnet or network addresses, you can segment the internetwork as required. Network protocol addressing and routing provide built-in scaling. When deciding whether to use routers or switches, remember to ask, "What problem am I trying to solve?" If your problem is protocol related rather than contention oriented, then routers are appropriate. Routers solve problems with excessive broadcasts, protocols that do not scale well, security issues, and network-layer addressing. Routers, however, are more expensive and harder to configure than switches.

Washington Project: Addressing
The district office should develop a complete TCP/IP addressing and naming convention scheme for all hosts, servers, and network interconnection devices. The implementation of unauthorized addresses should be prohibited. All computers located on the administrative networks should have static addresses. Curriculum computers should obtain addresses by utilizing Dynamic Host Configuration Protocol (DHCP). DHCP provides a mechanism for allocating IP addresses dynamically so that addresses can be reused when hosts no longer need them.

Using Routers to Impose Logical Structure. As shown in Figure 4-23, routers can be used to provide IP subnets to add structure to addresses. With bridges and switches, all unknown addresses must be flooded out of every port. With routers, hosts using protocols with network-layer addressing can solve the problem of finding other hosts without flooding. If the destination address is local, the sending host can encapsulate the packet in a data-link header and send a unicast frame directly to the station. The router does not see the frame and, of course, does not need to flood the frame. The sending host might have to use ARP, which would cause a broadcast, but the broadcast is only a local broadcast and is not forwarded by the router. If the destination is not local, then the sending station transmits the packet to the router. The router sends the frame to the destination or to the next hop, based on its routing table. Given this routing functionality, it is clear that large, scalable LANs need to incorporate some routers.

Using a Layer 3 Router for Segmentation. Figure 4-24 is an example of an implementation that has multiple physical networks. All data traffic from Network 1 destined for Network 2 has to go through the router. In this implementation, there are two broadcast domains. The two networks have unique Layer 3 IP addressing network/subnetwork addressing schemes.

In a structured Layer 1 wiring scheme, multiple physical networks are easy to create simply by patching the horizontal cabling and vertical cabling into the appropriate Layer 2 switch using patch cables. As we will see in future chapters, this implementation provides for robust security implementation. In addition, the router is the central point in the LAN for traffic destination.

Documenting the Logical and Physical Network Implementation

After you have developed the IP addressing scheme for the customer, you should document it by site and by network within the site, as shown in Table 4-2. A standard convention should be set for addressing important hosts on the network. This addressing scheme should be kept consistent throughout the entire network, as shown in Figure 4-25. By creating addressing maps, you can get a snapshot of the network, as shown in Figure 4-26. Creating physical maps of the network, as shown in Figure 4-27, helps you troubleshoot the network.

FIGURE 4-24
In this implementation, the router serves as the central point in the LAN for traffic destination, and robust security is implemented.

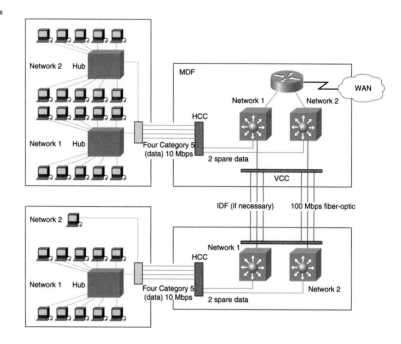

FIGURE 4-25
Networks with good documentation are easy to troubleshoot when problems occur.

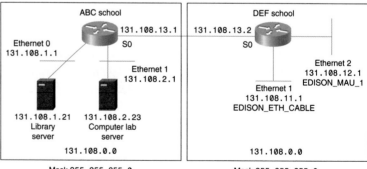

IP Network 131.108.0.0
Subnet Mask = 255.255.255.0
XYZ school district
ABC school
131.108.1.0
through
131.108.10.0
Subnet mask = 255.255.255.0
Router name = ABC Router
Ethernet 0 = 131.108.1.0
Ethernet 1 = 131.108.2.0
Ethernet 2 = 131.108.3.0
DEF school
131.108.11.0
through
131.108.21.0
Subnet mask = 255.255.255.0
Router name = DEF Router
Ethernet 0 = 131.108.11.0
Ethernet 1 = 131.108.12.0

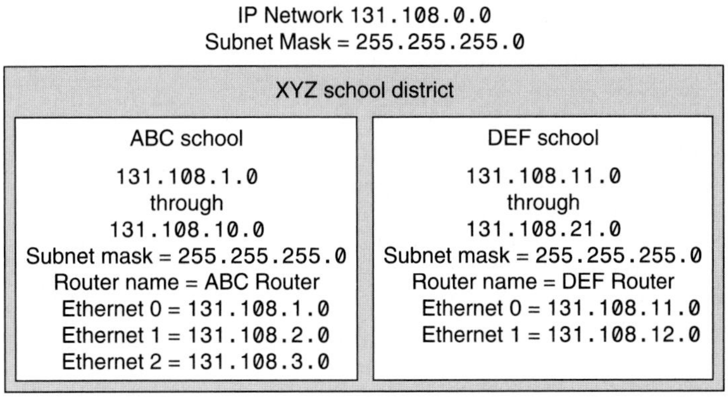

FIGURE 4-26
Networks with good documentation such as this reduce network problem load.

Router-1
WAN link
Rooms
Category 5
UTP
Ethernet 0
Ethernet 1
HCC1
Port 1
HCC2
MDF-1
Room 103
Building A
Include
cutsheets
MDF-1
Port 2-3
Port 6-7
MDF-2
VCC
Port 6-7
IDF1-1
IDF1-2
IDF-1
Room 217
Building J
HCC-3
HCC-4
Category 5
UTP

FIGURE 4-27
Physical maps indicate where MDFs and IDFs are located and where a host is connected to the network.

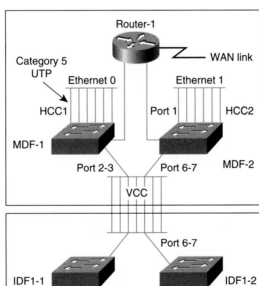

Summary

- One of the most critical factors in ensuring a fast and stable network is the design of the network. If a network is not designed properly, many unforeseen problems may arise, and network growth can be jeopardized.
- LAN design goals include functionality, scalability, adaptability, and manageability.
- Network design issues include function and placement of servers, collision detection, segmentation, and bandwidth versus broadcast domains.
- The design process includes the following:
    - Gathering the users requirements and expectations
    - Determining data traffic patterns now and in the future based on growth and server placements
    - Defining all the Layer 1, 2, and 3 devices, along with the LAN and WAN topology
    - Documenting the physical and logical network implementation

Washington School District Project Task: LAN Design

In this chapter, you have learned concepts that will help you begin the design process for the Washington School District network. As part of the LAN design process, you need to complete the following tasks:

1. Gather all information required to design a LAN for the Washington School District.

2. Design a LAN based on the addressing scheme for the Washington School District.

3. Develop and document an overall LAN design based on the user and district requirements.

You need to have the following items to properly design the Washington School District LAN and complete the tasks required:

- A user requirements document
- An overall design document, which includes a logical LAN design model of the school and a complete physical design document that includes
    - Detail of all MDFs/IDFs in the rooms, including a to-scale diagram
    - The number of HCCs, VCCs, and LAN switch ports required to meet the existing and projected growth needs

- Specifications on the type and quantity of cable media for all horizontal and vertical runs
- Specifications on security, VLANs, and the separation of staff and student networks
- The overall district IP addressing scheme

Chapter Review

Complete all the review questions to test your understanding of the topics and concepts covered in this chapter. Answers are listed in Appendix A, "Chapter Review Answer Key."

1. What are the four main goals of any network design?

2. What is the purpose of Layer 2 devices in a network design?

3. What is the purpose of Layer 3 devices in a network design?

4. What are the two major categories of servers that you should consider in a network design, and what are their purposes?

5. What are the main aspects of a network that should be documented and why?

6. Which of the following is likely to cause congestion?

   A. Internet access

   B. Central database access

   C. Video and image transmission

   D. All of the above

7. Which of the following is *not* a cause of excessive broadcasts?

   A. Too many client packets looking for services

   B. Too many server packets announcing services

   C. Too many routing table updates

   D. Too many network segments

8. A primary data link–layer design goal is the selection of _____ devices, such as bridges or LAN switches, used to connect _____ media to form LAN segments.

   A. Layer 3; Layer 2

   B. Layer 1; Layer 2

   C. Layer 2; Layer 1

   D. Layer 2; Layer 3

9. Which of the following specifications for 10BaseT is wrong?

   A. Data rate = 10 Mbps

   B. Max length = 400 meters

C. Signaling method = baseband

D. Media = Category 5 UTP

10. Which of the following are benefits of implementing Layer 3 devices in your LAN:

A. Allows segmentation of the LAN into unique physical and logical networks

B. Filters data-link broadcasts and multicasts and allows for WAN connectivity

C. Provides logical structure to the network

D. All of the above

Key Terms

10BaseT A 10-Mbps baseband Ethernet specification using two pairs of twisted-pair cabling (Category 3, 4, or 5): one pair for transmitting data and the other for receiving data. 10BaseT, which is part of the IEEE 802.3 specification, has a distance limit of approximately 100 meters per segment.

100BaseFX A 100-Mbps baseband Fast Ethernet specification using two strands of multimode fiber-optic cable per link. To guarantee proper signal timing, a 100BaseFX link cannot exceed 400 meters in length. Based on the IEEE 802.3 standard.

100BaseTX A 100-Mbps baseband Fast Ethernet specification using two pairs of either UTP or STP wiring. The first pair of wires is used to receive data; the second is used to transmit. To guarantee proper signal timing, a 100BaseTX segment cannot exceed 100 meters in length. Based on the IEEE 802.3 standard.

asymmetric switching A type of switching that provides switched connections between ports of unlike bandwidth, such as a combination of 10-Mbps and 100-Mbps ports.

ATM (Asynchronous Transfer Mode) An international standard for cell relay in which multiple service types (such as voice, video, or data) are conveyed in fixed-length (53-byte) cells. Fixed-length cells allow cell processing to occur in hardware, thereby reducing transit delays. ATM is designed to take advantage of high-speed transmission media, such as E3, SONET, and T3.

backbone cabling   Cabling that provides interconnections between wiring closets, between wiring closets and the POP, and between buildings that are part of the same LAN.

broadcast domain   The set of all devices that will receive broadcast frames originating from any device within the set. Broadcast domains are typically bounded by routers because routers do not forward broadcast frames.

catchment area   A zone that falls within an area that can be served by an internetworking device such as a hub.

Category 5 cabling   One of five grades of UTP cabling described in the EIA/TIA 568B standard. Category 5 cabling can transmit data at speeds up to 100 Mbps.

contention   An access method in which network devices compete for permission to access the physical medium.

EIA/TIA 568   A standard that describes the characteristics and applications for various grades of UTP cabling.

encapsulate   To wrap data in a particular protocol header. For example, Ethernet data is wrapped in a specific Ethernet header before network transit. Also, when bridging dissimilar networks, the entire frame from one network simply is placed in the header used by the data link layer protocol of the other network.

enterprise server   A server that supports all the users on a network by offering services such as e-mail or Domain Name System (DNS).

Ethernet   A baseband LAN specification invented by Xerox Corporation and developed jointly by Xerox, Intel, and Digital Equipment Corporation. Ethernet networks use CSMA/CD and run over a variety of cable types at 10 Mbps. Ethernet is similar to the IEEE 802.3 series of standards.

Fast Ethernet   Any of a number of 100-Mbps Ethernet specifications. Fast Ethernet offers a speed increase ten times that of the 10BaseT Ethernet specification, while preserving such qualities as frame format, MAC mechanisms, and MTU. Such similarities allow the use of existing 10BaseT applications and network management tools on Fast Ethernet networks. Based on an extension to the IEEE 802.3 specification.

fiber-optic cable   A physical medium capable of conducting modulated light transmission. Compared with other transmission media, fiber-optic cable is more expensive but is not susceptible to electromagnetic interference, and it is capable of higher data rates. Sometimes called *optical fiber.*

flooding   A traffic-passing technique used by switches and bridges in which traffic received on an interface is sent out all the interfaces of that device except the interface on which the information was originally received.

HCC (horizontal cross-connect)   A wiring closet where the horizontal cabling connects to a patch panel that is connected by backbone cabling to the MDF.

header   Control information placed before data when encapsulating that data for network transmission.

IDF (intermediate distribution facility)   A secondary communications room for a building using a star networking topology. The IDF is dependent on the MDF.

intranet   An internal network that is to be accessed by users who have access to an organization's internal LAN.

LAN (local-area network)   A high-speed, low-error data network covering a relatively small geographic area (up to a few thousand meters). LANs connect workstations, peripherals, terminals, and other devices in a single building or other geographically limited area. LAN standards specify cabling and signaling at the physical and data link layers of the OSI model. Ethernet, FDDI, and Token Ring are widely used LAN technologies.

MDF (main distribution facility)   The primary communications room for a building. The central point of a star networking topology where patch panels, hub, and router are located.

media   Plural of *medium*. The various physical environments through which transmission signals pass. Common network media include twisted-pair, coaxial, and fiber-optic cable, and the atmosphere (through which microwave, laser, and infrared transmission occurs). Sometimes called *physical media*.

network address   A network-layer address referring to a logical, rather than a physical, network device. Also called a *protocol address*.

protocol   A formal description of a set of rules and conventions that govern how devices on a network exchange information.

routing table   A table stored in a router or some other internetworking device that keeps track of routes to particular network destinations and, in some cases, metrics associated with those routes.

segmentation   The process of splitting a single collision domain into two or more collision domains in order to reduce collisions and network congestion.

star topology   A LAN topology in which endpoints on a network are connected to a common central switch by point-to-point links. A ring topology that is organized as a star implements a unidirectional closed-loop star, instead of point-to-point links.

unicast   A message sent to a single network destination.

UTP (unshielded twisted-pair)   A four-pair wire medium used in a variety of networks. UTP does not require the fixed spacing between connections that is necessary with coaxial-type connections. There are five types of UTP cabling commonly used: Category 1 cabling, Category 2 cabling, Category 3 cabling, Category 4 cabling, and Category 5 cabling.

VCC (vertical cross-connect)   A connection that is used to interconnect the various IDFs to the central MDF.

vertical cabling   *See* backbone cabling.

WAN (wide-area network)   A data communications network that serves users across a broad geographic area and often uses transmission devices provided by common carriers. Frame Relay, SMDS, and X.25 are examples of WAN technologies.

workgroup server   A server that supports a specific set of users and offers services, such as word processing and file sharing, which are services that only a few groups of people would need.

Objectives

After reading this chapter, you will be able to

- Describe the routing functions of the network layer and how these functions relate to path determination in a router
- Describe routed and routing protocols
- Describe interior and exterior protocols
- Describe routing protocol characteristics and configuration
- Describe IGRP features, operation, and configuration tasks

Routing Protocols: IGRP

Introduction

In Chapter 4, "LAN Design," you learned about LAN design goals and methodology. In addition, you learned about design considerations related to Layers 1, 2, and 3 of the Open System Interconnection (OSI) reference model. Reliability, connectivity, ease of use, ease of modification, and ease of implementation are other issues that need to be considered in building networks:

- To be reliable, a network must provide a means for error detection as well as the capability to correct the error.

- To provide connectivity, a network must be able to incorporate a variety of hardware and software products in such a way that they can function together.

- To be easy to use, a network must perform in such a way that users need have no concern for or knowledge of the network's structure or implementation.

- To be easy to modify, a network must allow itself to evolve and adapt as needs change or expand, or as new technologies emerge.

- Finally, to be easy to implement, a network must follow industry-wide networking standards, and it must allow for a variety of configurations that meet network users' needs.

In this chapter, you will learn how the use of routers can help you address these issues. In addition, this chapter discusses how routers can be used to connect two or more networks and how they are used to pass data packets between networks based on network protocol information. You will also learn that a router can have more than one Internet Protocol (IP) address because it is attached to more than one network. As you learned in *Cisco Systems Networking Academy: First-Year Companion Guide*, an important function of routers is to examine incoming data packets and make path selections based on information stored in their routing tables. In this chapter, you will learn more about how routers operate and what kinds of protocols they use. Finally, this chapter describes routing and IP routing protocols and discusses Cisco's proprietary implementation of Interior Gateway Routing Protocol (IGRP).

Washington Project: Routing Protocols and Implementing IGRP
The concepts covered in this chapter will help you understand routing protocols. Routing protocols route protocols (such as IGRP) through a network. This chapter will help you apply IGRP to the network design you have been creating for the Washington School District project. In addition, you will learn how to implement IGRP and all the IGRP-required configurations needed for the network implementations.

Network-Layer Basics

As you have learned, the network layer interfaces to networks and provides the best end-to-end packet delivery services to its user, the transport layer. The network layer sends packets from the source network to the destination network. To send packets from the source to the destination, path determination needs to occur at the network layer. This function is usually the responsibility of the router.

Network-Layer Path Determination

The path determination function enables a router to evaluate the available paths to a destination and to establish the best method for routing a packet. *Routing* refers to the process of choosing the best path over which to send packets and how to cross multiple physical networks. This is the basis of all Internet communication. Most routing protocols simply use the shortest and best path, and they use different methods to find the shortest and best path. The sections that follow explain some of the ways routing protocols find the shortest and best paths.

Packet routing in a network is similar to traveling by car: Routers, through the use of protocols, make path decisions based on routing tables, and people driving cars determine their paths by reading road signs.

Routing Tables

In IP networks, the router forwards packets from the source network to the destination network based on the IP routing table. After the router determines which path to use, it can proceed with switching the packet: It accepts the packet on one interface and forwards it to another interface that is the next hop on the best path to the packet's destination. This is why routing protocols are so important: Each router that handles the packet must know what to do with the packet.

Routing tables store information on possible destinations and how to reach each of the destinations. Routing tables need to store only the network portion of IP addresses for routing. This keeps the tables small and efficient.

Entries in the routing tables contain an IP address of the next hop along the route to the destination. Each entry specifies only one hop and points to a router that is directly connected, which means that it can be reached across a single network.

Routing protocols fill routing tables with a variety of information. For example, a router uses the destination/next-hop routing table when it receives an incoming packet. The router uses its routing table to check the destination address and attempts to associate the address with a next hop. A destination/next-hop routing table tells a router that a particular destination can be best reached by sending the packet to a particular router that represents the next hop on the way to the final destination.

Routers must communicate with each other in order to build tables through the use of routing protocols and through the transmission of a variety of messages. The routing update message is one such message. Routing updates generally consist of all or a portion of a routing table. By analyzing routing updates from all routers, a router can build a detailed picture of network topology. When routers understand the network topology, they can determine the best routes to network destinations.

Representing Distance with Metrics

It is important that a routing table be constantly updated, because its primary objective is to include the best information for the router. Each routing protocol interprets *best path* in its own way. The protocol generates a number—called the metric—for each path through the network. Typically, the smaller the metric, the better the path. Routing tables can also contain information about the desirability of a path. Routers compare metrics to determine the best routes. Metrics differ depending on the design of the routing protocol being used. A variety of common metrics are described later in this chapter.

A variety of metrics can be used to define the best path. Some routing protocols, such as Routing Information Protocol (RIP), use only one metric, and some routing protocols, such as IGRP, use a combination of metrics. The metrics most commonly used by routers are shown in Table 5-1.

TABLE 5-1   Commonly Used Metrics

Metric Type	Description
Hop count	The number of routers a packet must go through to reach a destination. The lower the hop count, the better the path. Path length is used to indicate the sum of the hops to a destination.

continues

TABLE 5-1   Commonly Used Metrics (Continued)

Metric Type	Description
Bandwidth	The data capacity of a link.
Delay	The length of time required to move a packet from source to destination.
Load	The amount of activity on a network resource, such as a router or link.
Reliability	The error rate of each network link.
Ticks	The delay on a data link using IBM PC clock ticks (approximately 55 milliseconds).
Cost	The arbitrary value, usually based on bandwidth, dollar expense, or other measurement, that is assigned by a network administrator.

The Network-Layer Communication Path

After examining a packet's destination protocol address, the router determines that it either knows or does not know how to forward the packet to the next hop. If the router does not know how to forward the packet, it typically drops the packet. If the router knows how to forward the packet, it changes the destination physical address to that of the next hop and transmits the packet.

The next hop may or may not be the ultimate destination host. If it is not the ultimate destination, the next hop is usually another router, which executes the same switching decision process as the previous router. This process is illustrated in Figure 5-1.

Addressing: The Network and the Host

The network address consists of a network portion and a host portion used by the router within the network cloud. To see whether the destination is on the same physical network, the network portion of the destination IP address is extracted and compared with the source's network address.

When a packet traverses a network, the source and destination IP addresses are never changed. An IP address is computed by the IP routing protocol and software, and is known as the next-hop address.

The network portion of the address is used to make path selections. A router is responsible for passing the packet to the next network along the path. The router uses the network portion of the address to make path selections.

FIGURE 5-1
As a packet moves through the network, its physical address changes, but its protocol address remains constant.

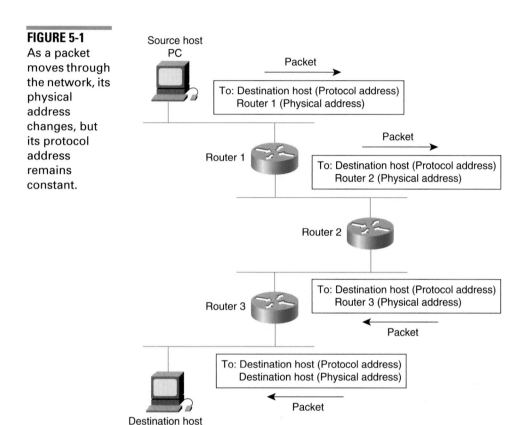

The switching function allows a router to accept a packet on one interface and forward it on a second interface. The path determination function enables the router to select the most appropriate interface for forwarding a packet.

Routed Versus Routing Protocols

Confusion about the terms *routed protocol* and *routing protocol* is common. Routed protocols are protocols that are routed over a network. Examples of such protocols are Transmission Control Protocol/Internet Protocol (TCP/IP) and Internetwork Packet Exchange (IPX). Routing protocols route routed protocols through a network. Examples of these protocols include IGRP, Enhanced IGRP, Open Shortest Path First (OSPF), Exterior Gateway Protocol (EGP), Border Gateway Protocol (BGP), OSI routing, Advanced Peer-to-Peer Networking (APPN), Intermediate System-to-Intermediate System (IS-IS), and

RIP. Put simply, computers (or *end systems*) use routed protocols, such as IP, to "talk to each other," whereas routers (or *intermediate systems*) use routing protocols to "talk to each other" about networks and paths.

Multiprotocol Routing

Routers are capable of multiprotocol routing, which means they support multiple independent routing protocols, such as RIP and IGRP. This capability allows a router to deliver packets from several routed protocols, such as TCP/IP and IPX, over the same data links.

Washington Project: Multiprotocol Routing
Based on user requirements, the Washington School District network needs to handle multiprotocol routing. The district requires that both TCP/IP and IPX routing protocols be handled over the network.

IP Routing Protocols

Routing is the process of determining where to send data packets destined for addresses outside the local network. Routers gather and maintain routing information to enable the transmission and receipt of such data packets. Routing information takes the form of entries in a routing table, with one entry for each identified route. Routing protocols allow a router to create and maintain routing tables dynamically and to adjust to network changes as they occur.

Routing protocols can be differentiated from one another based on several key characteristics:

- First, the particular goals of the protocol designer affect the operation of the resulting routing protocol.
- Second, there are various types of routing protocols. Each protocol has a different effect on network and router resources.
- Third, as discussed earlier in this chapter, routing protocols use a variety of metrics to identify the best routes.

Routing protocols are broadly divided into two classes: interior protocols and exterior protocols. Interior protocols are used for routing networks that are under a common network administration. All IP interior protocols must be specified with a list of associated networks before routing activities can begin. A routing process listens to updates from other routers on these networks and broadcasts its own routing information on those same networks. The interior protocols Cisco supports include RIP and IGRP. Exterior protocols are used to exchange routing information between networks that do not share a common administration. Exterior routing protocols include EGP and BGP. Exterior routing protocols require the following information before routing can begin:

- A list of neighbor (also called *peer*) routers with which to exchange routing information
- A list of networks to advertise as directly reachable

The following sections discuss routing protocol characteristics in more detail.

Washington Project: IGRP Design Goals

Throughout the rest of the chapter, you will learn the concepts and configuration techniques to help address the following design goals for IGRP implementation in the Washington School District network:

- The network should use stable routing, and no routing loops should occur.
- The network should quickly respond to changes in the network topology.
- The network should have low overhead, and IGRP itself should not use more bandwidth than is actually needed for its task.
- The network design should take into account error rates and level of traffic on different paths.

The Optimal Route

Optimal route refers to the ability of the routing protocol to select the best route. The best route depends on the metrics and metric weightings used to make the calculation. For example, one routing protocol might use the number of hops and the delay, but might weigh the delay more heavily in the calculation.

Simplicity and Efficiency

Routing protocols are also designed to be as simple and efficient as possible. Efficiency is particularly important when the software implementing the routing protocol must run on a computer with limited physical resources.

Robustness

Routing protocols must be robust. In other words, they should perform correctly in the face of unusual or unforeseen circumstances, such as hardware failures, high load conditions, and incorrect implementations. Because routers are located at network junction points, they can cause considerable problems when they fail. The best routing protocols are often those that have withstood the test of time and proven stable under a variety of network conditions.

Rapid Convergence

Routing protocols must converge rapidly. Convergence is the speed and ability of a group of networking devices running a specific routing protocol to agree on the topology of a network after a change in that topology. When a network event, such as a change in a network's topology, causes routes to either go down or become available, routers distribute routing update messages. Routing update messages are sent to networks, thereby causing the recalculation of optimal routes and eventually causing all routers to agree on these routes. Routing protocols that converge slowly can cause routing loops or network outages.

Figure 5-2 shows a routing loop. In this case, a packet arrives at Router 1 at Time T1. Router 1 has already been updated and so knows that the best route to the destination calls for Router 2 to be the next stop. Router 1 therefore forwards the packet to Router 2. Router 2 has not yet been updated and so believes that the best next hop is Router 1. Therefore, Router 2 forwards the packet back to Router 1. The packet will continue to bounce back and forth between the two routers until Router 2 receives its routing update or until the packet has been switched the maximum number of times allowed. Different routing protocols have different maximums; the network administrator usually can define lower maximums. For example, IGRP has a maximum of 255, it defaults to 100, and it is usually set to 50 or less.

FIGURE 5-2
Routing loops occur until the routing update has occurred or until the packet has been switched the maximum number of times allowed.

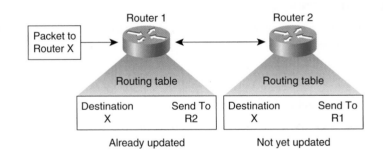

Flexibility

Routing protocols should also be flexible. In other words, they should quickly and accurately adapt to a variety of network circumstances. For example, assume that a network segment has gone down. Many routing protocols quickly select the next-best path for all routes that normally use a given segment. Routing protocols can be programmed to adapt to changes in network bandwidth, router queue size, network delay, and other variables.

Static Routing

Static routing protocols are hardly protocols at all. Before routing begins, the network administrator establishes static routing table mappings. These mappings do not change unless the network administrator changes them. Protocols that use static routes are simple to design and work well in environments where network traffic is predictable and network design is simple.

Because static routing systems cannot react to network changes, they are generally considered unsuitable for today's large, constantly changing networks. These networks require dynamic routing protocols.

Dynamic Routing

Dynamic routing protocols adjust to changing network circumstances. They do this by analyzing incoming routing update messages. If a message indicates that a network change has occurred, the routing software recalculates routes and sends out new routing update messages. These messages permeate the network, prompting routers to recalculate their routing tables accordingly.

Dynamic routing protocols can be supplemented with static routes where appropriate. For example, a gateway of last resort (that is, a router to which all unroutable packets are sent) may be designated. This router acts as a central storing place for all unroutable packets, ensuring that all messages are at least handled in some way.

Routing Approaches

As you have learned, most routing protocols can be classified into three basic approaches:

- The distance-vector routing approach determines the direction (vector) and distance to any link in the network. Examples of distance-vector routing protocols are IGRP and RIP.
- The link-state (also called shortest path first) approach re-creates the exact topology of the entire network (or at least the partition in which the router is situated). Examples of link-state routing protocols are OSPF, IS-IS, and NetWare Link Services Protocol (NLSP).
- The hybrid approach combines aspects of the link-state and distance-vector approaches. An example of a hybrid routing approach is Enhanced IGRP.

IP Routing Configuration

Each routing protocol must be configured separately. With any routing protocol, you must follow two basic steps:

1. Create the routing process with one of the router commands.
2. Configure the protocol specifics.

As you learned earlier, the interior protocols such as IGRP and RIP must have a list of networks specified before routing activities can begin. In addition, you learned that the routing process listens to updates from other routers on these networks and broadcasts its own routing information on those same networks. IGRP has the additional requirement of an autonomous system (AS) number.

Washington Project: AS Numbers

AS number consistency is a design issue. You need to have the same number throughout the Washington School District network. The AS is assigned a 16-bit number by the Internet Assigned Numbers Authority.

With any of the IP routing protocols, you need to create the routing process, associate networks with the routing process, and customize the routing protocol for your particular network. Choosing a routing protocol is a complex task. When choosing a routing protocol, you should consider the following:

- Network size and complexity
- Network traffic levels
- Security needs
- Reliability needs
- Network delay characteristics
- Organizational policies
- Organizational acceptance of change

Understanding IGRP Operation

IGRP is a Cisco proprietary protocol and was developed to supercede RIP. IGRP is a distance-vector interior routing protocol. Distance-vector routing protocols call for each router to send all or a portion of its routing table in a routing update message at regular intervals to each of its neighboring routers. As routing information spreads throughout the network, routers can calculate distances to all nodes within the network.

IGRP uses a combination of metrics. Network delay, bandwidth, reliability, and load are all factored into the routing decision. Network administrators can determine the settings for each of these metrics. IGRP uses either the settings determined by the administrator or the default settings to automatically calculate best routes.

IGRP provides a wide range for its metrics. For example, reliability and load can have any value between 1 and 255; bandwidth can have values reflecting speeds from 1200 bps to 10 Gbps; and delay can have any value from 1 to 2^{24}. Wide metric ranges allow an adequate metric setting in networks with widely varying performance characteristics. As a result, network administrators can influence route selection in an intuitive fashion. This is accomplished by weighting each of the four metrics—that is, telling the router how much to value a particular metric. The default values related to the weightings for IGRP give the most importance to bandwidth, which makes IGRP superior to RIP. In contrast, RIP does not weigh metrics because it only uses one.

Interior, System, and Exterior IGRP Routes

Cisco's principal goal in creating IGRP was to provide a robust protocol for routing within an autonomous system (AS). An AS is a collection of networks under common administration sharing a common routing strategy, as shown in Figure 5-3.

FIGURE 5-3
Autonomous systems are subdivided by areas.

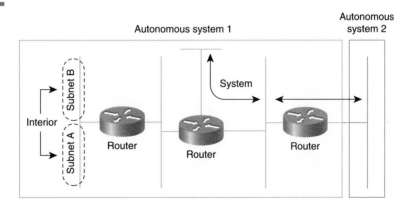

IGRP uses a combination of user-configurable metrics, including network delay, bandwidth, reliability, and load. IGRP advertises three types of routes: interior, system, and exterior (as shown in Figure 5-3). *Interior routes* are routes between subnets in the network attached to a router interface. If the network attached to a router is not subnetted, IGRP does not advertise interior routes. Additionally, subnet information is not included in IGRP updates, which poses a problem for noncontiguous IP subnets.

System routes are routes to networks within the AS. The router derives system routes from directly connected network interfaces and system route information provided by other routers that use IGRP. System routes do not include subnetting information.

Exterior routes are routes to networks outside the AS that are considered when identifying a gateway of last resort. The router chooses a gateway of last resort from the list of exterior routes that IGRP provides. The router uses the gateway of last resort if it does not have a better route for a packet and the destination is not a connected network. If the AS has more than one connection to an external network, different routers can choose different exterior routers as the gateway of last resort.

Creating the IGRP Routing Process

To configure IGRP, you need to create the IGRP routing process. The router commands needed to implement IGRP on a router are explained in this section. This section also describes the processes the routers go through to ensure that the neighbor routers are aware of the status of all networks in the AS, including the frequency with which routing table updates are sent and the effects of the updates on bandwidth utilization.

Engineering Journal: Configuring IGRP

To create the IGRP routing process, you need to perform the tasks described here, starting in global configuration mode.

Enable an IGRP routing process by using the command **router igrp**, which places you in router configuration mode. The full syntax of this command is as follows:

```
router igrp autonomous-system
```

The argument *autonomous-system* identifies the routes to other IGRP routers, and is used to tag the routing information passed along. You use the **no router igrp** command to shut down the routing process on the AS specified by the *autonomous-system* argument:

```
no router igrp autonomous-system
```

You associate networks with an IGRP routing process by using the command **network**. The full syntax of this command is as follows:

```
network network-number
```

The argument *network-number* is a network number, in dotted-decimal IP notation. Note that this number must not contain subnet information. You can specify multiple **network** commands.

When an IGRP routing process is configured, an AS number must be specified. This number may or may not be assigned. The AS number is used to tag updates belonging to one of up to four IGRP routing processes. You use the **no network** command with the network number to remove a network from the list:

```
no network network-number
```

In the following example, a router is configured for IGRP and assigned to AS 109. In the last two lines, two network commands assign the two networks to a list of networks to receive IGRP updates:

```
Router(config)# router igrp 109
network 131.108.0.0
network 192.31.7.0
```

IGRP sends updates to the interfaces in the specified networks. If an interface's network is not specified, it is not advertised in any IGRP updates.

Enhancing IGRP Stability

IGRP provides a number of features that are designed to enhance its stability, including the following:

- Holddowns
- Split horizons
- Poison reverse updates

These features are described in the following sections.

Holddowns

When a router learns that a network is further away than was previously known, or it learns that the network is down, the route to that network is placed into holddown. During the holddown period, the route is advertised, but incoming advertisements about that network from any router other than the one that originally advertised the network's new metric are ignored. This mechanism is often used to help avoid routing loops in the network, but has the effect of increasing the topology convergence time.

Holddowns are used to prevent regular update messages from reinstating a route that may have gone bad. When a router goes down, neighboring routers detect this via the lack of regularly scheduled update messages. These routers then calculate new routes and send routing update messages to inform their neighbors of the route change. This activity begins a wave of triggered updates that filter through the network. These triggered updates do not instantly arrive at every network device. It is therefore possible for Device A, which has not yet been informed of a network failure, to send a regular update message (indicating that a route that has just gone down is still good) to Device B, which has just been notified of the network failure. In this case, Device B would now contain (and potentially advertise) incorrect routing information.

Holddowns tell routers to hold down any changes that might affect routes for some period of time. The hold-down period is usually calculated to be just greater than the period of time necessary to update the entire network with a routing change. This can prevent routing loops caused by slow convergence.

Split Horizons

A split horizon occurs when a router tries to send information about a route back in the direction from which it came. For example, consider Figure 5-4. Router 1 initially advertises that it has a route to Network A. As a result, there is no reason for Router 2 to include this route back to Router 1 because Router 1 is closer to Network A. The split-horizon rule says that Router 2 should strike this route from any updates it sends to Router 1.

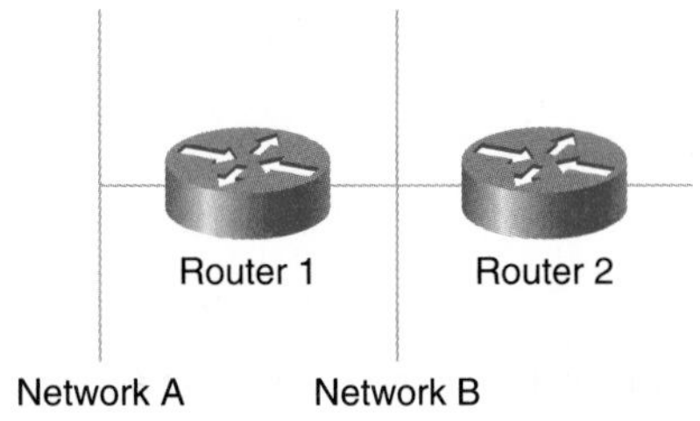

FIGURE 5-4
Because Router 1 is closer to Network A, Router 2 should strike updates to Router 1 about its route to Network 2.

The split-horizon rule helps prevent routing loops. For example, consider the case where Router 1's interface to Network A goes down. Without split horizons, Router 2 continues to inform Router 1 that it can get to Network A (through Router 1). If Router 1 does not have sufficient intelligence, it might actually pick up Router 2's route as an alternative to its failed direct connection, causing a routing loop. Although holddowns should prevent this, split horizons are implemented in IGRP because they provide extra protocol stability.

Poison Reverse Updates

Whereas split horizons should prevent routing loops between adjacent routers, poison reverse updates are intended to defeat larger routing loops. Increases in routing metrics generally indicate routing loops. Poison reverse updates are then sent to remove the route and place it in holddown. A router poisons the route by sending an update with a metric of infinity to a router that originally advertised a route to a network. Poisoning the route can help speed convergence.

Engineering Journal: The `timers basic` and `no metric holddown` Commands

The following descriptions of the **timers basic** and **no metric holddown** commands help you control routing updates.

The `timers basic` Command

timers basic lets you control how often IGRP sends updates. The default is once every 90 seconds. In order to allow for dropped packets, IGRP can't time out expired routes until several minutes have elapsed. When IGRP removes a route, it can't adopt a new one for several more minutes because of holddown.

The first thing to do is to speed up the time constants. Use 15 seconds instead of 90 for the basic time constant. This allows routes to expire after 45 seconds. All the other times decrease proportionally.

Actually, the expiration time turns out not to be as important as you might expect. Normally, routes don't just expire. They are killed because a keepalive fails on some interface. Keepalives normally occur every 10 seconds, so it takes 30 seconds to detect an interface down that way. You should use a keepalive of 4 on T1 lines where you care about speed of routing adjustment. This lets you detect a failure in 12 seconds.

The `no metric holddown` Command

The other critical parameter to change in order to accept a new route is **no metric holddown**. This disables holddowns, meaning that after a route has been removed, a new one is accepted immediately. There are good theoretical reasons for using holddowns. For example, there could be cases where, without holddowns, an old route can never get out of the system.

IGRP Metric Information

IGRP uses several types of metric information. For each path through an AS, IGRP records the segment with the lowest bandwidth, the accumulated delay, the smallest maximum transmission unit (MTU), and the reliability and load.

Variables are used to weight each metric, and bandwidth is by default given the most importance when calculating the best path. For a network of one medium (such as a network that uses all Ethernet), this metric reduces to a hop count. For a network of mixed media (for example, Ethernet and serial lines running from 9600 baud to T1 rates), the route with the lowest metric reflects the most desirable path to a destination.

IGRP Updates

A router running IGRP sends an IGRP update broadcast every 90 seconds. It declares a route inaccessible if it does not receive an update from the first router in the route within three update periods (270 seconds). After five update periods (450 seconds), the router removes the route from the routing table. IGRP uses flash update and poison reverse to speed up the convergence of the routing protocol.

Flash update is the sending of an update sooner than the standard periodic update interval of notifying other routers of a metric change. Poison reverse updates are intended to defeat larger routing loops that are caused by increases in routing metrics. The poison reverse updates are sent to remove a route and place it in holddown, which keeps new routing information from being used for a certain period of time.

Maximum Hop Count

IGRP has a maximum hop count of 255, which is normally set lower than the default 100. Because IGRP uses triggered updates, counting to 100 may not take too long. However, you should set the maximum hop count to something smaller, unless you have an enormous network. It should be a number at least as large as the maximum number of routers a route might ever have to go through in the network. If you exchange IGRP routing with an external network, the hop count must include your network plus that external network. When you compute hop count, take into account what the configuration would look like if a few lines went down.

Here's a sample router statement that uses all the features explained in this section; you should use your own network number in place of 128.6.0.0:

```
Router(config)# router igrp 46
timers basic 15 45 0 60
network 128.6.0.0
no metric holddown
metric maximum-hop 50
```

With this statement, routing generally adapts to change within 30 seconds, assuming that the keepalive interval, which is the period of time between messages sent by a network device, has been set to 4.

Summary

- Network-layer routing functions include network addressing and best path selection for traffic.
- Routing tables store information on possible destinations and how to reach each of the destinations.
- Routed protocols are protocols that are routed over a network, and routing protocols are protocols that implement routing protocols.
- Routing protocols can be either static or dynamic.

- Interior protocols are used for routing networks that are under a common network administration, and exterior protocols are used to exchange routing information between networks that do not share a common administration.

- IGRP is a distance-vector interior gateway protocol and uses a combination of user-configurable metrics including network delay, bandwidth, reliability, and load.

- You can improve the stability of IGRP by using holddowns, split horizons, and poison reverse updates.

- To configure IGRP, the only mandatory task is to create the IGRP routing process. Other tasks are optional.

Washington School District Project Task: Routing Protocols and Configuring IGRP

In this chapter, you have learned concepts and configuration processes that will help you implement IGRP as the routing protocol in the Washington School District network. As part of the IGRP configuration and implementation, you need to complete the following tasks:

> **NOTE**
>
> It is best to complete these activities in conjunction with an IGRP lab.

1. Identify and gather the information required to implement IGRP at the schools' networks and across the district network. Add the information you gather to the existing requirements and LAN design. (Hint: Consult the Washington School Project technical requirements.)

2. Identify and document the networks that will be advertised by the router in the school district and add that information to the requirements and LAN design. (Hint: Consult the Washington School Project technical requirements.)

3. Identify and document the IGRP AS number for the school district.

4. Write down the router command sequence needed to implement IGRP on the school's router.

5. Describe the process that the routers go through to ensure that the neighbor routers are aware of the status of all networks in the AS.

6. Identify the best settings for maximum hops, holddown timer, update timer, and so on. Also, document appropriate bandwidth settings for serial interfaces.

Chapter Review

Complete all the review questions to test your understanding of the topics and concepts covered in this chapter. Answers are listed in Appendix A, "Chapter Review Answer Key."

1. At what layer of the OSI model does path determination take place and what is that layer's function?

2. How does a router determine on which interface to forward a data packet?

3. What does the term *multiprotocol routing* mean?

4. What two basic router factors does a dynamic routing protocol depend on?

5. What does the term *convergence* mean in network implementation?

6. After a router determines which path to use for a packet, it can then proceed with which of the following?

    A. A broadcast

    B. Storing the packet in a routing table

    C. Choosing a routing protocol

    D. Switching the packet

7. The success of dynamic routing depends on which of the following?

    A. Manually entering routes

    B. Maintaining a routing table

    C. Periodic routing updates

    D. B and C

8. _____ routing protocols determine the direction and distance to any link in the internetwork; _____ routing protocols are also called shortest path first.

    A. Distance-vector; link-state

    B. Distance-vector; hybrid

    C. Link-state; distance-vector

    D. Dynamic; static

9. Which of the following is *not* a variable IGRP uses to determine a composite metric?

   A. Bandwidth

   B. Delay

   C. Load

   D. IGRP uses all of these.

10. To select IGRP as a routing protocol, which command do you use?

   A. `show igrp`

   B. `router network igrp`

   C. `enable igrp`

   D. `router igrp`

Key Terms

AS (autonomous system)   A collection of networks under common administration sharing a common routing strategy. Also referred to as a *routing domain*. The AS is assigned a 16-bit number by the Internet Assigned Numbers Authority.

bandwidth   The difference between the highest and lowest frequencies available for network signals. Also, the rated throughput capacity of a given network medium or protocol.

BGP (Border Gateway Protocol)   An interdomain routing protocol that replaces Exterior Gateway Protocol (EGP). BGP exchanges reachability information with other BGP systems and is defined by RFC 1163.

convergence   The speed and ability of a group of internetworking devices running a specific routing protocol to agree on the topology of an internetwork after a change in that topology.

cost   An arbitrary value, typically based on hop count, media bandwidth, or other measures, that is assigned by a network administrator and used to compare various paths through an internetwork environment. Cost values are used by routing protocols to determine the most favorable path to a particular destination: the lower the cost, the better the path.

delay   The time between the initiation of a transaction by a sender and the first response received by the sender. Also, the time required to move a packet from source to destination over a given path.

dynamic routing   Routing that adjusts automatically to network topology or traffic changes.

exterior protocol   A protocol that is used to exchange routing information between networks that do not share a common administration.

flash update   The process of the sending of an update sooner than the standard periodic update interval for notifying other routers of a metric change.

gateway of last resort   A router to which all unroutable packets are sent.

holddown   An IGRP feature that rejects new routes for the same destination for some period of time.

hop   The passage of a data packet between two network nodes (for example, between two routers).

hop count   A routing metric used to measure the distance between a source and a destination. RIP uses hop count as its sole metric.

interior protocol   A protocol that is used for routing networks that are under a common network administration.

IGRP (Interior Gateway Routing Protocol)   A protocol developed by Cisco to address the problems associated with routing in large, heterogeneous networks.

keepalive   A message sent by one network device to inform another network device that the virtual circuit between the two is still active.

load   The amount of activity on a network resource, such as a router or link.

metric   A standard of measurement (for example, path length) that is used by routing protocols to determine the optimal path to a destination.

MTU (maximum transmission unit)   Maximum packet size, in bytes, that a particular interface can handle.

multiprotocol routing   Routing in which a router delivers packets from several routed protocols, such as TCP/IP and IPX, over the same data links.

next-hop address   The IP address that is computed by the IP routing protocol and software.

path determination   The decision of which path traffic should take through the network cloud. Path determination occurs at the network layer of the OSI reference model.

poison reverse update   An IGRP feature intended to defeat larger routing loops. Poison reverse updates explicitly indicate that a network or subnet is unreachable, rather than imply that a network is unreachable by not including it in updates.

reliability   The ratio of expected to received keepalives from a link. If the ratio is high, the line is reliable. Used as a routing metric.

routed protocol   A protocol that can be routed by a router. A router must be able to interpret the logical internetwork as specified by that routed protocol. Examples of routed protocols include AppleTalk, DECnet, and IP.

routing protocol   A protocol that accomplishes routing through the implementation of a specific routing protocol. Examples of routing protocols include IGRP, OSPF, and RIP.

split horizon   An IGRP feature designed to prevent routers from picking up erroneous routes. Split horizon prevents loops between adjacent routers and keeps down the size of update messages.

static routing   Routing that is explicitly configured and entered into the routing table. Static routes take precedence over routes chosen by dynamic routing protocols.

tick   The delay on a data link using IBM PC clock ticks (approximately 55 milliseconds). One tick is $\frac{1}{18}$ second.

Objectives

After reading this chapter, you will be able to

- Define and describe the purpose and operation of ACLs

- Explain the processes involved in testing packets with ACLs

- Describe ACL configuration commands, global statements, and interface commands

- Define and explain the function and operation of wildcard masks bits and the wildcards **any** and **host**

- Describe standard ACLs

- Describe extended ACLs

- Describe named ACLs

- Monitor and verify selected ACL operations on the router

Chapter 6

ACLs

Introduction

Network administrators face a dilemma: They must figure out how to deny unwanted access to the network while allowing appropriate access. Although security tools, such as passwords, callback equipment, and physical security devices, are helpful, they often lack the flexibility of basic traffic filtering and the specific controls most administrators prefer. For example, a network administrator might want to allow users on the LAN to go out to the Internet through the LAN, but might not want the users outside the LAN using the Internet to Telnet in to the LAN.

Routers provide basic traffic filtering capabilities, such as blocking Internet traffic, with access control lists (ACLs). In this chapter, you will learn about using standard and extended ACLs as a means to control network traffic and how ACLs are used as part of a security solution. An ACL is a sequential collection of permit or deny statements that apply to addresses or upper-layer protocols. This chapter focuses on standard, extended, and named ACLs.

In addition, this chapter includes tips, considerations, recommendations, and general guidelines on how to use ACLs, and includes the commands and configurations needed to create ACLs. Finally, this chapter provides examples of standard and extended ACLs and how to apply ACLs to router interfaces.

Washington School District Project: ACLs
In this chapter, you will learn the concepts and configuration commands that will help you use and implement ACLs in the Washington School District network. In addition, as ACL concepts and commands are introduced, you will be able to apply ACLs in your network design and implementation.

ACL Overview

ACLs are lists of instructions you apply to a router's interface. These lists tell the router what kinds of packets to accept and what kinds of packets to deny. Acceptance and denial can be based on certain specifications, such as source address, destination address, and port number.

ACLs enable you to manage traffic and process specific packets by grouping the destination interface to an ACL. Grouping activates an ACL on a specific interface so that any traffic going through the interface is tested against the conditions contained in the ACL.

ACLs can be created for all routed network protocols, such as Internet Protocol (IP) and Internetwork Packet Exchange (IPX), to filter packets as the packets pass through a router. ACLs can be configured at the router to control access to a network or subnet. For example, in the Washington School District, ACLs could be used to prevent student traffic from entering the administrative network.

ACLs filter network traffic by controlling whether routed packets are forwarded or blocked at the router's interfaces. The router examines each packet to determine whether to forward or drop it, based on the conditions specified in the ACL. ACL conditions could be the source address of the traffic, the destination address of the traffic, the upper-layer protocol, or other information.

ACLs must be defined on a per-protocol basis. In other words, you must define an ACL for every protocol enabled on an interface if you want to control traffic flow for that protocol. (Note that some protocols refer to ACLs as *filters*.) For example, if your router interface were configured for IP, AppleTalk, and IPX, you would need to define at least three ACLs. As shown in Figure 6-1, ACLs can be used as a tool for network control by adding the flexibility to filter the packets that flow in or out of router interfaces.

FIGURE 6-1
Using ACLs, you can deny traffic based on packet tests, such as addressing or traffic type.

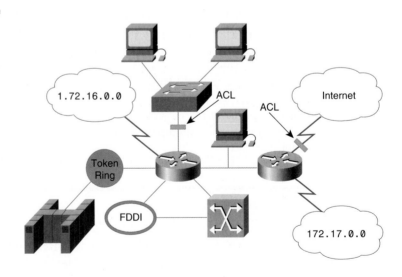

Reasons to Create ACLs

There are many reasons to create ACLs. For example, ACLs can be used to

- Limit network traffic and increase network performance. For example, ACLs can designate certain packets to be processed by a router before other traffic, on the basis of a protocol. This is referred to as queuing, which ensures that routers will not process packets that are not needed. As a result, queuing limits network traffic and reducing network congestion.

- Provide traffic flow control. For example, ACLs can restrict or reduce the contents of routing updates. These restrictions are used to limit information about specific networks from propagating through the network.

- Provide a basic level of security for network access. For example, ACLs can allow one host to access a part of your network and prevent another host from accessing the same area. In Figure 6-2, Host A is allowed to access the Human Resources network, and Host B is prevented from accessing the Human Resources network. If you do not configure ACLs on your router, all packets passing through the router could be allowed onto all parts of the network.

- Decide which types of traffic are forwarded or blocked at the router interfaces. For example, you can permit e-mail traffic to be routed, but at the same time block all Telnet traffic.

> **Washington Project: Using ACLs (Continued)**
>
> E-mail and DNS need to be available throughout the district, and these types of services should not allow any unauthorized access to the administration network.
>
> All the ACLs you create need to be controlled at the district office, and you need to review exceptions to the ACLs prior to implementation.

FIGURE 6-2
You can use ACLs to prevent traffic from being routed to a network.

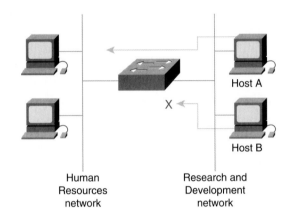

Host A

X ←

Host B

Human
Resources
network

Research and
Development
network

Creating an ACL in the Correct Order

The order in which you place ACL statements is important. When the router is deciding whether to forward or block a packet, the Cisco Internetwork Operating System (IOS) software tests the packet against each condition statement, in the order in which the statements were created. After a match is found, no more condition statements are checked.

If you create a condition statement that permits all traffic, no statements added later will ever be checked. If you need additional statements, you must delete the ACL and re-create it with the new condition statements. This is why it's a good idea to edit router configuration on a PC using a text editor and then Trivial File Transfer Protocol (TFTP) it to the router.

Using ACLs

You can create an ACL for each protocol you want to filter for each router interface. For some protocols, you create one ACL to filter inbound traffic, and one ACL to filter outbound traffic. Two main types of ACLs can be created: standard and extended ACLs. You'll learn about these later in the chapter.

After an ACL statement checks a packet for a match, the packet can be denied or permitted to use an interface in the access group.

Cisco IOS ACLs check the packet and upper-layer headers, as shown in Figure 6-3. For example, you could use a standard ACL to filter a packet on source address only.

FIGURE 6-3
ACLs check the
packet and
upper-layer
headers.

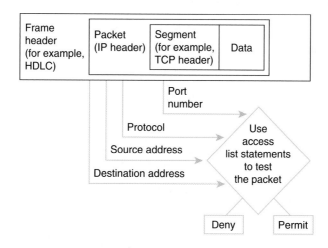

How ACLs Work

An ACL is a group of statements that define how packets

- Enter inbound interfaces
- Relay through the router
- Exit outbound interfaces of the router

As shown in Figure 6-4, the beginning of the communication process is the same, whether ACLs are used or not. As a packet enters an interface, the router checks to see whether the packet is routable or bridgeable. If the packet is neither routable nor bridgeable, the packet is dropped. If the packet is routable, a routing table entry then indicates a destination network, some routing metric or state, and the interface to use for forwarding the packet.

Next, the router checks whether the destination interface is grouped to an ACL. If it is not, the packet can be sent to the destination interface directly; for example, if it will use To0, which has no ACLs, the packet uses To0 directly.

ACL statements operate in sequential, logical order. If a packet header and an ACL statement match, the packet skips the rest of the statements. If a condition match is true, the packet is permitted or denied.

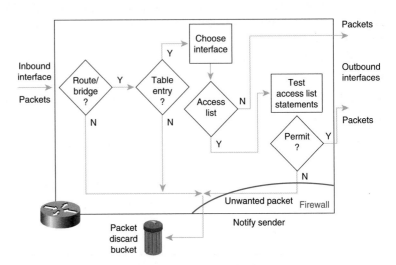

FIGURE 6-4
ACLs do not filter packets that originate in the router itself, but on packets from other sources.

In Figure 6-5, for instance, by matching the first test, a packet is denied access to the destination. It is discarded and dropped into the bit bucket, and it is not exposed to any ACL tests that follow.

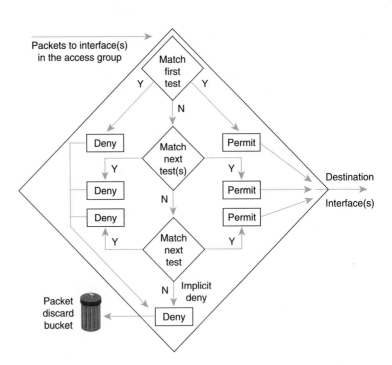

FIGURE 6-5
ACLs evaluate incoming packets and notify the sender if a packet is unwanted.

If the packet does not match conditions of the first test, it drops to the next ACL statement. Assume that a different packet's parameters match the next test, which is a permit statement; the permitted packet proceeds to the destination interface. Another packet does not match the conditions of the first or second test, but does match conditions of the next ACL statement; again, a permit results.

ACLs allow you to control what clients can access on your network. Conditions in an ACL file can

- Screen out certain hosts to either allow or deny access to part of your network

- Set up password authentication so that only users who supply a valid login and password can access part of the network

- Grant users permission to access part of the network for such things as an individual users' files or folders

<table>
<tr><td colspan="1" align="center">Washington Project: User Permission</td></tr>
<tr><td>You need to develop a user ID and password policy for all computers attached to the Washington School District administration LAN. This policy should be published and strictly enforced. Finally, you need make sure that all computers in the district network will have full access to the Internet.</td></tr>
</table>

ACL Configuration Tasks

In practice, ACL commands can be lengthy character strings. Key tasks covered in this section for creating ACLs include the following:

- You create ACLs by using the normal global router configuration process.

- Specifying an ACL number from 1 to 99 instructs the router to accept standard ACL statements. Specifying an ACL number from 100 to 199 instructs the router to accept extended ACL statements.

- You must carefully select and logically order the ACL. Permitted IP protocols must be specified; all other protocols should be denied.

- You should select which IP protocols to check; any other protocols are not checked. Later in the procedure, you can also specify an optional destination port for more precision.

- IP address filtering occurs through the use of ACL address wildcard masking to identify how to check or ignore corresponding address bits.

> **NOTE**
>
> For logical completeness, an ACL must have conditions that test true for all packets using the ACL. A final implied statement covers all packets for which conditions did not test true. This final test condition matches all other packets and results in a deny. Instead of proceeding in or out an interface, all remaining packets are dropped. So, if you want to avoid this, the last statement of your ACL should be a permit any. Note that the implicit deny any is not listed in your configuration file. Because this statement is not listed, some network administrators prefer to explicitly enter the deny statement, so that it appears in configuration information, which is good for record keeping.

You can understand the general ACL configuration commands by grouping the commands into two general steps:

Step 1   Define the ACL by using the following command:

```
Router(config)# access-list access-list-number
     {permit | deny} {test-conditions}
```

A global statement identifies the ACL. Specifically, the 1–99 range is reserved for standard IP. This number refers to the type of ACL. In Cisco IOS Release 11.2 or newer, ACLs can also use an ACL name, such as education_group, rather than a number.

The **permit** or **deny** term in the global ACL statement indicates how packets that meet the test conditions are handled by Cisco IOS software. **permit** usually means the packet will be allowed to use one or more interfaces that you will specify later.

The final term or terms specifies the test conditions used by the ACL statement.

Step 2   Next, you need to apply ACLs to an interface by using the **access-group** command, as in this example:

```
Router(config-if)# {protocol} access-group access-list-number
```

All the ACL statements identified by *access-list-number* are associated with one or more interfaces. Any packets that pass the ACL test conditions can be permitted to use any interface in the access group of interfaces.

> **NOTE**
>
> The **access-list** command is used when an ACL is being created, and the **access-group** command is used when the same ACL is being applied to an interface.

Grouping ACLs to Interfaces

Although each protocol has its own set of specific tasks and rules that are required to provide traffic filtering, in general most protocols require the two basic steps described in the section, "ACL Configuration Tasks." The first step is to create an ACL definition, and the second step is to apply the ACL to an interface.

ACLs are assigned to one or more interfaces and can filter inbound traffic or outbound traffic, depending on the configuration. Outbound ACLs are generally more efficient than inbound, and are therefore preferred. A router with an inbound ACL must check every packet to see whether it matches the ACL condition before switching the packet to an outbound interface.

Assigning a Unique Number to Each ACL

When configuring ACLs on a router, you must identify each ACL uniquely by assigning a number to the protocol's ACL. When you use a number to identify an ACL, the number must be within the specific range of numbers that is valid for the protocol.

You can specify ACLs by numbers for the protocols listed in Table 6-1. Table 6-1 also lists the range of ACL numbers that is valid for each protocol.

TABLE 6-1   Protocols with ACLs Specified by Numbers

Protocol	Range
IP	1–99
Extended IP	100–199
AppleTalk	600–699
IPX	800–899
Extended IPX	900–999
IPX Service Advertising Protocol	1000–1099

After you create a numbered ACL, you must assign it to an interface for it to be used. If you want to alter an ACL containing numbered ACL statements, you need to delete all the statements in the numbered ACL by using the command **no access-list** list-number.

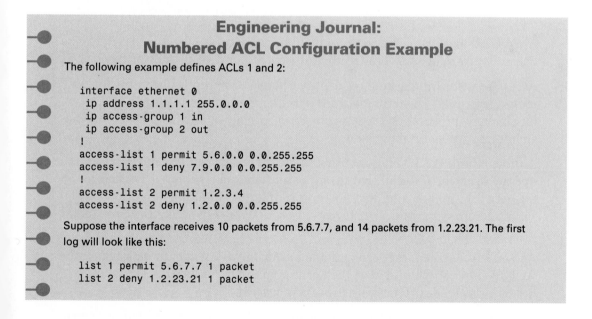

Engineering Journal:
Numbered ACL Configuration Example

The following example defines ACLs 1 and 2:

```
interface ethernet 0
 ip address 1.1.1.1 255.0.0.0
 ip access-group 1 in
 ip access-group 2 out
!
access-list 1 permit 5.6.0.0 0.0.255.255
access-list 1 deny 7.9.0.0 0.0.255.255
!
access-list 2 permit 1.2.3.4
access-list 2 deny 1.2.0.0 0.0.255.255
```

Suppose the interface receives 10 packets from 5.6.7.7, and 14 packets from 1.2.23.21. The first log will look like this:

```
list 1 permit 5.6.7.7 1 packet
list 2 deny 1.2.23.21 1 packet
```

Using Wildcard Mask Bits

A wildcard mask is a 32-bit quantity that is divided into four octets, with each octet containing 8 bits. A wildcard mask bit 0 means "check the corresponding bit value" and a wildcard mask bit 1 means "do not check (ignore) that corresponding bit value" (see Figure 6-6).

FIGURE 6-6
By carefully setting wild-card masks, you can select one or several IP addresses for permit or deny tests.

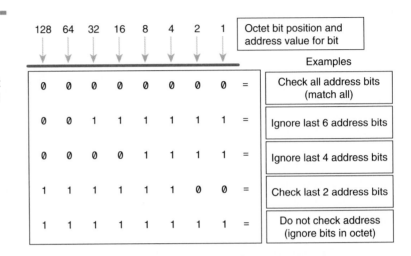

NOTE

Wildcard masking for ACLs operates differently from IP subnet masking. A zero in a bit position of the ACL mask indicates that the corresponding bit in the address must be checked; a one in a bit position of the ACL mask indicates that the corresponding bit in the address can be ignored. Thus, wildcard bit masks often look like inverted subnet masks (for example, 0.0.255.255 versus 255.255.0.0).

A wildcard mask is paired with an IP address. address bits uses the numbers one and zero to identify how to treat the corresponding IP address bits.

ACLs use wildcard masking to identify a single or multiple addresses for permit or deny tests. The term *wildcard masking* is a nickname for the ACL mask-bit matching process and comes from of an analogy of a wildcard that matches any other card in a poker game.

Although both are 32-bit quantities, wildcard masks and IP subnet masks operate differently. Recall that the zeros and ones in a subnet mask determine the network, subnet, and host portions of the corresponding IP address. The zeros and ones in a wildcard, as just noted, determine whether the corresponding bits in the IP address should be checked or ignored for ACL purposes.

As you have learned, the zero and one bits in an ACL wildcard mask cause the ACL to either check or ignore the corresponding bit in the IP address. In Figure 6-7, this wildcard masking process is applied.

Say you want to test an IP address for subnets that will be permitted or denied. Assume that the IP address is a Class B address (that is, the first two octets are the network number) with 8 bits of subnetting (the third octet is for subnets). You want to use IP wildcard mask bits to permit all packets from any host in the 172.30.16.0 to 172.30.31.0 subnets. Figure 6-7 shows an example of how to use the wildcard mask to do this.

FIGURE 6-7
The address 172.30.16.0 with the wild-card mask 0.0.15.255 matches subnets 172.30.16.0 to 172.30.31.0.

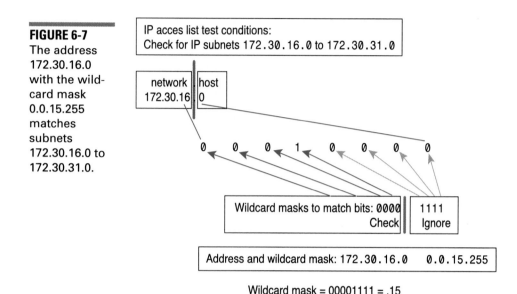

To begin, the wildcard mask checks the first two octets (172.30), using corresponding zero bits in the wildcard mask.

Because there is no interest in individual host addresses (a host ID does not have .00 at the end of the address), the wildcard mask ignores the final octet, using corresponding one bits in the wildcard mask.

In the third octet, the wildcard mask is 15 (00001111), and the IP address is 16 (00010000). The first four zeros in the wildcard mask tell the router to match the first four bits of the IP address (0001). Because the last four bits are ignored, all numbers in the range of 16 (00010000) to 31 (00011111) will match because they begin in the pattern 0001.

For the final (least-significant) four bits in this octet, the wildcard mask ignores the value because in these positions, the address value can be binary zero or binary one, and the corresponding wildcard bits are ones.

In this example, the address 172.30.16.0 with the wildcard mask 0.0.15.255 matches subnets 172.30.16.0 to 172.30.31.0. The wildcard mask does not match any other subnets.

Using the Wildcard any

Working with decimal representations of binary wildcard mask bits can be tedious. For the most common uses of wildcard masking, you can use abbreviations. These abbreviations reduce the amount of typing you need to do when configuring address test conditions. For example, say you want to specify that any destination address will be permitted in an ACL test. To indicate any IP address, you would enter 0.0.0.0, as shown in Figure 6-8; then, to indicate that the ACL should ignore (that is, allow without checking) any value, the corresponding wildcard mask bits for this address would be all ones (that is, 255.255.255.255). You can use the abbreviation **any** to communicate this same test condition to Cisco IOS ACL software. Instead of typing 0.0.0.0 255.255.255.255, you can use the word **any** by itself as the keyword.

For example, instead of using this:

```
Router(config)# access-list 1 permit 0.0.0.0  255.255.255.255
```

you can use this:

```
Router(config)# access-list 1 permit any
```

FIGURE 6-8
You can use the wildcard **any** instead of a long wildcard mask string when you want to match any address.

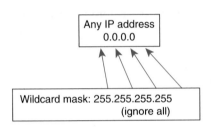

Using the Wildcard host

A second common condition where Cisco IOS permits an abbreviation in the ACL wildcard mask is when you want to match all the bits of an entire IP host address. For example, say you want to specify that a specific IP host address will be denied in an ACL test. To indicate a host IP address, you would enter the full address (for example, 172.30.16.29, as shown in Figure 6-9); then, to indicate that the ACL should check all the bits in the address, the corresponding wildcard mask bits for this address would be all zeros (that is, 0.0.0.0). You can use the abbreviation **host** to communicate this same test condition to Cisco IOS ACL software. In the example, instead of typing 172.30.16.29 0.0.0.0, you can use the word **host** in front of the address.

For example, instead of using this:

```
Router(config)# access-list 1 permit 172.30.16.29  0.0.0.0
```

you can use this:

```
Router(config)# access-list 1 permit host 172.30.16.29
```

FIGURE 6-9
An example of using the wild-card **host** in an ACL test condition is the string **host 172.30.16.29**.

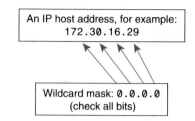

An IP host address, for example:
172.30.16.29

Wildcard mask: 0.0.0.0
(check all bits)

Standard ACLs

You use standard ACLs when you want to block all traffic from a network or a specific host, allow all traffic from a specific network, or deny protocol suites. Standard ACLs check the source address of packets that could be routed. The result permits or denies output for an entire protocol suite (for example, TCP/IP), based on the network, subnet, and host addresses. For example, in Figure 6-10, packets coming in E0 are checked for source address and protocol. If they are permitted, the packets are output through S0, which is grouped to the ACL. If they are not permitted, they are dropped.

FIGURE 6-10
Packets coming from E0 are checked for source address and protocol.

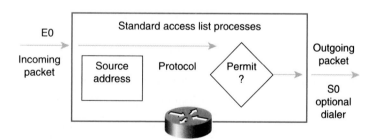

Standard ACL Examples

As you have learned, you use the standard version of the **access-list** global configuration command to define a standard ACL with a number. This command is used in global configuration command mode.

The full syntax of the command is

```
Router(config)# access-list access-list-number {permit | deny}
     source [source-wildcard] [log]
```

You use the **no** form of this command to remove a standard ACL. This is the syntax:

```
Router(config)# no access-list access-list-number
```

The following is a description of the parameters used in this syntax:

Parameter	Description
access-list-number	Number of an ACL. This is a decimal number from 1 to 99 (for a standard IP ACL).
deny	Denies access if the conditions are matched.
permit	Permits access if the conditions are matched.
source	Number of the network or host from which the packet is being sent. There are two ways to specify the *source*: • Use a 32-bit quantity in four-part, dotted-decimal format. • Use the keyword **any** as an abbreviation for a *source* and *source-wildcard* of 0.0.0.0 255.255.255.255.
source-wildcard	(Optional) Wildcard bits to be applied to the source. There are two ways to specify the *source-wildcard*: • Use a 32-bit quantity in four-part, dotted-decimal format. Place ones in the bit positions you want to ignore. • Use the keyword **any** as an abbreviation for a source and source-wildcard of 0.0.0.0 255.255.255.255. (Optional) Causes an informational `logging message` about the packet that matches the entry to be sent to the console. (The level of messages logged to the console is controlled by the `logging console` command.)
log	The message includes the ACL number, whether the packet was permitted or denied, the source address, and the number of packets. The message is generated for the first packet that matches, and then at five-minute intervals, including the number of packets permitted or denied in the prior five-minute interval.

You use the `show access-lists` EXEC command to display the contents of all ACLs. In addition, you use the `show access-lists` EXEC command to display the contents of one ACL.

The following example of a standard ACL allows access for hosts on the three specified networks:

```
access-list 1 permit 192.5.34.0  0.0.0.255
access-list 1 permit 128.88.0.0  0.0.255.255
access-list 1 permit 36.0.0.0  0.255.255.255
! (Note: all other access implicitly denied)
```

In the example, the wildcard bits apply to the host portions of the network addresses. Any host with a source address that does not match the ACL statements will be rejected.

To specify a large number of individual addresses more easily, you can omit the wildcard if it is all zeros. Thus, the following two configuration commands have the same effect:

```
access-list 2 permit 36.48.0.3
access-list 2 permit 36.48.0.3  0.0.0.0
```

The `ip access-group` command groups an existing ACL to an interface. Remember that only one ACL per port per protocol per direction is allowed. The format of the command is

```
Router(config)#ip access-group access-list-number {in | out}
```

Where the parameters have the following meanings:

Parameter	Description
access-list-number	Indicates the number of the ACL to be linked to this interface.
in | **out**	Selects whether the ACL is applied to the incoming or outgoing interface. If **in** or **out** is not specified, **out** is the default.

NOTE

To remove an ACL, first enter the **no ip access-group** command, including list number, for each interface where the list had been used, and then enter the **no access-list** command (with list number).

The standard ACL configuration examples in the following sections refer to the network shown in Figure 6-11. The first example permits traffic from source network 172.16.0.0. The second example denies traffic from a specific host with the address 172.16.4.13 and permits all other traffic. The third example denies traffic from a specific subnet with the address 172.16.4.0 and permits all other traffic.

Standard ACL Example 1: Permitting Traffic from a Source Network

In this example, the ACL allows only traffic from source network 172.16.0.0 to be forwarded. Non-172.16.0.0 network traffic is blocked. Example 6-1 shows how the ACL allows only traffic from source network 172.16.0.0 to be forwarded and non-172.16.0.0 to be blocked.

FIGURE 6-11
This network is an example of two subnets connected by a router.

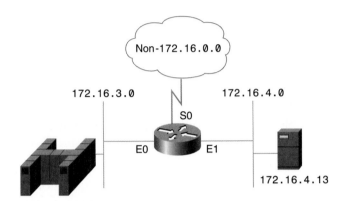

Example 6-1   Permitting Traffic from Source Network 172.16.0.0
```
access-list 1 permit 172.16.0.0  0.0.255.255
(implicit deny any - not visible in the list)
(access-list 1 deny 0.0.0.0  255.255.255.255)

interface ethernet 0
ip access-group 1 out
interface ethernet 1
ip access-group 1 out
```

The following are the fields in the output shown in Example 6-1:

Field	Description
1	ACL number; indicates that this is a simple list.
permit	Traffic that matches selected parameters will be forwarded.
172.16.0.0	IP address that will be used with the wildcard mask to identify the source network.
0.0.255.255	Wildcard mask; zeros indicate positions that must match and ones indicate "don't care" positions.

Also, in Example 6-1, the command `ip access-group 1 out` groups the ACL to an outgoing interface.

Standard ACL Example 2: Denying a Specific Host

Example 6-2 shows how an ACL is designed to block traffic from a specific address, 172.16.4.13, and to allow all other traffic to be forwarded on interface Ethernet 0. The first `access-list` command uses the deny parameter to deny traffic from the identified host. The address mask 0.0.0.0 in this line requires the test to match all bits.

Example 6-2   Denying a Specific Host

```
access-list 1 deny host 172.16.4.13  0.0.0.0
access-list 1 permit 0.0.0.0  255.255.255.255
(implicit deny any)
(access-list 1 deny 0.0.0.0  255.255.255.255)

interface ethernet 0
ip access-group 1
```

The following are the fields in the output shown in Example 6-2:

Field	Description
1	ACL number; indicates that this is a simple list.
Deny	Traffic that matches selected parameters will not be forwarded.
Host	Shorthand for the wildcard mask 0.0.0.0.
permit	Traffic that matches selected parameters will be forwarded.
0.0.0.0	IP address of the source host; all zeros indicate a placeholder.
255.255.255.255	Wildcard mask; zeros indicate positions that must match, ones indicate "don't care" positions. All ones in the mask indicates that all 32 bits will not be checked in the source address.

In the second `access-list` command, the 0.0.0.0 255.255.255.255 IP address/wildcard mask combination identifies traffic from any source. This combination can also be written using the keyword `any`. All zeros in the address indicate a placeholder, and all ones in the wildcard mask indicate that all 32 bits will not be checked in the source address.

Any packet that does not match the first line of the ACL will match the second one and be forwarded.

Standard ACL Example 3: Denying a Specific Subnet

Example 6-3 shows how an ACL is designed to block traffic from a specific subnet, 172.16.4.0, and to allow all other traffic to be forwarded. Note the wildcard mask, 0.0.0.255: The zeros in the first three octets indicate a "don't care" condition. Note also that the **any** abbreviation has been used for the IP address of the source.

Example 6-3   Denying a Specific Subnet

```
access-list 1 deny 172.16.4.0  0.0.0.255
access-list 1 permit any
(implicit deny any)
access-list 1 deny any

interface ethernet 0
ip access-group 1
```

The following are the fields in the output shown in Example 6-3:

Field	Description
1	This ACL is designed to block traffic from a specific subnet, 172.16.4.0, and to allow all other traffic to be forwarded.
deny	Traffic that matches selected parameters will not be forwarded.
172.16.4.0	IP address of the source subnet.
0.0.0.255	Wildcard mask; zeros indicate positions that must match, ones indicate don't-care positions. The mask with zeros in the first three octets indicates that those positions must match; the 255 in the last octet indicates a don't-care condition.
permit	Traffic that matches selected parameters will be forwarded.
any	Abbreviation for the IP address of the source; all zeros indicate a placeholder and the wildcard mask 255.255.255.255. All ones in the mask indicates that all 32 bits will not be checked in the source address.

Extended ACLs

Extended ACLs are used most often to test conditions because they provide a greater range of control than standard ACLs. You would use an extended ACL when you want to allow Web traffic but deny File Transfer Protocol (FTP) or Telnet from non-company networks. Extended ACLs check for both source and destination packet addresses. They also can check for specific protocols, port numbers, and other parameters. This gives you more flexibility to describe what checking the ACL will do. Packets can be permitted or denied output based on where the packet originated and based on its destination. For example, in Figure 6-10, the extended ACL can allow e-mail traffic from E0 to specific S0 destinations, while denying remote logins or file transfers.

In Figure 6-10, let's assume that Interface E0 has been grouped to an extended ACL. This would mean that you used precise, logical statements to create the ACL. Before a packet can proceed to that interface, it is tested by the ACL associated with that interface.

Based on the extended ACL tests, the packet can be permitted or denied. For inbound lists, this means that permitted packets will continue to be processed. For outbound lists, this means that permitted packets will be sent directly to E0. If test results deny permission, the packet will be discarded. The router's ACL provides firewall control to deny use of the E0 interface. When packets are discarded, some protocols return a packet to the sender, stating that the destination was unreachable.

For a single ACL, you can define multiple statements. Each of these statements should reference the same identifying name or number, to tie the statements to the same ACL. You can have as many condition statements as you want, limited only by the available memory. Of course, the more statements you have, the more difficult it will be to comprehend and manage your ACL. Therefore, documenting ACLs prevents confusion.

The standard ACL (numbered 1 to 99) might not provide the traffic-filtering control you need. Standard ACLs filter traffic based on a source address and mask. Standard ACLs also permit or deny the entire Transmission Control Protocol (TCP) protocol suite. You might need a more precise way to control traffic and access.

For more precise traffic-filtering control, you use extended ACLs. Extended ACL statements check for source address and for destination address. In addition, at the end of the extended ACL statement, you gain additional precision from a field that specifies the optional TCP or User Datagram Protocol (UDP) protocol port number. These can be the well-known port numbers for TCP/IP. A few of the most common port numbers are shown in Table 6-2.

TABLE 6-2   Common Port Numbers

Common Port Number (Decimal)	IP Protocol
20	FTP data
21	FTP program
23	Telnet
25	Simple Mail Transport Protocol (SMTP)
69	TFTP
53	DNS

You can specify the logical operation the extended ACL will perform on specific protocols. Extended ACLs use a number in the range 100 to 199.

Extended ACL Examples

The complete form of the `access-list` command is

```
Router(config)# access-list access-list-number {permit | deny}
    protocol source [source-mask destination destination-mask
    [operator operand] [established] [log]
```

Where the parameters have the following meanings:

Parameter	Description
access-list-number	Identifies the list using a number in the range 100 to 199.
permit | deny	Indicates whether this entry allows or blocks the specified address.
protocol	The protocol, such as IP, TCP, UDP, ICMP, GRE, or IGRP.
source and destination	Identifies source and destination addresses.
source-mask and destination-mask	Wildcard mask; zeros indicate positions that must match, ones indicate don't-care positions.
operator operand	lt, gt, eq, neq (less than, greater than, equal, not equal), and a port number.
established	Allows TCP traffic to pass if the packet uses an established connection (for example, has ACK bits set).

The `ip access-group` command links an existing extended ACL to an outbound or inbound interface. Remember that only one ACL per port, per protocol, per direction is allowed. The format of the command is

```
Router(config)# ip access-group access-list access-list-number {in | out}
```

Where the parameters have the following meanings:

Parameter	Description
access-list-number	Indicates the number of the ACL to be linked to this interface.
in | out	Selects whether the ACL is applied to the incoming or outgoing packet on the interface. If in or out is not specified, out is the default.

Destination and source addresses or specific protocols using extended ACLs need to be identified with numbers in the range 100 to 199. Upper-level TCP or UDP port numbers in addition to the other tests in extended ACLs need to be identified, with a number in the range 100 to 199. Reserved well-known port numbers are shown in Table 6-3.

TABLE 6-3   Reserved Well-Known Port Numbers

Decimal	Keyword	Description	
0		Reserved	
1–4		Unassigned	
20	FTP-DATA	FTP (data)	TCP
21	FTP	FTP	TCP
23	TELNET	Terminal connection	TCP
25	SMTP	SMTP	TCP
42	NAMESERVER	Host name server	UDP
53	DOMAIN	DNS	TCP/UDP
69	TFTP	TFTP	UDP
70		Gopher	TCP/IP
80		WWW	TCP
133–159		Unassigned	
160–223		Reserved	
161		FNP	UDP
224–241		Unassigned	
242–255		Unassigned	

The extended ACL configuration examples in the following sections refer to the network shown in Figure 6-11. The first example denies FTP for E0. The second example denies only Telnet out of E0 and permits all other traffic.

Extended ACL Example 1: Denying FTP for E0

Example 6-4 shows an extended ACL that blocks FTP traffic.

Example 6-4   Denying FTP for E0

```
access-list 101 deny tcp 172.16.4.0
    0.0.0.255 172.16.3.0  0.0.0.255  eq 21
access-list 101 permit ip 172.16.4.0
    0.0.0.255 0.0.0.0 255.255.255.255
(implicit deny any)
(access-list 101 deny ip 0.0.0.0
   255.255.255.255  0.0.0.0  255.255.255.255)

interface ethernet 0
ip access-group 101
```

The following are the fields in the output shown in Example 6-4:

Field	Description
101	ACL number; indicates extended ACL.
deny	Traffic that matches selected parameters will be blocked.
tcp	Transport-layer protocol.
172.16.4.0 and 0.0.0.255	Source address and mask; the first three octets must match, but the last octet does not matter.
172.16.3.0 and 0.0.0.255	Destination address and mask; the first three octets must match, but the last octet does not matter.
eq021	Specifies the well-known port number for FTP.
eq 20	Specifies the well-known port number for FTP data.

The `interface E0 access-group 101` command links ACL 101 to outgoing port interface E0. Note that this ACL does not deny FTP traffic; it only denies traffic on ports 20 and 21. FTP servers can easily be configured to work on different ports. You should understand that well-known port numbers are just that: well-known. There are no guarantees that services will be on those ports, although they usually are.

Example 6-5   Allowing Only Mail of Interface E0 and Denying All Other Traffic

```
access-list 101 permit tcp 172.16.4.0  0.0.0.255 any eq 25
(implicit deny any)
(access-list 101 deny ip 0.0.0.0  255.255.255.255
   0.0.0.0  255.255.255.255)

interface ethernet 0
ip access-group 101
```

The following are the fields in the output shown in Example 6-5:

Field	Description
101	ACL number; indicates extended ACL.
permit	Traffic that matches selected parameters will be forwarded.
tcp	Transport-layer protocol.
172.16.4.0 and 0.0.0.255	Source address and mask; the first three octets must match, but the last octet does not matter.
0.0.0.0 and 255.255.255.255	Destination address and mask; no octet values matter.
eq 25	Specifies well-known port number for SMTP.
access-group 101	Command links ACL 101 to outgoing port interface E0.

This example permits SMTP traffic (`eq 25`) from 172.16.4.0 being sent out interface E0. All traffic from any other source to any destination is permitted, as indicated by the keyword `any`. Interface E0 is configured with the `access-group 101 out` command; that is, ACL 101 is linked to outgoing port interface E0.

Using Named ACLs

Named ACLs allow standard and extended IP ACLs to be identified with an alphanumeric string (name) instead of the current numeric (1 to 199) representation. Named ACLs can be used to delete individual entries from a specific ACL. This enables you to modify your ACLs without deleting and then reconfiguring them. Use named ACLs when

- You want to intuitively identify ACLs using an alphanumeric name.
- You have more than 99 simple and 100 extended ACLs to be configured in a router for a given protocol.

Consider the following before implementing named ACLs:

- Named ACLs are not compatible with Cisco IOS releases prior to Release 11.2.
- You cannot use the same name for multiple ACLs. In addition, ACLs of different types cannot have the same name. For example, it is illegal to specify a standard ACL named George and an extended ACL with the same name.

To name the ACL, use the following command:

```
Router(config)# ip access-list {standard | extended} name
```

In ACL configuration mode, specify one or more conditions allowed or denied. The determines whether the packet is passed or dropped:

```
Router(config {std- | ext-}nacl)# deny {source [source-wildcard] | any}
```

or

```
Router(config {std- | ext-}nacl)# permit {source [source-wildcard] | any}
```

The following configuration creates a standard ACL named Internetfilter and an extended ACL named marketinggroup:

```
interface ethernet0/5
ip address 2.0.5.1 255.255.255.0
ip access-group Internetfilter out
ip access-group marketinggroup in
...
```

```
ip access-list standard Internetfilter
permit 1.2.3.4

deny any
ip access-list extended marketing_group
permit tcp any 171.69.0.0 0.255.255.255 eq telnet

deny tcp any any
deny udp any 171.69.0.0  0.255.255.255 lt 1024

deny ip any log
```

The deny Command

You use the **deny** ACL configuration command to set conditions for a named ACL. The full syntax for this command is

> **deny** {source [source-wildcard] | **any**} [log]

You use the **no** form of this command to remove a deny condition, using the following syntax:

> **no deny** {*source* [source-wildcard] | **any**}

The following example sets a deny condition for a standard ACL named Internetfilter:

```
ip access-list standard Internetfilter
 deny 192.5.34.0  0.0.0.255
 permit 128.88.0.0  0.0.255.255
 permit 36.0.0.0  0.255.255.255
 ! (Note: all other access implicitly denied)
```

The permit Command

You use the **permit** access-list configuration command to set conditions for a named ACL. The full syntax of this command is

> **permit** {source [*source-wildcard*] | **any**} [**log**]

You use the **no** form of this command to remove a condition from an ACL, using the following syntax

> **no permit** {*source* [*source-wildcard*] | **any**}

You use this command in access list configuration mode, following the **ip access-list** command, to define the conditions under which a packet passes the ACL.

The following example is for a standard ACL named Internetfilter:

```
ip access-list standard Internetfilter
deny 192.5.34.0  0.0.0.255
permit 128.88.0.0  0.0.255.255
permit 36.0.0.0  0.255.255.255
! (Note: all other access implicitly denied)
```

In this example, permit and deny statements have no number, and **no** removes the specific test from the named ACL:

```
Router(config {std- | ext-}nacl)# {permit | deny} {ip ACL test conditions}
{permit | deny} {ip ACL test conditions}
no {permit | deny} {ip ACL text conditions}
```

This example activates the IP named ACL on an interface:

```
Router(config-if)# ip access-group {name | 1-199 {in | out} }
```

The following is a configuration output example:

```
ip access-list extended come_on
permit tcp any 171.69.0.0 0.255.255.255 eq telnet

deny tcp any any
deny udp any 171.69.0.0 0.255.255.255 lt 1024

deny ip any any
interface ethernet0/5
ip address 2.0.5.1 255.255.255.0
ip access-group over_out out
ip access-group come_on in
ip access-list standard over_and
permit 1.2.3.4

deny any
```

Using ACLs with Protocols

ACLs can control most protocols on a Cisco router. You enter a number in the protocol number range as the first argument of the global ACL statement. The router identifies which ACL software to use based on this numbered entry. Many ACLs are possible for a protocol. You select a different number from the protocol number range for each new ACL; however, you can specify only one ACL per protocol per interface. For some protocols, you can group up to two ACLs to an interface: one inbound ACL and one outbound ACL. With other protocols, you group only one ACL, which checks both inbound and outbound packets. If the ACL is inbound, when the router receives a packet, the Cisco IOS software checks the ACL's condition statements for a match. If the packet is permitted, the software continues to process the packet. If the packet is denied, the software discards the packet by placing it in the bit bucket. If the ACL is outbound, after receiving and routing a packet to the outbound interface, the software checks the ACL's condition statements for a match. If the packet is permitted, the software transmits the packet. If the packet is denied, the software discards the packet by sending it to the bit bucket.

Engineering Journal:
Naming or Numbering an IP Protocol

The name or number of an IP protocol can be one of the keywords `eigrp`, `gre`, `icmp`, `igmp`, `igrp`, `ip`, `ipinip`, `nos`, `ospf`, `tcp`, or `udp`, or an integer in the range **0** to **255**, representing an IP protocol number. To match any Internet protocol (including ICMP, TCP, and UDP), use the keyword `ip`. The protocols and their corresponding numbers are listed in RFC 1700, along with port numbers.

Placing ACLs

As you learned earlier, ACLs are used to control traffic by filtering packets and eliminating unwanted traffic at a destination. Depending on where you place an ACL statement, you can reduce unnecessary traffic. Traffic that will be denied at a remote destination should not use network resources along the route to that destination.

Suppose an enterprise's policy aims to deny Telnet or FTP traffic on Router A to the switched Ethernet LAN on Router D's E1 port, as shown in Figure 6-12. At the same time, other traffic must be permitted. Several approaches can accomplish this policy. The recommended approach uses an extended ACL. It specifies both source and destination addresses. Place this extended ACL in Router A. Then, packets do not cross Router A's Ethernet, do not cross the serial interfaces of Routers B and C, and do not enter Router D. Traffic with different source and destination addresses can still be permitted.

The rule is to put the extended ACL as close as possible to the source of the traffic denied. Standard ACLs do not specify destination addresses, so you have to put the standard ACL as near the destination as possible. For example, as shown in Figure 6-12, you should place either a standard or an extended ACL on E0 of Router D to prevent traffic from Router A.

Using ACLs with Firewalls

ACLs should be used in firewall routers, which are often positioned between the internal network and an external network, such as the Internet. The firewall router provides a point of isolation so that the rest of the internal network structure is not affected. You can also use ACLs on a router positioned between two parts of the network to control traffic entering or exiting a specific part of the internal network.

> **NOTE**
>
> For most protocols, if you define an inbound ACL for traffic filtering, you should include precise ACL condition statements to permit routing updates. If you do not, you might lose communication from the interface when routing updates are blocked by the deny all traffic statement at the end of the ACL. This can be avoided by adding a permit any statement to the end of any ACL you create.

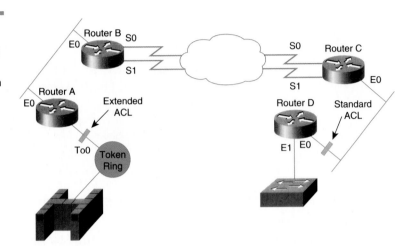

FIGURE 6-12
You should
place standard
ACLs close to
the destination
and extended
ACLs close to
the source.

To provide the security benefits of ACLs, you should at a minimum configure ACLs on border routers, which are routers situated on the boundaries of the network. This provides basic security from the outside network, or from a less controlled area of the network, into a more private area of the network.

On these border routers, ACLs can be created for each network protocol configured on the router interfaces. You can configure ACLs so that inbound traffic, outbound traffic, or both are filtered on an interface.

Washington Project: Firewall Implementation
The Internet connectivity you will need to implement in the Washington School District requires a double firewall implementation with all the applications that are exposed to the Internet residing on a public backbone network. You need to ensure that all connections initiated from the Internet into each school's private network will be refused.

Setting Up a Firewall Architecture

A firewall architecture is a structure that exists between you and the outside world to protect you from intruders. In most circumstances, intruders come from the global Internet and the thousands of remote networks it interconnects. Typically, a network firewall consists of several different machines, as shown in Figure 6-13.

In this architecture, the router that is connected to the Internet (that is, the exterior router) forces all incoming traffic to go to the application gateway. The router that is connected to the internal network (that is, the interior router) accepts packets only from the application gateway.

FIGURE 6-13
A typical firewall architecture protects a network from intruders from the Internet.

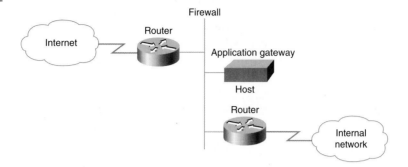

In effect, the gateway controls the delivery of network-based services both into and from the internal network. For example, only certain users might be allowed to communicate with the Internet, or only certain applications might be permitted to establish connections between an interior and exterior host.

If the only application that is permitted is mail, then only mail packets should be allowed through the router. This protects the application gateway and avoids overwhelming it with packets that it would otherwise discard.

Engineering Journal: Using a Firewall Router

This section uses the scenario illustrated in Figure 6-13 to describe the use of ACLs to restrict traffic to and from a firewall router.

Having a designated router act as a firewall is good because it clearly identifies the router's purpose as the external gateway and avoids encumbering other routers with this task. In the event that the internal network needs to isolate itself, the firewall router provides the point of isolation so that the rest of the internal network structure is not affected.

In the firewall router configuration that follows, subnet 13 of the Class B network is the firewall subnet, and subnet 14 provides the connection to the worldwide Internet via a service provider:

```
interface ethernet 0
ip address B.B.13.1 255.255.255.0
interface serial 0
ip address B.B.14.1 255.255.255.0
router igrp
network B.B.0.0
```

This simple configuration provides no security and allows all traffic from the outside world onto all parts of the network. To provide security on the firewall router, you need to use ACLs and access groups.

An ACL defines the actual traffic that will be permitted or denied, and an access group applies an ACL definition to an interface. ACLs can be used to deny connections that are known to be

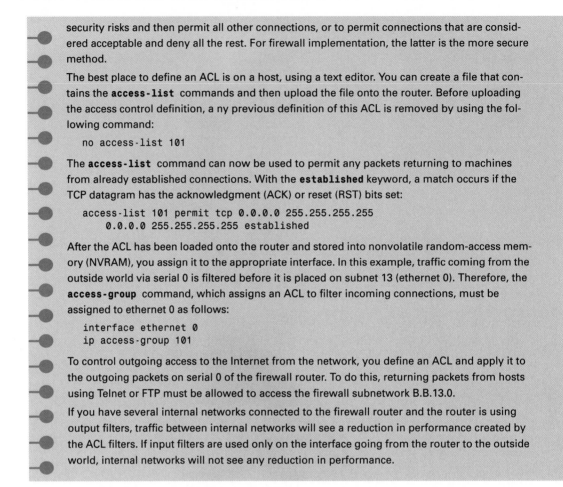

security risks and then permit all other connections, or to permit connections that are considered acceptable and deny all the rest. For firewall implementation, the latter is the more secure method.

The best place to define an ACL is on a host, using a text editor. You can create a file that contains the **access-list** commands and then upload the file onto the router. Before uploading the access control definition, a ny previous definition of this ACL is removed by using the following command:

```
no access-list 101
```

The **access-list** command can now be used to permit any packets returning to machines from already established connections. With the **established** keyword, a match occurs if the TCP datagram has the acknowledgment (ACK) or reset (RST) bits set:

```
access-list 101 permit tcp 0.0.0.0 255.255.255.255
    0.0.0.0 255.255.255.255 established
```

After the ACL has been loaded onto the router and stored into nonvolatile random-access memory (NVRAM), you assign it to the appropriate interface. In this example, traffic coming from the outside world via serial 0 is filtered before it is placed on subnet 13 (ethernet 0). Therefore, the **access-group** command, which assigns an ACL to filter incoming connections, must be assigned to ethernet 0 as follows:

```
interface ethernet 0
ip access-group 101
```

To control outgoing access to the Internet from the network, you define an ACL and apply it to the outgoing packets on serial 0 of the firewall router. To do this, returning packets from hosts using Telnet or FTP must be allowed to access the firewall subnetwork B.B.13.0.

If you have several internal networks connected to the firewall router and the router is using output filters, traffic between internal networks will see a reduction in performance created by the ACL filters. If input filters are used only on the interface going from the router to the outside world, internal networks will not see any reduction in performance.

Verifying ACLs

The **show ip interface** command displays IP interface information and indicates whether any ACLs are set. The **show access-lists** command displays the contents of all ACLs. By entering the ACL name or number as an option for this command, you can see a specific list, as shown in Example 6-6.

Example 6-6   Show IP Interface

```
Router> show

Ethernet0 is up, line protocol is up
    Internet address is 192.54.22.2, subnet mask is 255.255.255.0
    Broadcast address is 255.255.255.255
    Address determined by nonvolatile memory
    MTU is 1500 bytes
    Helper address is 192.52.71.4
```

```
Secondary address 131.192.115.2, subnet mask 255.255.255.0
Outgoing ACL 10 is set
Inbound ACL is not set
Proxy ARP is enabled
Security level is default
Split horizon is enabled
ICMP redirects are always sent
ICMP unreachables are never sent
ICMP mask replies are never sent
IP fast switching is enables
Gateway Discovery is diabled
IP accounting is disabled
TCP/IP header compression is disabled
Probe proxy name replies are disabled
Router>
```

Summary

- ACLs perform several functions within a Cisco router, including implementing security/access procedures.
- ACLs are used to control and manage traffic.
- For some protocols, you can apply up to two ACLs to an interface: one inbound ACL and one outbound ACL.
- With ACLs, after a packet is checked for a match with the ACL statement, it can be denied or permitted to use an interface in the access group.
- IP address bits uses the number one and the number zero to identify how to treat the corresponding IP address bits.
- The two main types of ACLs are standard ACLs and extended ACLs.
- ACLs can be configured for all routed network protocols to filter those protocols' packets as the packets pass through a router.
- ACLs are typically used in firewall routers, which are often positioned between the internal network and an external network such as the Internet.

Washington School District Project Task: Using ACLs

In this chapter, you have learned concepts and configuration process that will help you implement ACLs in the Washington School District network. In response to the network design and security requirements, you need to complete the following tasks:

1. Document why you would need ACLs and create a logical diagram describing the overall effect of these ACLs on the entire district network.

2. Document what type of ACL will be placed on the district router(s), and where they will be placed and why.

3. Document the router command sequence required to implement each ACL on each of the schools' routers.

4. Document the effect of each ACL as it relates to traffic flow across individual school LANs and the overall district network.

Chapter Review

Complete all the review questions to test your understanding of the topics and concepts covered in this chapter. Answers are listed in Appendix A, "Chapter Review Answer Key."

1. What is the purpose of ACLs?

2. What condition do standard ACLs use for IP data packets?

3. How do extended ACLs differ from standard ACLs?

4. How do ACLs compare each data packet to the conditions in the list?

5. How are standard and extended ACLs differentiated in the router?

6. Which of the following commands would you use to find out whether there are any ACLs set on an interface?

   A. `show running-config`

   B. `show ip protocols`

   C. `show ip interface`

   D. `show ip network`

7. What do you call the additional 32 bits of information in the `access-list` statement?

   A. Wildcard bits

   B. Access bits

   C. Zero bits

   D. One bits

8. Using `Router(config)# access-list 156.1.0.0 0.0.255.255` is equivalent to saying which of the following?

   A. "Deny my network only"

   B. "Permit a specific host"

   C. "Permit my network only"

   D. "deny a specific host"

9. When you issue a permit entry into an ACL that is accompanied by an implicit deny all, all traffic except that listed in the permit statement will be denied.

   A. True

   B. False

10. The `show access-lists` command is used to do which of the following?

A. Monitor whether ACLs are set

B. Monitor ACL statements

C. Monitor ACL debugging

D. Monitor groupings

Key Terms

ACL (access control list)   A list kept by a Cisco router to control access to or from the router for a number of services (for example, to prevent packets with a certain IP address from leaving a particular interface on the router).

bit bucket   The destination of discarded bits as determined by the router.

border router   A router situated at the edges, or end, of the network boundary, which provides a basic security from the outside network, or from a less controlled area of the network, into a more private area of the network.

DNS (Domain Name System)   A system used in the Internet for translating names of network nodes into addresses.

extended ACL (extended access control list)   An ACL that checks for source address and destination address.

firewall   A router or an access server, or several routers or access servers, designated as a buffer between any connected public networks and a private network. A firewall router uses access control lists and other methods to ensure the security of the private network.

queuing   A process in which ACLs can designate certain packets to be processed by a router before other traffic, on the basis of a protocol.

standard ACL (standard access control list)   An ACL that filters based on a source address and mask. Standard ACLs permit or deny the entire TCP/IP protocol suite.

wildcard mask   A 32-bit quantity used in conjunction with an IP address to determine which bits in an IP address should be ignored when comparing that address with another IP address. A wildcard mask is specified when setting up an ACL.

Objectives

After reading this chapter, you will be able to

- Explain how Cisco routers are used in NetWare networks
- Describe the Novell NetWare protocol suite
- Describe Novell IPX addressing
- Describe Novell encapsulation
- Explain how Novell uses RIP for routing
- Describe Service Advertising Protocol
- Configure both the router Ethernet and serial interfaces with IPX addresses
- Describe how to discover IPX addresses on remote routers
- Describe how to verify IPX operation and connectivity between routers
- Explain troubleshooting in IPX operations

Chapter 7

Novell IPX

Introduction

Novell NetWare is a network operating system (NOS), which connects PCs and other clients to NetWare servers. NetWare servers provide a variety of network services to their clients, including file sharing, printer sharing, directory services, and Internet access. Many NetWare servers function as application platforms for shared databases and as Internet and intranet servers. With more than 5 million networks and more than 50 million clients, Novell has the largest share of the NOS user base market.

In addition to Transmission Control Protocol/Internet Protocol (TCP/IP), Novell's Internetwork Packet Exchange (IPX) is another protocol that is commonly implemented in the networking industry. Until Novell's NetWare 5.0 release in 1998, all NetWare networks used IPX. As with AppleTalk, Novell migrated NetWare to IP. Therefore, IPX networks are networks that must still be supported due to their installed base. In this chapter, you will learn about Novell's IPX protocols, operation, and configuration.

Washington Project: IPX Implementation
In this chapter, you will learn how to implement Novell IPX in the Washington School District network. The school district needs a workgroup server in each computer lab at the school sites. The computer labs are located on the curriculum LAN segments of their respective sites. Both IP and IPX services need to be advertised across the school district network to other curriculum LAN segments.

Cisco Routers in NetWare Networks

Cisco and Novell have collaborated for many years to develop and improve NetWare-based networking. Although many of the NetWare protocols were initially designed for use on small, homogeneous LANs, Cisco has added features to optimize NetWare protocols performance in large and diverse networking environments. Cisco supports many unique enhancements to the basic NetWare protocol suite. These enhancements are part of the Cisco Internetwork Operating System (IOS) software.

The Novell NetWare Protocol Suite

Novell, Inc., developed and introduced NetWare in the early 1980s. NetWare uses a client/server architecture. Clients (sometimes called *workstations*) request services, such as file and printer access, from servers. Unlike in Windows NT networks, NetWare servers are dedicated servers and cannot be used as clients. Figure 7-1 shows the NetWare protocol suite, the media access protocols that NetWare and Cisco support, and the relationship between the NetWare protocols and the Open System Interconnection (OSI) reference model.

FIGURE 7-1

The NetWare protocol stack supports all common media access protocols.

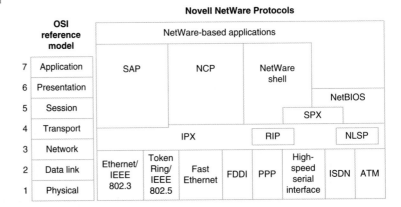

Novell IPX is a proprietary suite of protocols and includes the following:

- A datagram, which is a connectionless protocol that does not require an acknowledgment for each packet
- A Layer 3 protocol that defines the network and node addresses
- Novell Routing Information Protocol (RIP)—which is different from IP RIP—to facilitate the exchange of routing information
- Service Advertising Protocol (SAP) to advertise network services
- NetWare Core Protocol (NCP) to provide client-to-server connections and applications
- Sequenced Packet Exchange (SPX) service for Layer 4 connection-oriented services

IPX Overview

IPX is the NetWare Layer 3 protocol used to route packets through interconnected networks. IPX specifies a connectionless datagram, similar to IP packets in TCP/IP networks.

IPX is similar to TCP/IP and operates within the same network implementation as TCP/IP, provided that you have a multiprotocol router. Some of the characteristics of IPX are that

- It is used in a client/server environment.
- It uses the *network.node* IPX addressing structure.
- Its logical address contains an interface MAC address.
- IPX interface configuration supports multiple data-link encapsulations.
- Novell RIP uses the distance-vector metrics of ticks and hops.
- Service access point and Get Nearest Server (GNS) broadcasts connect clients and servers.

IPX uses dynamic distance-vector routing (such as RIP) or link-state routing (such as NetWare Link Services Protocol [NLSP]). IPX RIP sends routing updates every 60 seconds. RIP uses network delay and hop count as its routing metrics and is limited to a total of 16 hops.

Novell IPX Addressing

Novell IPX addressing uses a two-part address—the network number and the node number—as shown in Figure 7-2. The node number is usually the Media Access Control (MAC) address for a network interface in the end node. Novell IPX supports multiple logical networks on an individual interface; each network requires a single encapsulation type. The IPX network number, which is assigned by the network administrator, can be up to eight base 16 (hexadecimal) digits in length.

> **NOTE**
>
> To make best-path decisions, IPX uses a tick as the metric, which is the delay expected when using a particular length. One tick is $1/18$ second. If two paths have an equal tick count, IPX RIP uses the hop count. Although they are similar, Novell's version of RIP is not compatible with RIP implementations used in other networking protocol suites, such as TCP/IP.

FIGURE 7-2
A Novell IPX address has 80 bits: 32 bits for the network number and 48 bits for the node number.

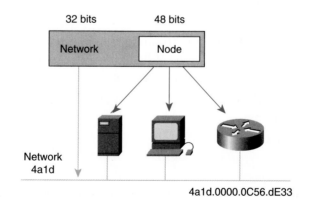

Figure 7-3 shows two IPX networks, 4a1d and 3f. The IPX node number is 12 hexadecimal digits in length. This number is usually the MAC address, obtained from a network interface that has a MAC address. The use of the

MAC address in the logical IPX address eliminates the need for Address Resolution Protocol (ARP). Serial interfaces use the MAC address of the Ethernet interface for their IPX node address. Figure 7-3 shows the IPX node 0000.0c56.de33 on the 4a1d network. Another node address is 0000.0c56.de34 on the 3f network.

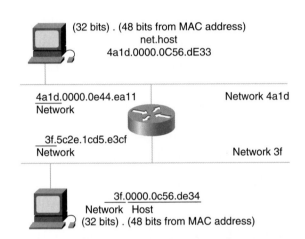

FIGURE 7-3
Each device in an IPX network has a unique address.

Regardless of whether you're using a LAN or a WAN interface, you assign the same IPX network numbers to the routers that are in use by the IPX devices. The way to obtain a Novell network address is to ask the network administrator for one. The network administrator must specify the correct IPX network address for the same network where you want to enable IPX on your Cisco router. On the Cisco router, you must use the same IPX network address as the address that already exists on that network, which is typically specified by the NetWare administrator. If you cannot obtain an IPX address from the network administrator, you can get the IPX address directly from a neighbor router. To do this, you Telnet to the neighbor router and use the `show protocols` or `show ipx interface` command.

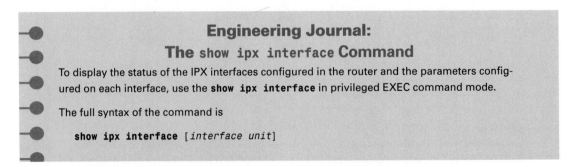

Engineering Journal:
The `show ipx interface` Command

To display the status of the IPX interfaces configured in the router and the parameters configured on each interface, use the `show ipx interface` in privileged EXEC command mode.

The full syntax of the command is

   `show ipx interface [interface unit]`

The argument *interface* is the interface and can be one of the following types: asynchronous, dialer, Ethernet (IEEE 802.3), FDDI, loopback, null, serial, Token Ring, or tunnel. The argument *unit* is the number of the interface. For example, `ethernet 0` specifies the first Ethernet interface.

The following is sample output from the **show ipx interface** command:

```
Router# show ipx interface ethernet 1
Ethernet1 is up, line protocol is up
  IPX address is C03.0000.0c05.6030, NOVELL-ETHER [up] line-up,
     RIPPQ: 0, SAPPQ : 0
  Delay of this Novell network, in ticks is 1
  IPXWAN processing not enabled on this interface.
  IPX SAP update interval is 1 minute(s)
```

The following are the fields shown in this output:

Field	Description
`Ethernet1 is…, line protocol is…`	The type of interface and whether it is currently active and inserted into the network (up) or inactive and not inserted (down).
`IPX address is…`	The network and node address of the local router interface, followed by the type of encapsulation configured on the interface and the interface's status.
`NOVELL-ETHER`	The type of encapsulation being used on the interface, if any.
`[up] line-up`	Indicates whether IPX routing is enabled or disabled on the interface. `line-up` indicates that IPX routing has been enabled with the **ipx routing** command. `line-down` indicates that it is not enabled. The word in square brackets provides more detail about the status of IPX routing when it is in the process of being enabled or disabled.
`RIPPQ:`	The number of packets in the RIP queue.
`SAPPQ:`	The number of packets in the SAP queue.
`Secondary address is…`	The address of a secondary network configured on this interface, if any, followed by the type of encapsulation configured on the interface and the interface's status. This line is displayed only if you have configured a secondary address with the **ipx network** command.
`Delay of this Novell network, in ticks…`	The value of the ticks field (configured with the **ipx delay** command).
`IPXWAN processing…`	Indicates whether IPXWAN processing has been enabled on this interface with the **ipx ipxwan** command.
`IPX SAP update interval`	Indicates the frequency of outgoing SAP updates (configured with the **ipx sap-interval** command).

> ### Washington Project: IPX Addressing Issues
>
> When planning IPX addressing, you do not need to worry about numbering hosts as you would for TCP/IP. This is because the host address for a workstation is usually the MAC address of that station's network interface card. However, you need to develop a scheme for the IPX network numbers in the Washington School District WAN. Remember that a router can't have two interfaces that belong to the same logical (IP, IPX, and so on) network, or subnet; therefore, you cannot use the same network number throughout the district WAN.
>
> When you develop your IPX network numbering scheme, keep in mind that IPX network numbers can be up to 32 bits (or 8 hexadecimal digits), but they usually contain leading zeros to "pad out" the address. For example, the number 21 can be used as a valid IPX network number because leading zeros can be added to expand 21 into 32 bits (written as 8 hexadecimal digits): 00000021.
>
> Some network administrators convert the IP network address to hexadecimal and use the result as the IPX network number. For example, the subnet 169.199.69.128 /27 would become A9C74580. But, there's no rule that says you have do this. You can use the leading zeros feature to create very simple IPX network numbers (such as 10, 20, 30, and so on).
>
> You will see later in this chapter that, because of Layer 2 issues, a router interface may need to exist on two logical networks—that is, have two network numbers simultaneously. After you have read about Novell frame encapsulation types, you should check the Washington School District requirements carefully to see if your addressing scheme needs to account for this.

Novell Encapsulations

NetWare supports multiple encapsulations (that is, frame types) for the Ethernet family of protocols, all of which are supported by Cisco routers.

Xerox, Intel, and Digital (known collectively as DIX) first released a standard for Ethernet in 1980, called *Ethernet Version I*. Two years later, DIX replaced this standard with *Ethernet Version II*, which is the standard encapsulation type for TCP/IP. Then, the Institute of Electrical and Electronic Engineers (IEEE) began work on an improved Ethernet frame in 1982. The 802.3 committee was responsible for work on this project, but Novell could not wait for the committee to officially release the new frame specification. In 1983, Novell released its frame specifications based on the incomplete work of the 802.3 committee. Novell called this frame type 802.3 (Ethernet 802.3); this specification is sometimes called *Ethernet raw* because the IEEE hadn't finished "cooking" it. Two years later, the IEEE finally released the final 802.3 specification, which included the logical link control (LLC) header. The LLC contains fields that identify service access points, and these fields make the IEEE's specification (now called 802.2) incompatible with Novell's 802.3. Because the IEEE 802.2 frame includes service access points, the Cisco IOS software refers to 802.2 as *ethernet sap* (Novell calls it *Ethernet_802.2*). Compatibility issues between 802.2 and 802.3 prompted the development of a fourth major frame type: *Ethernet SNAP*. The most important thing to remember about these four frame types is that they are not compatible with each other. If a Novell server uses 802.3 framing, and a Cisco router is configured to encapsulate using 802.2, then these two nodes cannot talk to each other.

The Cisco IOS software and Novell terms for these encapsulations are

- Ethernet 802.3 is also called raw Ethernet and is the default for NetWare versions 2 through 3.11.

- Ethernet 802.2 or sap (also called Novell Ethernet_802.2 or 802.3) is the standard IEEE frame format, including an 802.2 LLC header. With the release of NetWare 3.12 and 4.x, this encapsulation became Novell's new standard frame format and is also used for OSI routing.

- Ethernet II or arpa (also called Novell Ethernet_II or Ethernet Version II) uses the standard Ethernet Version II header and is used with TCP/IP.

- Ethernet SNAP or snap (also called Novell Ethernet_SNAP or snap) extends the IEEE 802.2 header by adding a Subnetwork Access Protocol (SNAP) header, which provides an "encapsulation type" code similar to that defined in the Ethernet Version II specification and used with TCP/IP and AppleTalk.

Cisco Encapsulation Names

Cisco hardware and Cisco IOS software support all the different Ethernet/ 802.3 encapsulations used by NetWare. Cisco equipment can tell the difference between these various packet types, regardless of how they are encapsulated. Multiple encapsulations are supported on a single LAN interface, allowing older and newer NetWare nodes to coexist on the same LAN segment as long as you configure multiple logical networks. Multiple IPX-encapsulation support reduces equipment expense, minimizes configuration complexity, and eases migration from one IPX encapsulation method to another.

When you configure an IPX network, you might need to specify an encapsulation type on the Novell servers and clients or on the Cisco router. Table 7-1 helps you specify the appropriate IPX encapsulation type by matching the Novell term to the equivalent Cisco IOS term for the same frame types.

TABLE 7-1   Cisco Encapsulation Names

Encapsulation Type	Novell IPX Name	Cisco IOS Name
Ethernet	Ethernet_802.3	novell-ether
	Ethernet_802.2	sap
	Ethernet_II	arpa
	Ethernet_SNAP	snap

continues

NOTE

Multiple IPX encapsulations can be specified on an interface, but only if multiple IPX network numbers have also been assigned. Although several IPX encapsulation types can share the same interface, Novell clients and servers with different IPX encapsulation types cannot communicate directly with each other.

NOTE

Make sure to use the Cisco name for the appropriate IPX encapsulation and that the IPX encapsulation types of the clients, servers, and routers all match. Also note that the default Ethernet IPX encapsulation type on Cisco routers does not match the default Ethernet IPX encapsulation type on Novell servers after NetWare 3.11.

TABLE 7-1   **Cisco Encapsulation Names (Continued)**

Encapsulation Type	Novell IPX Name	Cisco IOS Name
Token Ring	Token-Ring	sap
	Token-Ring_SNAP	snap
FDDI	FDDI_SNAP	snap
	FDDI_802.2	sap
	FDDI_RAW	novell-fddi

Washington Project: IPX Addressing and Encapsulation Types
When configuring routers for the Washington School District, you should note what Novell servers are connected to a router's interface. If those servers are running NetWare 3.12 or 4.x, then you must configure that interface to use ethernet sap as a frame type. If two NetWare servers connect to the same router port and use different frame types, then you have to configure the router interface for multiple framing types; thus, you must create multiple logical networks (that is, the interface will have two IPX addresses that have the same host number but different network numbers).

IPX Packet Format

The IPX packet is the basic unit of Novell NetWare networking. The following descriptions summarize the IPX packet fields:

Field	Description
Checksum	Indicates that the checksum is not used when this 16-bit field is set to ones (FFFF).
Packet length	Specifies the length in bytes of a complete IPX datagram. IPX packets can be any length, up to the media maximum transmission unit (MTU) size (no packet fragmentation is allowed).
Transport control	Indicates the number of routers through which the packet has passed. When this value reaches 16, the packet is discarded under the assumption that a routing loop might be occurring.
Packet type	Specifies which upper-layer protocol should receive the packet's information. It has two common values: • 5—Specifies SPX • 17—Specifies NCP

Novell Routing Using RIP

Connecting existing Novell LANs together and supporting large numbers of NetWare clients and servers presents special challenges in areas such as network management and scalability. Cisco IOS software provides several key features designed to make very large Novell networks possible.

Cisco IOS software supports the standard Novell RIP, which provides a basic solution for networking Novell LANs together. However, the frequent update messages, the slow convergence when the network topology changes, and the 16-hop hop count limitation of RIP make it a poor choice for larger networks or networks connected via WAN links.

Because Novell RIP is a distance-vector routing protocol, it uses two metrics to make routing decisions: ticks and hop count. Novell RIP checks its two distance-vector metrics by first comparing the ticks for path alternatives. If two or more paths have the same tick value, Novell RIP compares the hop count. If two or more paths have the same hop count, the router load shares. Load sharing is the use of two or more paths to route packets to the same destination evenly among multiple routers to balance the work and improve network performance.

Engineering Journal:
The `ipx maximum-paths` Command

To set the maximum number of equal-cost paths the router uses when forwarding packets, use the **ipx maximum-paths** in global configuration mode. The full syntax of this command is

    ipx maximum-paths paths

To restore the default value of 1, use the **no** form of this command:

    no ipx maximum-paths paths

The argument *paths* indicates the maximum number of equal-cost paths the router will use. The argument *paths* can be a value from 1 to 512. The default value is 1.

The **ipx maximum-paths** command is designed to increase throughput by allowing the router to choose among several equal-cost, parallel paths. (Note that when paths have differing costs, the router chooses lower-cost routes before higher-cost routes.) IPX load shares on a packet-by-packet basis in round-robin fashion, regardless of whether you are using fast switching or process switching. That is, the first packet is sent along the first path, the second packet along the second path, and so on. When the final path is reached, the next packet is sent to the first path, the next to the second path, and so on.

Limiting the number of equal-cost paths can save memory on routers with limited memory or very large configurations. Additionally, in networks with a large number of multiple paths and end systems with the limited ability to cache out-of-sequence packets, performance might suffer when traffic is split between many paths. In the following example, the router uses up to three parallel paths:

```
Router(config)# ipx maximum-paths 3
```

A router's Novell RIP routing table is different from its IP routing table because the router maintains a routing table for every IPX protocol that is enabled. Therefore, each IPX-enabled router periodically passes copies of its Novell RIP routing table to its direct neighbor. The neighbor IPX routers add distance vectors as required before passing copies of their Novell RIP tables to their own neighbors.

A "best information" split-horizon protocol prevents the neighbor from broadcasting Novell RIP tables about IPX information back to the networks from which it received that information. Novell RIP also uses an information aging mechanism to handle conditions where an IPX enabled router goes down without any exact message to its neighbors. Periodic updates reset the aging timer. Routing table updates are sent at 60-second intervals. This update frequency can cause excessive overhead traffic on some networks.

Engineering Journal:
The `ipx routing` Command

To enable IPX routing, use the **`ipx routing`** in global configuration mode. The full syntax of the command is

```
ipx routing [node]
```

To disable IPX routing, use the **no** form of this command:

```
no ipx routing [node]
```

The argument *node* indicates the node number of the router. This is a 48-bit value represented by a dotted triplet of four-digit hexadecimal numbers (*xxxx.xxxx.xxxx*).

If you omit *node,* the router uses the hardware MAC address currently assigned to it as its node address. This is the MAC address of the first Ethernet, Token Ring, or FDDI interface card. If no satisfactory interfaces are present in the router (such as only serial interfaces), you must specify *node*.

The **`ipx routing`** command enables the IPX RIP and SAP services on the router. If you omit the argument *node* and if the MAC address later changes, the IPX node address automatically changes to the new address. However, connectivity might be lost between the time that the MAC address changes and the time that the IPX clients and servers learn the router's new address. The following example enables IPX routing:

```
Router(config)# ipx routing
```

Engineering Journal:
Cisco's Enhanced IGRP

One of Cisco's greatest strengths for connecting NetWare LANs is the enhanced version of Cisco's Interior Gateway Routing Protocol (IGRP). Enhanced IGRP provides support for NetWare and AppleTalk networks, in addition to TCP/IP. Enhanced IGRP is a distance-vector routing protocol, but features the fast convergence on changes in the network topology of a link-state routing protocol. Enhanced IGRP issues routing updates only when the network topology changes, transmits only the changed information, and limits the distribution of the update information to those routers affected by the change. As a result, Enhanced IGRP provides low routing overhead, low router CPU utilization, and moderate memory requirements.

Unlike link-state protocols, Enhanced IGRP does not require networks to be designed with an explicit address hierarchy, which gives network administrators greater flexibility in connecting and extending existing networks. Enhanced IGRP also makes use of multiple metrics (delay, bandwidth, reliability, and load) to build a more accurate view of the overall network topology and make more efficient use of network bandwidth. Enhanced IGRP can reduce backbone traffic on large NetWare networks by as much as 40% to 50%. Many large public and private NetWare networks have been implemented using Enhanced IGRP on the network backbone because of its excellent scalability and performance.

To create an IPX Enhanced IGRP routing process, perform the following tasks:

Task	Command
Enable an IPX Enhanced IGRP routing process in global configuration mode.	`ipx router eigrp` *autonomous-system-number*
Enable Enhanced IGRP on a network in IPX router configuration mode.	`network` {*network-number* | `all`}

The following example enables RIP on Networks 1 and 2, and Enhanced IGRP on Network 1:

```
Router# ipx routing
!
interface ethernet 0
 ipx network 1
!
interface ethernet 1
 ipx network 2
!
ipx router eigrp 100
 network 1
```

The following example enables RIP on Network 2, and Enhanced IGRP on Network 1:

```
Router# ipx routing
!
interface ethernet 0
 ipx network 1
!
interface ethernet 1
```

```
    ipx network 2
    !
   ipx router eigrp 100
    ipx network 1
    !
   ipx router rip
    no ipx network 1
```

Service Advertising Protocol

NetWare's SAP allows network resources, including file and print servers, to advertise their network addresses and the services they provide. Each service is identified by a number, called a SAP identifier. SAP updates are sent every 60 seconds.

Intermediate network devices, like routers, listen to the SAP updates and build a table of all known services and associated network addresses. When a Novell client requests a particular network service, the router responds with the network address of the requested service. The client can then contact the service directly.

All the servers on NetWare networks can advertise their services and addresses. All versions of NetWare support SAP broadcasts to announce and locate registered network services. Adding, finding, and removing services on the network is dynamic because of SAP advertisements.

Each SAP service is an object type identified by a number. The following are examples:

Number	SAP Service
4	NetWare file server
7	Print server
24	Remote bridge server (router)

Workstations do not keep SAP tables—only routers and servers keep SAP tables. All servers and routers keep a complete list of the services available throughout the network in SAP tables. Like RIP, SAP also uses an aging mechanism to identify and remove SAP table entries that become invalid.

By default, service advertisements occur at 60-second intervals. However, although service advertisements might work well on a LAN, broadcasting services can require too much bandwidth to be acceptable on large networks, or in networks linked on WAN serial connections.

Routers do not forward SAP broadcasts. Instead, each router builds its own SAP table and forwards the SAP table to other routers. By default, this occurs every 60 seconds, but the router can use access control lists to control the SAPs accepted or forwarded.

Cisco IOS software also allows network administrators to display SAP table entries by name rather than by SAP identifier. By presenting network configuration information in a more readable format, this feature makes maintaining networks and diagnosing network problems easier.

Engineering Journal: Configurable RIP and SAP Update Timers and Packet Sizes

NetWare clients and servers rely on RIP and SAP update messages, both of which occur every 60 seconds by default, to transmit routing information and to provide current information on available network services. Once each minute, RIP and SAP update timers trigger broadcast packets to inform the network of changes in the internal tables of a particular device. These update packets can wreak havoc on network performance, however, particularly in the case of large, continually changing networks with relatively slow backbones.

Cisco IOS software supports configurable RIP and SAP update timers on a per-interface basis. By appropriately configuring the RIP and SAP update timers, network administrators can control the amount of traffic introduced to the network by RIP and SAP, thereby saving precious bandwidth.

Cisco IOS software also allows the size of the RIP and SAP packets to be increased (up to the MTU of the underlying network). By increasing the size of the RIP and SAP packets, the overall number of update packets can be reduced, making more efficient use of available bandwidth.

Get Nearest Server Protocol

NetWare clients automatically discover available network services because Novell servers and routers announce the services by using SAP broadcasts. One type of SAP advertisement is GNS, which enables a client to quickly locate the nearest server for login.

The NetWare client/server interaction begins when the client powers up and runs its client startup programs. These programs use the client's network adapter on the LAN and initiate the connection sequence for the NetWare command shell to use. The connection sequence is a broadcast that comes from a client using SAP. The nearest NetWare file server responds with another SAP; the protocol type is GNS. From that point on, the client can log in to the target server, make a connection, set the packet size, and proceed to use server resources.

If a NetWare server is located on the segment, it responds to the client request. The Cisco router does not respond to the GNS request. If there are no Net-Ware servers on the local network, the Cisco router responds with a server address from its own SAP table.

Cisco IOS software allows NetWare clients to be located on LAN segments where there are no servers. When a NetWare client wants to locate a NetWare server, it issues a NetWare GNS request. Cisco routers listen to NetWare traffic, identify eligible servers, and forward the GNS requests specifically to them. By filtering GNS packets, you can explicitly exclude selected servers, providing greater security and flexibility in network design.

In responding to GNS requests, Cisco IOS software can also distribute clients evenly among the available servers. For example, assume that Clients A and B both issue GNS requests, as shown in Figure 7-4. The Cisco router sends a GNS response to Client A, telling it to communicate with Server 1, and a GNS response to Client B, telling it to communicate with Server 2.

FIGURE 7-4
A GNS request
is a broadcast
from a client
needing a
server.

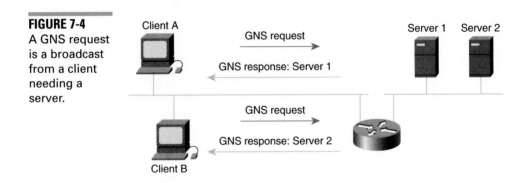

By supporting serverless LAN segments and distributing clients evenly among available servers, Cisco IOS software provides network-based load sharing, improves application availability, and minimizes the need to configure and manage large numbers of local servers, assuming that the servers are identical.

Novell IPX Configuration Tasks

Configuring the router for IPX routing involves both global and interface tasks.

Global IPX configuration tasks include the following:

- Start the IPX routing process.
- Enable load sharing if appropriate for your network.

Interface IPX configuration tasks include the following:

- Assign unique network numbers to each interface. Multiple network numbers can be assigned to an interface, allowing support of different encapsulation types.
- Set the optional IPX encapsulation type if it is different from the default.

These IPX configuration tasks are described in more detail in the following sections.

Novell IPX Global Configuration

As you learned earlier, the `ipx routing` command enables Novell IPX routing. If no node address is specified, the Cisco router uses the MAC address of the interface. If a Cisco router has only serial interfaces, an address must be specified. In addition, the `ipx maximum-paths` command enables load sharing. As previously stated, this is the maximum number of parallel paths to the destination; the default is 1 and the maximum is 512.

Assigning IPX Network Numbers to Interfaces

When assigning IPX network numbers to interfaces that support multiple IPX networks, you can also configure primary and secondary IPX networks.

The first logical network you configure on an interface is considered the *primary network*. Any additional networks are considered *secondary networks*. Again, each IPX network on an interface must use a distinct encapsulation, and it should match that of the clients and servers using the same network number. Assigning the second network number is necessary if an additional encapsulation type is linked to an individual network.

To assign network numbers to interfaces that support multiple IPX networks, you normally use subinterfaces. A subinterface is a mechanism that allows a single physical interface to support multiple logical interfaces or networks. That is, several logical interfaces or networks can be associated with a single hardware interface. Each subinterface must use a distinct encapsulation, and the encapsulation must match that of the clients and servers using the same network number.

Washington Project: Configuring Subinterfaces
If a router's interface needs to exist on two different IPX networks to accommodate two different frame types or two different IP subnets, and if you run out of host space, then you need to configure subinterfaces.

Engineering Journal: Subinterfaces

Subinterfaces are useful for IP and other protocols as well. It is possible that one physical interface on the router can belong to two different subnets. In addition, on an IPX network, it is imperative that all nodes speak the same frame type. So, when you have a mix of nodes speaking different frame types, subinterfaces are needed in IP. E0 can be on multiple subnets, and in IPX so E0 can speak multiple frame types. Therefore, you need to remember that, in order to speak *x* number of frame types, you must be on *x* number of logical networks.

The example shown in Figure 7-5 illustrates both the global configuration of Novell IPX and the assignment of network numbers to interfaces. The following describes the commands used in the example:

Command	Description
ipx routing	Selects IPX for routing, and starts IPX RIP.
ipx maximum-paths 2	Allows load sharing over parallel metric paths to the destination. The number of parallel paths used is limited to two.
interface ethernet 0.1	Indicates the first subinterface on interface E0.
encapsulation novell-ether	Specifies that Novell's unique frame format is used on this network segment. Cisco's keyword is **novell-ether**; Novell's terminology is **Ethernet_802.3.**
ipx network 9e	The network number assigned to subinterface E0.1.
interface ethernet 0.2	Indicates the second subinterface on interface E0.
ipx network 6c	The network number assigned to subinterface E0.2.
encapsulation sap	Specifies that Ethernet 802.2 frame format is used on this network segment. Cisco's keyword is **sap.**

FIGURE 7-5
A Novell IPX configuration example of assigning network numbers to interfaces.

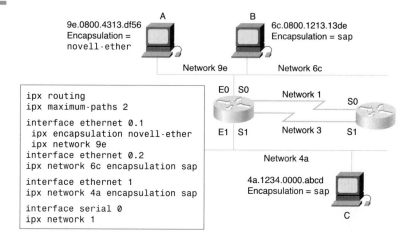

```
ipx routing
ipx maximum-paths 2

interface ethernet 0.1
 ipx encapsulation novell-ether
 ipx network 9e
interface ethernet 0.2
ipx network 6c encapsulation sap

interface ethernet 1
ipx network 4a encapsulation sap

interface serial 0
ipx network 1
```

Verifying IPX Operation

When IPX routing is configured, you can monitor and troubleshoot IPX by using the commands listed in Table 7-2.

TABLE 7-2   IPX Monitoring and Troubleshooting Commands

Command	Displays
Monitoring Commands	
show ipx interface	IPX status and parameters.
show ipx route	Routing table contents.
show ipx servers	IPX server list.
show ipx traffic	Number and type of packets
Troubleshooting Commands	
debug ipx routing activity	Information about RIP update packets.
debug ipx sap	Information about SAP update packets.
ping	Information about a particular node that is capable of responding to network requests.

Monitoring and Managing an IPX Network

Cisco IOS software includes a variety of tools for configuring, monitoring, and managing the network. These tools make NetWare networks easier to set up and can be essential when unforeseen network conditions are encountered.

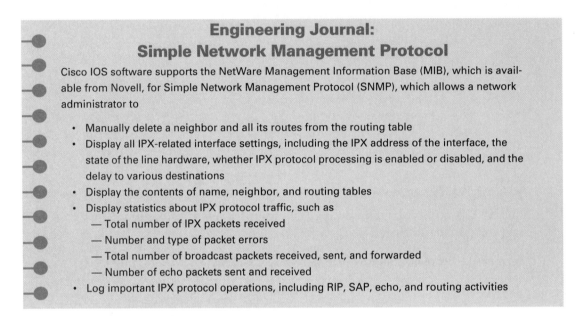

Engineering Journal:
Simple Network Management Protocol

Cisco IOS software supports the NetWare Management Information Base (MIB), which is available from Novell, for Simple Network Management Protocol (SNMP), which allows a network administrator to

- Manually delete a neighbor and all its routes from the routing table
- Display all IPX-related interface settings, including the IPX address of the interface, the state of the line hardware, whether IPX protocol processing is enabled or disabled, and the delay to various destinations
- Display the contents of name, neighbor, and routing tables
- Display statistics about IPX protocol traffic, such as
  — Total number of IPX packets received
  — Number and type of packet errors
  — Total number of broadcast packets received, sent, and forwarded
  — Number of echo packets sent and received
- Log important IPX protocol operations, including RIP, SAP, echo, and routing activities

Monitoring the Status of an IPX Interface

The `show ipx interface` command shows the status of IPX interface and IPX parameters configured on each interface.

In Example 7-1, the first highlighted line shows the IPX address, the type of encapsulation, and the status of the interface. The second highlighted area shows that the SAP filters are not set. The last highlighted line shows that fast switching is enabled.

Example 7-1   `show ipx interface` **Command Sample Output**

```
Router# show ipx interface ethernet 0
Ethernet0 is up, line protocol is up
  IPX address is 3010.aa00.0400.0284 NOVELL_ETHER [up] line-up RIPPQ: 0, SAPPQ: 0
  Delay of this Novel network, in ticks, is 1
  IPXWAN processing not enabled on this interface
  IPX SAP update interval is 1 minute(s)
  IPX type 20 propagation packet forwarding is disabled
  Outgoing access list is not set
  IPX Helper access list is not set
  SAP Input filter list is not set
  SAP Output filter list is not set
```

```
SAP Router filter list is not set
SAP GNS output filter list is not set
Input filter list is not set
Output filter list is not set
Router filter list is not set
Netbios Input host access list is not set
Netbios Input bytes access list is not set
Netbios Output host access list is not set
Netbios Output bytes access list is not set
Update time is 60 seconds
IPX accounting is disabled
IPX fast switching is configured (enabled)
IPX SSE switching is disabled
RIP packets received 1, RIP packets sent 10006
SAP packets received 1, SAP packets sent 6
```

You can manually set the tick metric to configure the tick delay on an interface. You use the command `ipx delay` *number,* where *number* is the ticks to associate with an interface. This command manually overrides the following defaults on the Cisco router:

- For LAN interfaces, 1 tick
- For WAN interfaces, 6 ticks

Monitoring IPX Routing Tables

The `show ipx route` command displays the contents of the IPX routing table.

In Example 7-2, the first highlighted line provides routing information for a remote network:

- The information was learned from a RIP update.
- The network is number 3030.
- The network is located six ticks or one hop away. This information is used to determine best routes. If there is a tie between ticks, hops are used to break the tie.
- The next hop in the path is router 3021.0000.0c03.13d3.
- The information was updated 23 seconds ago.
- The next-hop router is reachable out interface Serial1.
- There is an equal-metric route to a different next-hop router, reachable through interface Serial 0 (for load sharing).

The second line of highlighting provides information about a direct connection:

- The network number is 3010.
- The encapsulation type is NOVELL-ETHER.

Example 7-2   show ipx route Command Sample Output

```
Router# show ipx route
Codes: C - Connected primary network, c - Connected secondary network,
  R - RIP, E - EIGRP, S - Static, W - IPXWAN connected
5 total IPX routes

Up to 2 parallel paths allowed. Novell routing protocol variant in use

R Net 3030 [6/1] via 3021.0000.0c03.13d3, 23 sec, Serial1
    via 3020.0000.0c03.13d3, 23 sec, Serial0
C Net 3020 (X25), Serial0
C Net 3021 (HDLC), Serial1
C Net 3010 (NOVELL-ETHER), Ethernet0
C Net 3000 (NOVELL-ETHER), Ethernet1
```

The following describes the fields shown in Example 7-2:

Field	Description
Codes	Codes defining how the route was learned: c—Directly connected primary network. c—Directly connected secondary network. R—Route learned from a RIP update. E—Route learned from an Enhanced IGRP update. S—Statically defined route, defined via the **ipx route** command. W—Directly connected route, determined via IPXWAN.
5 Total IPX routes	The number of routes in the IPX routing table.
Parallel paths allowed	The maximum number of parallel paths for which the router has been configured with the **ipx maximum-paths** command.
Novell routing protocol variant in use	Indicates whether the router is using the IPX-compliant routing protocols (default).
Net 1	The network to which the route goes.
[6/1]	*Delay/Metric. Delay* is the number of IBM clock ticks reported to the destination network. *Metric* is the number of hops reported to the same network. *Delay* is used as the primary routing metric, and *Metric* (hop count) is used as a tie breaker.
via network.node	The address of a router that is the next hop to the remote network.
Age	The amount of time, in hours, minutes, and seconds, that has elapsed since information about this network was last received.

Field	Description
Uses	The number of times this network has been looked up in the routing table. This field is incremented when a packet is process-switched, even if the packet is eventually filtered and not sent. Therefore, this field represents a fair estimate of the number of times a route gets used.
Ethernet0	The interface through which packets to the remote network will be sent.
(NOVELL-ETHER) (HDLC) (SAP)(SNAP)	The encapsulation (frame) type. This is shown only for directly connected

Monitoring the Novell IPX Servers

The `show ipx servers` command lists the IPX servers discovered through SAP advertisements. The output of the `show ipx servers` command shows the following information:

- The service learned about the server from a SAP update
- The server name, network location, device address, and source socket number
- The ticks and hops for the route (taken from the routing table)
- The number of hops (taken from the SAP protocol)
- The interface through which to reach the server

To list the IPX servers discovered through SAP advertisements, use the `show ipx servers` in user EXEC mode. The full syntax of this command is:

```
show ipx servers [sorted [name | net | type]]
```

The following describes the keywords used in the command:

Keyword	Description
sorted	(Optional) Sorts the display of IPX servers according to the keyword that follows.
name	(Optional) Displays the IPX servers alphabetically by server name.
net	(Optional) Displays the IPX servers numerically by network number.
type	(Optional) Displays the IPX servers numerically by SAP service type. This is the default.

Example 7-3 is sample output from the show ipx servers command.

Example 7-3   **show ipx servers Command Sample Output**

```
Router> show ipx servers
Codes: P - Periodic, I - Incremental, H - Holddown, S - Static
1 Total IPX Servers
Table ordering is based on routing and server info
Type  Name                     Net Address     Port    Route Hops Itf
P     4 MAXINE         AD33000.0000.1b04.0288:0451 332800/ 1   2  Et3
```

The following describes the fields shown in Example 7-3:

Field	Description
Codes	Codes defining how the server was learned: • P—The server information was learned via the normal periodic SAP updates. • I—The server information was learned by using the incremental SAP capability in IPX Enhanced IGRP. • H—The server is believed to have gone down, and the router will no longer advertise this server's services. • S—The server is defined statically, via the **ipx sap** command.
Total IPX Servers and server info	The number of servers in the list.
Table order is based on routing and server info	Entries listed are based on the routing information associated with this SAP. Server information is used as a tie breaker.
Type	The SAP service number.
Name	The server name.
Net	The network number of the server.
Address	The node address of the server.
Port	The socket number.
Route	The metric/hop count for the route to the network.
Hops	The SAP-advertised number of hops from the router to the server's network.
Itf	The interface through which this server was first discovered.

Monitoring IPX Traffic

You use the `show ipx traffic` command to get information about the number and type of IPX packets received and transmitted by the router.

Notice in Example 7-4 that a large percentage of the total number of packets received and sent were RIP advertisements because this sample was taken from a lab network with essentially no user traffic on it. This output shows how much overhead traffic IPX generates.

Example 7-4   `show ipx traffic` Command Sample Output

```
Router# show ipx traffic
Rcvd:   32124925 total, 1691992 format errors, 0 checksum errors,
            67 bad hop count,
        18563 packets pitched, 452467 local destination, 0 multicast
Bcast:  452397 received, 1237193 sent
Sent:   2164776 generated, 31655567 forwarded
        0 encapsulation failed, 2053 no route
SAP:    3684 SAP requests, 10382 SAP replies
        259288 SAP advertisements received, 942564 sent
        0 SAP flash updates sent, 0 SAP poison sent
        0 SAP format errors
RIP:    0 RIP format errors
Echo:   Rcvd 0 requests, 0 replies
        Sent 0 requests, 0 replies
        4252 unknown, 0 SAPs throttled, freed NDB len 0
Watchdog:
        0 packets received, 0 replies spoofed
Queue lengths:
        IPX input: 1, SAP 0, RIP 0, GNS 0
        Total length for SAP throttling purposes: 1/(no preset limit)
IGRP:   Total received 0, sent 0
        Updates received 0, sent 0
        Queries received 0, sent 0
        Replies received 0, sent 0
        SAPs received 0, sent 0
```

The following describes the fields that might possibly be shown in Example 7-4:

Field	Description
Rcvd:	A description of the packets the router has received.
644 total	The total number of packets the router has received.
1705 format errors	The number of bad packets discarded (for example, packets using a frame type not configured on an interface).
0 checksum errors	The number of packets containing a checksum error.
0 bad hop count	The number of packets discarded because their hop count exceeded 16 (that is, the packets timed out).

Field	Description
0 packets pitched	The number of times the router has discarded packets. This can happen when a type 20 propagation or all-networks broadcast fails the `ipx type-20-input-checks` command; when a type 20 propagation packet handling detects a loop, detects an excessive hop count, or is malformed; when RIP or SAP packets are received for the wrong network; when the router receives its own broadcast; or when the router receives local packets from the wrong source network.
644 local destination	The number of packets sent to the local broadcast address or specifically to the router.
0 multicast	The number of packets received that were addressed to multiple destinations.
Bcast:	A description of the broadcast packets the router has received and sent.
589 received	The number of broadcast packets received.
324 sent	The number of broadcast packets sent. It includes broadcast packets the router is either forwarding or has generated.
Sent:	A description of the packets that the router generated and then sent, and the ones the router has received and then routed to other destinations.
380 generated	The number of packets the router transmitted that it generated itself.
0 forwarded	The number of packets the router transmitted that it forwarded from other sources.
0 encapsulation failed	The number of packets the router was unable to encapsulate.
4 no route	The number of times the router could not locate in the routing table a route to the destination.
SAP:	A description of the SAP packets the router has sent and received.
1 SAP requests	The number of SAP requests the router has received.
1 SAP replies	The number of SAP replies the router has sent in response to SAP requests.

Field	Description
61 SAP advertisements received	The number of SAP advertisements the router has received from another router.
120 sent	The number of SAP advertisements the router has generated and then sent.
0 SAP flash updates sent	The number of SAP advertisements the router has generated and then sent as a result of a change in its routing table.
0 SAP poison sent	The number of times the router has generated an update indicating that a service is no longer reachable.
0 SAP format errors	The number of SAP advertisements that were incorrectly formatted.
RIP:	A description of the RIP packets the router has sent and received.
0 RIP format errors	The number of RIP packets that were incorrectly formatted.
Echo:	A description of the `ping` replies and requests the router has sent and received.
Rcvd 55 request 0 replies	The number of `ping` requests and replies received by the router.
Sent 0 requests, 55 replies	The number of `ping` requests and replies sent by the router.
0 unknown	The number of unrecognized packets sent to the router.
0 SAPs throttled	The number of SAP packets discarded because they exceeded buffer capacity.
freed NDB length	The number of network descriptor blocks (NDBs) that have been removed from the network but still need to be removed from the router's routing table.
Watchdog:	A description of the watchdog packets the router has handled.
0 packets received	The number of watchdog packets the router has received from IPX servers on the local network.
0 replies spoofed	The number of times the router has responded to a watchdog packet on behalf of the remote client.
Queue lengths	A description of outgoing packets currently in buffers that are waiting to be processed.

Field	Description
IPX input	The number of incoming packets waiting to be processed.
SAP	The number of incoming SAP packets waiting to be processed.
RIP	The number of incoming RIP packets waiting to be processed.
GNS	The number of incoming GNS packets waiting to be processed.
Total length for SAP throttling purposes	The maximum number of incoming RIP and SAP packets allowed in the buffer. Any SAP request packets received beyond this number are discarded.
unknown counter	The number of packets the router was unable to forward, for example, because no route was available.

Troubleshooting IPX Routing

Cisco IOS software supports a `debug` command and a `ping` command, allowing network administrators to view and track almost any aspect of network traffic. Cisco's `debug` support can be essential to network administrators in monitoring, managing, and troubleshooting Novell networks.

The `debug ipx routing activity` command displays information about IPX routing update packets that are transmitted or received.

A router sends an update every 60 seconds. Each update packet can contain up to 50 entries. If there are more than 50 entries in the routing table, the update includes more than 1 packet.

In Example 7-5, the router is sending updates but not receiving them. Updates received from other routers would also appear in this listing.

Example 7-5   `debug ipx routing activity` Command Sample Output

```
Router# debug ipx routing activity
IPX routing debugging is on
Router#
IPXRIP: positing full update to 3010.ffff.ffff.ffff via Ethernet0 (broadcast)
IPXRIP: positing full update to 3000.ffff.ffff.ffff via Ethernet1 (broadcast)
IPXRIP: positing full update to 3020.ffff.ffff.ffff via Serial0 (broadcast)
IPXRIP: positing full update to 3021.ffff.ffff.ffff via Serial1 (broadcast)
IPXRIP: sending update to 3020.ffff.ffff.ffff via Serial0
IPXRIP: arc=3020.0000.0c03.14d8m dst=3020.ffff.ffff.ffff, packet sent
  network 3021, hops 1, delay 6
  network 3010, hops 1, delay 6
  network 3000, hops 1, delay 6
IPXRIP: sending update to 3021.ffff.ffff.ffff via Serial1
IPXRIP: arc=3021.0000.0c03.14d8m dst=3021.ffff.ffff.ffff, packet sent
```

```
    network 3020, hops 1, delay 6
    network 3010, hops 1, delay 6
    network 3000, hops 1, delay 6
 IPXRIP: sending update to 3010.ffff.ffff.ffff via Ethernet0
 IPXRIP: arc=3010.aa00.0400.0284, dst=3010.ffff.ffff.ffff, packet sent
    network 3030, hops 2, delay 7
    network 3020, hops 1, delay 1
    network 3021, hops 1, delay 1
    network 3000, hops 1, delay 1
 IPXRIP: sending update to 3000.ffff.ffff.ffff via Ethernet1
```

Troubleshooting IPX SAP

The **debug ipx sap** command displays information about IPX SAP packets that are transmitted or received.

Like RIP updates, these SAP updates are sent every 60 seconds and may contain multiple packets. As shown in Example 7-6, each SAP packet appears as multiple lines in the output, including a packet summary message and a service detail message.

Example 7-6   **debug ipx sap** **Command Sample Output**

```
Router# debug ipx sap
IPX SAP debugging is on
Router#
NovellSAP: at 0023F778
I SAP Response type 0x2 len 160 arc:160.0000.0c00.070d
dest:160.ffff.ffff.ffff(452)
type 0x4, "HELLO2", 199.0002.0004.0006(451), 2 hops
type 0x4, "HELLO1", 199.0002.0004.0008(451), 2 hops
Novell SAP: sending update to 160
NovellSAP: at 169080
O SAP Update type 0x2 len 96 ssoc; 0x452 dest: 160.ffff.ffff.ffff(452)
Novell: type 0x4 "Magnolia", 42.0000.0000.0000(451), 2 hops
```

SAP responses may be one of the following:

- 0x1—General query
- 0x2—General response
- 0x3—GNS request
- 0x4—GNS response

In each line of the SAP response of the sample output, the address and distance of the responding or target router is listed.

The IPX ping Command

Cisco IOS software provides an IPX version of the **ping** command to aid in network troubleshooting. The **ping** command enables network administrators to verify that a particular node is capable of responding to network requests. This feature helps determine whether a physical path exists through a station that is causing network problems. IPX `ping` is a Novell standard and can be used with Novell clients and servers and network devices.

The Privileged IPX `ping` Command. To check host reachability and network connectivity, use the `ping` in privileged EXEC command mode. The full syntax of the command is

    ping [ipx] [network.node]

The following is a description of the parameters used in this command:

Parameter	Description
ipx	(Optional) Specifies the IPX protocol.
network.node	(Optional) The address of the system to `ping`.

The privileged `ping` command provides a complete `ping` facility for users who have system privileges.

The privileged `ping` command works only on Cisco routers running IOS Release 8.2 or later. Novell IPX devices do not respond to this command.

You cannot `ping` a router from itself. To abort a `ping` session, type the escape sequence. By default, this is Ctrl-^-6 -X. You enter this by simultaneously pressing the Ctrl, Shift, and 6 keys, letting go, and then pressing the X key.

Table 7-3 describes the test characters displayed in `ping` responses.

TABLE 7-3   ping Response Test Characters

ping Test Character	Meaning
!	Each exclamation point indicates the receipt of a reply from the target address.
.	Each period indicates that the network server timed out while waiting for a reply from the target address.
U	A destination unreachable error protocol data unit (PDU) was received.
C	A congestion experienced packet was received.
I	A user interrupted the test.
?	An unknown packet type.
&	Packet lifetime exceeded.

The sample display in Example 7-7 shows input to and output from the privileged `ping` command.

Example 7-7   Privileged `ping` Command Output

```
Router# ping
Protocol [ip]: ipx
Target Novell Address: 211.0000.0c01.f4cf
Repeat Count [5]:
Datagram Size [100]:
Timeout in seconds [2]:
Verbose [n]:
Type escape sequence to abort.
Sending 5 100-byte Novell echoes to 211.0000.0c01.f4cf, timeout is 2
seconds.
!!!!!
Success rate is 100%, round trip min/avg/max  = 1/2/4 ms.
```

The User IPX `ping` Command. To check host reachability and network connectivity, use the user-level `ping` command in EXEC command mode. As opposed to the privileged `ping` command, the user-level `ping` command provides a basic `ping` facility for users who do not have system privileges. This command is equivalent to a simplified form of the privileged `ping` command. It sends five 100-byte `ping` packets.

The full syntax of the command is

> `ping [ipx] {host | address}`

The following is a description of the parameters used in the syntax:

Parameter	Description
`ipx`	(Optional) Specifies the IPX protocol.
`host`	The host name of the system to `ping`.
`address`	The address of the system to `ping`.

The user-level `ping` command works only on Cisco routers running IOS Release 8.2 or later. Novell IPX devices do not respond to this command.

You cannot `ping` a router from itself. If the system cannot map an address for a host name, it returns an `%Unrecognized host or address` error message.

Example 7-8 shows input to and output from the user-level `ping` command:

Example 7-8   User-Level `ping` Command Output

```
Router> ping ipx 211.0000.0c01.f4cf
Type escape sequence to abort.
Sending 5, 100-byte Novell Echoes to 211.0000.0c01.f4cf, timeout is 2 seconds:
...
Success rate is 0 percent (0/5)
```

Summary

- Novell IPX is a proprietary suite of protocols and includes the following:

  — A datagram, connectionless protocol that does not require an acknowledgment for each packet.

  — A Layer 3 protocol that defines the network and internode addresses.

- Novell NetWare uses RIP to facilitate the exchange of routing information and SAP to advertise network services. NetWare uses NCP to provide client-to-server connections and applications, and SPX for Layer 4 connection-oriented services.

- IPX is the NetWare Layer 3 protocol and specifies a connectionless datagram, similarly to an IP packet in TCP/IP networks.

- The default encapsulation types on Cisco router interfaces and their keywords are Ethernet (novell-ether), Token Ring (sap), and FDDI (snap).

- Novell RIP is a distance-vector routing protocol and uses two metrics to make routing decisions: ticks and hop count.

- NetWare's SAP allows network resources to advertise their network addresses and the services they provide.

- GNS enables a client to locate the nearest server for login.

- The router configuration for IPX routing involves both global and interface tasks.

Washington School District Project Task: Configuring Novell IPX

In this chapter, you have learned concepts and configuration processes that will help you implement IPX in the Washington School District network. As part of the IPX configuration and implementation, you need to complete the following tasks:

NOTE

These tasks should be completed in conjunction with the IPX lab activities. Consult with your instructor to assist you with these tasks.

1. Document the changes in the network design to conform with the users' IPX requirements.

2. Document the changes in the router configuration to conform with the users' requirements.

3. List the appropriate router commands needed to implement IPX in the network implementation.

Chapter Review

Complete all the review questions to test your understanding of the topics and concepts covered in this chapter. Answers are listed in Appendix A, "Chapter Review Answer Key."

1. In an IPX network, what is used for the host address?

2. What command do you use to set the maximum number of equal-cost paths the router uses when forwarding packets?

3. What command mode must the router be in before you can issue the `ipx routing` command?

4. What command do you issue to verify IPX address assignment on a router?

5. What command displays information about IPX SAP packets that are transmitted or received?

6. A Novell IPX address has 80 bits: 32 for the _____ and 48 for the _____.

   A. network number; IP address

   B. node number; MAC address

   C. network number; node number

   D. MAC address; node number

7. When you configure an IPX network, you may need to specify an encapsulation type on which of the following?

   A. Just the Novell servers

   B. Just the Cisco routers

   C. Sometimes A and B

   D. Always A and B

8. Novell NetWare uses _____ to facilitate the exchange of routing information and _____ to advertise network services.

   A. NCP; RIP

   B. RIP; SAP

   C. SPX; NCP

   D. SAP; RIP

9. The syntax for configuring Novell IPX globally is which of the following?

   A. `ipx routing [node]`

   B. `router ipx`

   C. `ipx route [node]`

   D. `router rip`

10. Fill in the commands: _____ displays IPX status and parameters; _____ displays the contents of the IPX routing table; and _____ lists servers discovered through SAP advertisements.

   A. `show ipx traffic; show ipx route; show ipx routing activity`

   B. `show ipx interface; show ipx route; show ipx servers`

   C. `show ipx interface; show ipx; show ipx servers`

   D. `show ipx; show ipx route; show ipx`

Key Terms

Cisco IOS (Internetwork Operating System) software   Cisco system software that provides common functionality, scalability, and security for all products under the CiscoFusion architecture. The Cisco IOS software allows centralized, integrated, and automated installation and management of internetworks, while ensuring support for a wide variety of protocols, media, services, and platforms.

client   A node or software program (front-end device) that requests services from a server.

client/server   The architecture of the relationship between a workstation and a server in a network.

Enhanced IGRP (Enhanced Interior Gateway Routing Protocol)   An advanced version of IGRP developed by Cisco. Provides superior convergence properties and operating efficiency, and combines the advantages of link-state protocols with those of distance-vector protocols.

encapsulate   To wrap data in a particular protocol header. For example, Ethernet data is wrapped in a specific Ethernet header before network transit. Also, when bridging dissimilar networks, the entire frame from one network is simply placed in the header used by the data link–layer protocol of the other network.

frame   A logical grouping of information sent as a data link–layer unit over a transmission medium. Often refers to the header and trailer, used for synchronization and error control, that surround the user data contained in the unit.

GNS (Get Nearest Server)   A request packet sent by a client on an IPX network to locate the nearest active server of a particular type. An IPX network client issues a GNS request to solicit either a direct response from a connected server or a response from a router that tells it where on the internetwork the service can be located. GNS is part of IPX SAP.

hexadecimal (base 16)   A number representation using the digits 0 through 9, with their usual meaning, plus the letters A through F, to represent hexadecimal digits with values 10 to 15. The rightmost digit counts ones, the next counts multiples of 16, the next is $16^2=256$, and so on.

IPX (Internetwork Packet Exchange)   A NetWare network-layer (Layer 3) protocol used for transferring data from servers to workstations. IPX is similar to IP and XNS.

load sharing   The use of two or more paths to route packets to the same destination evenly among multiple routers to balance the work and improve network performance.

MAC (Media Access Control) address   A standardized data link–layer address that is required for every port or device that connects to a LAN. Other devices in the network use these addresses to locate specific ports in the network and to create and update routing tables and data structures. MAC addresses are each 6 bytes long, and they are controlled by the IEEE. Also known as a hardware address, a MAC-layer address, or a physical address.

NetWare   A popular distributed NOS developed by Novell. Provides transparent remote file access and numerous other distributed network services.

NLSP (NetWare Link Services Protocol)   A link-state routing protocol based on IS-IS. The Cisco implementation of NLSP also includes MIB variables and tools to redistribute routing and SAP information between NLSP and other IPX routing protocols.

NOS (network operating system)   The operating system used to run a network such Novell NetWare and Windows NT.

routing metric   A method by which a routing protocol determines that one route is better than another. This information is stored in routing tables. Metrics include bandwidth, communication cost, delay, hop count, load, MTU, path cost, and reliability. Sometimes referred to simply as a metric.

SAP (Service Advertising Protocol)   An IPX protocol that provides a means of informing network clients, via routers and servers, of available network resources and services.

server   A node or software program that provides services to clients.

service access point   A field defined by the IEEE 802.2 specification that is part of an address specification.

SPX (Sequenced Packet Exchange)   A reliable, connection-oriented protocol that supplements the datagram service provided by network-layer protocols. Novell derived this commonly used NetWare transport protocol from the SPP of the XNS protocol suite.

subinterface   One of a number of virtual interfaces on a single physical interface.

Objectives

After reading this chapter, you will be able to

- Describe the purpose and function of WANs
- Describe the various WAN devices
- Describe WAN operation
- Understand WAN encapsulation formats
- Understand WAN link options

Chapter 8

WANs

Introduction

This chapter introduces the various protocols and technologies used in wide-area network (WAN) environments. You will learn about the basics of WANs, including common WAN technologies, types of wide-area services, encapsulation formats, and link options. In this chapter, you also will learn about point-to-point links, circuit switching, packet switching, virtual circuits, dialup services, and WAN devices.

Washington Project: WAN Implementation
The Washington School District WAN should connect all school and administrative offices with the district office for the purpose of delivering data. The information presented in this chapter will help you understand and design a district WAN that connects all the schools and administrative offices. In addition, you will be able to apply related concepts to the WAN design as you work through the chapter.

WAN Technology Overview

A WAN is a data communications network that operates beyond a LAN's geographic scope. One way that a WAN is different from a LAN is that, with a WAN, you must subscribe to an outside WAN service provider, such as a regional Bell operating company (RBOC) to use WAN carrier network services. A WAN uses data links, such as Integrated Services Digital Network (ISDN)and Frame Relay, that are provided by carrier services to access bandwidth over wide-area geographies. A WAN connects the locations of an organization to each other, to locations of other organizations, to external services (such as databases), and to remote users. WANs generally carry a variety of traffic types, such as voice, data, and video.

WAN technologies function at the three lowest layers of the OSI reference model: the physical layer, the data link layer, and the network layer. Figure 8-1 illustrates the relationship between the common WAN technologies and the OSI reference model.

WAN Services

Telephone and data services are the most commonly used WAN services. Telephone and data services are connected from the building point of presence (POP) to the WAN provider's central office (CO). The CO is the local telephone company office to which all local loops in a given area connect and in which circuit switching of subscriber lines occurs.

FIGURE 8-1
WAN technologies operate at the three lowest levels of the OSI reference model.

An overview of the WAN cloud (shown in Figure 8-2) organizes WAN provider services into three main types:

- Call setup—Call setup sets up and clears calls between telephone users. Also called signaling, call setup uses a separate telephone channel not used for other traffic. The most commonly used call setup is Signaling System 7 (SS7), which uses telephone control messages and signals between the transfer points along the way to the called destination.

- Time-division multiplexing (TDM)—Information from many sources has bandwidth allocation on a single medium. Circuit switching uses signaling to determine the call route, which is a dedicated path between the sender and the receiver. By multiplexing traffic into fixed time slots, TDM avoids congested facilities and variable delays. Basic telephone service and ISDN use TDM circuits.

- Frame Relay—Information contained in frames shares bandwidth with other WAN Frame Relay subscribers. Frame Relay is statistical multiplexed service, unlike TDM, which uses Layer 2 identifiers and permanent virtual circuits. In addition, Frame Relay packet switching uses Layer 3 routing with sender and receiver addressing contained in the packet.

FIGURE 8-2
There are three types of WAN service providers.

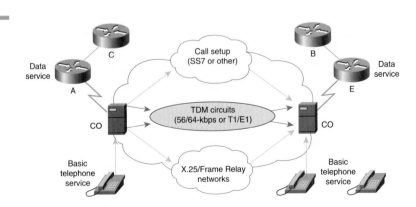

WAN Service Providers

Advances in technology over the past decade have made a number of additional WAN solutions available to network designers. When you're selecting an appropriate WAN solution, you should discuss the costs and benefits of each with your service providers.

When your organization subscribes to an outside WAN service provider for network resources, the provider gives connection requirements to the subscriber, such as the type of equipment to be used to receive services. As shown Figure 8-3, the following are the most commonly used terms associated with the main parts of WAN services:

■ Customer premises equipment (CPE)—Devices physically located on the subscriber's premises. Includes both devices owned by the subscriber and devices leased to the subscriber by the service provider.

■ Demarcation (or demarc)—The point at which the CPE ends and the local loop portion of the service begins. Often occurs at the POP of a building.

■ Local loop (or "last-mile")—Cabling (usually copper wiring) that extends from the demarc into the WAN service provider's central office.

■ CO switch—A switching facility that provides the nearest point of presence for the provider's WAN service.

■ Toll network—The collective switches and facilities (called trunks) inside the WAN provider's cloud. The caller's traffic may cross a trunk to a primary center, then to a sectional center, and then to a regional- or international-carrier center as the call travels the long distance to its destination.

FIGURE 8-3
An organization makes connections to destinations as point-to-point calls.

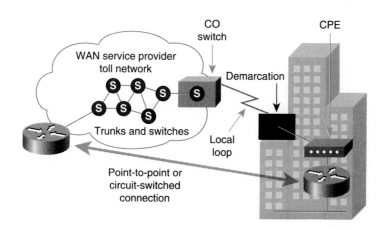

A key interface in the customer site occurs between the data terminal equipment (DTE) and the data circuit-terminating equipment (DCE). Typically, the DTE is the router, and the DCE is the device used to convert the user data from the DTE into a form acceptable to the WAN service's facility. As shown in Figure 8-4, the DCE is the attached modem, channel service unit/data service unit (CSU/DSU), or terminal adapter/network termination 1 (TA/NT1).

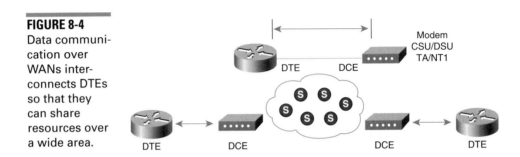

FIGURE 8-4
Data communication over WANs interconnects DTEs so that they can share resources over a wide area.

The WAN path between the DTEs is called the link, circuit, channel, or line. The DCE primarily provides an interface for the DTE into the communication link in the WAN cloud. The DTE/DCE interface acts as a boundary where responsibility for the traffic passes between the WAN subscriber and the WAN provider.

The DTE/DCE interface uses various protocols (such as HSSI and v.35) that establish the codes that the devices use to communicate with each other. This communication determines how call setup operates and how user traffic crosses the WAN.

WAN Virtual Circuits

A virtual circuit is a logical circuit, as opposed to a point-to-point circuit, created to ensure reliable communication between two network devices. Two types of virtual circuits exist: switched virtual circuits (SVCs) and permanent virtual circuits (PVCs).

SVCs are virtual circuits that are dynamically established on demand and terminated when transmission is complete. Communication over an SVC consists of three phases: circuit establishment, data transfer, and circuit termination. The establishment phase involves creating the virtual circuit between the source and destination devices. Data transfer involves transmitting data between the devices over the virtual circuit, and the circuit-termination phase involves tearing down the virtual circuit between the source and destination devices. SVCs are used in situations where data transmission between devices is sporadic. SVCs increase bandwidth used due to the circuit establishment and termination phases, but decrease the cost associated with constant virtual-circuit availability.

A PVC is a permanently established virtual circuit that consists of one mode: data transfer. PVCs are used in situations where data transfer between devices is constant. PVCs decrease the bandwidth use associated with the establishment and termination of virtual circuits, but increase costs due to constant virtual-circuit availability.

Washington Project: WAN Technology Design
The WAN technology required for the Washington District network is a Frame Relay PVC. You should add the Frame Relay PVC to the Washington network design. In addition, you should implement a Frame Relay link to the Internet.

WAN Signaling Standards and Capacity

WAN links can be ordered from the WAN provider at various speeds that are stated in bits per second (bps) capacity. This bps capacity determines how fast data can be moved across the WAN link. WAN bandwidth is often provisioned in the United States by using the North American Digital Hierarchy, shown in Table 8-1.

TABLE 8-1 WAN Link Types and Bandwidth

Line Type	Signal Standard	Bit Rate Capacity
56	DSO	56 kbps
64	DSO	64 kbps
T1	DS1	1.544 Mbps
E1	ZM	2.048 Mbps
E3	M3	34.064 Mbps
J1	Y1	2.048 Mbps
T3	DS3	44.736 Mbps
OC-1	SONET	51.84 Mbps
OC-3	SONET	155.54 Mbps
OC-9	SONET	466.56 Mbps
OC-12	SONET	622.08 Mbps
OC-18	SONET	933.12 Mbps

continues

TABLE 8-1   WAN Link Types and Bandwidth (Continued)

Line Type	Signal Standard	Bit Rate Capacity
OC-24	SONET	1244.16 Mbps
OC-36	SONET	1866.24 Mbps
OC-48	SONET	2488.32 Mbps

WAN Devices

WANs use numerous types of devices, including the following:

- Routers, which offer many services, including networking and WAN interface ports.
- WAN switches, which connect to WAN bandwidth for voice, data, and video communication.
- Modems, which interface voice-grade services. Modems include CSUs/DSUs and TA/NT1 devices that interface ISDN services.
- Communication servers, which concentrate dial-in and dial-out user communication.

Figure 8-5 shows the icons used for these WAN devices.

FIGURE 8-5
The main WAN devices are routers, WAN switches, modems, and communication servers.

Router   WAN switch   Modem CSU/DSU TA/NT1   Communication server

Routers

Routers are devices that implement the network service. They provide interfaces for a wide range of links and subnetworks at a wide range of speeds. Routers are active and intelligent network nodes and thus can participate in managing the network. Routers manage networks by providing dynamic control over resources and supporting the tasks and goals for networks. These are connectivity, reliable performance, management control, and flexibility.

WAN Switches

A WAN switch is a multiport networking device, which typically switches such traffic as Frame Relay, X.25, and Switched Multimegabit Data Service (SMDS). WAN switches operate at the data link layer of the OSI reference model. Figure 8-6 illustrates two routers at remote ends of a WAN that are connected by WAN switches. In this example, the switches filter, forward, and flood frames based on the destination address of each frame.

Washington Project: Deployment of Switches
As part of the Washington School District network design and implementation, you need to determine what type of switches to obtain, how many of them to obtain, and where to place them in the network. Possible locations include the MDFs and IDFs in the school locations and at the main district office. Additionally, you need to determine what types of switches are needed, such as LAN or WAN switches, and whether they need to be Layer 2 or Layer 3 switches. Finally, you need to determine the segmentation and security required to establish the types, number, and placement of switches in the network.

FIGURE 8-6
WAN switches can connect two routers at remote ends of a WAN.

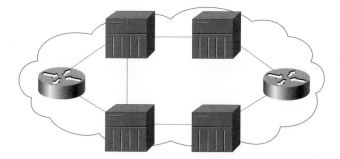

Modems

A modem is a device that interprets digital and analog signals by modulating and demodulating the signal, enabling data to be transmitted over voice-grade telephone lines. At the source, digital signals are converted to a form suitable for transmission over analog communication facilities. At the destination, these analog signals are returned to their digital form. Figure 8-7 illustrates a simple modem-to-modem connection through a WAN.

CSUs/DSUs

A CSU/DSU is a digital-interface device—or sometimes two separate digital devices—that adapts the physical interface on a DTE device (such as a terminal) to the interface of a DCE device (such as a switch) in a switched-carrier network. Figure 8-8 illustrates the placement of the CSU/DSU in a WAN implementation. Sometimes, CSUs/DSUs are integrated in the router box.

FIGURE 8-7
A WAN can handle analog and digital signals through a modem connection.

FIGURE 8-8
In a WAN, the CSU/DSU is placed between the switch and the terminal.

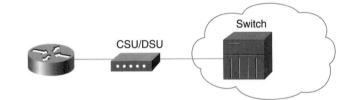

Washington Project: Deployment of CSUs/DSUs
As part of the Washington School District network design and implementation, you need to determine what kind of CSU/DSUs to obtain, how many of them to obtain, and where to place them in the network. Possible locations include the MDFs in the school locations and at the main district office, where the WAN links will be terminated. Keep in mind that CSUs/DSUs need to be located close to routers.

ISDN Terminal Adapters

An ISDN TA is a device used to connect ISDN Basic Rate Interface (BRI) connections to other interfaces. A TA is essentially an ISDN modem. Figure 8-9 illustrates the placement of a TA in an ISDN environment.

FIGURE 8-9
In a WAN, the TA connects the ISDN to other interfaces, such as the switches.

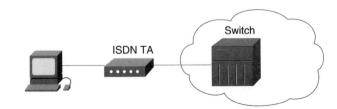

WANs and the OSI Reference Model

WANs use the OSI reference model layered approach to encapsulation, just as LANs do, but they are mainly focused on the physical and data link layers. WAN standards typically describe both physical-layer delivery methods and data link-layer requirements, including addressing, flow control and encapsulation. WAN standards are defined and managed by a number of recognized authorities, including the following agencies:

- International Telecommunication Union-Telecommunication Standardization Sector (ITU-T), formerly the Consultative Committee for International Telegraph and Telephone (CCITT)
- International Organization for Standardization (ISO)
- Internet Engineering Task Force (IETF)
- Electronic Industries Association (EIA)
- Telecommunications Industries Association (TIA)

The WAN Physical Layer

WAN physical-layer protocols describe how to provide electrical, mechanical, operational, and functional connections for WAN services. Most WANs require an interconnection that is provided by a communications service provider (such as an RBOC), an alternative carrier (such as an Internet service provider), or a post, telephone, and telegraph (PTT) agency.

The WAN physical layer also describes the interface between the DTE and the DCE. Typically, the DCE is the service provider, and the DTE is the attached device, as shown in Figure 8-10.

FIGURE 8-10

The service provider circuit typically terminates at a DTE (for example, a router), and a DCE (for example, at the customer site).

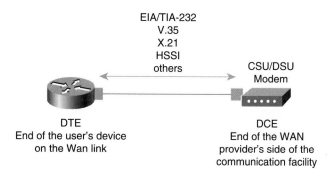

EIA/TIA-232
V.35
X.21
HSSI
others

CSU/DSU
Modem

DTE
End of the user's device
on the Wan link

DCE
End of the WAN
provider's side of the
communication facility

Several physical-layer standards define the rules governing the interface between the DTE and the DCE:

- EIA/TIA-232 —A common physical-layer interface standard, developed by EIA and TIA, that supports unbalanced circuits at signal speeds of up to 64 kbps. It closely resembles the V.24 specification, and was formerly known as RS-232. This standard has been in place for many years.

- EIA/TIA-449—A popular physical-layer interface developed by EIA and TIA. It is essentially a faster (up to 2 Mbps) version of EIA/TIA-232, capable of longer cable runs.

- EIA/TIA-612/613—A standard describing High Speed Serial Interface (HSSI), which provides access to services at T3 (45 Mbps), E3 (34 Mbps), and Synchronous Optical Network (SONET) STS-1 (51.82 Mbps) rates. The actual rate of the interface depends on the external DSU and the type of service to which it is connected.

- V.24—An ITU-T standard for a physical-layer interface between DTE and DCE.

- V.35—An ITU-T standard describing a synchronous, physical-layer protocol used for communications between a network access device and a packet network. V.35 is most commonly used in the United States and in Europe, and is recommended for speeds up to 48 kbps.

- X.21—An ITU-T standard for serial communications over synchronous digital lines. The X.21 protocol is used primarily in Europe and Japan.

- G.703—An ITU-T electrical and mechanical specification for connections between telephone company equipment and DTE using British Naval connectors (BNCs) and operating at E1 data rates.

- EIA-530—Two electrical implementations of EIA/TIA-449: RS-422 (for balanced transmission) and RS-423 (for unbalanced transmission).

The WAN Data Link Layer

The WAN data link layer defines how data is encapsulated for transmission to remote sites. WAN data-link protocols describe how frames are carried between systems on a single data path.

Figure 8-11 shows the common data-link encapsulations associated with WAN lines, which are:

- Frame Relay—By using simplified encapsulation with no error correction mechanisms over high-quality digital facilities, Frame Relay can transmit data very rapidly compared to the other WAN protocols.

- Point-to-Point Protocol (PPP)—Described by RFC 1661, PPP was developed by the IETF. PPP contains a protocol field to identify the network-layer protocol.

- ISDN—A set of digital services that transmits voice and data over existing phone lines.

- Link Access Procedure, Balanced (LAPB)—For packet-switched networks, LAPB is used to encapsulate packets at Layer 2 of the X.25 stack. It can also be used over a point-to-point link if the link is unreliable or there is an inherent delay associated with the link, such as in a satellite link. LAPB provides reliability and flow control on a point-to-point basis.

- Cisco/IETF—Used to encapsulate Frame Relay traffic. The *cisco* option is proprietary and can be used only between Cisco routers.

- High-Level Data Link Control (HDLC)—An ISO standard, HDLC might not be compatible between different vendors because of the way each vendor has chosen to implement it. HDLC supports both point-to-point and multipoint configurations.

FIGURE 8-11
The choice of encapsulation protocol depends on the WAN technology and the communicating equipment.

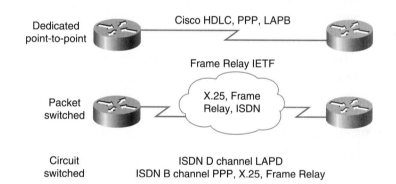

WAN Frame Encapsulation Formats

The two most common point-to-point WAN encapsulations are HDLC and PPP. All the serial line encapsulations share a common frame format, which has the following fields, as shown in Figure 8-12:

- Flag—Indicates the beginning of the frame and is set to the hexadecimal (base 16) pattern 7F.

- Address—A 1- or 2-byte field to address the end station in multidrop environments.

- Control—Indicates whether the frame is an information, a supervisory, or an unnumbered type frame. It also contains specific function codes.

- Data—The encapsulated data.

- FCS—The frame check sequence (FCS).
- Flag—The trailing 7E flag identifier.

FIGURE 8-12
Point-to-point encapsulations generally are used on dedicated WAN lines.

PPP

Flag	Address	Control	Protocol	LCP	FCS	Flag

HDLC

Flag	Address	Control	Propietary	Data	FCS	Flag

Each WAN connection type uses a Layer 2 protocol to encapsulate traffic while it is crossing the WAN link. To ensure that the correct encapsulation protocol is used, you need to configure the Layer 2 encapsulation type to use for each serial interface on a router. The choice of encapsulation protocol depends on the WAN technology and the communicating equipment. Encapsulation protocols that can be used with the WAN connection types covered in this chapter are PPP and HDLC.

PPP Encapsulation

PPP is a standard serial-line encapsulation method (described in RFC 1332 and RFC 1661). This protocol can, among other things, check for link quality during connection establishment. In addition, there is support for authentication through Password Authentication Protocol (PAP) and Challenge Handshake Authentication Protocol (CHAP). PPP is covered in depth in Chapter 10, "PPP."

Engineering Journal:
PPP Link Negotiation

PPP ensures interoperability between networking vendors by using several additional protocols, including the following:

- LCP for negotiating basic line interoperability
- A family of network control protocols for negotiating individual Layer 3 protocols and their options (such as IP Control Protocol [IPCP] for IP and options such as compression)

When the PPP link is negotiated, a link control protocol is negotiated to establish the link, and then additional network control protocols are negotiated.

You can use the command **show interfaces** to check the status of the LCP and the network control protocol and to test the interoperability of the network layers. There are also excellent **debug ppp** commands for troubleshooting.

To configure the serial line to use PPP, use the `encapsulation ppp` command, as follows:

```
Router(config)# interface serial 0
Router(config-if)# encapsulation ppp
```

HDLC Encapsulation

HDLC is a data link–layer protocol derived from the Synchronous Data Link Control (SDLC) encapsulation protocol. HDLC is Cisco's default encapsulation for serial lines. This implementation is very streamlined; there is no windowing or flow control, and only point-to-point connections are allowed. The address field is always set to all ones. Furthermore, a 2-byte proprietary type code is inserted after the control field, which means that HDLC framing is not interoperable with other vendors' equipment.

If both ends of a dedicated-line connection are routers or access servers running Cisco Internetwork Operating System (IOS) software, HDLC encapsulation typically is used. Because HDLC encapsulation methods may vary, you should use PPP with devices that are not running Cisco IOS software.

Washington Project: PPP Encapsulation
Although both PPP and HDLC are appropriate frame types for point-to-point connections, you should use PPP on point-to-point links in the Washington School District network. PPP offers the following advantages: • Interoperability between networking vendors • LCP for negotiating basic line interoperability • A family of network control protocols for negotiating individual Layer 3 protocols

WAN Link Options

In general, as shown in Figure 8-13, two types of WAN link options are available: dedicated lines and switched connections. Switched connections, in turn, can be either circuit switched or packet switched. The following sections describe these types of link options.

Dedicated Lines

Dedicated lines, also called *leased lines*, provide full-time service. Dedicated lines typically are used to carry data, voice, and occasionally video. In data network design, dedicated lines generally provide core or backbone connectivity between major sites or campuses, as well as LAN-to-LAN connectivity.

Dedicated lines generally are considered reasonable design options for WANs. With dedicated lines, you need a router port and a circuit for each remote site.

When dedicated line connections are made, a router port is required for each connection, along with a CSU/DSU and the actual circuit from the service provider. The cost of dedicated-line solutions can become significant when they are used to connect many sites.

FIGURE 8-13
There are different types of circuit-switched or packet-switched connections.

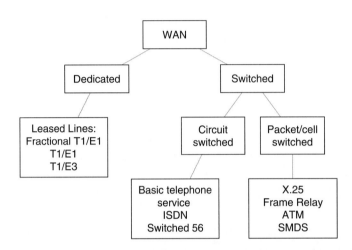

Dedicated, full-time connectivity is provided by point-to-point serial links. Connections are made using the router's synchronous serial ports with typical bandwidth use of up to 2 Mbps (E1) available through the use of a CSU/DSU. Different encapsulation methods at the data link layer provide flexibility and reliability for user traffic. Dedicated lines of this type are ideal for high-volume environments with a steady-rate traffic pattern. Use of available bandwidth is a concern because you have to pay for the line to be available even when the connection is idle.

Washington Project: Dedicated Lines
The Washington School District should use dedicated lines for its WAN core. You need to determine how many links this will involve and what kinds of equipment must be purchased (such as CSUs/DSUs).

Dedicated lines also are referred to as point-to-point links because their established path is permanent and fixed for each remote network reached through the carrier facilities. A point-to-point link provides a single, pre-established WAN communications path from the customer premises through a carrier network, such as a telephone company, to a remote network. The service provider reserves point-to-point links for the private use of the customer. Figure 8-14 illustrates a typical point-to-point link through a WAN.

FIGURE 8-14
A typical point-
to-point link
operates
through a WAN
to a router, and
to end sys-
tems on both
ends of the
link.

Packet-Switched Connections

Packet switching is a WAN switching method in which network devices share a single point-to-point link to transport packets from a source to a destination across a carrier network, as shown in Figure 8-15. Frame Relay, SMDS, and X.25 are all examples of packet-switched WAN technologies.

FIGURE 8-15
Packet switch-
ing transfers
packets across
a carrier net-
work.

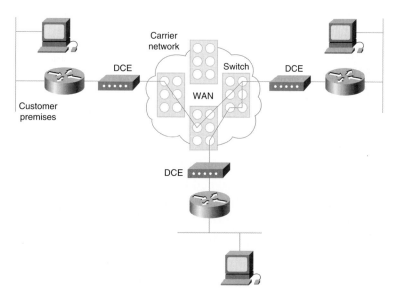

Switched networks can carry variable-size frames (packets) or fixed-size cells. The most common packet-switched network type is Frame Relay.

Frame Relay

Frame Relay was designed to provide high-speed, reliable links. As a result, Frame Relay does not offer much error checking or reliability, but expects upper-layer protocols to attend to these issues.

Frame Relay is a packet-switching data communications technology that can connect multiple network devices on a multipoint WAN, as shown in Figure 8-16. The design of Frame Relay WANs can affect certain aspects (such as split horizon) of higher-layer protocols such as IP, IPX, and Apple-Talk. Frame Relay is called a *non-broadcast multiaccess technology* because it has no broadcast channel. Broadcasts are transmitted through Frame Relay by sending packets to all network destinations.

FIGURE 8-16
Frame Relay is a packet-switched data network technology designed to be simpler and faster than older technologies (such as X.25) that connect multiple network devices.

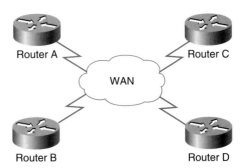

Frame Relay defines the connection between a customer DTE and a carrier DCE. The DTE is typically a router, and the DCE is a Frame Relay switch. (In this case, DTE and DCE refer to the data link layer, not the physical layer.) Frame Relay access is at 56 kbps, 64 kbps, or 1.544 Mbps.

Frame Relay is a cost-effective alternative to point-to-point WAN designs. Each site can be connected to every other by a virtual circuit. Each router needs only one physical interface to the carrier. Frame Relay is implemented mostly as a carrier-provided service but can also be used for private networks.

Frame Relay service is offered through a PVC. A PVC is an unreliable data link. A data-link connection identifier (DLCI) identifies a PVC. The DLCI number is a local identifier between the DTE and the DCE that identifies the logical circuit between the source and destination devices. The DLCI contract specifies the committed information rate (CIR) provided by the carrier, which is the rate, in bits per second, at which the Frame Relay switch agrees to transfer data. (These topics are covered in depth in Chapter 12, "Frame Relay.")

As you'll learn further in Chapter 12, "Frame Relay," two common topologies can be used in a Frame Relay solution:

- Fully meshed topology—Every Frame Relay network device has a PVC to every other device on the multipoint WAN. Any update sent by one device is seen by every other. If this design is used, the entire Frame Relay WAN can be treated as one data link.

- Partially meshed topology—This is also often called a star topology or hub-and-spokes topology. In a partially meshed topology, not every device on the Frame Relay cloud has a PVC to every other device.

Circuit-Switched Connections

Circuit switching is a WAN switching method in which a dedicated physical circuit is established, maintained, and terminated through a carrier network for each communication session. Used extensively in telephone company networks, circuit switching operates much like a normal telephone call. ISDN is an example of a circuit-switched WAN technology.

Circuit-switched connections from one site to another are brought up when needed and generally require low bandwidth. Basic telephone service connections are generally limited to 28.8 kbps without compression, and ISDN connections are limited to 64 or 128 kbps. Circuit-switched connections are used primarily to connect remote users and mobile users to corporate LANs. They are also used as backup lines for higher-speed circuits, such as Frame Relay and dedicated lines.

DDR

Dial-on-demand routing (DDR) is a technique in which a router can dynamically initiate and close circuit-switched sessions when transmitting end stations need them. When the router receives traffic destined for a remote network, a circuit is established, and the traffic is transmitted normally. The router maintains an idle timer that is reset only when interesting traffic is received. (*Interesting traffic* refers to traffic the router needs to route.) If the router receives no interesting traffic before the idle timer expires, however, the circuit is terminated. Likewise, if uninteresting traffic is received and no circuit exists, the router drops the traffic. When the router receives interesting traffic, it initiates a new circuit.

DDR enables you to make a standard telephone connection or an ISDN connection only when required by the volume of network traffic. DDR may be less expensive than a dedicated-line or multipoint solutions. DDR means that the connection is brought up only when a specific type of traffic initiates the call or when you need a backup link. These circuit-switched calls, indicated by the broken lines in Figure 8-17, are placed using ISDN networks. DDR is a substitute for dedicated lines when full-time circuit availability is not required. In addition, DDR can be used to replace point-to-point links and switched multi-access WAN services.

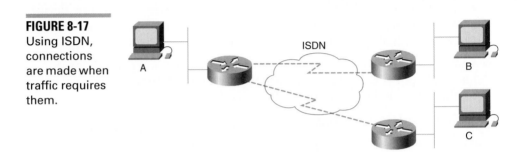

FIGURE 8-17
Using ISDN, connections are made when traffic requires them.

DDR can be used to provide backup load sharing and interface backup. For example, you might have several serial lines, but you want the second serial line to be used only when the first line is very busy so that load sharing can occur. When your WAN lines are used for critical applications, you might want a DDR line configured in case the primary lines go down. In this case, the secondary line enables itself so traffic can still get across.

Compared to LAN or campus-based networking, the traffic that uses DDR is typically low volume and periodic. DDR initiates a WAN call to a remote site only when there is traffic to transmit.

When you configure for DDR, you must enter configuration commands that indicate what protocol packets make-up interesting traffic to initiate the call. To do this, you enter access control list statements to identify the source and destination addresses, and you choose specific protocol selection criteria for initiating the call. Then you must establish the interfaces where the DDR call initiates. This step designates a dialer group. The dialer group associates the results of the access control list specification of interesting packets to the router's interfaces for dialing a WAN call.

ISDN

Telephone companies developed ISDN with the intention of creating a totally digital network. ISDN devices include the following:

- Terminal Equipment 1 (TE1)—Designates a device that is compatible with the ISDN network. A TE1 connects to an NT of either Type 1 or Type 2.
- Terminal Equipment 2 (TE2)—Designates a device that is not compatible with ISDN and requires a TA.
- TA—Converts standard electrical signals into the form used by ISDN so that non-ISDN devices can connect to the ISDN network.

- NT Type 1 (NT1)—Connects four-wire ISDN subscriber wiring to the conventional two-wire local loop facility.

- NT Type 2 (NT2)—Directs traffic to and from different subscriber devices and the NT1. The NT2 is an intelligent device that performs switching and concentrating.

As shown in Figure 8-18, ISDN interface reference points include the following:

- The S/T interface defines the interface between a TE1 and an NT. The S/T also is used to define the TA-to-NT interface.

- The R interface defines the interface between a TE2 and the TA.

- The U interface defines the two-wire interface between the NT and the ISDN cloud.

FIGURE 8-18
ISDN is an end-to-end digital network technology used for voice, data, fax, and video.

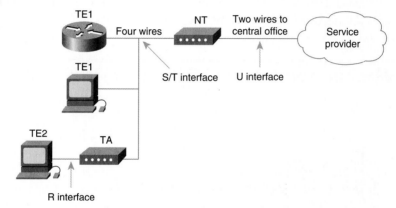

There are two ISDN services: BRI and Primary Rate Interface (PRI). ISDN BRI operates mostly over the copper twisted-pair telephone wiring in place today. ISDN BRI delivers a total bandwidth of a 144-kbps line into three separate channels. Two of the channels, called B (bearer) channels, operate at 64 kbps and are used to carry voice or data traffic. The third channel, the D (delta) channel, is a 16-kbps signaling channel used to carry instructions that tell the telephone network how to handle each of the B channels. ISDN BRI often is referred to as *2B+D*. ISDN is covered in depth in Chapter 11, "ISDN."

ISDN provides great flexibility to the network designer because of its capability to use each of the B channels for separate voice or data applications. For example, one ISDN 64-kbps B channel can download a long document from the corporate network while the other B channel browses a Web page. When you're designing a WAN, you should be careful to select equipment that has the right feature to take advantage of ISDN's flexibility.

Summary

- A WAN is used to interconnect LANs that are separated by a large geographic distance.

- A WAN provides a data path between routers and the LANs that each router supports.

- Many types of WAN services are available to the WAN subscriber, which must know how to interface to the WAN provider's service.

- WAN devices include WAN switches, modems, and ISDN TAs.

- A WAN mainly operates at the OSI physical and data link layers.

- WAN encapsulation formats include PPP and HDLC encapsulation.

- WAN link options include dedicated lines such as point-to-point links, packet-switched connections such as Frame Relay, and circuit-switched connections such as DDR and ISDN.

Washington School District Project Task: WANs

In this chapter, you have learned about the WAN technologies that enable you to interconnect all the individual Washington School District sites into the WAN topology.

You need to complete the following tasks:

1. Select WAN services for the district WAN.

2. Determine the costs and the range of WAN services.

3. Document the WAN design.

Chapter Review

Complete all the review questions to test your understanding of the topics and concepts covered in this chapter. Answers are listed in Appendix A, "Chapter Review Answer Key."

1. How many data paths are used by WAN data-link protocols to frames to carry frames between systems?

   A. Two

   B. One

   C. Four

   D. Undetermined

2. At what layer of the OSI reference model would you find the DCE or DTE equipment?

   A. The network layer

   B. The data link layer

   C. The physical layer

   D. The transport layer

3. A CSU/DSU generally is used as what type of equipment?

   A. Router

   B. DTE

   C. Switch

   D. DCE

4. Which of the following encapsulation types is associated with synchronous serial lines?

   A. PPP

   B. HDLC

   C. Frame Relay

   D. All of the above

5. What encapsulation type would you select for a link if speed were the most important factor?

   A. Frame Relay

   B. PPP

C. HDLC

D. SLIP

6. Devices that are located at a service subscriber's site are referred to as what?

    A. Customer owned equipment

    B. Subscriber devices

    C. Customer premises equipment

    D. Subscriber premises equipment

7. The WAN path between DTEs is known as what?

    A. The link

    B. The circuit

    C. The channel

    D. All of the above

8. Which WAN services can be used with a router?

    A. Frame Relay

    B. ISDN

    C. PPP

    D. All of the above

9. Which of the following is an example of a packet-switched protocol?

    A. ISDN

    B. Frame Relay

    C. PPP

    D. HDLC

10. Which protocol does PPP use for establishing and maintaining point-to-point connections?

    A. HDLC

    B. LCP

    C. LAPD

    D. Cisco IETF

Key Terms

ATM (Asynchronous Transfer Mode)   An international standard for cell relay in which multiple service types (such as voice, video, or data) are conveyed in fixed-length (53-byte) cells. Fixed-length cells allow cell processing to occur in hardware, thereby reducing transit delays. ATM is designed to take advantage of high-speed transmission media such as E3, SONET, and T3.

B channel (bearer channel)   In ISDN, a full-duplex, 64-kbps channel used to send user data.

carrier network   A service provider's network.

CIR (committed information rate)   The rate, in bits per second, at which the Frame Relay switch agrees to transfer data.

Cisco IOS (Internetwork Operating System) software   Cisco system software that provides common functionality, scalability, and security for all products under the CiscoFusion architecture. Cisco IOS software allows centralized, integrated, and automated installation and management of internetworks, while ensuring support for a wide variety of protocols, media, services, and platforms.

CO (central office)   The local telephone company office to which all local loops in a given area connect and in which circuit switching of subscriber lines occurs.

CPE (customer premises equipment)   Terminating equipment, such as terminals, telephones, and modems, supplied by the telephone company, installed at customer sites, and connected to the telephone company network.

CSU/DSU (channel service unit/digital service unit)   A digital interface device that connects end-user equipment to the local digital telephone loop.

DCE (data circuit-terminating equipment)   The device used to convert the user data from the DTE into a form acceptable to the WAN service's facility.

D channel (delta channel)   A full-duplex, 16-kbps (BRI) or 64-kbps (PRI) ISDN channel.

DDR (dial-on-demand routing)   A technique with which a router can dynamically initiate and close circuit-switched sessions as transmitting end stations need them.

demarcation   The point at which the CPE ends and the local loop portion of the service begins. Often occurs at the POP of a building.

DLCI (data-link connection identifier)   A value that specifies a PVC or an SVC in a Frame Relay network. In the basic Frame Relay specification, DLCIs are locally significant (that is, connected devices can use different values to specify the same connection). In the LMI extended specification, DLCIs are globally significant (that is, DLCIs specify individual end devices).

DTE (data terminal equipment)   A device at the user end of a user-to-network interface that serves as a data source, destination, or both. A DTE connects to a data network through a DCE device (for example, a modem) and typically uses clocking signals generated by the DCE. DTEs include such devices as computers, protocol translators, and multiplexers.

EIA (Electronic Industries Association)   A group that specifies electrical transmission standards. EIA and TIA have developed numerous well-known communications standards together, including EIA/TIA-232 and EIA/TIA-449.

Frame Relay   An industry-standard, switched data link–layer protocol that handles multiple virtual circuits using HDLC encapsulation between connected devices. Frame Relay is more efficient than X.25, the protocol for which it is generally considered a replacement.

fully meshed topology   A topology in which every Frame Relay network device has a PVC to every other device on the multipoint WAN.

hexadecimal (base 16)   A number representation using the digits 0 through 9, with their usual meaning, plus the letters A through F, to represent hexadecimal digits with values 10 to 15. The rightmost digit counts ones, the next counts multiples of 16, the next is $16^2=256$, and so on.

IETF (Internet Engineering Task Force)   A task force consisting of more than 80 working groups responsible for developing Internet standards. The IETF operates under the auspices of ISOC.

LAPB (Link Access Procedure, Balanced)   A data link–layer protocol in the X.25 protocol stack. LAPB is a bit-oriented protocol derived from HDLC.

local loop   Cabling (usually copper wiring) that extends from the demarc into the WAN service provider's central office.

modem (modulator-demodulator)   A device that converts digital and analog signals. At the source, a modem converts digital signals to a form suitable for transmission over analog communication facilities. At the destination, the analog signals are returned to their digital form. Modems allow data to be transmitted over voice-grade telephone lines.

NT1 (network termination 1)   A type of device that interfaces with ISDN services.

partially meshed topology   A topology in which not every device on the Frame Relay cloud has a PVC to every other device.

point-to-point link   A link that provides a single, pre-established WAN communications path from the customer premises through a carrier network, such as a telephone company, to a remote network. Also called a dedicated line or a leased line.

POP (point of presence)   The point of interconnection between the communication facilities provided by the telephone company and the building's main distribution facility.

PTT (post, telephone, and telegraph)   A government agency that provides telephone services. PTTs exist in most areas outside North America and provide both local and long-distance telephone services.

PVC (permanent virtual circuit)   A virtual circuit that is permanently established. PVCs save bandwidth associated with circuit establishment and teardown in situations where certain virtual circuits must exist all the time.

RBOC (regional Bell operating company)   A local or regional telephone company that owns and operates telephone lines and switches in one of seven U.S. regions. The RBOCs were created by the divestiture of AT&T.

reliability   The ratio of expected to received keepalives from a link. If the ratio is high, the line is reliable. Used as a routing metric.

SDLC (Synchronous Data Link Control)   An SNA data link–layer communications protocol. SDLC is a bit-oriented, full-duplex serial protocol that has spawned numerous similar protocols, including HDLC and LAPB.

SS7 (Signaling System 7)   A standard common channel signaling system developed by Bellcore. It uses telephone control messages and signals between the transfer points along the way to the called destination.

star topology   A LAN topology in which endpoints on a network are connected to a common central switch by point-to-point links. A ring topology that is organized as a star implements a unidirectional closed-loop star, instead of point-to-point links.

SVC (switched virtual circuit)   A virtual circuit that is dynamically established on demand and is torn down when transmission is complete. SVCs are used in situations in which data transmission is sporadic.

TA (terminal adapter)   A device used to connect ISDN BRI connections to existing interfaces such as EIA/TIA-232. Essentially, an ISDN modem.

TDM (time-division multiplexing) A circuit-switching signal used to determine the call route, which is a dedicated path between the sender and the receiver.

TIA (Telecommunications Industries Association) An organization that develops standards relating to telecommunications technologies. Together, TIA and EIA have formalized standards, such as EIA/TIA-232, for the electrical characteristics of data transmission.

toll network The collective switches and facilities (called trunks) inside the WAN provider's cloud.

virtual circuit A logical circuit created to ensure reliable communication between two network devices. A virtual circuit is defined by a VPI/VCI pair, and can be either permanent (a PVC) or switched (an SVC). Virtual circuits are used in Frame Relay and X.25. In ATM, a virtual circuit is called a virtual channel. Sometimes abbreviated VC.

WAN (wide-area network) A data communications network that serves users across a broad geographic area and often uses transmission devices provided by common carriers. Frame Relay, SMDS, and X.25 are examples of WAN technologies.

X.25 An ITU-T standard that defines how connections between DTEs and DCEs are maintained for remote terminal access and computer communications in public data networks. Frame Relay has superseded X.25 to some degree.

Objectives

After reading this chapter, you will be able to

- Describe WAN communication
- Describe the process and considerations for designing a WAN
- Describe the process for gathering user requirements for WAN design
- Describe the benefits of using a hierarchical design model, and identify and describe the three layers of the hierarchical model
- Describe the placement of ISDN and Frame Relay
- Describe how placement of enterprise servers and workgroup servers affects traffic patterns across the WAN
- Describe backbone service requirements
- Describe the benefits of switches and Layer 2 services
- Describe the benefits of routers and Layer 3 services
- Describe multiple- and single-protocol routing
- Identify and describe WAN reliability options

Chapter 9

WAN Design

Introduction

Today's network administrators must manage complex wide-area networks (WANs) in order to support the growing number of software applications that are built around Internet Protocol (IP) and the Web. These WANs require network resources and higher-performance networking technologies. WANs are complex environments involving multiple media, multiple protocols, and interconnection to other networks such as the Internet that need many protocols and features in order to permit growth and manageability.

Despite improvements in equipment performance and media capabilities, WAN design is becoming more difficult. Carefully designing WANs can reduce problems associated with growing networking environment. To design reliable, scalable WANs, network designers must keep in mind that each WAN has specific design requirements. This chapter provides an overview of the methodologies utilized to design WANs.

Washington Project: WAN Design
In this chapter, you will learn about WAN design processes that will enable you to implement WAN services requirements into the Washington School District network design. The district WAN should connect all school and administrative offices with the district office for the purpose of delivering data.

WAN Communication

WAN communication occurs between geographically separated areas. When a local end station wants to communicate with a remote end station (that is, an end station located at a different site), information must be sent over one or more WAN links. Routers within WANs are connection points of a network. These routers determine the most appropriate path through the network for the required data streams.

As you learned in Chapter 8, "WANs," WAN communication is often called a service because the network provider often charges users for the WAN services it provides. Circuit-switching and packet-switching technologies are two types of

WAN services, each of which has advantages and disadvantages. For example, circuit-switched networks offer users dedicated bandwidth that cannot be infringed upon by other users. In contrast, packet switching is a WAN switching method in which network devices share a single point-to-point link to transport packets from a source to a destination across a carrier network. Packet-switched networks have traditionally offered more flexibility and used network bandwidth more efficiently than circuit-switched networks.

Traditionally, relatively low throughput, high delay, and high error rates have characterized WAN communication. WAN connections are also characterized by the cost of renting media (that is, wire) from a service provider to connect two or more campuses together. Because the WAN infrastructure is often rented from a service provider, WAN network designs must optimize the cost of bandwidth and bandwidth efficiency. For example, all technologies and features used in WANs are developed to meet the following design requirements:

- Optimize WAN bandwidth
- Minimize cost
- Maximize the effective service to the end users

Recently, traditional shared-media networks are being overtaxed because of the following new network requirements:

- Network usage has increased as enterprises utilize client/server, multimedia, and other applications to enhance productivity.
- The rate of change in application requirements has accelerated and will continue to do so (for example, Internet "push" technologies).
- Network costs continue to increase, creating even more pressure to contain expenditures.
- Applications increasingly require distinct network qualities of service due to services they provide end users.
- An unprecedented number of connections are being established among offices of all sizes, remote users, mobile users, international sites, customers/suppliers, and the Internet.
- The explosive growth of corporate intranets and extranets has created a greater demand for bandwidth.
- The increased use of enterprise servers continues to grow to serve the business needs of organizations.

Compared to current WANs, the new WAN infrastructures must be more complex, must be based on new technologies, and must be able to handle an ever-increasing (and rapidly changing) application mix with required and guaranteed service levels. In addition, with a 300% traffic increase expected in the next five years, enterprises will feel even greater pressure to contain WAN costs.

Network designers are using WAN technologies to support these new requirements. WAN connections generally handle important information and are optimized for price and performance bandwidth. The routers connecting the campuses, for example, generally apply traffic optimization, multiple paths for redundancy, dial backup for disaster recovery, and quality of service (QoS) for critical applications. Table 9-1 summarizes the various WAN technologies that support such WAN requirements.

TABLE 9-1   Summary of WAN Technologies

WAN Technology	Typical Uses
Leased line	Leased lines can be used for Point-to-Point Protocol (PPP) networks and hub-and-spokes topologies, or for backup for another type of link.
Integrated Services Digital Network (ISDN)	ISDN can be used for cost-effective remote access to corporate networks. It provides support for voice and video as well as a backup for another type of link.
Frame Relay	Frame Relay provides a cost-effective, high-speed, low-latency mesh topology between remote sites. It can be used in both private and carrier-provided networks.

LAN/WAN Integration

Distributed applications need increasingly more bandwidth, and the explosion of Internet use is driving many LAN architectures to the limit. Voice communications have increased significantly, with more reliance being placed on centralized voice mail systems for verbal communications. The network is the critical tool for information flow. Networks are being required to cost less, yet support the emerging applications and larger number of users with increased performance.

Until now, local- and wide-area communications have remained logically separate. In the LAN, bandwidth is free and connectivity is limited only by hardware and implementation costs. In the WAN, bandwidth is the overriding cost, and delay-sensitive traffic such as voice has remained separate from data.

Internet applications such as voice and real-time video require better, more predictable LAN and WAN performance. These multimedia applications are fast becoming an essential part of the business productivity toolkit. As companies begin to consider implementing new intranet-based, bandwidth-intensive multimedia applications—such as video training, videoconferencing, and voice over IP—the impact of these applications on the existing networking infrastructure will become a serious concern.

For example, if a company has relied on its corporate network for business-critical IP traffic and wants to integrate an online video-training application, the network must be able to provide guaranteed QoS. This QoS must deliver the multimedia traffic, but does not allow it to interfere with the business-critical traffic. Consequently, network designers need greater flexibility in solving multiple internetworking problems without creating multiple networks or writing off existing data communication investments.

The First Steps in Designing a WAN

Designing a WAN can be a challenging task. The discussions that follow outline several areas that you should carefully consider when planning a WAN implementation. The steps described here can lead to improved WAN cost and performance. Businesses can continually improve their WANs by incorporating these steps into the planning process.

Two primary goals drive WAN design and implementation:

- Application availability—Networks carry application information between computers. If the applications are not available to network users, the network is not doing its job.

- Total cost of ownership—Information Systems (IS) department budgets often run in the millions of dollars. As large businesses increasingly rely on electronic data for managing business activities, the associated costs of computing resources will continue to rise. A well-designed WAN can help to balance these objectives. When properly implemented, the WAN infrastructure can optimize application availability and allow the cost-effective use of existing network resources.

In general, WAN design needs to take into account three general factors:

- Environmental variables—Environmental variables include the location of hosts, servers, terminals, and other end nodes; the projected traffic for the environment; and the projected costs for delivering different service levels.

- Performance constraints—Performance constraints consist of network reliability, traffic throughput, and host/client computer speeds (for example, network interface cards and hard drive access speeds).

■ Networking variables—Networking variables include the network topology, line capacities, and packet traffic. Characterizing network traffic is critical to successful WAN planning, but few planners perform this key step well, if at all.

Engineering Journal:
Traffic Characterization

In WAN design, nothing is more critical than characterizing the types of traffic that will be carried by the WAN.

Types of traffic include

- Voice/fax
- Transaction data (for example, SNA)
- Client/server data
- Messaging (for example, e-mail)
- File transfers
- Batch data
- Network management
- Videoconferencing

Analyzing and categorizing traffic is the basis for key design decisions. Traffic drives capacity, and capacity drives cost. Time-proven processes for measuring and estimating traffic exist for traditional networks, but not for WANs.

Traffic characteristics include

- Peak and average volume
- Connectivity and volume flows
- Connection orientation
- Latency tolerance, including length and variability
- Network availability tolerance
- Error rate tolerance
- Priority
- Protocol type
- Average packet length

Because many network planners do not have the planning and design techniques needed to deal with WAN traffic complexities and uncertainties, they typically "guesstimate" bandwidth capacity, which results in costly, over-engineered networks or poorly performing, under-engineered ones.

The overall goal of WAN design is to minimize cost based on these elements while delivering service that does not compromise established availability requirements. You face two primary concerns: availability and cost. These issues are essentially at odds. Any increase in availability must generally be reflected as an increase in cost. Therefore, you must carefully weigh the relative importance of resource availability and overall cost.

The first step in the design process is to understand the business requirements, which is covered in the following sections. WAN requirements must reflect the goals, characteristics, business processes, and policies of the business in which they operate.

Gathering Requirements

When designing a WAN, you need to start by gathering data about the business structure and processes. Next, you need to determine who the major players will be in helping you design the network. You need to speak to major users and find out their geographic location, their current applications, and their plans for the future. The final network design should reflect the user requirements.

In general, users primarily want application availability in their networks. The chief components of application availability are response time, throughput, and reliability:

- Response time is the time between entry of a command or keystroke and the host system's execution of the command or delivery of a response. Applications in which fast response time is considered critical include interactive online services, such as automated tellers and point-of-sale machines.

- Throughput-intensive applications generally involve file-transfer activities. However, throughput-intensive applications also usually have low response-time requirements. Indeed, they can often be scheduled at times when response-time-sensitive traffic is low (for example, after normal work hours).

- Although reliability is always important, some applications have genuine requirements that exceed typical needs. Organizations that require nearly 100% uptime conduct all activities online or over the telephone. Financial services, securities exchanges, and emergency, police, and military operations are a few examples. These situations imply a requirement for a high level of hardware and redundancy. Determining the cost of any downtime is essential in determining the relative importance of reliability to your network.

You can assess user requirements in a number of ways. The more involved your users are in the process, the more likely your evaluation will be accurate. In general, you can use the following methods to obtain this information:

- User community profiles—Outline what different user groups require. This is the first step in determining network requirements. Although many general users have roughly the same requirements of an e-mail system, they may have different needs from users sharing print servers in a finance department.

- Interviews, focus groups, and surveys—Build a baseline for implementing a network. Understand that some groups might require access to common servers. Others might want to allow external access to specific internal computing resources. Certain organizations might require IS support systems to be managed in a particular way, according to some external standard.

  The least formal method of obtaining information is to conduct interviews with key user groups. Focus groups can also be used to gather information and generate discussion among different organizations with similar (or dissimilar) interests. Finally, formal surveys can be used to get a statistically valid reading of user sentiment regarding a particular service level.

- Human factors tests—The most expensive, time-consuming, and possibly revealing method of assessing user requirements is to conduct a test involving representative users in a lab environment. This is most applicable when you're evaluating response time requirements. For example, you might set up working systems and have users perform normal remote host activities from the lab network. By evaluating user reactions to variations in host responsiveness, you can create benchmark thresholds for acceptable performance.

After gathering data about the corporate structure, you need to determine where information flows in the company. Find out where shared data resides and who uses it. Determine whether data outside the company is accessed.

Make sure you understand the performance issues of any existing network. If time permits, analyze the performance of the existing network.

Washington Project: Understanding the Customer

First and foremost, you must understand your customers; in the case of the Washington School District, your customers include teachers, students, staff members, and administrators.

You need to determine whether the district has documented policies in place. You need to answer questions like the following:

- Has district data been declared mission critical?
- Have district operations been declared mission critical?
- What protocols are allowed on the district network?

Washington Project: Understanding the Customer (Continued)
• Are only certain desktop hosts supported in the district?
Mission-critical data and operations are considered key to the business, and access to them is critical to the business running on a daily basis. You need to determine who in the district has authority over mission-critical data and operations, along with addressing, naming, topology design, and configuration. Some districts have a central Management Information System (MIS) department that controls everything. Some districts have very small MIS departments and, therefore, must pass on authority to departments.

Analyzing Requirements

You need to analyze network requirements, including the customer's business and technical goals. What new applications will be implemented? Are any applications Internet based? What new networks will be accessed? What are the success criteria? (How will you know if the new design is successful?)

Availability measures the usefulness of the network. Many things affect availability, including throughput, response time, and access to resources. Every customer has a different definition of *availability*. You can increase availability by adding more resources. Resources drive up cost. Network design seeks to provide the greatest availability for the least cost.

Washington Project: Analyzing Availability
You need to find out what availability means to your customers, who in the Washington School District are teachers, students, administrators, and staff members. When analyzing your the district's technical requirements, estimate the traffic load caused by applications and by normal protocol behavior (for example, a new node joining the network). Estimate worst-case traffic load during the busiest times for users and during regularly scheduled network services, such as file server backups. This will help you understand what availability means to your customers.

The objective of analyzing requirements is to determine, for representative sites, the average and peak data rates for each source over time. Try to characterize activity throughout a normal work day in terms of the type of traffic passed, level of traffic, response time of hosts, time to execute file transfers, and so on. You can also observe utilization on existing network equipment over the test period.

Engineering Journal: Traffic Measurement

Depending on the traffic type, you should use one of the following four techniques to analyze and measure traffic:

- Network management software—For some types of traffic, you can use network management software to analyze traffic statistics.
- Existing measurements—You can place network analysis equipment on servers, and analyze packet flows from router statistics for existing network segments.
- The estimation process—Where existing measurements cannot be attained (for example, the application does not yet exist), you can use an estimation process. You should work with the application developers and the network administrator to estimate transaction rates, lengths, and flows to derive traffic statistics.
- Comparative sources—You can find a known source that is likely to have similar characteristics and adjust the traffic statistics accordingly.

If the tested network's characteristics are close to those of the new network, you can try estimating to the new network's number of users, applications, and topology. This is a best-guess approach to traffic estimation given the unavailability of tools to characterize detailed traffic behavior.

In addition to passively monitoring an existing network, you can measure activity and traffic generated by a known number of users attached to a representative test network and then calculate findings to your anticipated population.

One problem with defining workloads on networks is that it is difficult to accurately pinpoint traffic load and network device performance as functions of the number of users, type of application, and geographic location. This is especially true without a real network in place.

Washington Project: Analyzing Network Traffic Load and Traffic Problems

Before you develop a district network structure and provision hardware, you need to determine the network traffic load that the district WAN needs to handle. You should determine all the sources of traffic and define what source characteristics must be ascertained. At this step, it is very important to define the sources in sufficient detail that source traffic can be measured or estimated.

Additionally, you need to evaluate applications that might cause traffic problems in the Washington School District WAN. The following applications can generate large volumes of traffic and therefore can cause network problems such as congestion:

- Internet access
- Computers loading software from a remote site
- Anything that transmits images or video

> **Washington Project: Analyzing Network Traffic**
> **Load and Traffic Problems (Continued)**
>
> - Central database access
>
> - Department file servers
>
> The introduction of new sources or applications into the Washington School District WAN must be projected, along with likely growth rates. Obviously, this step requires considerable consultation with district end users and application developers. Finally, district network management data is an important source that you should not overlook because it could take up more than 15% of the total traffic volume.

Consider the following factors that influence the dynamics of the network:

- The time-dependent nature of network access—Peak periods can vary; measurements must reflect a range of observations that includes peak demand.

- Differences associated with type of traffic—Routed and bridged traffic place different demands on network devices and protocols; some protocols are sensitive to dropped packets; some application types require more bandwidth.

- The random nature of network traffic—Exact arrival time and specific effects of traffic are unpredictable.

Each traffic source has its own metric, and each must be converted to bits per second. You should standardize traffic volumes to obtain per-user volumes. Finally, you should apply a factor to account for protocol overhead, packet fragmentation, traffic growth, and safety margin. By varying this factor, you can conduct what-if analyses. For example, you could run Microsoft Office from a server, and then analyze the traffic volume generated from users sharing the application on the network. This volume will help you determine the bandwidth and server requirements to install Microsoft Office on the network.

Sensitivity Testing

From a practical point of view, sensitivity testing involves breaking stable links and observing what happens. When working with a test network, this is relatively easy. You can disturb the network by removing an active interface, and monitor how the change is handled by the network: how traffic is rerouted, the speed of convergence, whether any connectivity is lost, and whether problems arise in handling specific types of traffic. You can also change the level of traffic on a network to determine the effects on the network when traffic levels approach media saturation.

Identifying and Selecting Networking Capabilities

After you understand your networking requirements, you must identify and then select the specific capabilities that fit your computing environment. The following sections help you identify and then select the specific capabilities that fit your computing environment.

Identifying and Selecting a Networking Model

Hierarchical models for network design allow you to design networks in layers. To understand the importance of layering, consider the Open System Interconnection (OSI) reference model, which is a layered model for understanding and implementing computer communications. By using layers, the OSI reference model simplifies the tasks required for two computers to communicate. Hierarchical models for network design also use layers to simplify the task required for internetworking. Each layer can be focused on specific functions, thereby allowing the networking designer to choose the right systems and features for the layer.

Using a hierarchical design can facilitate changes. Modularity in network design allows you to create design elements that can be replicated as the network grows. Because each element in the network design requires change, the cost and complexity of making the upgrade is constrained to a small subset of the overall network. In large flat or meshed network architectures, changes tend to affect a large number of systems. You can also facilitate the identification of failure-points in a network by structuring the network into small, easy-to-understand elements. Network mangers can easily understand the transition points in the network, which helps identify failure points.

The Hierarchical Network Design Model

Network designs tend to follow one of two general design strategies: mesh or hierarchical. In a mesh structure, the network topology is flat; all routers perform essentially the same functions, and there is usually no clear definition of where specific functions are performed. Expansion of the network tends to proceed in a haphazard, arbitrary manner. In a hierarchical structure the network is organized in layers that each have one or more specific functions. Benefits to using a hierarchical model include the following:

- Scalability—Networks that follow the hierarchical model can grow much larger without sacrificing control or manageability because functionality is localized and potential problems can be recognized more easily. An example of a very large-scale hierarchical network design is the Public Switched Telephone Network.

- Ease of implementation—A hierarchical design assigns clear functionality to each layer, thereby making network implementation easier.

- Ease of troubleshooting—Because the functions of the individual layers are well defined, the isolation of problems in the network is less complicated. Temporarily segmenting the network to reduce the scope of a problem also is easier.

- Predictability—The behavior of a network using functional layers is fairly predictable, which makes capacity planning for growth considerably easier; this design approach also facilitates modeling of network performance for analytical purposes.

- Protocol support—The mixing of current and future applications and protocols is much easier on networks that follow the principles of hierarchical design because the underlying infrastructure is already logically organized.

- Manageability—All the benefits listed here contribute to greater manageability of the network.

Using the Hierarchical Design Model

A hierarchical network design includes the following three layers:

- The core layer (also called the backbone), which provides optimal transport between sites
- The distribution layer, which provides policy-based connectivity
- The access layer, which provides workgroup and user access to the network

Figure 9-1 shows a high-level view of the various aspects of a hierarchical network design.

Three-Layer Model Components

A layer is identified as a point in the network where an OSI reference model Layer 3 (network layer) boundary occurs: The three layers are bound by Layer 3 devices or other devices that separate the network into broadcast domains. As shown in Figure 9-1, the three-layer model consists of core, distribution, and access layers, each of which has specific functions:

- Core layer—The core layer provides fast wide-area connections between geographically remote sites, tying a number of campus networks together in a corporate or enterprise WAN. Core links are usually point-to-point, and there are rarely any hosts in the core layer. Core services (for example, T1/T3, Frame Relay, SMDS) typically are leased from a telecom service provider.

- Distribution layer—The distribution layer gives network services to multiple LANs within a WAN environment. This layer is where the WAN backbone network is found, and it is typically based on Fast Ethernet. This layer is implemented on large sites and is used to interconnect buildings.

- Access layer—The access layer is usually a LAN or a group of LANs, typically Ethernet or Token Ring, that provide users with frontline access to network services. The access layer is where almost all hosts are attached to the network, including servers of all kinds and user workstations. Chapter 4, "LAN Design," focuses on the design of the access layer.

FIGURE 9-1
A hierarchical network design presents three layers—core, distribution, and access—with each layer providing different functionality.

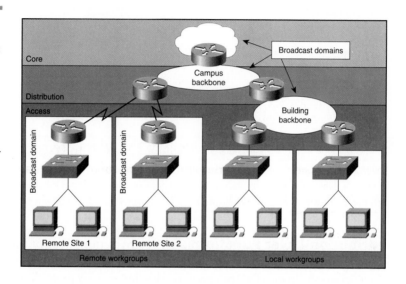

A three-layer model can meet the needs of most enterprise networks. However, not all environments require a full three-layer hierarchy—a one- or two-layer design may be adequate. Even in these cases, however, a hierarchical structure should be maintained to allow these one- or two-layer hierarchical networks to expand to three layers if the need arises. The following sections discuss in more detail the functions of the three layers. Then, we'll move on to discuss one- and two-layer hierarchies.

Core-Layer Functions. The core layer's function is to provide a fast path between remote sites, as shown in Figure 9-2. This layer of the network should not perform any packet manipulation, such as using access control lists and performing filtering, that would slow down the switching of packets. The core layer is, therefore, usually implemented as a WAN. The WAN may need redundant paths so that the network can withstand individual circuit outages and continue to function. Load sharing and rapid convergence of routing protocols may also be important design features. Efficient use of bandwidth in the core is nearly always a concern.

FIGURE 9-2
The core layer optimizes transport between remote sites by creating redundant paths and providing load sharing, effective use of bandwidth, and rapid convergence.

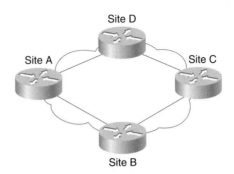

Site D

Site A

Site C

Site B

Washington Project: The WAN Core

The WAN core for the Washington School District network should be a high-speed switching backbone designed to switch packets as quickly as possible. School locations should connect into the WAN core based on proximity to the core from the school locations.

Distribution-Layer Functions. The distribution layer of the network is the demarcation point between the access and core layers and helps to define and differentiate the core. The purpose of this layer is to provide boundary definition, and it is the layer at which packet manipulation occurs. In the WAN environment, the distribution layer can include several functions, such as the following:

- Address or area aggregation
- Departmental or workgroup access
- Broadcast/multicast domain definition
- Virtual LAN (VLAN) routing
- Any media transitions that need to occur
- Security

The distribution layer would include the campus backbone with all its connecting routers, as shown in Figure 9-3. Because policy is typically implemented at this level, we can say that the distribution layer provides policy-based connectivity. *Policy-based connectivity* means that the Layer 3 routers are programmed to allow on the campus backbone only traffic that the network manager has determined acceptable. Note that good network design practice would not put end stations (such as servers) on the backbone. Not putting end stations on the backbone frees up the backbone to act strictly as a transit path for traffic between workgroups in different buildings, or from workgroups to campus-wide servers.

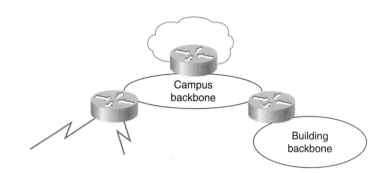

In non-campus environments, the distribution layer can be a redistribution point between routing domains or the point between static and dynamic routing protocols. It can also be the point at which remote sites access the corporate network. The distribution layer can be summarized as the layer that provides policy-based connectivity.

Access-Layer Functions. The access layer is the point at which local end users are allowed into the network, as shown in Figure 9-4. This layer can also use access control lists or filters to further optimize the needs of a particular set of users. In the campus environment, access-layer functions can include the following:

- Shared bandwidth
- Switched bandwidth
- MAC-layer filtering
- Microsegmentation

The access layer connects users into LANs, and LANs into WAN backbones or WAN links. This approach enables designers to distribute services across the CPUs of devices operating at this layer. The access layer allows logical segmentation of the network and grouping of users based on a function. Traditionally, this segmentation is based on organizational boundaries (such as Marketing, Administration, or Engineering). However, from a network management and control perspective, the main function of the access layer is to isolate broadcast traffic to the individual workgroup or LAN. (You studied this layer in great detail in Chapter 4, "LAN Design.") In non-campus environments, the access layer can give remote sites access to the corporate network via some wide-area technology, such as Frame Relay, ISDN, or leased lines, which are covered in the following chapters.

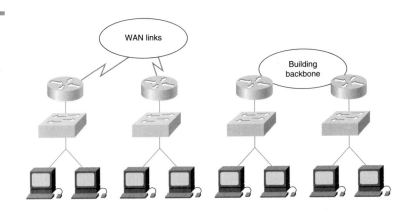

FIGURE 9-4
The access layer connects workgroups to backbones.

One-Layer Design

Not all networks require a three-layer hierarchy. A key design decision becomes the placement of servers: They can be distributed across multiple LANs or concentrated in a central server farm location. Figure 9-5 shows a distributed server design. A one-layer design is typically implemented if there are only a few remote locations in the company, and access to applications is mainly done via the local LAN to the site file server. Each site is its own broadcast domain.

Two-Layer Design

In a two-layer design, a WAN link is used to interconnect separate sites, as shown in Figure 9-6. Inside the site, multiple LANs may be implemented, with each LAN segment being its own broadcast domain. The router at Site A becomes a concentration point from WAN links.

FIGURE 9-5
A one-layer design is sufficient in many smaller networks.

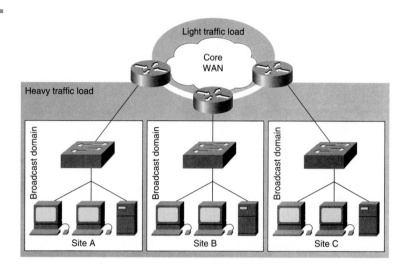

FIGURE 9-6
In a two-layer design, VLANs can be implemented to create separate logical networks.

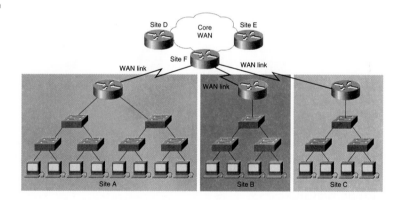

Washington Project: The Two-Layer Hierarchical Model

The Washington School District WAN should be based on a two-layer hierarchical model. Three regional hubs should be established—one each at the district office, the service center, and Shaw Butte Elementary School—in order to form a fast WAN core network.

Hierarchical WAN Design Advantages

One of the advantages of a hierarchical WAN design is that it provides a method for controlling data traffic patterns by putting Layer 3 routing points throughout the network. Because routers have the ability to determine paths from the source host to destination hosts based on Layer 3 addressing, data traffic flows up the hierarchy only as far as it needs to find the destination host, as shown in Figure 9-7.

FIGURE 9-7
Routers are data path decision points.

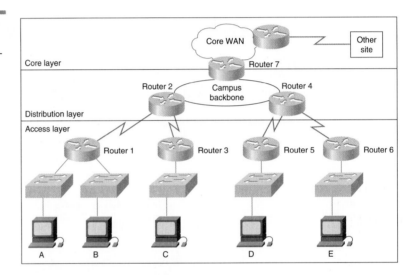

If Host A were to establish a connection to Host B, the traffic from this connection would travel to Router 1 and be forwarded back down to Host B. Notice in Figure 9-8 that this connection does not require that any traffic be placed on the link between Router 1 and Router 2, thus conserving the bandwidth on that link.

In a two-layer WAN hierarchy, which is shown in Figure 9-9, the traffic only travels up the hierarchy as far as needed to get to the destination, thus conserving bandwidth on other WAN links.

Server Placement

The placement of servers as it relates to who will be accessing them affects traffic patterns in the WAN. If you place an enterprise server in the access layer of Site 1, as shown in Figure 9-10, all traffic destined for that is forced to go across links between Routers 1 and 2. This consumes major quantities of bandwidth from Site 1.

FIGURE 9-8
Data flows up the hierarchy based on source/destination addressing.

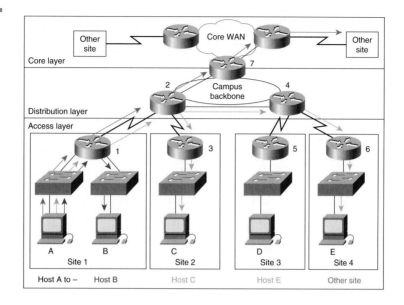

FIGURE 9-9
The traffic patterns in a two-layer WAN hierarchy are governed by host source and destination addresses, and path determinations of the router.

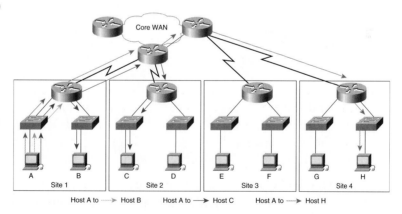

If you place the enterprise server at a higher layer in the hierarchy, as shown in Figure 9-11, the traffic on the link between Routers 1 and 2 is reduced and is available for users at Site 1 to access other services. In Figure 9-12, a workgroup server is placed at the access layer of the site where the largest concentration of users is located, and traffic crossing the WAN link to access this server is limited. Thus, more bandwidth is available to access resources outside the site.

FIGURE 9-10
Unnecessary
traffic con-
sumes band-
width; in this
case, the
server is poorly
placed and
causes the
unnecessary
traffic.

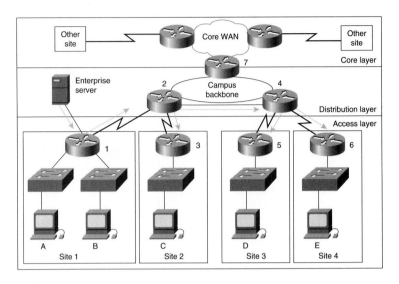

FIGURE 9-11
Moving servers
to correct loca-
tions frees up
bandwidth.

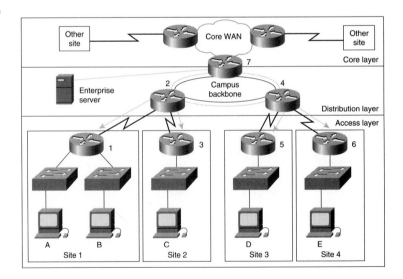

Frame Relay and ISDN WAN Links

It is not uncommon for remote sites to access the WAN core layer by using
WAN technologies other than dedicated links. As shown inFigure 9-13, Frame
Relay and ISDN are two such alternatives. If a remote site is small and has low
demand for access to services in the corporate network, ISDN would be a logical choice for this implementation. Perhaps another remote site cannot get

access to dedicate WAN links from its service provider, but has access to Frame Relay. In either case, an entry point needs to be established for these types of WAN connections to the WAN core. These entry points should be established on a router that is directly connected to the WAN core, which allows the remote sites complete access to the enterprise network without adding unnecessary data traffic to other sites.

FIGURE 9-12
Placement of servers should be based on user needs.

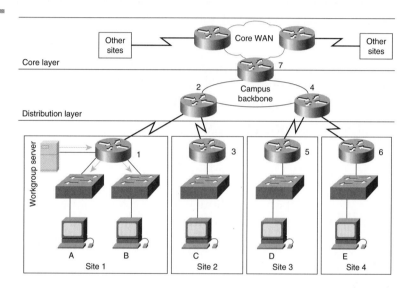

FIGURE 9-13
Different WAN technologies can be used to access the WAN core.

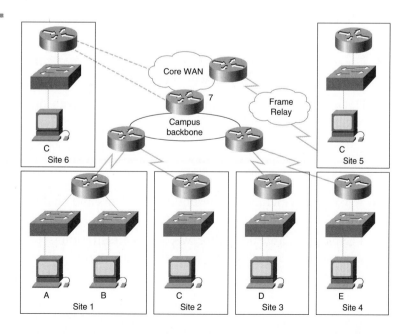

Washington Project: The Frame Relay Link

You should provide access to the Internet or any other outside network connections through the Washington School District office by using a Frame Relay WAN link. For security purposes, no other connections should be permitted.

Washington School District Project Task: WAN Design

In this chapter, you have learned about the WAN design process, so now you can focus on interconnecting all the individual Washington School District sites into a WAN topology that satisfies the users' requirements.

Complete the following tasks:

1. Create a WAN design that includes the following:

    - WAN link speeds and upgrade path

    - A model of traffic flow between schools showing a two- or three-layer WAN hierarchy

    - A list of additional equipment, such as CSUs/DSUs (channel service units/data service units) and router interfaces required to implement the districtwide WAN

    - A list of what kind of redundancy is needed to ensure WAN uptime

    (Hint: Consult the Washington School District Project technical requirements.)

2. Document all the router commands necessary for reconfiguration of routers in order to implement the WAN design.

3. Document how a WAN implementation affects routing updates between routers.

Summary

- WAN design includes gathering requirements and analyzing requirements such as availability and traffic load.

- The most scalable design for WAN implementation is a hierarchical model, with each layer performing a particular function.

- The hierarchical design model consists of core-layer functions, distribution-layer functions, and access-layer functions.

- Enterprise WANs can be made up of several different WAN technologies, such as Frame Relay and ISDN.

- Placement of servers is critical for controlling traffic patterns across the WAN.

Chapter Review

Complete all the review questions to test your understanding of the topics and concepts covered in this chapter. Answers are listed in Appendix A, "Chapter Review Answer Key."

1. Which of the following are initial concerns in a WAN design?

   A. Determining whether data outside the company is accessed

   B. Determining who is involved in the design from the customer standpoint

   C. Determining where shared data resides and who uses it

   D. All of the above

2. When analyzing network load requirements, you should check worst-case traffic load during what time of the day?

   A. The busiest time

   B. The least busiest time

   C. During network backups

   D. After regular work hours

3. When designing the WAN, where should application servers be placed?

   A. On the enterprise backbone

   B. Close to the users

   C. Near the point of presence

   D. Any place the designer chooses

4. Which of the following is not a benefit of a hierarchical design model?

   A. Scalability

   B. Ease of implementation

   C. A flat topology

   D. Ease of troubleshooting

5. In most cases, when designing the core layer, your main concern should be which of the following?

   A. Efficient use of bandwidth

   B. Workgroup access

    C. Server placement

    D. Enterprise server placement

6. Which of the following would be placed on the network backbone?

    A. Server

    B. Routers

    C. Workstations

    D. Application servers

7. Which layer connects users into the LAN?

    A. Workgroup

    B. Core

    C. Access

    D. Distribution

8. Which layer connects a LAN into a WAN link?

    A. Distribution

    B. Workgroup

    C. Core

    D. Access

9. In a one-layer design, the placement of what device becomes extremely important?

    A. Server

    B. Router

    C. Workstation

    D. Switch

10. In a two-layer design, what device would you use to segment the LAN into individual broadcast domains?

    A. Switches

    B. Routers

    C. Hubs

    D. Repeaters

Key Terms

access layer   The layer at which a LAN or a group of LANs, typically Ethernet or Token Ring, provides users with frontline access to network services.

circuit   A communications path between two or more points.

circuit switching   A switching system in which a dedicated physical circuit path must exist between the sender and the receiver for the duration of the "call." Used heavily in the telephone company network. Circuit switching can be contrasted with contention and token passing as a channel-access method, and with message switching and packet switching as a switching technique.

core layer   The layer that provides fast wide-area connections between geographically remote sites, tying a number of campus networks together in a corporate or enterprise WAN.

dedicated link   A communications link that is indefinitely reserved for transmissions, rather than switched as transmission is required.

distribution layer   The layer in which the distribution of network services occurs to multiple LANs within a WAN environment. This layer is where the WAN backbone network is found, typically based on Fast Ethernet.

enterprise network   A corporation, agency, school, or other organization's network that ties together its data, communication, computing, and file servers.

Frame Relay   An industry-standard, switched data link–layer protocol that handles multiple virtual circuits using HDLC encapsulation between connected devices. Frame Relay is more efficient than X.25, the protocol for which it is generally considered a replacement.

leased line   A transmission line reserved by a communications carrier for the private use of a customer. A leased line is a type of dedicated line.

link   A network communications channel consisting of a circuit or transmission path and all related equipment between a sender and a receiver. Most often used to refer to a WAN connection. Sometimes referred to as a line or a transmission link.

packet switching   A networking method in which nodes share bandwidth with each other by sending packets.

T1   A digital WAN carrier facility that transmits DS-1-formatted data at 1.544 Mbps through the telephone-switching network, using AMI or B8ZS coding.

T3   A digital WAN carrier facility that transmits DS-3-formatted data at 44.736 Mbps through the telephone switching network.

WAN link   A WAN communications channel consisting of a circuit or transmission path and all related equipment between a sender and a receiver.

Objectives

After reading this chapter, you will be able to

- Identify and describe the basic components defining PPP communication
- Define and describe the use of LCP and NCP frames in PPP
- Understand the process for configuring and verifying PPP
- Describe and explain PPP authentication
- Define and describe the use of password authentication
- Define and describe the use of CHAP

PPP

Introduction

You studied wide-area network (WAN) technologies in Chapter 8, "WANs"—now it is important to understand that WAN connections are controlled by protocols that perform the same basic functions as Layer 2 LAN protocols, such as Ethernet. In a LAN environment, in order to move data between any two nodes or routers, a data path must be established, and flow control procedures must be in place to ensure delivery of data. This is also true in the WAN environment and is accomplished by using WAN protocols.

In this chapter, you will learn about the basic components, processes, and operations that define Point-to-Point Protocol (PPP) communication. In addition, this chapter discusses the use of Link Control Protocol (LCP) and Network Control Program (NCP) frames in PPP. Finally, you will learn how to configure and verify the configuration of PPP. Along with PPP authentication, you will learn to use of Password Authentication Protocol (PAP) and Challenge Handshake Authentication Protocol (CHAP).

Washington Project: Applying PPP
In Chapter 8, you learned about WAN design and developed the Washington School District's WAN design to allow connectivity between all sites in the district. Without a Layer 2 protocol, the physical WAN links have no mechanism to transmit data and implement flow control. In this chapter you will apply PPP as the data link–layer protocol to be used in the district WAN implementation.

PPP Overview

In the late 1980s, Serial Line Internet Protocol (SLIP) was blocking the Internet's growth. PPP was created to solve remote Internet connectivity problems. Additionally, PPP was needed to dynamically assign IP addresses and allow for multiple protocols to ride on top. PPP provides router-to-router and host-to-network connections over both synchronous and asynchronous circuits (see Figure 10-1).

PPP is the most widely used and most popular WAN protocols because it offers all the following features:

- Control of data link setup
- Assignment and management of IP addresses

- Network protocol multiplexing
- Link configuration and link quality testing
- Error detection
- Option negotiation for capabilities such as network-layer address negotiation and data compression negotiation

FIGURE 10-1
PPP provides reliable connections between routers.

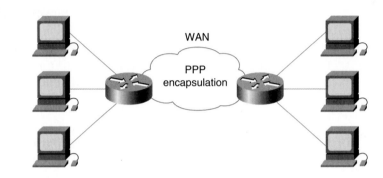

PPP Components

PPP addresses the problems of Internet connectivity by using three main components:

- A method for encapsulating datagrams over serial links. PPP uses High-Level Data Link Control (HDLC) as a basis for encapsulating datagrams over point-to-point links.
- An LCP to establish, configure, and test the data-link connection.
- A family of NCPs for establishing and configuring different network-layer protocols. PPP is designed to allow the simultaneous use of multiple network-layer protocols. Today, PPP supports other protocols besides IP, including Internetwork Packet Exchange (IPX) and DECnet. As shown in Figure 10-2, PPP uses its NCP component to encapsulate multiple protocols.

PPP Layer Functions

PPP uses a layered architecture, as shown in Figure 10-3. With its lower-level functions, PPP can use

- Synchronous physical media, such as those that connect Integrated Services Digital Network (ISDN) networks (which are covered in Chapter 11, "ISDN").
- Asynchronous physical media, such as those that use basic telephone service for modem dialup connections.

FIGURE 10-2
PPP can carry packets from several protocol suites by using NCP.

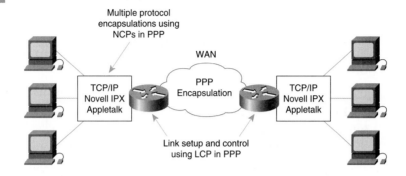

FIGURE 10-3
PPP is a data link–layer protocol with network-layer services.

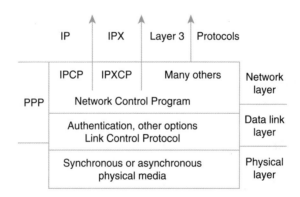

With its higher-level functions, PPP carries packets from several network-layer protocols in NCPs. These higher-layer protocols include the following:

- BCP—Bridge Control Protocol
- IPCP—Internet Protocol Control Protocol
- IPXCP—Internetwork Packet Exchange Control Protocol

These are functional fields containing standardized codes to indicate the network-layer protocol type that PPP encapsulates.

PPP Frame Formats

As shown in Figure 10-4, the fields of a PPP frame are as follows:

- Flag—Indicates the beginning or end of a frame and consists of the binary sequence 01111110.
- Address—Consists of the standard broadcast address, which is the binary sequence 11111111. PPP does not assign individual station addresses.

- Control—1 byte that consists of the binary sequence 00000011, which calls for transmission of user data in an unsequenced frame. A connectionless link service similar to that of Logical Link Control (LLC) Type 1 is provided.

- Protocol—2 bytes that identify the protocol encapsulated in the data field of the frame.

- Data—0 or more bytes that contain the datagram for the protocol specified in the Protocol field. The end of the data field is found by locating the closing flag sequence and allowing 2 bytes for the frame check sequence (FCS) field. The default maximum length of the data field is 1,500 bytes.

- FCS—Normally 16 bits (2 bytes). Refers to the extra characters added to a frame for error control purposes.

FIGURE 10-4
PPP uses the frame structure of the International Organization for Standardization (ISO) HDLC procedures.

Field length, in bytes

	1	1	1	1	Variable	2 or 4
	Flag	Address	Control	Protocol	Data	FCS

PPP Session Establishment

PPP provides a method of establishing, configuring, maintaining, and terminating a point-to-point connection. In order to establish communications over a point-to-point link, PPP goes through four distinct phases:

1. Link establishment and configuration negotiation—An originating PPP node sends LCP frames to configure and test the data link.

2. Link-quality determination—The link is established and negotiated. Note that this is an optional phase.

3. Network-layer protocol configuration negotiation—The originating PPP node sends NCP frames to choose and configure network-layer protocols. The chosen network-layer protocols—such as TCP/IP, Novell IPX, and AppleTalk—are configured, and packets from each network-layer protocol are sent.

4. Link termination—The link remains configured for communications until LCP or NCP frames close the link or until some external event occurs (for example, an inactivity timer expires or a user intervenes).

There are three classes of LCP frames:

- Link establishment frames—Used to establish and configure a link.
- Link termination frames—Used to terminate a link.
- Link maintenance frames—Used to manage and debug a link.

LCP frames are used to accomplish the work of each of the LCP phases, which are described in the following sections.

Phase 1: Link Establishment and Configuration Negotiation

In the link establishment and configuration negotiation phase, each PPP device sends LCP packets to configure and test the data link. LCP packets contain a configuration option field that allows devices to negotiate on the use of options, such as the maximum receive unit, compression of certain PPP fields, and the link authentication protocol. If a configuration option is not included in an LCP packet, the default value for that configuration option is assumed.

Before any network-layer datagrams (for example, IP) can be exchanged, LCP must first open the connection and negotiate the configuration parameters. This phase is complete when a configuration acknowledgment frame has been sent and received.

Phase 2: Link-Quality Determination

LCP allows an optional link-quality determination phase following the link establishment and configuration negotiation phase. In the link-quality determination phase, the link is tested to determine whether the link quality is good enough to bring up network-layer protocols.

In addition, after the link has been established and the authentication protocol decided on, the client or user workstation can be authenticated. Authentication, if used, takes place before the network-layer protocol configuration phase begins. LCP can delay transmission of network-layer protocol information until this phase is completed.

PPP supports two authentication protocols: PAP and CHAP. Both of these protocols are detailed in RFC 1334, "PPP Authentication Protocols." These protocols are covered later in this chapter, in the section "PPP Authentication."

Phase 3: Network-Layer Protocol Configuration Negotiation

When LCP finishes the link-quality determination phase, network-layer protocols can be separately configured by the appropriate NCP and can be brought up and taken down at any time.

In this phase, the PPP devices send NCP packets to choose and configure one or more network-layer protocols (such as IP). When each of the chosen network-layer protocols has been configured, datagrams from each network-layer protocol can be sent over the link. If LCP closes the link, it informs the network-layer protocols so that they can take appropriate action. When PPP is configured, you can check its LCP and NCP states by using the `show interfaces` command.

Phase 4: Link Termination

LCP can terminate the link at any time. This is usually done at the request of a user but can happen because of a physical event, such as the loss of a carrier or a timeout.

Washington Project: Enabling PPP Encapsulation
You can enable PPP on serial lines to encapsulate IP and other network-layer protocol datagrams. To do so, enable PPP encapsulation in interface configuration mode, using the `encapsulation ppp` command: • Enter interface configuration mode for the desired interface. • Configure the interface for PPP encapsulation: `Router(config)# encapsulation ppp`

PPP Authentication

As you have learned, the authentication phase of a PPP session is optional. After the link has been established, and the authentication protocol decided on, the peer can be authenticated. If it is used, authentication takes place before the network-layer protocol configuration phase begins.

The authentication options require that the calling side of the link enter authentication information to help ensure that the user has the network administrator's permission to make the call. Peer routers exchange authentication messages.

When configuring PPP authentication, you can select PAP or CHAP. In general, CHAP is the preferred protocol. A brief description of each follows:

- PAP—As shown in Figure 10-5, PAP provides a simple method for a remote node to establish its identity, using a two-way handshake. After the PPP link establishment phase is complete, a username/password pair is repeatedly sent by the remote node across the link until authentication is acknowledged or the connection is terminated.

  PAP is not a strong authentication protocol. Passwords are sent across the link in clear text, and there is no protection from playback or repeated trial-and-error attacks. The remote node is in control of the frequency and timing of the login attempts.

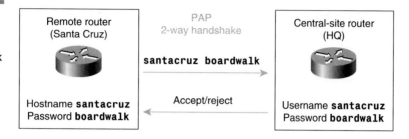

FIGURE 10-5
PAP is activated only upon initial link establishment.

- CHAP—CHAP is used to periodically verify the identity of the remote node, using a three-way handshake, as shown in Figure 10-6. This is done upon initial link establishment and can be repeated any time after the link has been established. CHAP offers features such as periodic verification to improve security; this makes CHAP more effective than PAP. PAP verifies only once, which makes it vulnerable to hacks and modem playback. Further, PAP allows the caller to attempt authentication at will (without first receiving a challenge), which makes it vulnerable to brute-force attacks, whereas CHAP does not allow a caller to attempt authentication without a challenge.

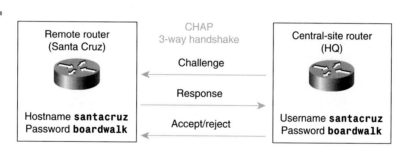

FIGURE 10-6
CHAP is used at the startup of a link, and periodically after that, to verify the identity of the remote node by using a three-way handshake.

After the PPP link establishment phase is complete, the host sends a challenge message to the remote node. The remote node responds with a value. The host checks the response against its own value. If the values match, the authentication is acknowledged. Otherwise, the connection is terminated.

CHAP provides protection against playback attacks through the use of a variable challenge value that is unique and unpredictable. The use of repeated challenges is intended to limit the time of exposure to any single attack. The local router (or a third-party authentication server, such as Netscape Commerce Server) is in control of the frequency and timing of the challenges.

Configuring PPP Authentication

To configure PPP authentication, do the following:

Step 1 On each router, define the username and password to expect from the remote router:

```
Router(config)#username name password secret
```

The arguments are described as follows:

name—This is the host name of the remote router. Note that it is case sensitive.

secret—On Cisco routers, the *secret* password must be the same for both routers.

Engineering Journal: Adding a Username

You should add a username entry for each remote system that the local router communicates with and requires authentication from. The remote device must also have a username entry for the local router.

To enable the local router to respond to remote CHAP challenges, one username name entry must be the same as the host name entry that has already been assigned to the device. With CHAP, you should use secret passwords that are known only to the authenticator and peer.

Step 2 Enter interface configuration mode for the desired interface.

Step 3 Configure the interface for PPP encapsulation:

```
Router(config-if)# encapsulation ppp
```

Step 4 Configure PPP authentication:

```
Router(config-if)# ppp authentication {chap | chap pap | pap chap | pap}
```

Step 5 If CHAP and PAP are enabled, then the first method specified is requested during the link negotiation phase. If the peer suggests using the second method or simply refuses the first method, then the second method is tried.

NOTE

When PPP is configured, you can check its LCP and NCP states by using the **show interfaces** command.

Step 6 In Cisco IOS Release 11.1 or later, if you choose PAP and are configuring the router that will send the PAP information (in other words, the router responding to a PAP request), you must enable PAP on the interface. PAP is disabled by default; to enable PAP, use the following command:

```
Router(config-if)# ppp pap sent-username username password password
```

Configuring CHAP Authentication

The following methods can be used to simplify CHAP configuration tasks on the router:

- You can use the same host name on multiple routers—When you want remote users to think they are connecting to the same router when authenticating, configure the same host name on each router:

```
Router(config-if)# ppp chap hostname hostname
```

- You can use a password to authenticate to an unknown host—To limit the number of username/password entries in the router, configure a password that will be sent to hosts that want to authenticate the router:

```
Router(config-if)# ppp chap password secret
```

This password is not used when the router authenticates a remote device.

Summary

- PPP is the most widely used WAN protocol.
- PPP addresses the problems of Internet connectivity by providing an LCP and a family of NCPs to negotiate optional configuration parameters and facilities.
- A PPP session has four phases:
  — Link establishment
  — Link quality determination
  — Network-layer protocol configuration
  — Link termination
- You can select PAP or CHAP when configuring PPP authentication.
- PAP is not a strong authentication protocol.
- CHAP provides protection against playback attacks through the use of a variable challenge value that is unique and unpredictable.
- You configure the interface for PPP encapsulation by using the **encapsulation ppp** command.
- When PPP is configured, you can check its LCP and NCP states by using the **show interfaces** command.

Washington School District Project Task: PPP

In this chapter, you learned concepts and configuration processes that will help you configure PPP in the Washington School District network. As part of the configuration, you need to complete the following tasks:

1. Apply PPP to the existing WAN designs.

2. Document the changes in the router configurations in order to implement PPP on the routers.

3. Document the router commands necessary to implement PPP on the router interfaces.

Chapter Review

Complete all the review questions to test your understanding of the topics and concepts covered in this chapter. Answers are listed in Appendix A, "Chapter Review Answer Key."

1. PPP is generally considered to be the successor to what protocol?

2. PPP supports which physical interfaces?

3. Which of the following is the network-layer protocol supported by PPP?

   A. Novell IPX

   B. TCP/IP

   C. AppleTalk

   D. All of the above

4. NCPs are used by PPP to do which of the following?

   A. Establish links

   B. Encapsulate multiple protocols

   C. Convert packets into cells

   D. Establish connections

5. In a PPP frame, what field identifies whether you have encapsulated IPX or TCP/IP?

   A. Flag

   B. Control

   C. Protocol

   D. FCS

6. When you're running PPP, LCP is responsible for which of the following?

   A. Establishment, maintenance, and termination of the point-to-point connection

   B. Maintenance of several links

   C. Router updates

   D. Compression

7. How many phases are involved in PPP session establishment?

   A. Two

   B. Three

   C. Four

   D. One

8. What type of handshaking occurs when PAP is the selected PPP authentication protocol?

   A. One-way

   B. Two-way

   C. Three-way

   D. Four-way

9. What command on the router can you use to check the LCP and NCP states for PPP?

   A. `router> show interfaces`

   B. `router(config)# show interfaces`

   C. `router# show interfaces`

   D. `router(config-if)# show interfaces`

10. When would PPP most likely be used at a local workstation for Internet connectivity?

    A. When the workstation is directly connected to a LAN

    B. When the workstation is directly connected to a router

    C. When the workstation needs dialup access to the Internet

    D. It will never be used on a workstation

Key Terms

asynchronous circuit   A signal that is transmitted without precise clocking. Such signals generally have different frequencies and phase relationships. Asynchronous transmissions usually encapsulate individual characters in control bits (called start and stop bits) that designate the beginning and end of each character.

CHAP (Challenge Handshake Authentication Protocol)   A security feature supported on lines using PPP encapsulation that prevents unauthorized access. CHAP does not itself prevent unauthorized access, but it identifies the remote end; the router or access server then determines whether that user is allowed access.

LCP (Link Control Protocol)   A protocol that provides a method of establishing, configuring, maintaining, and terminating the point-to-point connection.

LLC (logical link control)   The higher of the two data link–layer sublayers defined by the IEEE. The LLC sublayer handles error control, flow control, framing, and MAC-sublayer addressing. The most prevalent LLC protocol is IEEE 802.2, which includes both connectionless and connection-oriented variants.

NCP (Network Control Program)   A program that routes and controls the flow of data between a communications controller and other network resources.

PAP (Password Authentication Protocol)   An authentication protocol that allows PPP peers to authenticate one another. The remote router attempting to connect to the local router is required to send an authentication request. Unlike CHAP, PAP passes the password and host name or username in cleartext (that is, unencrypted). PAP does not itself prevent unauthorized access, but it identifies the remote end; the router or access server then determines whether that user is allowed access. PAP is supported only on PPP lines.

PPP (Point-to-Point Protocol)   A successor to SLIP, a protocol that provides router-to-router and host-to-network connections over synchronous and asynchronous circuits.

SLIP (Serial Line Internet Protocol)   A standard protocol for point-to-point serial connections using a variation of TCP/IP. The predecessor of PPP.

synchronous circuit   A signal that is transmitted with precise clocking. Such signals have the same frequency, with individual characters encapsulated in control bits (called start bits and stop bits) that designate the beginning and end of each character.

Objectives

After reading this chapter, you will be able to

- Describe ISDN and its components
- Describe ISDN standards
- Describe ISDN encapsulation
- Describe ISDN uses
- Describe BRI and PRI
- Describe ISDN configuration tasks
- Describe dial-on-demand routing

Chapter 11

ISDN

Introduction

Many types of WAN technologies can be implemented to solve connectivity issues for users who need access to geographically distant locations. In Chapter 10, "PPP," you learned about Point-to-Point Protocol (PPP). In this chapter, you will learn about the services, standards, components, operation, and configuration of Integrated Services Digital Network (ISDN) communication. ISDN is specifically designed to solve the problems of small offices or dialin users that need more bandwidth than traditional telephone dialin services can provide; ISDN also provides backup links.

Telephone companies developed ISDN with the intention of creating a totally digital network. ISDN was developed to use the existing telephone wiring system, and it works very much like a telephone. When you make a data call with ISDN, the WAN link is brought up for the duration of the call and is taken down when the call is completed; it's very similar to how you call a friend on the phone and then hang up when you are done talking.

Washington Project: ISDN Connectivity
In this chapter, you will learn the concepts and configuration process needed to implement an ISDN connection in the Washington School District WAN. You need to provide an ISDN connection for a remote site that needs part-time connectivity to the district.

ISDN Overview

ISDN was developed to provide digital services over existing telephone wiring; these services can deliver not just voice, but data, text, graphics, music, video, and information. ISDN is generally viewed as an alternative to leased lines, which can be used for telecommuting and networking small and remote offices into LANs.

Telephone companies developed ISDN as part of an effort to standardize subscriber services, User-Network Interface (UNI), and network capabilities. Standardizing subscriber services makes it more possible to ensure international compatibility. The ISDN standards define the hardware and call setup schemes for end-to-end digital connectivity, which help achieve the goal of worldwide connectivity by ensuring that ISDN networks easily communicate with one another.

ISDN's ability to bring digital connectivity to local sites has many benefits, including the following:

- ISDN can carry a variety of user traffic signals. ISDN provides access to digital video, packet-switched data, and telephone network services.

- ISDN offers much faster call setup, using out-of-band (D, or delta, channel) signaling, than modem connections. For example, a duration of less than one second can be sufficient to make some ISDN calls.

- ISDN provides a faster data transfer rate than modems by using the bearer channel (B channel). With multiple B channels, ISDN offers users more bandwidth on WANs (for example, two B channels equals 128 kbps) than some leased lines.

ISDN can provide a clear data path over which to negotiate PPP links.

However, you should ensure in the design phase that the equipment selected has the feature set that takes advantage of ISDN's flexibility. In addition, you must keep in mind the following ISDN design issues:

- Security issues—Because network devices can now be connected over the Public Switched Telephone Network (PSTN), it is crucial to design and confirm a robust security model for protecting the network.

- Cost-containment issues—A primary goal of selecting ISDN for your network is to avoid the cost of full-time data services (such as leased lines or Frame Relay). Therefore, it is very important to evaluate your data traffic profiles and monitor ISDN usage patterns to ensure that your WAN costs are controlled.

ISDN Components

ISDN components include terminals, terminal adapters (TAs), network-termination (NT) devices, line-termination equipment, and exchange-termination equipment. Table 11-1 provides a summary of the ISDN components. ISDN terminals come in two types, as shown in Figure 11-1. Specialized ISDN terminals are referred to as terminal equipment type 1 (TE1). Non-ISDN terminals such as data terminal equipment (DTE) that predate the ISDN standards are referred to as terminal equipment type 2 (TE2). TE1s connect to the ISDN network through a four-wire, twisted-pair digital link. TE2s connect to the ISDN network through a TA. The ISDN TA can be either a standalone device or a board inside the TE2. If the TE2 is implemented as a standalone device, it connects to the TA via a standard physical-layer interface.

Beyond the TE1 and TE2 devices, the next connection point in the ISDN network is the network termination type 1 (NT1) or network termination type 2 (NT2) device. These are network-termination devices that connect the four-wire subscriber wiring to the conventional two-wire local loop. In North America, the NT1 is a customer premises equipment (CPE) device. In most parts of the world besides North America, the NT1 is part of the network provided by the carrier. The NT2 is a more complicated device, typically found in digital private branch exchanges (PBXs), that performs Layer 2 and Layer 3 protocol functions services. An NT1/2 device also exists; it is a single device that combines the functions of an NT1 and an NT2.

TABLE 11-1   ISDN Components

Component	Description
Terminal equipment type 1 (TE1)	Designates a device that is compatible with the ISDN network. A TE1 connects to a network termination of either type 1 or type 2.
Terminal equipment type 2 (TE2)	Designates a device that is not compatible with ISDN and requires a terminal adapter.
Terminal adapter (TA)	Converts standard electrical signals into the form used by ISDN so that non-ISDN devices can connect to the ISDN network.
Network termination type 1 (NT1)	Connects four-wire ISDN subscriber wiring to the conventional two-wire local loop facility.
Network termination type 2 (NT2)	Directs traffic to and from different subscriber devices and the NT1. The NT2 is an intelligent device that performs switching and concentrating.

ISDN Reference Points

Before you can connect devices that perform specific functions, the devices need to support specific interfaces. Because CPEs can include one or more functions, the interfaces they use to connect to other devices that support other functions can vary. As a result, the standards do not define interfaces in terms of hardware, but refer to them as reference points. Reference points are a series of specifications that define the connection between specific devices, depending on their function in the end-to-end connection. It is important to know about these interface types because a CPE device, such as a router, can support different reference types, which could result in the need for additional equipment.

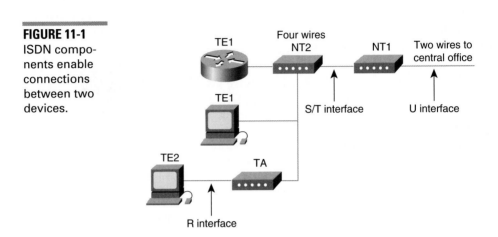

FIGURE 11-1
ISDN compo-
nents enable
connections
between two
devices.

Table 11-2 provides a summary of the reference points that affect the customer side of the ISDN connection (see Figure 11-2).

TABLE 11-2   ISDN Reference Points

Reference Point	Description
R	References the connection between a non–ISDN-compatible device and a TA.
S	References the points that connect into the NT2 or customer switching device. It is the interface that enables calls between the various parts of the CPE.
T	Electrically identical to the S interface, a T interface references the outbound connection from the NT2 to the ISDN network or NT1.
U	References the connection between the NT1 and the ISDN network owned by the phone company. The U reference point is relevant only in North America, where the NT1 function is not provided by the service provider.

A sample ISDN configuration is shown in Figure 11-3, where three devices are attached to an ISDN switch at the central office (CO). Two of these devices are ISDN compatible, so they can be attached through an S reference point to

NT2 devices. The third device (a standard, non-ISDN telephone) attaches through the R reference point to a TA. Although they are not shown, similar user stations are attached to the far-right ISDN switch.

FIGURE 11-2
Reference points define logical interfaces between functional groupings, such as TAs and NT1s.

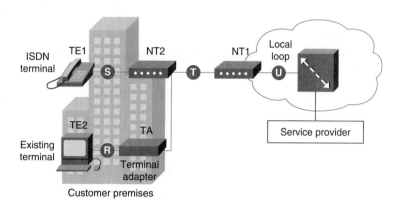

FIGURE 11-3
Several devices can access different types of networks through an ISDN switch.

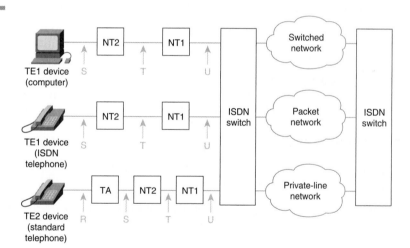

Washington Project: ISDN Equipment and Media

You need to identify what additional equipment and media will be necessary in order to implement an ISDN link in the Washington School District WAN design.

ISDN Switch Types

For proper ISDN operation, it is important that the correct switch type is configured on the ISDN device. ISDN service providers use a variety of switch types for their ISDN services. Services offered by carriers vary considerably from nation to nation and region to region. Just like modems, each switch type operates slightly differently and has a specific set of call setup requirements. As a result, before you can connect a router to an ISDN service, you must be aware of the switch types used at the CO. You specify this information during router configuration so the router can place ISDN network-level calls and send data.

ISDN Service Profile Identifiers

In addition to learning about the switch type your service provider uses, you also need to know what service profile identifiers (SPIDs) are assigned to your connection. The ISDN carrier provides a SPID to identify the line configuration of the ISDN service. SPIDs are a series of characters (that can look like phone numbers) that identify you to the switch at the CO. After you're identified, the switch links the services you ordered to the connection.

ISDN Standards

Work on standards for ISDN began in the late 1960s. A comprehensive set of ISDN recommendations was published in 1984 and is continuously updated by the Consultative Committee for International Telegraph and Telephone (CCITT)—now the International Telecommunication Union Telecommunication Standardization Sector (ITU-T). ITU-T groups and organizes the ISDN protocols as described in Table 11-3.

TABLE 11-3 ISDN Protocols

Protocols that Begin with This Letter	Are Used for These Purposes
E	These protocols recommend telephone network standards for ISDN. For example, the E.164 protocol describes international addressing for ISDN.
I	These protocols deal with concepts, terminology, and general methods. The I.100 series includes general ISDN concepts and the structure of other I-series recommendations; the I.200 series deals with service aspects of ISDN; the I.300 series describes network aspects; the I.400 series describes how the UNI is provided.

TABLE 11-3   ISDN Protocols (Continued)

Protocols that Begin with This Letter	Are Used for These Purposes
Q	These protocols cover how switching and signaling should operate. The term signaling in this context means the process of call setup used. Q.921 describes the ISDN data-link processes of Link Access Procedure on the D channel (LAPD), which functions like Layer 2 processes in the Open System Interconnection (OSI) reference model. Q.931 specifies OSI reference model Layer 3 functions.

Q.931 recommends a network layer between the terminal endpoint and the local ISDN switch. This protocol does not impose an end-to-end recommendation. The various ISDN providers and switch types can and do use various implementations of Q.931. Other switches were developed before the standards groups finalized this standard.

Because switch types are not standard, when configuring the router, you need to specify the ISDN switch you are connecting to. In addition, Cisco routers have **debug** commands to monitor Q.931 and Q.921 processes when an ISDN call is initiated or being terminated.

ISDN and the OSI Reference Model

ISDN is addressed by a suite of ITU-T standards spanning the physical, data link, and network layers of the OSI reference model:

- The physical layer—The ISDN Basic Rate Interface (BRI) physical-layer specification is defined in ITU-T I.430. The ISDN Primary Rate Interface (PRI) physical-layer specification is defined in ITU-T I.431.
- The data link layer—The ISDN data link-layer specification is based on LAPD and is formally specified in ITU-T Q.920 and ITU-T Q.921.
- The network layer—The ISDN network layer is defined in ITU-T Q.930 and ITU-T Q.931. Together these two standards specify user-to-user, circuit-switched, and packet-switched connections.

The ISDN Physical Layer

ISDN physical-layer (Layer 1) frame formats differ depending on whether the frame is outbound (from terminal to network—the NT frame format) or inbound (from network to terminal—the TE frame format). Both of the frames are 48 bits long, of which 36 bits represent data. Both physical-layer frame formats are shown in Figure 11-4. The bits of an ISDN physical-layer frame are used as follows:

- Framing bit—Provides synchronization.
- Load balancing bit—Adjusts the average bit value.
- Echo of previous D channel bit—Used for contention resolution when several terminals on a passive bus contend for a channel.
- Activation bit—Activates devices.
- Spare bit—Unassigned.
- B1 channel bits, B2 channel bits, and D channel bits—Used for user data.

FIGURE 11-4
ISDN physical-layer frame formats are 48 bits long, of which 36 bits represent data

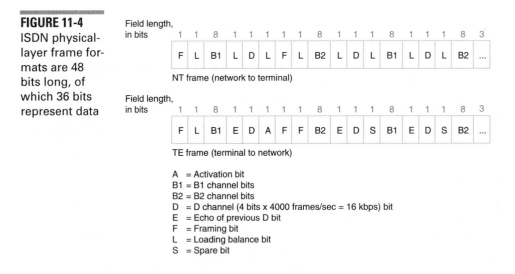

Multiple ISDN user devices can be physically attached to one circuit. In this configuration, collisions can result if two terminals transmit simultaneously. ISDN therefore provides features to determine link contention. These features are part of the ISDN D channel, which is described in more detail later in this chapter.

The ISDN Data Link Layer

Layer 2 of the ISDN signaling protocol is LAPD. LAPD is similar to High-Level Data Link Control (HDLC) and Link Access Procedure, Balanced (LAPB). As the expansion of the LAPD abbreviation—Link Access Procedure on the D channel—indicates, it is used across the D channel to ensure that control and signaling information flows and is received properly (see Figure 11-5).

FIGURE 11-5
The LAPD frame format is very similar to that of HDLC.

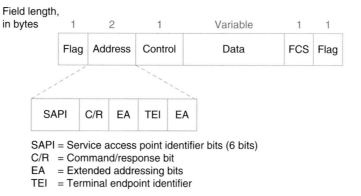

Field length, in bytes

1	2	1	Variable	1	1
Flag	Address	Control	Data	FCS	Flag

SAPI	C/R	EA	TEI	EA

SAPI = Service access point identifier bits (6 bits)
C/R = Command/response bit
EA = Extended addressing bits
TEI = Terminal endpoint identifier

The LAPD *flag* and *control* fields are identical to those of HDLC. The LAPD *address* field can be either 1 or 2 bytes long. If the extended address bit of the first byte is set, the address is 1 byte; if it is not set, the address is 2 bytes. The first address field byte contains the *service access point identifier* (SAPI), which identifies the portal at which LAPD services are provided to Layer 3. The command/response (C/R) bit indicates whether the frame contains a command or a response. The *terminal endpoint identifier* (TEI) field identifies either a single terminal or multiple terminals. A TEI of all ones indicates a broadcast.

The ISDN Network Layer

Two Layer 3 specifications are used for ISDN signaling: ITU-T I.450 (also known as ITU-T Q.930) and ITU-T I.451 (also known as ITU-T Q.931). Together, these protocols support user-to-user, circuit-switched, and packet-switched connections. A variety of call establishment, call termination, information, and miscellaneous messages are specified, including setup, connect, release, user information, cancel, status, and disconnect. Figure 11-6 shows the typical stages of an ISDN circuit-switched call.

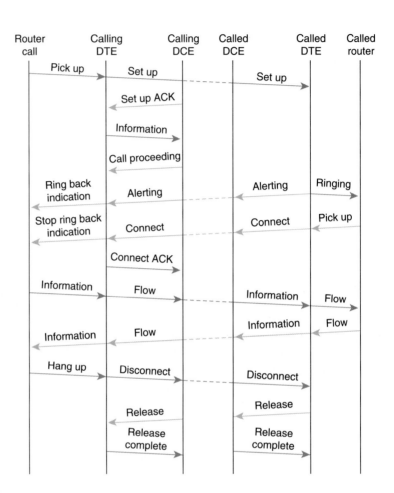

FIGURE 11-6
ISDN circuit switching includes a variety of call stages.

ISDN Encapsulation

When you're deploying remote access solutions, several encapsulation choices are available. The two most common are PPP and HDLC. ISDN defaults to HDLC. However, PPP is much more robust than HDLC because it provides an excellent mechanism for authentication and negotiation of compatible link and protocol configuration. With PPP, you can enable Challenge Handshake Authentication Protocol (CHAP), a popular authentication protocol for call screening. One of the other encapsulations for end-to-end ISDN is LAPD.

ISDN interfaces allow only a single encapsulation type. Once an ISDN call has been established, the router can use an ISDN cloud to carry any of the network-layer protocols required, such as IP to multiple destinations.

PPP

Most networking designs use PPP for encapsulation. PPP is a powerful and modular peer-to-peer mechanism used to establish data links, provide security, and encapsulate data traffic. PPP is negotiated between the networking peers each time a connection is established. PPP links can then be used by network protocols such as IP and IPX to establish network connectivity.

PPP is an open standard specified by RFC 1661. PPP was designed with several features that make it particularly useful in remote access applications. PPP uses Link Control Protocol (LCP) to initially establish the link and agree on configuration. There are built-in security features in the protocol; Password Authentication Protocol (PAP) and CHAP make robust security design easier.

PPP consists of several components:

- PPP framing—RFC 1662 discusses the implementation of PPP in HDLC-like framing. There are differences in the way PPP is implemented on asynchronous and synchronous links.

  When one end of the link uses synchronous PPP (such as an ISDN router) and the other uses asynchronous PPP (such as an ISDN TA connected to a PC serial port), two techniques are available to provide framing compatibility. The preferable method is to enable synchronous-to-asynchronous PPP frame conversion in the ISDN TA.

- LCP—PPP LCP provides a method of establishing, configuring, maintaining, and terminating a point-to-point connection. Before any network-layer datagrams (for example, IP) can be exchanged, LCP must first open the connection and negotiate configuration parameters. This phase is complete when a configuration acknowledgment frame has been both sent and received.

- PPP authentication—PPP authentication is used to provide primary security on ISDN and other PPP encapsulated links. The PPP authentication protocols (PAP and CHAP) are defined in RFC 1334 (and you can find more information about them in Chapter 10, "PPP"). After LCP has established the PPP connection, you can implement an optional authentication protocol before proceeding to the negotiation and establishment of the Network Control Programs. If authentication is needed, it must be negotiated as an option at the LCP establishment phase. Authentication can be bidirectional (each side authenticates the other) or unidirectional (one side, typically the called side, authenticates the other).

PPP authentication is enabled with the `ppp authentication` interface command. PAP and CHAP can be used to authenticate the remote connection. CHAP is considered a superior authentication protocol because it uses a three-way handshake to avoid sending the password in cleartext on the PPP link.

ISDN Uses

ISDN has many uses in networking, as shown in Figure 11-7. The following sections discuss the following ISDN uses:

- Remote access
- Remote nodes
- Small office/home office (SOHO) connectivity

FIGURE 11-7
One use of ISDN is for SOHO dialup connectivity.

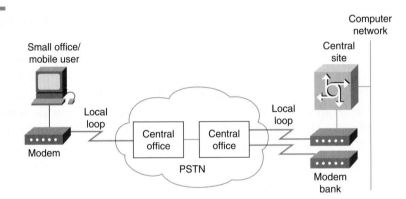

Remote Access

Remote access involves connecting users located at remote locations through dialup connections. The remote location can be a telecommuter's home, a mobile user's hotel room, or a small remote office. The dialup connection can be made via an analog connection using basic telephone service or via ISDN. Connectivity is affected by speed, cost, distance, and availability.

Remote access links generally represent the lowest-speed link in the enterprise. Any improvements in speed are desirable. The cost of remote access tends to be relatively low, especially for basic telephone service. ISDN service fees can vary widely, and they often depend on the geographic area, service availability, and billing method. There may be distance limitations, such as being out of a geographic range, with regard to dialup services, especially with ISDN.

Remote Nodes

With the remote nodes method, as shown in Figure 11-8, the users connect to the local LAN at the central site for the duration of the call. Aside from having a lower-speed connection, the user sees the same environment the local user sees. The connection to the LAN is typically through an access server. This device usually combines the functions of a modem and those of a router. When the remote user is logged in, he or she can access servers at the local LAN as if they were local.

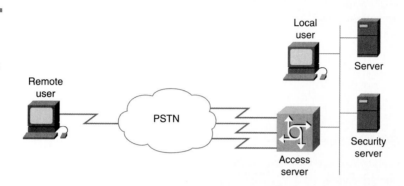

FIGURE 11-8
With ISDN, a remote user can appear as a network node.

This method offers many advantages. It is the most secure and flexible, and it is the most scalable. Only one PC is required for the remote user, and many client software solutions are available. The only additional hardware required at the remote location is a modem. The main disadvantage of this method is the additional administrative overhead required to support the remote user. Because of its many advantages, this solution is used in the remainder of the design examples in this chapter.

The full-time telecommuter/teleworker is one who normally works out of the home. This user is usually a power user who needs access to the enterprise networks for large amounts of time. This connection should be reliable and available at all times. Such a requirement would generally point to ISDN as the connection method, as shown in Figure 11-9. With this solution, the ISDN connection can be used to service any phone needs, as well as to connect the workstation.

Washington Project: ISDN Requirement
A small remote site will require connectivity to the Washington School District WAN from time to time. You should use ISDN technology to make the small site a remote node on the WAN.

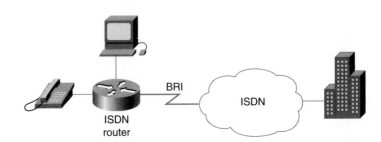

FIGURE 11-9
For an ISDN
connection,
components
include an
ISDN router
and client soft-
ware.

SOHO Connectivity

A small office or home office consisting of a few users requires a connection
that provides faster, more reliable connectivity than an analog dialup connection. In the configuration shown in Figure 11-10, all the users at the remote
location have equal access to services located at the corporate office through
an ISDN router. This offers to the casual or full-time SOHO sites the capability to connect to the corporate site or the Internet at much higher speeds than
are available over phone lines and modems.

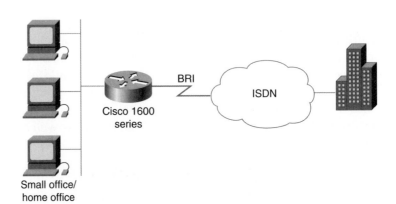

FIGURE 11-10
SOHO sites can
be supported
economically
with ISDN.

SOHO designs typically involve dialup only (SOHO-initiated connections)
and can take advantage of emerging address translation technology to simplify
design and support. Using these features, the SOHO site can support multiple
devices, but appears as a single IP address.

FIGURE 11-13
The BRI local
loop is con-
nected to ISDN.

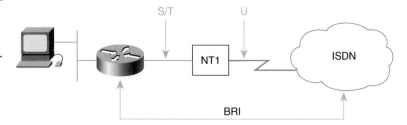

BRI Hardware

Two common types of ISDN CPE are available for BRI services: LAN routers and PC TAs. Some BRI devices offer integrated NT1s and integrated TAs for analog telephones.

ISDN LAN routers provide routing between ISDN BRI and the LAN by using dial-on-demand routing (DDR). DDR automatically establishes and releases circuit-switched calls, providing transparent connectivity to remote sites based on networking traffic. DDR also controls establishment and release of secondary B channels based on load thresholds. Multilink PPP is used to provide bandwidth aggregation when using multiple B channels. Some ISDN applications may require the SOHO user to take direct control over ISDN calls.

PC TAs connect to PC workstations either by the PC bus or externally through the communications ports (such as RS-232) and can be used similarly to analog (such as V.34) internal and external modems.

PC TAs can provide a single PC user with direct control over ISDN session initiation and release, similar to using an analog modem. Automated mechanisms must be provided to support the addition and removal of the secondary B channel. Cisco 200 Series PC cards can provide ISDN services to a PC.

ISDN Configuration Tasks

You must specify global and interface parameters to prepare the router for operation in an ISDN environment.

Global parameter tasks include the following:

- Select the switch that matches the ISDN provider's switch at the CO. This requirement is necessary because, despite standards, signaling specifics differ regionally and nationally.

- Set destination details. This involves indicating static routes from the router to other ISDN destinations and establishing the criteria for interesting packets in the router that initiate an ISDN call to the appropriate destination.

Interface parameter tasks include the following:

- Select interface specifications. Specify the interface type BRI and the number for this ISDN BRI port. The interface uses an IP address and subnet mask.

- Configure ISDN addressing with DDR dialer information and any ID supplied by the ISDN service provider. Indicate that the interface is part of the dialer group, using the interesting packets set globally. Additional commands place the ISDN call to the appropriate destination.

- Following interface configuration, you can define optional features, including time to wait for the ISDN carrier to respond to the call and seconds of idle time before the router times out and drops the call.

- Next, BRI configuration involves configuration of ISDN, switch type, and ISDN SPIDs. The following section provides examples and descriptions of ISDN configuration tasks.

Engineering Journal: ISDN Commands

The **interface bri** *interface-number* command designates the interface used for ISDN on a router acting as a TE1. If the router does not have a native BRI (that is, it is a TE2 device), it must use an external ISDN terminal adapter. On a TE2 router, use the command **interface serial** *interface-number*.

Use the **encapsulation ppp** command if you want PPP encapsulation for your ISDN interface. This is the case if you want any of the rich LCP options that PPP offers (for example, CHAP authentication). You must use PPP PAP or CHAP if you will receive calls from more than one dialup source.

Configuring ISDN BRI

To configure BRI and enter interface configuration mode, use the **interface bri** command in global configuration mode. The full syntax of the command is

```
interface bri number
```

The *number* argument describes the port, connector, or interface card number. The numbers are assigned at the factory at the time of installation or when added to a system, and can be displayed by using the **show interfaces** command.

Example 11-1 configures BRI 0 to call and receive calls from two sites, use PPP encapsulation on outgoing calls, and use CHAP authentication on incoming calls.

Example 11-1   Receiving Calls from Two Sites
```
interface bri 0
encapsulation ppp
no keepalive
dialer map ip 131.108.36.10 name EB1 234
dialer map ip 131.108 36.9 name EB2 456
dialer-group 1
isdn spid1 0146334600
isdn spid2 0146334610
isdn T200 1000
ppp authentication chap
```

Defining a Switch Type

Before using ISDN BRI, you must define the `isdn switch-type` global command to specify the CO switch to which the router connects.

The Cisco IOS command output shown in Example 11-2 helps illustrate the supported BRI switch types (in North America, the most common types are 5ESS, DMS100, and NI-1).

Example 11-2   Supported BRI Switch Types
```
kdt-3640(config)# isdn switch-type ?
  basic-1tr6    1TR6 switch type for Germany
  basic-5ess    AT&T 5ESS switch type for the U.S.
  basic-dms100  Northern DMS-100 switch type
  basic-net3    NET3 switch type for the UK and Europe
  basic-ni1     National ISDN-1 switch type
  basic-nwnet3  NET3 switch type for Norway
  basic-nznet3  NET3 switch type for New Zealand
  basic-ts013   TS013 switch type for Australia
  ntt           NTT switch type for Japan
  vn2           VN2 switch type for France
  vn3           VN3 and VN4 switch types for France
```

> **NOTE**
>
> For Cisco IOS releases up to 11.2, the configured ISDN switch type is a global command (note that this also means you cannot use BRI and PRI cards in the same Cisco IOS chassis). In Cisco IOS 11.3T or later, multiple switch types in a single Cisco IOS chassis are supported.

To configure a CO switch on the ISDN interface, use the `isdn switch-type` command in global configuration command mode. The full syntax of the command is

```
isdn switch-type switch-type
```

The argument `switch-type` indicates the service provider switch type. `switch-type` defaults to **none**, which disables the switch on the ISDN interface. To disable the switch on the ISDN interface, specify `isdn switch-type none`.

The following example configures the AT&T 5ESS switch type:

```
isdn switch-type basic-5ess
```

Defining SPIDs

SPIDs allow multiple ISDN devices, such as voice and data devices, to share the local loop. In many cases, such as when you're configuring the router to connect to a DMS-100, you need to input the SPIDs.

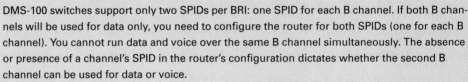

Engineering Journal: DMS-100 Switches

DMS-100 switches support only two SPIDs per BRI: one SPID for each B channel. If both B channels will be used for data only, you need to configure the router for both SPIDs (one for each B channel). You cannot run data and voice over the same B channel simultaneously. The absence or presence of a channel's SPID in the router's configuration dictates whether the second B channel can be used for data or voice.

Remember that ISDN is typically used for dialup connectivity. The SPIDs are processed during each call setup operation.

You use the **isdn spid2** command in interface configuration mode to define at the router the SPID number that has been assigned by the ISDN service provider for the B2 channel. The full syntax of the command is

```
isdn spid2 spid-number [ldn]
```

You use the **no isdn spid2** command to disable the specified SPID, thereby preventing access to the switch. If you include the LDN in the **no** form of this command, the access to the switch is permitted, but the other B channel might not be able to receive incoming calls. The full syntax of the command is

```
no isdn spid2 spid-number [ldn]
```

The *spid-number* argument indicates the number identifying the service to which you have subscribed. This value is assigned by the ISDN service provider and is usually a 10-digit telephone number with some extra digits. By default, no SPID number is defined.

Engineering Journal: The ldn Argument

The *ldn* argument is optional and indicates the local directory number (LDN), as delivered by the service provider in the incoming setup message. This is a seven-digit number also assigned by the service provider.

This command is required for DMS-100 and National ISDN-1 (NI-1) switches only. You must define the LDN if you want to receive any incoming calls on the B1 channel. The ISDN switch checks for the LDN to determine whether both channels can be used to transmit and receive data. If the LDN is not present, then only the B2 channel can be used for full-duplex communication. However, the other channel can still be used for making outgoing calls.

The following example defines, on the router, a SPID and an LDN for the B2 channel:

```
isdn spid2 415555121202 5551214
```

Each SPID points to line setup and configuration information. When a device attempts to connect to the ISDN network, it performs a D channel Layer 2 initialization process that causes a TEI to be assigned to the device. The device then attempts D channel Layer 3 initialization. If SPIDs are necessary but not configured or are configured incorrectly on the device, the Layer 3 initialization fails, and the ISDN services cannot be used.

There is no standard format for SPIDs. As a result, SPID numbers vary depending on the switch vendor and the carrier.

A typical Cisco IOS SPID configuration is as follows:

```
interface bri 0
isdn spid1 0835866201 8358662
isdn spid2 0835866401 8358664
```

These commands also specify the LDN, which is the seven-digit number assigned by the service provider and used for call routing. The LDN is not necessary for establishing ISDN-based connections, but it must be specified if you want to receive incoming calls on a B2 channel. The LDN is required only when two SPIDs are configured (for example, when you're connecting to a DMS or NI1 switch). Each SPID is associated with an LDN. Configuring the LDN causes incoming calls to the B2 channel to be answered properly. If the LDN is not configured, incoming calls to the B2 channel might fail.

BRI Configuration Example

This section is based on the output shown in Example 11-3, which shows a BRI configuration.

Example 11-3 A Sample BRI Configuration

```
! set up switch type, static route and dialer for ISDN on Cisco A
isdn switch-type basic-5ess
ip route 172.16.29.0.255.255.255.0 172.16.126.2
dialer-list 1 protocol ip permit
!
! configure BRI interface for PPP; set address and mask
interface bri 0
ip address 172.16.126.1 255.255.255.0
!
! refer to protocols in dialer-list to identify interesting packets
dialer-group 1
!
! select call start, stop, and other ISDN provider details
dialer wait-for-carrier time 15
dialer idle-timeout 300
isdn spid1 0145678912
! call setup details for router
dialer map ip 172.16.126.2 name cisco-b 445
```

The following is a description of the commands and parameters shown in Example 11-3:

Command/Parameter	Description
isdn switch-type	Selects the AT&T switch as the CO ISDN switch type for this router.
dialer-list 1 protocol ip per-mit	Associates permitted IP traffic with the dialer group 1. The router will not start an ISDN call for any other packet traffic with dialer group 1.
interface bri 0	Selects an interface with TA and other ISDN functions on the router.
encapsulation ppp	Uses PPP encapsulation on the selected interface.
dialer-group 1	Associates the BRI 0 interface with dialing access group 1.
dialer wait-for-carrier-time	Specifies a 15-second maximum time for the provider to respond after the call initiates.
dialer idle-timeout	The number of seconds of idle time before the router drops the ISDN call. Note that a long duration is configured to delay termination.

The following is a description of the *dialer map* parameters shown in Example 11-3:

dialer map Parameter	Description
ip	Name of protocol.
172.16.126.2	Destination address.
name	An identification for the remote side router. Refers to the called router.
445	ISDN connection number used to reach this DDR destination.

Confirming BRI Operations

To confirm BRI operations, use the **show isdn status** command to inspect the status of your BRI interfaces. In Example 11-4, the TEIs have been successfully negotiated and ISDN Layer 3 (end-to-end) is ready to make or receive calls.

Example 11-4   `show isdn status` **Command Output**

```
kdt-1600#show isdn status
The current ISDN Switchtype = basic-ni1
ISDN BRI0 interface
    Layer 1 Status:
        ACTIVE
    Layer 2 Status:
        TEI = 109, State = MULTIPLE_FRAME_ESTABLISHED
        TEI = 110, State = MULTIPLE_FRAME_ESTABLISHED
    Spid Status:
        TEI 109, ces = 1, state = 8(established)
            spid1 configured, spid1 sent, spid1 valid
            Endpoint ID Info: epsf = 0, usid = 1, tid = 1
        TEI 110, ces = 2, state = 8(established)
            spid2 configured, spid2 sent, spid2 valid
            Endpoint ID Info: epsf = 0, usid = 3, tid = 1
    Layer 3 Status:
        0 Active Layer 3 Call(s)
    Activated dsl 0 CCBs = 0
    Total Allocated ISDN CCBs = 0
```

Dial-on-Demand Routing

When building networking applications, you must determine how ISDN connections will be initiated, established, and maintained. DDR creates connectivity between ISDN sites by establishing and releasing circuit-switched connections as needed by networking traffic. DDR can provide network routing and directory services in numerous ways to provide the illusion of full-time connectivity over circuit-switched connections.

To provide total control over when the DDR connections are made, you must carefully consider the following issues:

- Which sites can initiate connections based on traffic?

- Is dialout required to SOHO sites? Is dialout required for network or workstation management? Which sites can terminate connections based on idle links?

- How are directory services and routing tables supported across an idle connection?

- What applications need to be supported over DDR connections? For how many users do they need to be supported?

- What unexpected protocols might cause DDR connections? Can they be filtered?

Verifying DDR Operation

The following commands can be used to verify that DDR is operating:

Command	Description
ping/telnet	When you ping or Telnet a remote site or when interesting traffic triggers a link, the router sends a change in link status message to the console.
show dialer	Used to obtain general diagnostic information about an interface configured for DDR, such as the number of times the dialer string has been successfully reached, and the idle timer and the fast idle timer values for each B channel. Current call-specific information is also provided, such as the length of the call and the number and name of the device to which the interface is currently connected.
show isdn active	Use this command when using ISDN. It shows that a call is in progress and lists the numbered call.
show isdn status	Used to show the statistics of the ISDN connection.
show ip route	Displays the routes known to the router, including static and dynamically learned routes.

Troubleshooting DDR Operation

The following commands can be used to troubleshoot DDR operation:

Command	Description
debug isdn q921	Verifies that you have a connection to the ISDN switch.
debug dialer	Shows such information as what number the interface is dialing.
clear interface	Used to clear a call that is in progress. In a troubleshooting situation, it is sometimes useful to clear historical statistics to track the current number of successful calls relative to failures. Use this command with care. It sometimes requires that you clear both the local and remote routers.

You troubleshoot SPID problems by using the **debug isdn q921** command. In Example 11-5, you can see that **isdn spid1** was rejected by the ISDN switch.

Example 11-5 Troubleshooting SPID Problems

```
kdt-1600# debug isdn q921
ISDN Q921 packets debugging is on
kdt-1600# clear interface bri 0
```

```
kdt-1600#
*Mar  1 00:09:03.728: ISDN BR0: TX -> SABMEp sapi = 0  tei = 113
*Mar  1 00:09:04.014: ISDN BR0: RX <- IDREM  ri = 0  ai = 127
*Mar  1 00:09:04.018: %ISDN-6-LAYER2DOWN:
        Layer 2 for Interface BRI0, TEI 113 changed to down
*Mar  1 00:09:04.022: %ISDN-6-LAYER2DOWN:
        Layer 2 for Interface BR0, TEI 113 changed to down
*Mar  1 00:09:04.046: ISDN BR0: TX -> IDREQ  ri = 44602  ai = 127
*Mar  1 00:09:04.049: ISDN BR0: RX <- IDCKRQ  ri = 0  ai = 113
*Mar  1 00:09:05.038: ISDN BR0: RX <- IDCKRQ  ri = 0  ai = 113
*Mar  1 00:09:06.030: ISDN BR0: TX -> IDREQ  ri = 37339  ai = 127
*Mar  1 00:09:06.149: ISDN BR0: RX <- IDREM  ri = 0  ai = 113
*Mar  1 00:09:06.156: ISDN BR0: RX <- IDASSN  ri = 37339  ai = 114
*Mar  1 00:09:06.164: ISDN BR0: TX -> SABMEp sapi = 0  tei = 114
*Mar  1 00:09:06.188: ISDN BR0: RX <- UAf sapi = 0  tei = 114
*Mar  1 00:09:06.188: %ISDN-6-LAYER2UP:
        Layer 2 for Interface BR0, TEI 114 changed to up
*Mar  1 00:09:06.200: ISDN BR0: TX ->
        INFOc sapi = 0  tei = 114  ns = 0  nr = 0  i =
                0x08007B3A06383932393833
*Mar  1 00:09:06.276: ISDN BR0: RX <-
        INFOc sapi = 0  tei = 114  ns = 0  nr = 1  i =
                0x08007B080382E43A
*Mar  1 00:09:06.283: ISDN BR0: TX -> RRr sapi = 0  tei = 114  nr = 1
*Mar  1 00:09:06.287: %ISDN-4-INVALID_SPID: Interface BR0,
    Spid1 was rejected
```

You check the status of the Cisco 700 ISDN line with the `show status` command, as shown in Example 11-6.

Example 11-6   Checking the Status of the Cisco 700 ISDN Line

```
kdt-776> show status
Status    01/04/1995 18:15:15
Line Status
  Line Activated
  Terminal Identifier Assigned    SPID Accepted
  Terminal Identifier Assigned    SPID Accepted
Port Status    Interface Connection Link
  Ch:  1      Waiting for Call
  Ch:  2      Waiting for Call
```

Summary

- ISDN provides an integrated voice/data capability that uses the public switched network.

- ISDN components include terminals, TAs, NT devices, and ISDN switches.

- ISDN reference points define logical interfaces between functional groupings, such as TAs and NT1s.

- ISDN is addressed by a suite of ITU-T standards, spanning the physical, data link, and network layers of the OSI reference model.

- The two most common encapsulation choices for ISDN are PPP and HDLC.
- ISDN has many uses, including remote access, remote nodes, and SOHO connectivity.
- There are two ISDN services: BRI and PRI.
- ISDN BRI delivers a total bandwidth of a 144-kbps line into three separate channels.
- BRI configuration involves the configuration of a BRI interface, an ISDN switch type, and ISDN SPIDs.
- DDR establishes and releases circuit switched connections as needed.

Washington School District Project Task: ISDN

In this chapter, you have learned concepts and configuration processes that will help you implement IGRP as the routing protocol in the Washington School District network. As part of the ISDN configuration and implementation, you need to complete the following tasks:

1. Document changes in the router configurations in order to implement ISDN on the routers.

2. Document the use of ISDN in the WAN design, including providing the following:

- A drawing of the implementation with all major reference points
- A description of overall bandwidth available to the site and how data communications will take place
- A description of all data communications equipment needed to accomplish the implementation

3. Document the router commands needed to implement ISDN on the router.

Chapter Review

Complete all the review questions to test your understanding of the topics and concepts covered in this chapter. Answers are listed in Appendix A, "Chapter Review Answer Key."

1. What is the top speed at which ISDN operates?

2. How many B channels does ISDN use?

3. How many D channels does ISDN use?

4. The ISDN service provider must provide the phone number and what type of identification number?

5. Which channel does ISDN use for call setup?

6. At the central site, what device can be used to provide the connection for dialup access?

   A. Switch

   B. Router

   C. Bridge

   D. Hub

7. For which of the following locations would ISDN service not be adequate?

   A. A large concentration of users at a site

   B. A small office

   C. A single-user site

   D. None of the above

8. Protocols that begin with E are used to specify what?

   A. Telephone network standards

   B. Switching and signaling

   C. ISDN concepts

   D. It is not used with ISDN

9. If you want to use CHAP for authentication when using ISDN, what protocol should you select?

   A. HDLC

   B. SLIP

C. PPP

D. PAP

10. On a router, which of the following commands do you use to set the ISDN switch type?

A. Router> `isdn switch-type`

B. Router# `isdn switch-type`

C. Router(config-if)# `isdn switch-type`

D. Router(config)# `isdn switch-type`

Key Terms

2B+D   In reference to the ISDN BRI service, two B channels and one D channel.

B channel (bearer channel)   In ISDN, a full-duplex, 64-kbps channel used to send user data.

BRI (Basic Rate Interface)   An ISDN interface composed of two B channels and one D channel for circuit-switched communication of voice, video, and data.

CO (central office)   The local telephone company office to which all local loops in a given area connect and in which circuit switching of subscriber lines occurs.

CPE (customer premises equipment)   Terminating equipment, such as terminals, telephones, and modems, supplied by the telephone company, installed at customer sites, and connected to the telephone company network.

D channel (delta channel)   A full-duplex, 16-kbps (BRI) or 64-kbps (PRI) ISDN channel.

ISDN (Integrated Services Digital Network)   A communication protocol, offered by telephone companies, that permits telephone networks to carry data, voice, and other source traffic.

LAPB (Link Access Procedure, Balanced)   A data link-layer protocol in the X.25 protocol stack. LAPB is a bit-oriented protocol derived from HDLC.

LAPD (Link Access Procedure on the D channel)   An ISDN data link-layer protocol for the D channel. LAPD was derived from LAPB and is designed primarily to satisfy the signaling requirements of ISDN basic access. Defined by ITU-T Recommendations Q.920 and Q.921.

NT1 (network termination type 1)   A device that connects four-wire ISDN subscriber wiring to the conventional two-wire local loop facility.

NT2 (network termination type 2)   A device that directs traffic to and from different subscriber devices and the NT1. The NT2 is an intelligent device that performs switching and concentrating.

PBX (private branch exchange)   A digital or an analog telephone switchboard located on the subscriber premises and used to connect private and public telephone networks.

PRI (Primary Rate Interface)   An ISDN interface to primary rate access. Primary rate access consists of a single 64-kbps D channel plus 23 (T1) or 30 (E1) B channels for voice or data.

Q.931   A protocol that recommends a network layer between the terminal endpoint and the local ISDN switch. Q.931 does not impose an end-to-end recommendation. The various ISDN providers and switch types can and do use various implementations of Q.931.

reference point   A specification that defines the connection between specific devices, depending on their function in the end-to-end connection.

signaling   In the ISDN context, the process of call setup used, such as call establishment, call termination, information, and miscellaneous messages, including setup, connect, release, user information, cancel, status, and disconnect.

SOHO (small office/home office)   A small office or home office consisting of a few users requiring a connection that provides faster, more reliable connectivity than an analog dialup connection.

SPID (service profile identifier)   A number that some service providers use to define the services to which an ISDN device subscribes. The ISDN device uses the SPID when accessing the switch that initializes the connection to a service provider.

TA (terminal adapter)   A device used to connect ISDN BRI connections to existing interfaces, such as EIA/TIA-232. Essentially, an ISDN modem.

TE1 (terminal equipment type 1)   A device that is compatible with the ISDN network. A TE1 connects to a network termination of either type 1 or type 2.

TE2 (terminal equipment type 2)   A device that is not compatible with ISDN and requires a terminal adapter.

UNI (User-Network Interface)   A specification that defines an interoperability standard for the interface between products (a router or a switch) located in a private network and the switches located within the public carrier networks. Also used to describe similar connections in Frame Relay networks.

Objectives

After reading this chapter, you will be able to

- Describe the operation of Frame Relay
- Describe the functions of DLCIs in Frame Relay
- Describe Cisco's implementation of Frame Relay
- Describe the process for configuring and verifying Frame Relay
- Describe the Frame Relay subinterfaces
- Describe how Frame Relay uses subinterfaces to solve the problem of split horizon

Chapter 12

Frame Relay

Introduction

You learned about Point-to-Point Protocol (PPP) in Chapter 10, "PPP," and Integrated Services Digital Network (ISDN) in Chapter 11, "ISDN." You learned that PPP and ISDN are two types of WAN technologies that can be implemented to solve connectivity issues for locations that need access to geographically distant locations. In this chapter, you will learn about another type of WAN technology, Frame Relay, that can be implemented to solve connectivity issues for users who need access to geographically distant locations.

In this chapter, you will learn about Frame Relay services, standards, components, and operation. In addition, this chapter describes the configuration tasks for Frame Relay service, along with the commands for monitoring and maintaining a Frame Relay connection.

Washington Project: Implementing Frame Relay
In this chapter, you will learn the concepts and configuration procedures that enable you to add Frame Relay to the Washington School District network design. In addition, you will learn the steps to implement a Frame Relay link to the Internet per the specification in the technical requirements document. This is the final step in your design and implementation of the district network.

Frame Relay Technology Overview

Frame Relay is a Consultative Committee for International Telegraph and Telephone (CCITT) and American National Standards Institute (ANSI) standard that defines the process for sending data over a public data network (PDN). It is a data-link technology that is streamlined to provide high performance and efficiency. It operates at the physical and data link layers of the OSI reference model, but it relies on upper-layer protocols such as TCP for error correction.

Frame Relay was originally conceived as a protocol for use over ISDN interfaces. Today, Frame Relay is an industry-standard, switched data link-layer protocol that handles multiple virtual circuits using High-Level Data Link Control (HDLC) encapsulation between connected devices. Frame Relay uses virtual circuits to make connections through a connection-oriented service.

The network providing the Frame Relay interface can be either a carrier-provided public network or a network of privately owned equipment, serving a single enterprise. Frame Relay provides a packet-switching data communication capability that is used across the interface between user devices (such as routers, bridges, and host machines) and network equipment (such as switching nodes). As you have learned, user devices are often referred to as data terminal equipment (DTE), whereas network equipment that interfaces to DTE is often referred to as data circuit-terminating equipment (DCE), as shown in Figure 12-1.

FIGURE 12-1
Frame Relay defines the interconnection process between a router and the service provider's local access switching equipment.

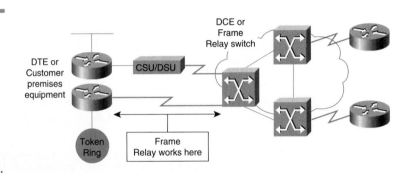

Frame Relay Terminology

Following are some terms that are used in this chapter to discuss Frame Relay:

- Local access rate—The clock speed (port speed) of the connection (local loop) to the Frame Relay cloud. It is the rate at which data travels into or out of the network.

- data-link connection identifier (DLCI)—As shown in Figure 12-2, a DLCI is number that identifies the logical circuit between the source and destination device. The Frame Relay switch maps the DLCIs between each pair of routers to create a permanent virtual circuit.

- Local management interface (LMI)—A signaling standard between the customer premises equipment (CPE) device and the Frame Relay switch that is responsible for managing the connection and maintaining status between the devices. LMIs can include support for a keepalive mechanism, which verifies that data is flowing; a multicast mechanism, which can provide the network server with its local DLCI; multicast addressing, providing a few DLCIs to be used as multicast (multiple destination) addresses and the ability to give DLCIs global (whole Frame Relay network) significance, rather than just local significance (DLCIs used only to the local switch); and a status mechanism, which provides an ongoing status on the

DLCIs known to the switch. There are several LMI types, and routers need to be told which LMI type is being used. Three types of LMIs are supported: `cisco`, `ansi`, and `q933a`.

FIGURE 12-2
The DLCI value identifies the logical connection that is multiplexed into the physical channel.

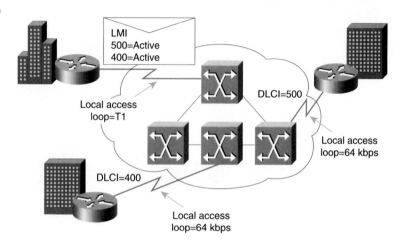

- Committed information rate (CIR)—The CIR is the guaranteed rate, in bits per second, that the service provider commits to providing.

- Committed burst—The maximum number of bits that the switch agrees to transfer during any committed rate measurement interval.

- Excess burst—The maximum number of uncommitted bits that the Frame Relay switch attempts to transfer beyond the CIR. Excess burst is dependent on the service offerings available by the vendor, but is typically limited to the port speed of the local access loop.

- Forward explicit congestion notification (FECN)—When a Frame Relay switch recognizes congestion in the network, it sends an FECN packet to the destination device, indicating that congestion has occurred.

- Backward explicit congestion notification (BECN)—As shown in Figure 12-3, when a Frame Relay switch recognizes congestion in the network, it sends a BECN packet to the source router, instructing the router to reduce the rate at which it is sending packets. If the router receives any BECNs during the current time interval, it decreases the transmit rate by 25%.

- Discard eligibility (DE) indicator—When the router detects network congestion, the Frame Relay switch will drop packets with the DE bit set first. The DE bit is set on the oversubscribed traffic (that is, the traffic that was received after the CIR was met).

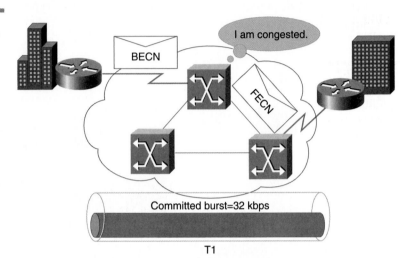

FIGURE 12-3
A Frame Relay switch sends BECN packets to reduce congestion.

Frame Relay Operation

Frame Relay can be used as an interface to either a publicly available carrier-provided service or to a network of privately owned equipment. You deploy a public Frame Relay service by putting Frame Relay switching equipment in the central office of a telecommunications carrier. In this case, users get economic benefits from traffic-sensitive charging rates, and don't have to spend the time and effort to administer and maintain the network equipment and service.

No standards for interconnecting equipment inside a Frame Relay network currently exist. Therefore, the support of Frame Relay interfaces does not necessarily dictate that the Frame Relay protocol is used between the network devices. Thus, traditional circuit switching, packet switching, or a hybrid approach combining these technologies can be used, as shown in Figure 12-4.

The lines that connect user devices to the network equipment can operate at a speed selected from a broad range of data rates. Speeds between 56 kbps and 2 Mbps are typical, although Frame Relay can support lower and higher speeds.

Frame Relay DLCIs

As an interface between user and network equipment (see Figure 12-5), Frame Relay provides a means for multiplexing many logical data conversations (referred to as *virtual circuits*) through a shared physical medium by assigning DLCIs to each pair of DTE devices.

FIGURE 12-4
You can use Frame Relay as an interface to a network by interconnecting equipment such as Frame Relay switches and routers.

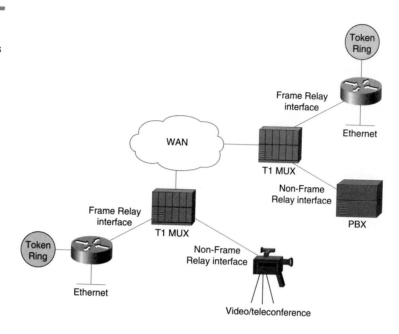

FIGURE 12-5
This single physical connection provides direct connectivity to each device on a network.

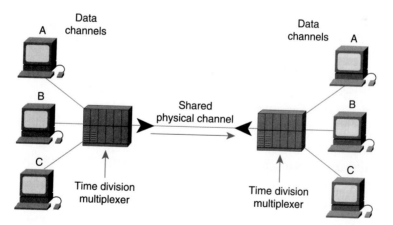

Frame Relay's multiplexing provides more flexible and efficient use of available bandwidth. Therefore, Frame Relay allows users to share bandwidth at a reduced cost. For example, say you have a WAN using Frame Relay, and the Frame Relay is equivalent to a group of roads. The phone company usually owns and maintains the roads. You can choose to rent out a road (or path) exclusively for your company (dedicated), or you can pay less to rent a path on shared roads. Of course, Frame Relay could also be run entirely over private networks; however, it's rarely used in this manner.

Frame Relay standards address permanent virtual circuits (PVCs) that are administratively configured and managed in a Frame Relay network. Frame Relay PVCs are identified by DLCIs, as shown in Figure 12-6. Frame Relay DLCIs have local significance. That is, the values themselves are not unique in the Frame Relay WAN. Two DTE devices connected by a virtual circuit might use a different DLCI value to refer to the same connection, as shown in Figure 12-6.

FIGURE 12-6
The end devices at two different ends of a connection can use different DLCI numbers to refer to the same connection.

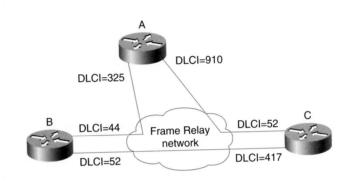

When Frame Relay provides a means for multiplexing many logical data conversations, first, the service provider's switching equipment constructs a table mapping a DLCI value to outbound ports. When a frame is received, the switching device analyzes the connection identifier and delivers the frame to the associated outbound port. Finally, the complete path to the destination is established before the first frame is sent.

Frame Relay Frame Format

The Frame Relay frame format is shown in Figure 12-7. The flag fields indicate the beginning and end of the frame. Following the leading flag field are 2 bytes of address information. 10 bits of these 2 bytes make up the actual circuit ID (that is, the DLCI).

The following are the Frame Relay frame fields:

- Flag—Indicates the beginning and the end of the Frame Relay frame.
- Address—Indicates the length of the Address field. Although Frame Relay addresses are currently all 2 bytes long, the address bits allow for the possible extension of address lengths in the future. The eighth bit of each byte of the address field is used to indicate the address. The address contains the following information:
  — DLCI Value —Indicates the DLCI value. Consists of the first 10 bits of the Address field.

— Congestion Control—The last 3 bits in the address field, which control the Frame Relay congestion notification mechanisms. These are the FECN, BECN, and discard eligible (DE) bits..

■ Data—Variable-length field that contains encapsulated upper-layer data.

■ FCS—Frame check sequence (FCS), used to ensure the integrity of transmitted data.

FIGURE 12-7
The flag fields delimit the beginning and end of the frame.

Field length, in bytes	1	2	Variable	2	1
	Flag	Address, including DLCI, FECN, BECN, and DE bits	Data	FCS	Flag

Frame Relay Addressing

In Figure 12-8, assume two PVCs, one between Atlanta and Los Angeles, and one between San Jose and Pittsburgh. Los Angeles uses DLCI 22 to refer to its PVC with Atlanta, whereas Atlanta refers to the same PVC as DLCI 82. Similarly, San Jose uses DLCI 22 to refer to its PVC with Pittsburgh. The network uses internal mechanisms to keep the two locally significant PVC identifiers distinct.

FIGURE 12-8
An example of the use of DLCIs in a Frame Relay network.

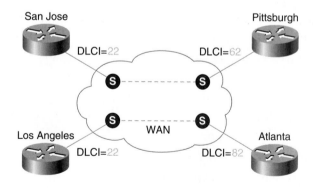

Cisco's Implementation of Frame Relay: LMI

There was a major development in Frame Relay's history in 1990, when Cisco Systems, StrataCom, Northern Telecom, and Digital Equipment Corporation formed a group to focus on Frame Relay technology development and accelerate the introduction of interoperable Frame Relay products. This group developed a specification conforming to the basic Frame Relay protocol, but extended it with features that provide additional capabilities for complex internetworking environments. These Frame Relay extensions are referred to as LMI.

LMI Operation

The main purpose of the LMI process is

- To determine the operational status of the various PVCs that the router knows about
- To transmit keepalive packets to ensure that the PVC stays up and does not shut down due to inactivity (see Figure 12-9)
- To tell the router what PVCs are available
- Three LMI types can be invoked by the router commands: `ansi`, `cisco`, and `q933a`.

FIGURE 12-9
LMI provides for management of connections.

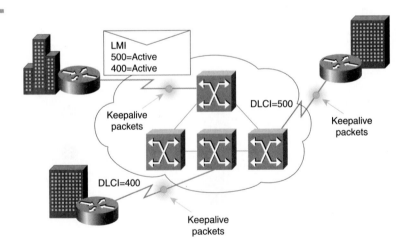

LMI Extensions

In addition to the basic Frame Relay protocol functions for transferring data, the Frame Relay specification includes LMI extensions that make supporting large, complex internetworks easier. Some LMI extensions are referred to as *common* and are expected to be implemented by everyone who adopts the specification. Other LMI functions are referred to as optional. A summary of the LMI extensions follows:

- Virtual circuit status messages (common)—Provide communication and synchronization between the network and the user device, periodically reporting the existence of new PVCs and the deletion of already existing PVCs, and generally providing information about PVC integrity. Virtual circuit status messages prevent the sending of data over PVCs that no longer exist.

- Multicasting (optional)—Allows a sender to transmit a single frame but have it delivered by the network to multiple recipients. Thus, multicasting supports the efficient conveyance of routing protocol messages and address resolution protocols that typically must be sent to many destinations simultaneously.

- Global addressing (optional)—Gives connection identifiers global rather than local significance, allowing them to be used to identify a specific interface to the Frame Relay network. Global addressing makes the Frame Relay network resemble a local-area network (LAN) in terms of addressing; address resolution protocols therefore perform over Frame Relay exactly as they do over a LAN.

- Simple flow control (optional)—Provides for an XON/XOFF flow control mechanism that applies to the entire Frame Relay interface. It is intended for devices whose higher layers cannot use the congestion notification bits and that need some level of flow control.

LMI Frame Format

The Frame Relay specification also includes the LMI procedures. LMI messages are sent in frames distinguished by an LMI-specific DLCIs (defined in the consortium specification as DLCI = 1023). The LMI frame format is shown in Figure 12-10.

After the flag and LMI DLCI fields, the LMI frame contains 4 mandatory bytes. The first of the mandatory bytes (*unnumbered information indicator*) has the same format as the LAPB *unnumbered information* (UI) frame indicator, with the poll/final bit set to zero. The next byte is referred to as the *protocol discriminator*, which is set to a value that indicates LMI. The third mandatory byte (*call reference*) is always filled with zeros.

The final mandatory byte is the *message type* field. Two message types have been defined: *Status-enquiry* messages and status messages. *Status* messages respond to status-enquiry messages. *Keepalives* (messages sent through a connection to ensure that both sides will continue to regard the connection as active) and PVC status messages are examples of these messages and are the common LMI features that are expected to be a part of every implementation that conforms to the Frame Relay specification.

FIGURE 12-10
In LMI frames, the basic protocol header is the same as in normal Frame Relay frames.

Together, status and status-enquiry messages help verify the integrity of logical and physical links. This information is critical in a routing environment because routing protocols make decisions based on link integrity.

Next is an information element (IE) field of a variable number of *bytes*. Following the message type field is some number of IEs. Each IE consists of a 1-byte *IE identifier*, an *IE length* field, and 1 or more bytes containing actual data.

Global Addressing

In addition to the common LMI features, several optional LMI extensions are extremely useful in an internetworking environment. The first important optional LMI extension is *global addressing*. With this extension, the values inserted in the DLCI field of a frame are globally significant addresses of individual end-user devices (for example, routers). This is implemented as shown in Figure 12-8.

As noted earlier, the basic (nonextended) Frame Relay specification supports only values of the DLCI field that identify PVCs with local significance. In this case, there are no addresses that identify network interfaces, or nodes attached to these interfaces. Because these addresses do not exist, they cannot be discovered by traditional address resolution and discovery techniques. This means that with normal Frame Relay addressing, static maps must be created to tell routers which DLCIs to use to find a remote device and its associated internetwork address.

In Figure 12-8, note that each interface has its own identifier. Suppose that Pittsburgh must send a frame to San Jose. The identifier for San Jose is 22, so Pittsburgh places the value 22 in the DLCI field and sends the frame into the

Frame Relay network. At the exit point, the DLCI field contents are changed by the network to 62 to reflect the source node of the frame. Each router interface has a distinct value as its node identifier, so individual devices can be distinguished. This permits routing in complex environments. Global addressing provides significant benefits in a large, complex network. The Frame Relay network now appears to the routers on its periphery like any LAN.

Multicasting

Multicasting is another valuable optional LMI feature. Multicast groups are designated by a series of four reserved DLCI values (1019 to 1022). Frames sent by a device using one of these reserved DLCIs are replicated by the network and sent to all exit points in the designated set. The multicasting extension also defines LMI messages that notify user devices of the addition, deletion, and presence of multicast groups. In networks that take advantage of dynamic routing, routing information must be exchanged among many routers. Routing messages can be sent efficiently by using frames with a multicast DLCI. This allows messages to be sent to specific groups of routers.

Inverse ARP

The Inverse ARP mechanism allows the router to automatically build the Frame Relay map, as shown in Figure 12-11. The router learns the DLCIs that are in use from the switch during the initial LMI exchange. The router then sends an Inverse ARP request to each DLCI for each protocol configured on the interface if the protocol is supported. The return information from the Inverse ARP is then used to build the Frame Relay map.

FIGURE 12-11
The router learns the DLCIs from the Frame Relay switch and sends and Inverse ARP request to each DLCI.

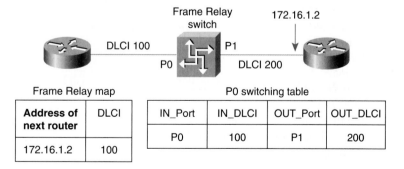

Frame Relay Mapping

The router next-hop address determined from the routing table must be resolved to a Frame Relay DLCI, as shown in Figure 12-12. The resolution is done through a data structure called a *Frame Relay map*. The routing table is then used to supply the next-hop protocol address or the DLCI for outgoing traffic. This data structure can be statically configured in the router, or the Inverse ARP feature can be used for automatic setup of the map.

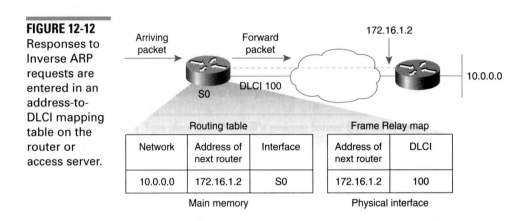

FIGURE 12-12
Responses to Inverse ARP requests are entered in an address-to-DLCI mapping table on the router or access server.

Frame Relay Switching Tables

The Frame Relay switching table consists of four entries: two for incoming port and DLCI, and two for outgoing port and DLCI, as shown in Figure 12-13. The DLCI could, therefore, be remapped as it passes through each switch; the fact that the port reference can be changed is why the DLCI does not change even though the port reference might change.

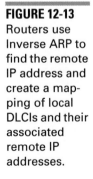
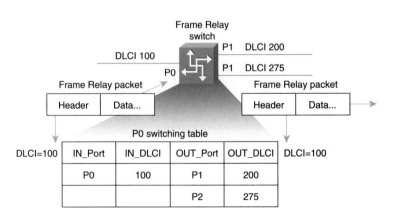

FIGURE 12-13
Routers use Inverse ARP to find the remote IP address and create a mapping of local DLCIs and their associated remote IP addresses.

Engineering Journal:
Frame Relay Operation Summary

Now that you have learned the basic Frame Relay operations, you can use the following steps, which are illustrated in Figures 12-14 and 12-15 to implement Frame Relay:

FIGURE 12-14
If Inverse ARP is not working, or the remote router does not support Inverse ARP, you need to configure the routes (that is, the DLCIs and IP addresses) of the remote routers.

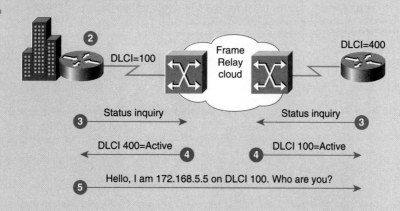

FIGURE 12-15
The router changes the status of each DLCI, based on the response from the Frame Relay switch.

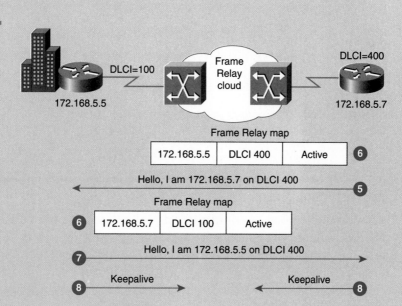

Step 1   Order Frame Relay service from a service provider, or create a private Frame Relay cloud.

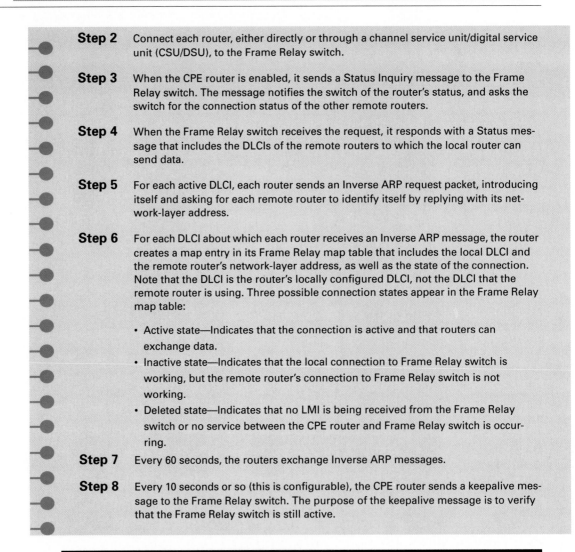

Step 2   Connect each router, either directly or through a channel service unit/digital service unit (CSU/DSU), to the Frame Relay switch.

Step 3   When the CPE router is enabled, it sends a Status Inquiry message to the Frame Relay switch. The message notifies the switch of the router's status, and asks the switch for the connection status of the other remote routers.

Step 4   When the Frame Relay switch receives the request, it responds with a Status message that includes the DLCIs of the remote routers to which the local router can send data.

Step 5   For each active DLCI, each router sends an Inverse ARP request packet, introducing itself and asking for each remote router to identify itself by replying with its network-layer address.

Step 6   For each DLCI about which each router receives an Inverse ARP message, the router creates a map entry in its Frame Relay map table that includes the local DLCI and the remote router's network-layer address, as well as the state of the connection. Note that the DLCI is the router's locally configured DLCI, not the DLCI that the remote router is using. Three possible connection states appear in the Frame Relay map table:

- Active state—Indicates that the connection is active and that routers can exchange data.
- Inactive state—Indicates that the local connection to Frame Relay switch is working, but the remote router's connection to Frame Relay switch is not working.
- Deleted state—Indicates that no LMI is being received from the Frame Relay switch or no service between the CPE router and Frame Relay switch is occurring.

Step 7   Every 60 seconds, the routers exchange Inverse ARP messages.

Step 8   Every 10 seconds or so (this is configurable), the CPE router sends a keepalive message to the Frame Relay switch. The purpose of the keepalive message is to verify that the Frame Relay switch is still active.

Frame Relay Subinterfaces

To enable the sending of complete routing updates in a Frame Relay network, you can configure the router with logically assigned interfaces called *subinterfaces*. Subinterfaces are logical subdivisions of a physical interface. In a subinterface configuration, each PVC can be configured as a point-to-point connection, which allows the subinterface to act as a dedicated line, as shown in Figure 12-16.

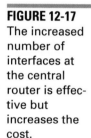

FIGURE 12-16
Routing updates can be sent out through sub-interfaces as if they were from separate physical interfaces.

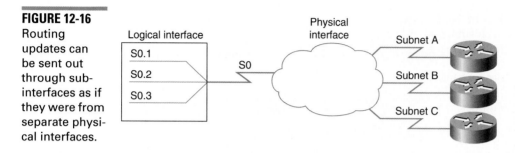

Early implementation of Frame Relay required that a router (that is, a DTE device) have a WAN serial interface for every PVC, as shown in Figure 12-17.

FIGURE 12-17
The increased number of interfaces at the central router is effective but increases the cost.

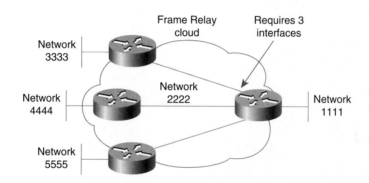

By logically dividing a single physical WAN serial interface into multiple virtual subinterfaces, the overall cost of implementing a Frame Relay network can be reduced. As shown in Figure 12-18, a single router interface can service may remote locations through individual unique suberinterfaces.

Split Horizon Routing Environments

In split horizon routing environments, routes learned on one subinterface can be advertised on another subinterface. Therefore, split horizon reduces routing loops by not allowing a routing update received on one physical interface to be advertised through the same physical interface (see Figure 12-19). As a result, if a remote router sends an update to the headquarters router that is connecting multiple PVCs over a single physical interface, the headquarters router cannot advertise that route through the same physical interface to other remote routers (see Figure 12-20).

FIGURE 12-18
Each subinterface is considered a unique network and a unique DLCI number.

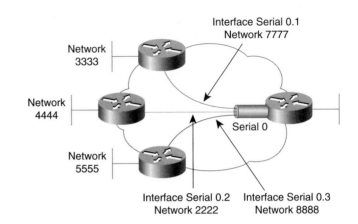

Interface Serial 0.1
Network 7777

Network 3333

Network 4444

Serial 0

Network 5555

Interface Serial 0.2
Network 2222

Interface Serial 0.3
Network 8888

FIGURE 12-19
With split horizon, if a router learns a protocol's route on an interface, it does not send information about that route back on that interface.

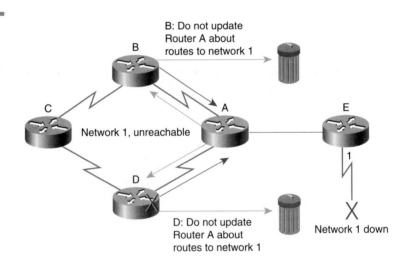

B: Do not update Router A about routes to network 1

B

C

A

E

Network 1, unreachable

1

D

D: Do not update Router A about routes to network 1

Network 1 down

Resolving Reachability Issues with Subinterfaces

You can configure subinterfaces to support the following connection types:

- Point-to-point—A single subinterface is used to establish one PVC connection to another physical interface or subinterface on a remote router. In this case, the interfaces would be in the same subnet, and each interface would have a single DLCI. Each point-to-point connection is its own subnet. In this environment, broadcasts are not a problem because the routers are point-to-point and act like a leased line.

- Multipoint—A single subinterface is used to establish multiple PVC connections to multiple physical interfaces or subinterfaces on remote routers. In this case, all the participating interfaces would be in the same subnet, and each interface would have its own local DLCI. In this environment, because the subinterface is acting like a regular Frame Relay network, routing updates are subject to split horizon.

FIGURE 12-20
With split horizon, routing updates received at a central router cannot be advertised out the same physical interface to other routers.

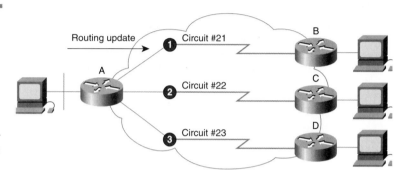

Configuring Basic Frame Relay

A basic Frame Relay configuration assumes that you want to configure Frame Relay on one or more physical interfaces (see Figure 12-21), and that LMI and Inverse ARP are supported by the remote router(s). In this type of environment, the LMI notifies the router about the available DLCIs. Inverse ARP is enabled by default, so it does not appear in configuration output. Use the following steps to configure basic Frame Relay:

Step 1   Select the interface and go into interface configuration mode:

```
router(config)# interface serial 0
```

Step 2   Configure a network-layer address, for example, an IP address:

```
router(config-if)# ip address 192.168.38.40 255.255.255.0
```

Step 3   Select the encapsulation type used to encapsulate data traffic end-to-end:

```
router(config-if)# encapsulation frame-relay [cisco | ietf]
```

where

cisco is the default, which you use if connecting to another Cisco router.

ietf is used for connecting to a non-Cisco router.

Step 4   If you're using Cisco IOS Release 11.1 or earlier, specify the LMI type used by the Frame Relay switch:

`router(config-if)# `**`frame-relay lmi-type {ansi | cisco | q933i}`**

where **cisco** is the default.

With IOS Release 11.2 or later, the LMI type is autosensed, so no configuration is needed.

Step 5   Configure the bandwidth for the link:

`router(config-if)# bandwidth `*`kilobits`*

This command affects routing operation by protocols such as IGRP, because it is used to define the metric of the link.

Step 6   If Inverse ARP was disabled on the router, reenable it (Inverse ARP is on by default):

`router(config-if)# frame`-relay **`inverse-arp`** [protocol] [dlci]

where

protocol is the supported protocols, including IP, IPX, AppleTalk, DECnet, VINES, and XNS.

dlci is the DLCI on the local interface that you want to exchange Inverse ARP messages.

FIGURE 12-21
When you have reliable connections to the local Frame Relay switch at both ends of the PVC, it is time to start planning the Frame Relay configuration.

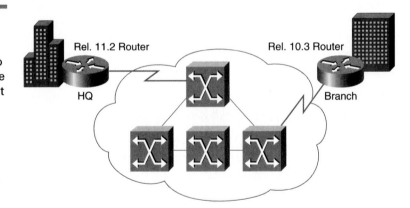

> ## Engineering Journal:
> ## Configuring Security
>
> Use the following steps to configure the router with some security measures, such as the router host name and the password used to prevent unauthorized access to the router:
>
> **Step 1** Configure the router with a host name, which is used in prompts and default configuration filenames. For PPP authentication, the host name entered with this command must match the username of the central site router:
>
> ```
> Router(config)# hostname 1600
> ```
>
> **Step 2** Specify a password to prevent unauthorized access to the router:
>
> ```
> 1600(config)# enable password 1600user
> ```

Verifying Frame Relay Operation

After configuring Frame Relay, you can verify that the connections are active by using the following **show** commands:

Command	Description
show interfaces serial	Displays information about the multicast DLCI, the DLCIs used on the Frame Relay–configured serial interface, and the LMI DLCI used for the LMI.
show frame-relay pvc	Displays the status of each configured connection as well as traffic statistics. This command is also useful for viewing the number of BECN and FECN packets received by the router.
show frame-relay map	Displays the network-layer address and associated DLCI for each remote destination that the local router is connected to.
show frame-relay lmi	Displays LMI traffic statistics. For example, it shows the number of status messages exchanged between the local router and the Frame Relay switch.

Confirming That the Line Is Up

Complete the following steps to confirm that the line is up:

Step 1 From the privileged EXEC command mode, enter the
show interfaces serial 0 command, as follows:

```
1600# show interfaces serial 0
Serial0 is up, line protocol is up
Hardware is QUICC Serial
MTU 1500 bytes, BW 1544 Kbit,
    DLY 20000 usec, rely 255/255, load 1/255
```

```
Encapsulation FRAME-RELAY,
    loopback not set, keepalive set (10 sec)
LMI enq sent 163, LMI stat recvd 136,
    LMI upd recvd 0, DTE LMI up
LMI enq recvd 39, LMI stat sent 0, LMI upd sent 0
LMI DLCI 1023 LMI type is CISCO frame relay DTE
Broadcast queue 0/64, broadcasts sent/dropped 27/0,
    interface broadcasts 28
Last input 00:00:01, output 00:00:05, output hang never
Last clearing of "show interface" counters never
Input queue: 0/75/0 (size/max/drops);
    Total output drops: 0
Queuing strategy: weighted fair
Output queue: 0/64/0 (size/threshold/drops)
Conversations 0/1 (active/max active)
Reserved Conversations 0/0 (allocated/max allocated)
5 minute input rate 0 bits/sec, 0 packets/sec
5 minute output rate 0 bits/sec, 0 packets/sec
1813 packets input, 109641 bytes, 0 no buffer
Received 1576 broadcasts, 0 runts, 0 giants
13 input errors, 0 CRC, 13 frame, 0 overrun,
    0 ignored, 0 abort
1848 packets output, 117260 bytes, 0 underruns
0 output errors, 0 collisions, 32 interface resets
0 output buffer failures, 0 output buffers swapped out
29 carrier transitions
DCD=up DSR=up DTR=up RTS=up CTS=up
```

Step 2   Confirm that the following messages (shown in bold above) appear in the command output:

— `Serial0 is up`, `line protocol is up`—The Frame Relay connection is active.

— `LMI enq sent 163`, `LMI stat recvd 136`—The connection is sending and receiving data. The number shown in your output will probably be different.

— `LMI type is CISCO`—The LMI type is configured correctly for the router.

Step 3   If the message does not appear in the command output, take the following steps:

— Confirm with the Frame Relay service provider that the LMI setting is correct for your line.

— Confirm that keepalives are set and that the router is receiving LMI updates.

Step 4   To continue configuration, reenter global configuration mode.

Confirming the Frame Relay Maps

Complete the following steps to confirm the Frame Relay maps:

Step 1 From privileged EXEC mode, enter the `show frame-relay map` command. Confirm that the `status defined, active` message (shown in bold in the example) appears for each serial subinterface:

```
1600# show frame-relay map
Serial0.1 (up): point-to-point dlci, dlci 17(0x11,0x410),
    broadcast,
status defined, active
```

Step 2 If the message does not appear, follow these steps:

— Confirm that the central-site router is connected and configured.

— Check with the Frame Relay carrier to verify that the line is operating correctly.

Step 3 To continue configuration, reenter global configuration mode.

Confirming Connectivity to the Central Site Router

Complete the following steps to confirm connectivity to the central site router:

Step 1 From privileged EXEC mode, enter the `ping` command, followed by the IP address of the central site router.

Step 2 Note the percentage in the `Success rate...` line (shown in bold in the example):

```
1600# ping 192.168.38.40
Type escape sequence to abort.
Sending 5, 100-byte ICMP Echos to 192.168.38.40,
    timeout is 2 seconds:
!!!!!
Success rate is 100 percent (5/5),
    round-trip min/avg/max = 32/32/32 ms
1600#
```

If the success rate is 10% or greater, this verification step is successful.

Step 3 To continue configuration, reenter global configuration mode.

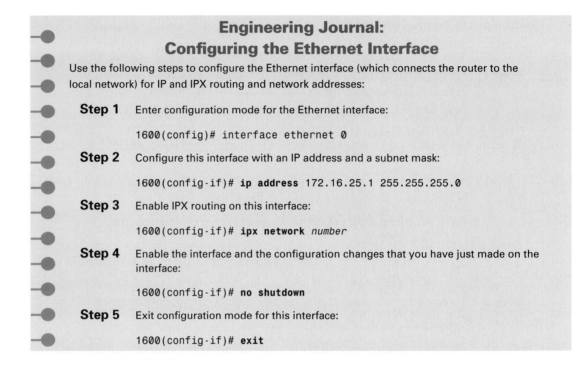

Engineering Journal:
Configuring the Ethernet Interface

Use the following steps to configure the Ethernet interface (which connects the router to the local network) for IP and IPX routing and network addresses:

Step 1   Enter configuration mode for the Ethernet interface:

```
1600(config)# interface ethernet 0
```

Step 2   Configure this interface with an IP address and a subnet mask:

```
1600(config-if)# ip address 172.16.25.1 255.255.255.0
```

Step 3   Enable IPX routing on this interface:

```
1600(config-if)# ipx network number
```

Step 4   Enable the interface and the configuration changes that you have just made on the interface:

```
1600(config-if)# no shutdown
```

Step 5   Exit configuration mode for this interface:

```
1600(config-if)# exit
```

Configuring the Serial Interface for a Frame Relay Connection

Use the following steps to configure the serial interface for Frame Relay packet encapsulation:

Step 1   Enter configuration mode for the serial interface:
```
1600(config)# interface serial 0
```
Step 2   Set the encapsulation method on this interface to Frame Relay:
```
1600(config-if)# encapsulation frame-relay
```
Step 3   Enable the configuration changes on this interface:
```
1600(config-if)# no shutdown
```

Verifying Frame Relay Configuration

You can verify your configuration to this point by confirming that an active PVC is active on the Frame Relay line, as follows:

Step 1   Wait 60 seconds after entering the `encapsulation frame-relay` command.

Step 2 From privileged EXEC mode, enter the `show frame-relay pvc` command.

Step 3 Confirm that the PVC STATUS=ACTIVE message (shown in bold in the following example) appears in the command output:

```
1600# show frame-relay pvc
PVC Statistics for interface Serial0 (Frame Relay DTE)
DLCI = 17, DLCI USAGE = LOCAL, PVC STATUS = ACTIVE, INTERFACE =
Serial0.1
input pkts 45 output pkts 52 in bytes 7764
out bytes 9958 dropped pkts 0 in FECN pkts 0
in BECN pkts 0 out FECN pkts 0 out BECN pkts 0
in DE pkts 0 out DE pkts 0
pvc create time 00:30:59, last time pvc status changed 00:19:21
```

Step 4 Record the number shown in the DLCI = message. (In this example, the number is 17.) You use this number to finish configuring the Frame Relay interface.

Step 5 If there is no output after entering the command, use the `show interfaces serial 0` command to determine whether the serial interface is active. An example of this command is in the next section, "Configuring the Point-to-Point Frame Relay Connection." The first line of the command output should be this:

```
Serial0 is up, line protocol is up
```

If the first line of the command output is Serial0 is up, line protocol is down, then you should confirm that the LMI type for the Frame Relay switch is correct by checking for the LMI type is CISCO message in the same command output.

Step 6 To continue configuration, reenter global configuration mode.

Engineering Journal:
Configuring Command-Line Access to the Router

Use the following steps to configure some parameters that control access to the router, including the type of terminal line used with the router, how long the router waits for a user entry before it times out, and the password used to start a terminal session with the router:

Step 1 Specify the console terminal line:

```
1600(config)#  line console 0
```

Step 2 Set the interval so that the EXEC command interpreter waits until user input is detected:

```
1600(config-line)#  exec-timeout 5
```

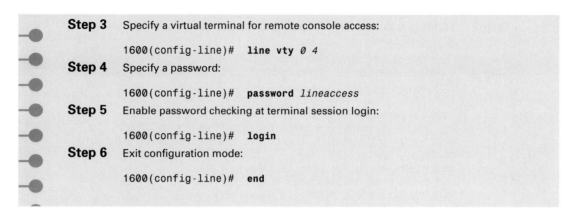

Step 3   Specify a virtual terminal for remote console access:

1600(config-line)#   **line vty 0 4**

Step 4   Specify a password:

1600(config-line)#   **password** *lineaccess*

Step 5   Enable password checking at terminal session login:

1600(config-line)#   **login**

Step 6   Exit configuration mode:

1600(config-line)#   **end**

Configuring Subinterfaces

To configure subinterfaces on a physical interface as shown in Figure 12-22, do the following:

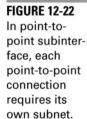

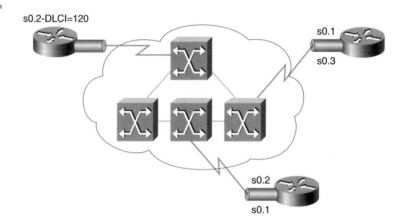

FIGURE 12-22 In point-to-point subinterface, each point-to-point connection requires its own subnet.

Step 1   Select the interface that you want to create subinterfaces on and get into interface configuration mode.

Step 2   Remove any network-layer address assigned to the physical interface. If the physical interface has an address, frames will not be received by the local subinterfaces.

Step 3   Configure Frame Relay encapsulation, as discussed in the "Configuring Basic Frame Relay" section.

Step 4   Select the subinterface you want to configure:

```
router(config-if)# interface serial number.subinterface-number
    {multipoint | point-to-point}
```

where

number.subinterface-number is the subinterface number in the range 1 to 4294967293. The interface number that precedes the period must match the interface number to which this subinterface belongs.

multipoint is used if you want the router to forward broadcasts and routing updates that it receives. Select this if routing IP and you want all routers in same subnet (see Figure 12-23).

FIGURE 12-23
With a multi-point configuration, you need only a single network or subnet.

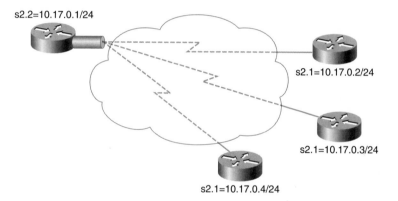

s2.2=10.17.0.1/24

s2.1=10.17.0.2/24

s2.1=10.17.0.3/24

s2.1=10.17.0.4/24

point-to-point is used if you do not want the router to forward broadcasts or routing updates and if you want each pair of point-to-point routers to have its own subnet (see Figure 12-24).

You are required to select either **multipoint** or **point-to-point**; there is no default.

Step 5   Configure a network-layer address on the subinterface. If the subinterface is point-to-point, and you are using IP, you can use the **ip unnumbered** command:

```
router(config-if)# ip unnumbered interface
```

If you use this command, it is recommended that the interface is the loopback interface. This is because the Frame Relay link will not work if this command is pointing to an interface that is not fully operational, and a loopback interface is not very likely to fail.

Step 6 If you configured the subinterface as multipoint or point-to-point, you must configure the local DLCI for the subinterface to distinguish it from the physical interface:

```
router(config-if)# frame-relay interface-dlci dlci-number
```
where

`dlci-number` defines the local DLCI number being linked to the subinterface. This is the only way to link an LMI-derived PVC to a subinterface because LMI does not know about subinterfaces.

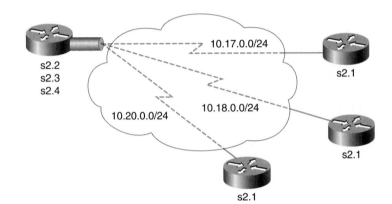

FIGURE 12-24
In a point-to-point subinterface configuration, subinterfaces act as leased line.

NOTE

If you defined a subinterface for point-to-point communication, you cannot reassign the same subinterface number to be used for multipoint communication without first rebooting the router. Instead you can avoid using that subinterface number and use a different subinterface number.

This command is required for all point-to-point subinterfaces. It is also required for multipoint subinterfaces for which Inverse ARP is enabled. It is not required for multipoint subinterfaces configured with static route maps.

Do not use this command on physical interfaces.

Configuring Optional Commands

The following commands can be used when necessary for enhanced router operation:

```
router(config-if)# frame-relay map protocol protocol-address dlci
    [broadcast] [ietf | cisco | payload-compress packet-by-packet]
```

The following is a description of this syntax:

Parameter	Description
protocol	Defines the supported protocol, bridging, or logical link control.
protocol-address	Defines the network-layer address of the destination router interface.

Parameter	Description
dlci	Defines the local DLCI used to connect to the remote protocol address.
broadcast	(Optional) Forwards broadcasts to this address when multicast is not enabled. Use this if you want the router to forward routing updates.
ietf | cisco	(Optional) Select the Frame Relay encapsulation type for use. Use **ietf** only if the remote router is a non-Cisco router. Otherwise, use **cisco**.
payload-compress packet-by-packet	(Optional) Packet-by-packet payload compression using the Stacker method.

Normally, Inverse ARP is used to request the next-hop protocol address for a specific connection. Responses to Inverse ARP are entered in an address-to-DLCI map (that is, Frame Relay map) table, as shown in Figure 12-25. The table is then used to route outgoing traffic. When Inverse ARP is not supported by the remote router, when configuring OSPF over Frame Relay, or when you want to control broadcast traffic while using routing, you must define the address-to-DLCI table statically. The static entries are referred to as *static maps.*

FIGURE 12-25
Responses to the Inverse ARP request of the next-hop protocol address are entered in an address-to-DLCI map.

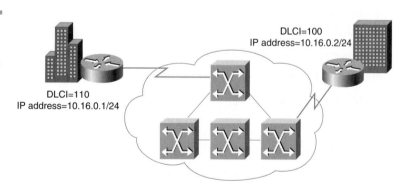

DLCI=100
IP address=10.16.0.2/24

DLCI=110
IP address=10.16.0.1/24

With Frame Relay, you can increase or decrease the keepalive interval. You can extend or reduce the interval at which the router interface sends keepalive messages to the Frame Relay switch. The default is 10 seconds, and the following is the syntax:

```
router(config-if)# keepalive number
```

where *number* is the value, in seconds, that is usually 2 to 3 seconds faster (that is, a shorter interval) than the setting of the Frame Relay switch to ensure proper synchronization.

If an LMI type is not used in the network, or when you are doing back-to-back testing between routers, you need to specify the DLCI for each local interface by using the following command:

```
router(config-if)# frame-relay local-dlci number
```

where *number* is the DLCI on the local interface to be used.

Summary

- Frame Relay WAN technology provides a flexible method of connecting LANs over Frame Relay WAN links.

- Frame Relay provides a packet-switching data communication capability that is used across the interface between user devices (such as routers, bridges, and host machines) and network equipment (such as switching nodes).

- Frame Relay uses virtual circuits to establish connections across the WAN.

The main purposes of the LMI process are to

- Determine the operational status of the various PVCs that the router knows about

- Transmit keepalive packets to ensure that the PVC stays up and does not shut down due to inactivity

- Tell the router what PVCs are available

- The Inverse ARP mechanism allows the router to automatically build the Frame Relay map

- The router next-hop address determined from the routing table must be resolved to a Frame Relay DLCI

Frame Relay can divide a single physical WAN interface into multiple subinterfaces.

- In split-horizon routing environments, routes learned on one subinterface can be advertised on another subinterface.

Washington School District Project Task: Frame Relay

In this chapter, you have learned concepts and configuration processes that will help you implement a Frame Relay data link in the Washington School District network. As part of the configuration and implementation, you need to complete the following tasks:

1. Document the insertion of Frame Relay in the WAN implementation, including:

   - DLCI numbers

   - The value of the CIR

   - A description of all data communication equipment needed to accomplish implementation.

2. Document the router commands needed to implement Frame Relay on the router.

Chapter Review

Complete all the review questions to test your understanding of the topics and concepts covered in this chapter. Answers are listed in Appendix A, "Chapter Review Answer Key."

1. How does Frame Relay handle multiple conversations on the same physical connection?

   A. It duplexes the conversations.

   B. It multiplexes the circuits.

   C. It converts it to an ATM cell.

   D. Multiple conversations are not allowed.

2. Which of the following protocols are used by Frame Relay for error correction?

   A. Physical and data-link protocols

   B. Upper-layer protocols

   C. Lower-layer protocols

   D. Frame Relay does not do error correction

3. Which of the following does Frame Relay do to make its DLCIs global?

   A. It broadcasts them.

   B. It sends out unicasts.

   C. It sends out multicasts.

   D. DLCIs can't become global.

4. Which of the following is the data rate at which the Frame Relay switch agrees to transfer data?

   A. Committed information rate

   B. Data transfer rate

   C. Timing rate

   D. Baud Rate

5. Which of the following assigns DLCI numbers?

   A. The end user

   B. The network root

C. A DLCI server

D. The service provider

6. DLCI information is included in which of the following fields of the Frame Relay header?

   A. The flag field

   B. The address field

   C. The data field

   D. The checksum field

7. Which of the following does Frame Relay use to keep PVCs active?

   A. Point-to-point connections

   B. Windows sockets

   C. Keepalives

   D. They become inactive

8. How does Frame Relay use Inverse ARP requests?

   A. It maps IP addresses to MAC addresses.

   B. It maps MAC addresses to IP addresses.

   C. It maps MAC addresses to network addresses.

   D. It uses the IP address-to-DLCI mapping table.

9. Which of the following does Frame Relay use to determine the next hop?

   A. An ARP table

   B. A RIP routing table

   C. A Frame Relay map

   D. A IGRP routing table

10. For which of the following does Frame Relay use split horizon?

    A. To increase router updates

    B. To prevent routing loops

    C. To raise convergence times

    D. Frame Relay does not use split horizon

Key Terms

BECN (backward explicit congestion notification) A bit set by a Frame Relay network in frames traveling in the opposite direction of frames encountering a congested path. DTE devices receiving frames with the BECN bit set can request that higher-level protocols take flow control action as appropriate.

DLCI (data-link connection identifier) A value that specifies a PVC or an SVC in a Frame Relay network. In the basic Frame Relay specification, DLCIs are locally significant (that is, connected devices can use different values to specify the same connection). In the LMI extended specification, DLCIs are globally significant (that is, DLCIs specify individual end devices).

FECN (forward explicit congestion notification) A bit set by a Frame Relay network to inform DTE devices receiving the frame that congestion was experienced in the path from source to destination. DTE devices receiving frames with the FECN bit set can request that higher-level protocols take flow-control action as appropriate.

Frame Relay An industry-standard, switched data link-layer protocol that handles multiple virtual circuits using HDLC encapsulation between connected devices. Frame Relay is more efficient than X.25, the protocol for which it is generally considered a replacement.

LMI (Local Management Interface) A set of enhancements to the basic Frame Relay specification. LMI includes support for a keepalive mechanism, which verifies that data is flowing; a multicast mechanism, which provides the network server with its local DLCI and the multicast DLCI; global addressing, which gives DLCIs global rather than local significance in Frame Relay networks; and a status mechanism, which provides an ongoing status report on the DLCIs known to the switch.

local access rate The clock speed (port speed) of the connection (local loop) to the Frame Relay cloud. It is the rate at which data travels into or out of the network.

media Plural of medium. The various physical environments through which transmission signals pass. Common network media include twisted-pair, coaxial, and fiber-optic cable, and the atmosphere (through which microwave, laser, and infrared transmission occurs). Sometimes called physical media.

PDN (public data network) A network operated either by a government (as in Europe) or by a private concern to provide computer communications to the public, usually for a fee. PDNs enable small organizations to create a WAN without all the equipment costs of long-distance circuits.

PVC (permanent virtual circuit)   A virtual circuit that is permanently established. PVCs save bandwidth associated with circuit establishment and teardown in situations where certain virtual circuits must exist all the time.

Chapter Review Answer Key

This appendix contains the answers to the chapter review questions at the end of each chapter.

Chapter 1

1. C. The physical layer

2. A. It sends data by using flow control.

3. B. Path determination and switching

4. C. Distance-vector and link-state

5. A. Converged

6. Each layer depends on the service function of the OSI reference model layer below it. To provide this service, the lower layer uses encapsulation to put the PDU from the upper layer into its data field; then, it can add whatever headers and trailers the layer will use to perform its function.

7. Transport-layer services allow reliable data transport between hosts and destinations. To obtain such reliable transport of data, a connection-oriented relationship is used between the communicating end systems.

8. ICMP is implemented by all TCP/IP hosts. ICMP messages are carried in IP datagrams and are used to send error and control messages. Examples of ICMP messages are `ping` and `destination unreachable`.

9. Windowing is a method to control the amount of information transferred end-to-end. Windowing is an end-to-end agreement between sender and receiver on how much data will be sent between acknowledgments.

10. The network layer provides best-effort end-to-end packet delivery. The network layer sends packets from the source network to the destination network based on the IP routing table.

Chapter 2

1. B. A data frame

2. B. 800 ns

3. D. A (Dedicated paths between sender and receiver hosts) and B (Multiple traffic paths within the switch)

4. D. Multiport bridges operating at Layer 2

5. A. Client/server network traffic where the "fast" switch port is connected to the server

6. B. Cut-through; store-and-forward

7. D. Redundant network paths, without suffering the effects of loops in the network

8. In store-and-forward switching, the entire frame is received before any forwarding takes place, whereas, in cut-through switching, the switch reads the destination address before receiving the entire frame. The frame then starts to be forwarded before the entire frame arrives.

9. In half-duplex Ethernet, the transmit (TX) and the receive (RX) circuits contend for the right to use the same single shared medium. In full-duplex Ethernet, TX and RX are separate circuits and, therefore, there is no contending for the right to transmit data across the media.

10. The main function of the Spanning-Tree Protocol is to allow redundant switched/bridged paths without suffering the effects of loops in the network.

Chapter 3

1. VLAN benefits include tighter network security with establishment of secure user groups, better management and control of broadcast activity, microsegmentation of the network, and the relocation of workgroup servers into secured, centralized locations.

2. Broadcast traffic within one VLAN is not transmitted outside the VLAN. Conversely, adjacent ports do not receive any of the broadcast traffic generated from other VLANs.

3. Port-centric VLANs, static VLANs, and dynamic VLANs

4. VLAN frame tagging is an approach that places a unique VLAN identifier in the header of each frame as it is forwarded throughout the network backbone.

5. A. The ability to increase networks without creating collisions domains

6. D. All of the above

7. C. Hub; switch

8. D. They automatically configure ports when new stations are added.

9. D. All of the above are criteria by which VLANs can be created.

10. A. Switches do not need to be configured.

Chapter 4

1. The four main goals of any network design are functionality, scalability, adaptability, and manageability.

2. The purpose of Layer 2 devices in the network is to provide flow control, error detection, and error correction, and to reduce congestion in the network.

3. Implementation of Layer 3 devices, such as routers, allows for segmentation of the LAN into unique physical and logical networks. Routers also allow for connectivity to WANs, such as the Internet.

4. The two major categories of servers in a network design are enterprise servers and workgroup servers. Enterprise servers support all the users on the network, such as those using e-mail or DNS. Workgroup servers support a specific set of users.

5. Any network documentation should include a physical network map, a logical network map, and an addressing map. Having these dramatically decreases problem resolution time.

6. D. All of the above

7. D. Too many network segments

8. C. Layer 2; Layer 1

9. B. Max length = 400 meters

10. D. All of the above

Chapter 5

1. Path determination occurs at Layer 3, the network layer. The path determination function enables a router to evaluate the available paths to a destination and to establish the preferred path of a packet across the network.

2. The router examines the packet header to determine the destination network and then references the routing table that associates networks with outgoing interfaces.

3. In multiprotocol routing, routers are capable of supporting multiple independent routing protocols and maintaining routing tables for several routed protocols concurrently. This capability allows a router to deliver packets from several routed protocols, such as IP and IPX, over the same data links.

4. The success of dynamic routing depends on two basic router functions:

   - Maintenance of a routing table

   - Timely distribution of knowledge—in the form of routing updates—to other routers (that is, convergence)

5. When all routers in a network are operating with the same knowledge, the network is said to have converged.

6. D. Switching the packet

7. D. B (Maintaining a routing table) and C (Periodic routing updates)

8. A. Distance-vector; link-state

9. D. IGRP uses all of these.

10. D. `router igrp`

Chapter 6

1. ACLs offer another powerful tool for network data packet control. ACLs filter the packet flow that flows in or out of a router's interfaces.

2. Standard ACLs check the source address of packets that could be routed. The result permits or denies output of the packet, based on the network, subnet, or host address.

3. Extended ACLs permit or deny with more precision than do standard ACLs. Extended ACLs check for both source and destination packet addresses. They also can check for specific protocols, port numbers, and other parameters.

4. ACL statements operate in sequential, logical order. They evaluate packets from the top of the list, down to the last statement in the list. Only if the packet does not match conditions of the first test does it drop to the next ACL statement.

5. Standard ACLs are identified with a number in the range 1 to 99. Extended ACLs are identified with a number in the range 100 to 199.

6. C. `show ip interface`

7. A. Wildcard bits

8. C. "Permit my network only"

9. A. True

10. B. Monitor ACL statements

Chapter 7

1. A MAC address

2. `ipx maximum-paths`

3. Global configuration mode

4. `show ipx interface`

5. `debug ipx sap`

6. C. Network number; node number

7. D. Always A (Novell servers) and B (Cisco routers)

8. B. RIP; SAP

9. A. `ipx routing` [*node*]

10. B. `show ipx interface; show ipx route; show ipx servers`

Chapter 8

1. B. One
2. C. The physical layer
3. D. DCE
4. D. None of the above
5. A. Frame Relay
6. C. Customer premises equipment
7. D. All of the above
8. D. All of the above
9. B. Frame Relay
10. B. LCP

Chapter 9

1. D. All of the above
2. A. The busiest time
3. B. Close to the users
4. C. A flat topology
5. A. Efficient use of bandwidth
6. B. Routers
7. C. Access
8. D. Access
9. A. Server
10. B. Routers

Chapter 10

1. SLIP
2. Asynchronous serial, ISDN, and synchronous serial

3. D. All of the above

4. B. Encapsulate multiple protocols

5. C. Protocol

6. A. Establishment, maintenance, and termination of the point-to-point connection

7. C. Four

8. B. Two-way

9. C. `router# `**`show interfaces`**

10. C. When the workstation needs dialup access to the Internet

Chapter 11

1. 128 kpbs

2. 2 B channels

3. 1 D channel

4. An SPID

5. The D channel

6. B. Router

7. A. A large concentration of users at the site

8. A. Telephone network standards

9. C. PPP

10. D. `router(config)# `**`isdn switch-type`**

Chapter 12

1. B. It multiplexes the circuits.

2. B. Upper-layer protocols

3. C. It sends out multicasts.

4. A. Committed information rate

5. D. The service provider

6. B. The address field

7. C. Keepalives

8. D. It uses the IP address-to-DLCI mapping table.

9. C. A Frame Relay map

10. B. To prevent routing loops

Command Summary

This appendix contains a summary of the commands used in this book and is intended to provide a quick reference. Each command is listed with a short description. In addition, this table contains cross-references to the chapter in which the command is introduced and explained. This appendix should add to your understanding of the commands used to configure Cisco routers.

Command	Description	Chapter
`access-group`	Applies access control lists (ACLs) to an interface.	6
`access-list`	Defines a standard IP ACL.	6
`clear interface`	Resets the hardware logic on an interface.	11
`debug dialer`	Shows such information as what number the interface is dialing.	11
`debug ipx routing activity`	Displays information about Routing Information Protocol (RIP) update packets.	7
`debug ipx sap`	Displays information about Service Advertising Protocol (SAP) update packets.	7
`debug isdn q921`	Displays data link-layer (Layer 2) access procedures that are taking place at the router on the D channel (LAPD) of its Integrated Services Digital Network (ISDN) interface.	11
`debug ppp`	Displays information on traffic and exchanges in an internetwork implementing Point-to-Point Protocol (PPP).	8
`deny`	Sets the conditions for a named IP ACL.	6
`dialer-group`	Controls access by configuring an interface to belong to a specific dialing group.	11
`dialer idle-timeout`	Specifies the idle time before the line is disconnected.	11
`dialer-list protocol`	Defines a DDR dialer list to control dialing by protocol or by a combination of protocol and ACL.	11

Command	Description	Chapter
`dialer map`	Configures a serial interface to call one or multiple sites.	11
`dialer wait-for-carrier-time`	Specifies how long to wait for a carrier.	11
`enable password`	Specifies a password to prevent unauthorized access to the router.	12
`encapsulation frame-relay`	Enables Frame Relay encapsulation.	12
`encapsulation novell-ether`	Specifies that Novell's unique frame format is used on a network segment.	7
`encapsulation ppp`	Sets PPP as the encapsulation method used by a serial or ISDN interface.	8, 10, 11
`encapsulation sap`	Specifies that Ethernet 802.2 frame format is used on a network segment. Cisco's keyword is `sap`.	7
`end`	Exits configuration mode.	12
`exec-timeout`	Sets the interval that the EXEC command interpreter waits until user input is detected.	12
`exit`	Exits any configuration mode or closes an active terminal session and terminates the EXEC.	12
`frame-relay local-dlci`	Enables the Local Management Interface (LMI) mechanism for serial lines using Frame Relay encapsulation.	12
`hostname`	Configures the router with a host name, which is used in prompts and default configuration filenames.	12
`interface`	Configures an interface type and enters interface configuration mode.	6, 7, 8, 11
`interface serial`	Selects the interface and enters interface configuration mode.	12
`ip access-group`	Controls access to an interface.	6
`ip address`	Sets the logical network address of the interface.	1, 6, 12

Command	Description	Chapter
`ip unnumbered`	Enables Internet Protocol (IP) processing on a serial interface without assigning an explicit IP address to the interface.	12
`ipx delay`	Sets the tick count.	7
`ipx ipxwan`	Enables the IPXWAN protocol on a serial interface.	7
`ipx maximum-paths`	Sets the number of equal-cost paths the Cisco IOS software uses when forwarding packets.	7
`ipx network`	Enables Internetwork Packet Exchange (IPX) routing on a particular interface and optionally selects the type of encapsulation (framing).	7, 12
`ipx router`	Specifies the routing protocol to use.	7
`ipx routing`	Enables IPX routing.	7
`ipx sap-interval`	Configures less frequent SAP updates over slow links.	7
`ipx type-20-input-checks`	Restricts the acceptance of IPX type 20 propagation packet broadcasts.	7
`isdn spid1`	Defines at the router the service profile identifier (SPID) number that has been assigned by the ISDN service provider for the B1 channel.	11
`isdn spid2`	Defines at the router the SPID number that has been assigned by the ISDN service provider for the B2 channel.	11
`isdn switch-type`	Specifies the central office switch type on the ISDN interface.	11
`keepalive`	Enables the LMI mechanism for serial lines using Frame Relay encapsulation.	12
`line console`	Configures a console port line.	12
`line vty`	Specifies a virtual terminal for remote console access.	12
`login`	Enables password checking at terminal session login.	12

Command	Description	Chapter
`metric holddown`	Keeps new IGRP routing information from being used for a certain period of time.	5
`network`	Assigns a NIC-based address to which the router is directly connected. Associates networks with an IGRP routing process. Enables Enhanced IGRP on a network in IPX router configuration mode.	1, 5, 7
`network-number`	Specifies a directly connected network.	1
`permit`	Sets conditions for a named IP ACL.	6
`ping`	Sends ICMP echo request packets to another node on the network. Checks host reachability and network connectivity. Diagnoses basic network connectivity.	1, 7, 11, 12
`ppp authentication`	Enables Challenge Handshake Authentication Protocol (CHAP) or Password Authentication Protocol (PAP) or both, and specifies the order in which CHAP and PAP authentication are selected on the interface.	10, 11
`ppp chap hostname`	Creates a pool of dialup routers that all appear to be the same host when authenticating with CHAP.	10
`ppp chap password`	Configures a password that will be sent to hosts that want to authenticate the router. This command limits the number of username/password entries in the router.	10
`ppp pap sent-username`	Enables remote PAP support for an interface and uses `sent-username` and `password` in the PAP authentication request packet to the peer.	10
`protocol`	Defines an IP routing protocol, which can be either RIP, Interior Gateway Routing Protocol (IGRP), Open Shortest Path First (OSPF), or Enhanced IGRP.	1
`router igrp`	Enables an IGRP routing process.	5
`router rip`	Selects RIP as the routing protocol.	1

Command	Description	Chapter
`show access-lists`	Displays the contents of all current ACLs.	6
`show dialer`	Displays general diagnostics for serial interfaces configured for DDR.	11
`show frame-relay lmi`	Displays statistics about the LMI.	12
`show frame-relay map`	Displays the current map entries and information about the connections.	12
`show frame-relay pvc`	Displays statistics about PVCs for Frame Relay interfaces.	12
`show interfaces`	Displays statistics for all interfaces configured on the router or access server.	8, 10, 11
`show interfaces serial`	Displays information about a serial interface.	12
`show ip interface`	Lists a summary of an interface's IP information and status.	6
`show ip route`	Displays the current state of the routing table.	11
`show ipx interface`	Displays the status of the IPX interfaces configured in the Cisco IOS software and the parameters configured on each interface.	7
`show ipx route`	Displays the content of the IPX routing table.	7
`show ipx servers`	Displays the IPX server list.	7
`show ipx traffic`	Displays the number and type of packets.	7
`show isdn active`	Displays current call information, including called number, the time until the call is disconnected, AOC charging units used during the call, and whether the AOC information is provided during calls or at the end of calls.	11
`show isdn status`	Displays the status of all ISDN interfaces or, optionally, a specific digital signal link (DSL) or a specific ISDN interface.	11
`show protocols`	Displays the configured protocols.	7

Command	Description	Chapter
`show spantree`	Displays spanning-tree information for a virtual local-area network (VLAN).	2
`show status`	Displays the current status of the ISDN line and both B channels.	11
`term ip netmask-format`	Specifies the format in which network masks are displayed in **show** command output.	1
`timers basic`	Controls how often IGRP sends updates.	5
`username password`	Specifies the password to be used in CHAP caller identification and PAP.	10

Movie Index

The following table lists the movies you'll find on this book's CD-ROM:

Movie	Description	Chapter
Movie 1.1	**The OSI Model Conceptual Framework** Protocols enabling communication	1
Movie 1.2	**IP Routing Table** Destination network address and next-hop pairs	1
Movie 1.3	**Router Function** Path determination	1
Movie 1.4	**Determining Network Address** The IP destination retrieves an internal subnet mask	1
Movie 1.5	**Router Can't Deliver** ICMP destination unreachable message	1
Movie 1.6	**Reachability** TCP/IP host sends ICMP echo request	1
Movie 1.7	**Address Resolution** Finding MAC address	1
Movie 1.8	**Connection-Oriented Services** Three phases—connection establishment, data transfer, and connection termination	1
Movie 1.9	**Three-Way Handshake** Sequence of messages exchanged to ensure transmission synchronization	1
Movie 1.10	**TCP Host Sends Packet** Window size	1
Movie 1.11	**Windowing** Window size, acknowledgment	1
Movie 1.12	**PAR** Positive acknowledgment and retransmission	1

Movie	Description	Chapter
Movie 1.13	**Distance-Vector Protocols** Routing updates	1
Movie 1.14	**OSPF Routers** Link-state advertisements	1
Movie 1.15	**Link-State Protocols** A complex database of topology information	1
Movie 2.1	**Ethernet and 802.3 LANs** Broadcast networks	2
Movie 2.2	**CSMA/CD LANs** Ethernet and 802.3	2
Movie 2.3	**Collisions** Backoff protocols that determine when to retransmit	2
Movie 2.4	**Repeater Advantages** Repeater cleans, amplifies, and resends	2
Movie 2.5	**Repeater Disadvantages** Can't filter traffic	2
Movie 2.6	**Bridge Examines MAC Addresses** Store-and-forward devices	2
Movie 2.7	**LAN Switching** Dedicated collision-free communication between devices	2
Movie 2.8	**Symmetric Switching** Switch connections between ports of equal bandwidth	2
Movie 2.9	**Asymmetric Switching** Switch connections between ports with different bandwidth	2
Movie 2.10	**Store-and-Forward Switching** Copies frame on board, checks frame's length and CRC	2
Movie 2.11	**Cut-Through Switching** Switch reads the destination address before receiving the entire frame	2

Movie	Description	Chapter
Movie 3.1	**Broadcast Transmission** Source node to network	3
Movie 3.2	**Route Processor** Using routing protocols to determine optimum paths	3
Movie 5.1	**Router Function** Sending data packets	5
Movie 5.2	**Path Switching** The network layer finds a path to the destination	5
Movie 5.3	**IGRP** Multipath routing	5
Movie 5.4	**Multicast Transmission** Data packets sent through network	5
Movie 5.5	**IGRP Update** Timer controls frequency of router update messages	5
Movie 7.1	**Sending Packets Through Network** Paths selected dynamically	7
Movie 7.2	**Large Novell Installations** Hundreds of file, print, and gateway services available	7
Movie 7.3	**Novell NetWare** Based on client/server architecture	7
Movie 7.4	**Simple Split Horizon** Prevents routing loops	7
Movie 7.5	**SAP** Network resources advertise services	7
Movie 8.1	**WAN Technology** Identify WAN components	8
Movie 8.2	**Data** Goes through layers, is given a header at each layer, and is passed on to next layer	8

Movie	Description	Chapter
Movie 8.3	**Sending Packets Through Network** Paths selected dynamically	8
Movie 8.4	**DLCIs Become Unique Network Addresses for DTE Devices** Frame Relay network changes to reflect origin of source	8
Movie 8.5	**Dial Backup** Activates backup serial line to be used when traffic is too heavy or when primary line fails	8
Movie 8.6	**ISDN BRI Service** B channel and D channel	8
Movie 10.1	**PPP Components** Three components: HDLC Encapsulation, Link Control Protocol, Network Control Programs (NCPs)	10
Movie 10.2	**PPP Link Establishment** Establish communications	10
Movie 10.3	**PPP Configuration Acknowledgement** Negotiate parameters	10
Movie 10.4	**LCP: Link Quality Determination** Test links	10
Movie 10.5	**Network-Layer Protocols** Configuration by appropriate NCP	10
Movie 10.6	**LCP Link Termination** LCP can terminate the link at any time	10
Movie 11.1	**ISDN Applications** Integration of telecommuting services	11
Movie 12.1	**Congestion Handled by FECN** Frame Relay switch recognizes congestion in the network	12

This glossary defines many of the terms and abbreviations related to networking. It includes all the key terms used throughout the book, as well as many other terms related to networking. As with any growing technical field, some terms evolve and take on several meanings. Where necessary, multiple definitions and abbreviation expansions are presented. Multiword terms are alphabetized as if there were no spaces; hyphenated terms, as if there were no hyphens.

Terms in this glossary typically are defined under their abbreviations. Each abbreviation expansion is listed separately, with a cross-reference to the abbreviation entry. In addition, many definitions contain cross-references to related terms.

We hope that this glossary adds to your understanding of internetworking technologies.

Numerics

2B+D *In reference to the ISDN BRI service, two B channels and one D channel.*

4B/5B local fiber *4-byte/5-byte local fiber. Fibre Channel physical medium used for FDDI and ATM. Supports speeds of up to 100 Mbps over multimode fiber.*

4-byte/5-byte local fiber *See 4B/5B local fiber.*

8B/10B local fiber *8-byte/10-byte local fiber. Fiber Channel physical medium that supports speeds up to 149.76 Mbps over multimode fiber.*

8-byte/10-byte local fiber *See 8B/10B local fiber.*

10Base2 *A 10-Mbps baseband Ethernet specification using 50-ohm thin coaxial cable. 10Base2, which is part of the IEEE 802.3 specification, has a distance limit of 185 meters per segment. See also Ethernet and IEEE 802.3.*

10Base5 *A 10-Mbps baseband Ethernet specification using standard (thick) 50-ohm baseband coaxial cable. 10Base5, which is part of the IEEE 802.3 baseband physical-layer specification, has a distance limit of 500 meters per segment. See also Ethernet and IEEE 802.3.*

10BaseF *A 10-Mbps baseband Ethernet specification that refers to the 10BaseFB, 10BaseFL, and 10BaseFP standards for Ethernet over fiber-optic cabling. See also 10BaseFB, 10BaseFL, 10BaseFP, and Ethernet.*

10BaseFB   *A 10-Mbps baseband Ethernet specification using fiber-optic cabling. 10BaseFB is part of the IEEE 10BaseF specification. It is not used to connect user stations, but provides a synchronous signaling backbone that allows additional segments and repeaters to be connected to the network. 10BaseFB segments can be up to 2000 meters long. See also 10BaseF and Ethernet.*

10BaseFL   *A 10-Mbps baseband Ethernet specification using fiber-optic cabling. 10BaseFL is part of the IEEE 10BaseF specification and, although able to interoperate with FOIRL, is designed to replace the FOIRL specification. 10BaseFL segments can be up to 1000 meters long if used with FOIRL, and up to 2000 meters if 10BaseFL is used exclusively. See also 10BaseF and Ethernet.*

10BaseFP   *A 10-Mbps fiber-passive baseband Ethernet specification using fiber-optic cabling. 10BaseFP is part of the IEEE 10BaseF specification. It organizes a number of computers into a star topology without the use of repeaters. 10BaseFP segments can be up to 500 meters long. See also 10BaseF and Ethernet.*

10BaseT   *A 10-Mbps baseband Ethernet specification using two pairs of twisted-pair cabling (Category 3, 4, or 5): one pair for transmitting data and the other for receiving data. 10BaseT, which is part of the IEEE 802.3 specification, has a distance limit of approximately 100 meters per segment. See also Ethernet and IEEE 802.3.*

10Broad36   *A 10-Mbps broadband Ethernet specification using broadband coaxial cable. 10Broad36, which is part of the IEEE 802.3 specification, has a distance limit of 3600 meters per segment. See also Ethernet and IEEE 802.3.*

100BaseFX   *A 100-Mbps baseband Fast Ethernet specification using two strands of multimode fiber-optic cable per link. To guarantee proper signal timing, a 100BaseFX link cannot exceed 400 meters in length. Based on the IEEE 802.3 standard. See also 100BaseX, Fast Ethernet, and IEEE 802.3.*

100BaseT   *A 100-Mbps baseband Fast Ethernet specification using UTP wiring. Like the 10BaseT technology on which it is based, 100BaseT sends link pulses over the network segment when no traffic is present. However, these link pulses contain more information than do those used in 10BaseT. Based on the IEEE 802.3 standard. See also 10BaseT, Fast Ethernet, and IEEE 802.3.*

100BaseT4   *A 100-Mbps baseband Fast Ethernet specification using four pairs of Category 3, 4, or 5 UTP wiring. To guarantee proper signal timing, a*

100BaseT4 segment cannot exceed 100 meters in length. Based on the IEEE 802.3 standard. See also Fast Ethernet and IEEE 802.3.

100BaseTX *A 100-Mbps baseband Fast Ethernet specification using two pairs of either UTP or STP wiring. The first pair of wires is used to receive data; the second is used to transmit. To guarantee proper signal timing, a 100BaseTX segment cannot exceed 100 meters in length. Based on the IEEE 802.3 standard. See also 100BaseX, Fast Ethernet, and IEEE 802.3.*

100BaseX *A 100-Mbps baseband Fast Ethernet specification that refers to the 100BaseFX and 100BaseTX standards for Fast Ethernet over fiber-optic cabling. Based on the IEEE 802.3 standard. See also 100BaseFX, 100BaseTX, Fast Ethernet, and IEEE 802.3.*

100VG-AnyLAN *A 100-Mbps Fast Ethernet and Token Ring media technology using four pairs of Category 3, 4, or 5 UTP cabling. This high-speed transport technology, developed by Hewlett-Packard, can be made to operate on existing 10BaseT Ethernet networks. Based on the IEEE 802.12 standard. See also IEEE 802.12.*

A

A&B bit signaling *A procedure used in T1 transmission facilities in which each of the 24 T1 subchannels devotes 1 bit of every sixth frame to the carrying of supervisory signaling information.*

ABM *Asynchronous Balanced Mode. An HDLC (and derivative protocol) communication mode supporting peer-oriented, point-to-point communications between two stations, where either station can initiate transmission.*

access layer *The layer at which a LAN or a group of LANs, typically Ethernet or Token Ring, provide users with frontline access to network services.*

access method *1. Generally, the way in which network devices access the network medium. 2. Software within an SNA processor that controls the flow of information through a network.*

ACK *See acknowledgment.*

acknowledgment *A notification sent from one network device to another to acknowledge that some event (for example, receipt of a message) has occurred. Sometimes abbreviated ACK.*

ACL (access control list) *A list kept by a Cisco router to control access to or from the router for a number of services (for example, to prevent packets with a certain IP address from leaving a particular interface on the router). See also extended ACL and standard ACL.*

active monitor *A device responsible for performing maintenance functions on a Token Ring network. A network node is selected to be the active monitor if it has the highest MAC address on the ring. The active monitor is responsible for such ring maintenance tasks as ensuring that tokens are not lost and that frames do not circulate indefinitely.*

adapter *See NIC.*

address *A data structure or logical convention used to identify a unique entity, such as a particular process or network device.*

address mapping *A technique that allows different protocols to interoperate by translating addresses from one format to another. For example, when routing IP over X.25, the IP addresses must be mapped to the X.25 addresses so that the IP packets can be transmitted by the X.25 network.*

address mask *A bit combination used to describe which portion of an address refers to the network or subnet and which part refers to the host. Sometimes referred to simply as mask.*

address resolution *Generally, a method for resolving differences between computer addressing schemes. Address resolution usually specifies a method for mapping network layer (Layer 3) addresses to data link layer (Layer 2) addresses.*

Address Resolution Protocol *See ARP.*

adjacency *A relationship formed between selected neighboring routers and end nodes for the purpose of exchanging routing information. Adjacency is based on the use of a common media segment.*

Advanced Research Projects Agency *See ARPA.*

advertising *A router process in which routing or service updates are sent so that other routers on the network can maintain lists of usable routes.*

AEP (AppleTalk Echo Protocol) *A protocol used to test connectivity between two AppleTalk nodes. One node sends a packet to another node and receives a duplicate, or echo, of that packet.*

AFP (AppleTalk Filing Protocol) *A presentation-layer protocol that allows users to share data files and application programs that reside on a file server. AFP supports AppleShare and Mac OS file sharing.*

agent *1. Generally, software that processes queries and returns replies on behalf of an application. 2. In NMSs, a process that resides in all managed devices and reports the values of specified variables to management stations.*

algorithm *See protocol.*

ANSI (American National Standards Institute) *A voluntary organization composed of corporate, government, and other members that coordinates standards-related activities, approves U.S. national standards, and develops positions for the U.S. in international standards organizations. ANSI helps develop international and U.S. standards relating to, among other things, communications and networking. ANSI is a member of the IEC and the International Organization for Standardization.*

API (application programming interface) *A specification of function-call conventions that defines an interface to a service.*

AppleTalk *A series of communications protocols designed by Apple Computer consisting of two phases. Phase 1, the earlier version, supports a single physical network that can have only one network number and be in one zone. Phase 2 supports multiple logical networks on a single physical network and allows networks to be in more than one zone. See also zone.*

application *A program that performs a function directly for a user. FTP and Telnet clients are examples of network applications.*

application layer *Layer 7 of the OSI reference model. This layer provides network services to user applications. For example, a word processing application is serviced by file transfer services at this layer. See also OSI reference model.*

APPN (Advanced Peer-to-Peer Networking) *An enhancement to the original IBM SNA architecture. APPN handles session establishment between peer nodes, dynamic transparent route calculation, and traffic prioritization for APPC traffic.*

ARA (AppleTalk Remote Access) *A protocol that provides Macintosh users direct access to information and resources at a remote AppleTalk site.*

area *A logical set of network segments (CLNS, DECnet, or OSPF based) and their attached devices. Areas are usually connected to other areas via routers, making up a single autonomous system.*

ARP (Address Resolution Protocol) *An Internet protocol used to map an IP address to a MAC address. Defined in RFC 826. Compare with RARP.*

ARPA (Advanced Research Projects Agency) *A research and development organization that is part of the U.S. Department of Defense. ARPA is responsible for numerous technological advances in communications and networking. ARPA evolved into DARPA, and then back into ARPA again in 1994.*

ARPANET *Advanced Research Projects Agency Network. A landmark packet-switching network established in 1969. ARPANET was developed in the 1970s by BBN and funded by ARPA (and later DARPA). It eventually evolved into the Internet. The term ARPANET was officially retired in 1990.*

AS (autonomous system) *A collection of networks under common administration sharing a common routing strategy. Also referred to as a routing domain. The AS is assigned a 16-bit number by the Internet Assigned Numbers Authority.*

ASBR (autonomous system boundary router) *An ABR located between an OSPF autonomous system and a non-OSPF network. ASBRs run both OSPF and another routing protocol, such as RIP. ASBRs must reside in a nonstub OSPF area.*

ASCII (American Standard Code for Information Interchange) *An 8-bit code (7 bits plus parity) for character representation.*

asymmetric switching *A type of switching that provides switched connections between ports of unlike bandwidth, such as a combination of 10-Mbps and 100-Mbps ports.*

Asynchronous Balanced Mode *See ABM.*

asynchronous circuit *A signal that is transmitted without precise clocking. Such signals generally have different frequencies and phase relationships. Asynchronous transmissions usually encapsulate individual characters in control bits (called start and stop bits) that designate the beginning and end of each character. See also synchronous circuit.*

Asynchronous Transfer Mode *See ATM.*

ATM (Asynchronous Transfer Mode) *An international standard for cell relay in which multiple service types (such as voice, video, or data) are conveyed in fixed-length (53-byte) cells. Fixed-length cells allow cell processing to occur in hardware, thereby reducing transit delays. ATM is designed to take advantage of high-speed transmission media, such as E3, SONET, and T3.*

ATM Forum *An international organization jointly founded in 1991 by Cisco Systems, NET/ADAPTIVE, Northern Telecom, and Sprint that develops and promotes standards-based implementation agreements for ATM technology. The ATM Forum expands on official standards developed by ANSI and ITU-T, and develops implementation agreements in advance of official standards.*

ATP (AppleTalk Transaction Protocol) *A transport-level protocol that provides a loss-free transaction service between sockets. The service allows exchanges between two socket clients in which one client requests the other to perform a particular task and to report the results. ATP binds the request and response together to ensure the reliable exchange of request/response pairs.*

attenuation *Loss of communication signal energy.*

AUI (attachment unit interface) *An IEEE 802.3 interface between a MAU and a network interface card. The term AUI can also refer to the rear panel port to which an AUI cable might attach, such as those found on a Cisco LightStream Ethernet access card. Also called a transceiver cable.*

AURP (AppleTalk Update-Based Routing Protocol) *A method of encapsulating AppleTalk traffic in the header of a foreign protocol, allowing the connection of two or more discontiguous AppleTalk internetworks through a foreign network (such as TCP/IP) to form an AppleTalk WAN. This connection is called an AURP tunnel. In addition to its encapsulation function, AURP maintains routing tables for the entire AppleTalk WAN by exchanging routing information between exterior routers.*

authentication *In security, the verification of the identity of a person or process.*

B

backbone *The structural core of the network, which connects all the components of the network so that communication can occur.*

backbone cabling *Cabling that provides interconnections between wiring closets, between wiring closets and the POP, and between buildings that are part of the same LAN.*

backoff *The retransmission delay enforced when a collision occurs.*

balanced-hybrid routing protocol *A protocol that combines aspects of the link-state and distance-vector protocols. See also link-state routing protocol and distance-vector routing protocol.*

bandwidth *The difference between the highest and lowest frequencies available for network signals. Also, the rated throughput capacity of a given network medium or protocol.*

bandwidth reservation *The process of assigning bandwidth to users and applications served by a network. It involves assigning priority to different flows of traffic based on how critical and delay sensitive they are. This makes the best use of available bandwidth, and if the network becomes congested, lower-priority traffic can be dropped. Sometimes called bandwidth allocation.*

Banyan VINES *See VINES.*

Basic Rate Interface *See BRI.*

B channel (bearer channel) *In ISDN, a full-duplex, 64-kbps channel used to send user data. See also 2B+D, D channel, E channel, and H channel.*

BECN (backward explicit congestion notification) *A bit set by a Frame Relay network in frames traveling in the opposite direction of frames encountering a congested path. DTE devices receiving frames with the BECN bit set can request that higher-level protocols take flow control action as appropriate. See also FECN.*

best-effort delivery *Delivery that occurs when a network system does not use a sophisticated acknowledgment system to guarantee reliable delivery of information.*

BGP (Border Gateway Protocol) *An interdomain routing protocol that replaces EGP. BGP exchanges reachability information with other BGP systems and is defined by RFC 1163.*

binary *A numbering system characterized by ones and zeros (1 = on; 0 = off).*

bit *A binary digit used in the binary numbering system. Can be zero or one. See also byte.*

bit bucket *The destination of discarded bits as determined by the router.*

BOOTP (Bootstrap Protocol) *A protocol used by a network node to determine the IP address of its Ethernet interfaces to affect network booting.*

bootstrap *A simple, preset operation to load instructions that in turn cause other instructions to be loaded into memory, or cause entry into other configuration modes.*

Bootstrap Protocol *See BOOTP.*

border router *A router situated at the edges, or end, of the network boundary, which provides a basic security from the outside network, or from a less controlled area of the network into a more private area of the network.*

BPDU (bridge protocol data unit) *A Spanning-Tree Protocol hello packet that is sent out at configurable intervals to exchange information among bridges in the network.*

BRI (Basic Rate Interface) *An ISDN interface composed of two B channels and one D channel for circuit-switched communication of voice, video, and data. Compare with PRI.*

bridge *A device that connects and passes packets between two network segments that use the same communications protocol. Bridges operate at the data link layer (Layer 2) of the OSI reference model. In general, a bridge filters, forwards, or floods an incoming frame based on the MAC address of that frame.*

bridging *A technology in which a bridge connects two or more LAN segments.*

broadcast *A data packet that is sent to all nodes on a network. Broadcasts are identified by a broadcast address. Compare with multicast and unicast. See also broadcast address, broadcast domain, and broadcast storm.*

broadcast address *A special address reserved for sending a message to all stations. Generally, a broadcast address is a MAC destination address of all ones. Compare with multicast address and unicast address. See also broadcast.*

broadcast domain *The set of all devices that will receive broadcast frames originating from any device within the set. Broadcast domains are typically bounded by routers because routers do not forward broadcast frames. See also broadcast.*

broadcast storm *An undesirable network event in which many broadcasts are sent simultaneously across all network segments. A broadcast storm uses substantial network bandwidth and, typically, causes network timeouts. See also broadcast.*

bus topology *A linear LAN architecture in which transmissions from network stations propagate the length of the medium and are received by all other stations. Compare with ring topology, star topology, and tree topology.*

byte *A series of consecutive binary digits that are operated on as a unit (for example, an 8-bit byte). See also bit.*

C

cable range *A range of network numbers that is valid for use by nodes on an extended AppleTalk network. The cable range value can be a single network number or a contiguous sequence of several network numbers. Node addresses are assigned based on the cable range value.*

caching *A form of replication in which information learned during a previous transaction is used to process later transactions.*

call setup time *The time required to establish a switched call between DTE devices.*

CAM (content-addressable memory) *Memory that maintains an accurate and functional forwarding database.*

carrier *An electromagnetic wave or alternating current of a single frequency, suitable for modulation by another, data-bearing signal.*

carrier network *A service provider's network.*

catchment area *A zone that falls within an area that can be served by an internetworking device, such as a hub.*

Category 1 cabling *One of five grades of UTP cabling described in the EIA/TIA 568B standard. Category 1 cabling is used for telephone communications and is not suitable for transmitting data. See also UTP.*

Category 2 cabling *One of five grades of UTP cabling described in the EIA/ TIA 568B standard. Category 2 cabling is capable of transmitting data at speeds up to 4 Mbps. See also UTP.*

Category 3 cabling *One of five grades of UTP cabling described in the EIA/ TIA 568B standard. Category 3 cabling is used in 10BaseT networks and can transmit data at speeds up to 10 Mbps. See also UTP.*

Category 4 cabling *One of five grades of UTP cabling described in the EIA/ TIA 568B standard. Category 4 cabling is used in Token Ring networks and can transmit data at speeds up to 16 Mbps. See also UTP.*

Category 5 cabling *One of five grades of UTP cabling described in the EIA/ TIA 568B standard. Category 5 cabling can transmit data at speeds up to 100 Mbps. See also UTP.*

CCITT (Consultative Committee for International Telegraph and Telephone) *An international organization responsible for the development of communications standards. Now called the ITU-T. See ITU-T.*

CDDI (Copper Distributed Data Interface) *An implementation of FDDI protocols over STP and UTP cabling. CDDI transmits over relatively short distances (about 100 meters), providing data rates of 100 Mbps using a dual-ring architecture to provide redundancy. Based on the ANSI Twisted-Pair Physical Medium Dependent (TPPMD) standard. Compare with FDDI.*

Challenge Handshake Authentication Protocol *See CHAP.*

CHAP (Challenge Handshake Authentication Protocol) *A security feature supported on lines using PPP encapsulation that prevents unauthorized access. CHAP does not itself prevent unauthorized access, but it identifies the remote end; the router or access server then determines whether that user is allowed access.*

CIDR (classless interdomain routing) *A technique supported by BGP and based on route aggregation. CIDR allows routers to group routes together in order to cut down on the quantity of routing information carried by the core routers. With CIDR, several IP networks appear to networks outside the group as a single, larger entity.*

CIR (committed information rate) *The rate, in bits per second, at which the Frame Relay switch agrees to transfer data.*

circuit *A communications path between two or more points.*

circuit group *A grouping of associated serial lines that link two bridges. If one of the serial links in a circuit group is in the spanning tree for a network, any of the serial links in the circuit group can be used for load balancing. This load-balancing strategy avoids data ordering problems by assigning each destination address to a particular serial link.*

circuit switching *A switching system in which a dedicated physical circuit path must exist between the sender and the receiver for the duration of the "call." Used heavily in the telephone company network. Circuit switching can be contrasted with contention and token passing as a channel-access method, and with message switching and packet switching as a switching technique.*

Cisco IOS (Internetwork Operating System) software *Cisco system software that provides common functionality, scalability, and security for all products under the CiscoFusion architecture. The Cisco IOS software allows centralized, integrated, and automated installation and management of internetworks, while ensuring support for a wide variety of protocols, media, services, and platforms.*

client *A node or software program (front-end device) that requests services from a server. See also server.*

client/server *The architecture of the relationship between a workstation and a server in a network.*

client/server application *An application that is stored centrally on a server and accessed by workstations, thus making it easy to maintain and protect.*

client/server computing *Distributed computing (processing) network systems in which transaction responsibilities are divided into two parts: client (front end) and server (back end). Both terms (client and server) can be applied to software programs or actual computing devices. Also called distributed computing (processing). Compare with peer-to-peer computing.*

client/server model *A common way to describe network services and the model user processes (programs) of those services. Examples include the nameserver/nameresolver paradigm of the DNS and fileserver/file-client relationships such as NFS and diskless hosts.*

CMIP (Common Management Information Protocol) *An OSI network management protocol created and standardized by ISO for the monitoring and control of heterogeneous networks. See also CMIS.*

CMIS (Common Management Information Services) *An OSI network management service interface created and standardized by ISO for the monitoring and control of heterogeneous networks. See also CMIP.*

CO (central office) *The local telephone company office to which all local loops in a given area connect and in which circuit switching of subscriber lines occurs.*

coaxial cable *Cable consisting of a hollow outer cylindrical conductor that surrounds a single inner wire conductor. Two types of coaxial cable are currently used in LANs: 50-ohm cable, which is used for digital signaling, and 75-ohm cable, which is used for analog signal and high-speed digital signaling.*

coding *Electrical techniques used to convey binary signals.*

collision *In Ethernet, the result of two nodes transmitting simultaneously. The frames from each device collide and are damaged when they meet on the physical medium.*

collision domain *In Ethernet, the network area within which frames that have collided are propagated. Repeaters and hubs propagate collisions; LAN switches, bridges, and routers do not.*

common carrier *A licensed, private utility company that supplies communication services to the public at regulated prices.*

concentrator *See hub.*

congestion *Traffic in excess of network capacity.*

congestion avoidance *A mechanism by which an ATM network controls traffic entering the network to minimize delays. To use resources most efficiently, lower-priority traffic is discarded at the edge of the network if conditions indicate that it cannot be delivered.*

connectionless *Data transfer without the existence of a virtual circuit. Compare with connection-oriented. See also virtual circuit.*

connection-oriented *Data transfer that requires the establishment of a virtual circuit. See also connectionless and virtual circuit.*

console *A DTE through which commands are entered into a host.*

contention *An access method in which network devices compete for permission to access the physical medium.*

convergence *The speed and ability of a group of internetworking devices running a specific routing protocol to agree on the topology of an internetwork after a change in that topology.*

core layer *The layer that provides fast wide-area connections between geographically remote sites, tying a number of campus networks together in a corporate or enterprise WAN.*

cost *An arbitrary value, typically based on hop count, media bandwidth, or other measures, that is assigned by a network administrator and used to compare various paths through an internetwork environment. Cost values are used by routing protocols to determine the most favorable path to a particular destination: the lower the cost, the better the path.*

count to infinity *A problem that can occur in routing algorithms that are slow to converge, in which routers continuously increment the hop count to particular networks. Typically, some arbitrary hop-count limit is imposed to prevent this problem.*

CPE (customer premises equipment) *Terminating equipment, such as terminals, telephones, and modems, supplied by the telephone company, installed at customer sites, and connected to the telephone company network.*

CSMA/CD (carrier sense multiple access collision detect) *A media-access mechanism wherein devices ready to transmit data first check the channel for a carrier. If no carrier is sensed for a specific period of time, a device can transmit. If two devices transmit at once, a collision occurs and is detected by all colliding devices. This collision subsequently delays retransmissions from those devices for some random length of time. CSMA/CD access is used by Ethernet and IEEE 802.3.*

CSU/DSU (channel service unit/digital service unit) *A digital interface device that connects end-user equipment to the local digital telephone loop.*

cut sheet *A rough diagram indicating where cable runs are located and the numbers of rooms they lead to.*

cut-through *A packet-switching approach that streams data through a switch so that the leading edge of a packet exits the switch at the output port before the packet finishes entering the input port. A device using cut-through packet switching reads, processes, and forwards packets as soon as the destination address is looked up and the outgoing port is determined. Also known as on-the-fly packet switching.*

D

DARPA (Defense Advanced Research Projects Agency) *The U.S. government agency that funded research for and experimentation with the Internet. Evolved from ARPA, and then, in 1994, back to ARPA. See also ARPA.*

DAS (dual attachment station) *A device attached to both the primary and the secondary FDDI rings. Dual attachment provides redundancy for the FDDI ring: If the primary ring fails, the station can wrap the primary ring to the secondary ring, isolating the failure and retaining ring integrity. Also called a Class A station. Compare with SAS.*

data *Upper-layer protocol data.*

data flow control layer *Layer 5 of the SNA architectural model. This layer determines and manages interactions between session partners, particularly data flow. Corresponds to the session layer of the OSI reference model. See also data link control layer, path control layer, physical control layer, presentation services layer, transaction services layer, and transmission control layer.*

datagram *A logical grouping of information sent as a network-layer unit over a transmission medium without prior establishment of a virtual circuit. IP datagrams are the primary information units in the Internet. The terms cell, frame, message, packet, and segment are also used to describe logical information groupings at various layers of the OSI reference model and in various technology circles.*

data link control layer *Layer 2 in the SNA architectural model. Responsible for the transmission of data over a particular physical link. Corresponds roughly to the data link layer of the OSI reference model. See also data flow control layer, path control layer, physical control layer, presentation services layer, transaction services layer, and transmission control layer.*

data link layer *Layer 2 of the OSI reference model. This layer provides reliable transit of data across a physical link. The data link layer is concerned* with physical addressing, network topology, line discipline, error notification, ordered delivery of frames, and flow control. The IEEE has divided this layer into two sublayers: the MAC sublayer and the LLC sublayer. Sometimes simply called link layer. Roughly corresponds to the data link control layer of the SNA model. See also OSI reference model.

DCE (data circuit-terminating equipment) *The device used to convert the user data from the DTE into a form acceptable to the WAN service's facility. Compare with DTE.*

D channel (delta channel) *A full-duplex, 16-kbps (BRI) or 64-kbps (PRI) ISDN channel. See also B channel, D channel, E channel, and H channel.*

DDN (Defense Data Network) *A U.S. military network composed of an unclassified network (MILNET) and various secret and top-secret networks. DDN is operated and maintained by DISA.*

DDP (Datagram Delivery Protocol) *An AppleTalk network-layer protocol responsible for the socket-to-socket delivery of datagrams over an AppleTalk internetwork.*

DDR (dial-on-demand routing) *A technique with which a router can dynamically initiate and close circuit-switched sessions as transmitting end stations need them.*

DECnet *A group of communications products (including a protocol suite) developed and supported by Digital Equipment Corporation. DECnet/OSI (also called DECnet Phase V) is the most recent iteration and supports both OSI protocols and proprietary Digital protocols. Phase IV Prime supports inherent MAC addresses that allow DECnet nodes to coexist with systems running other protocols that have MAC address restrictions.*

DECnet Routing Protocol *See DRP.*

dedicated link *A communications link that is indefinitely reserved for transmissions, rather than switched as transmission is required. See also leased line.*

default route *A routing table entry that is used to direct frames for which a next hop is not explicitly listed in the routing table.*

delay *The time between the initiation of a transaction by a sender and the first response received by the sender. Also, the time required to move a packet from source to destination over a given path.*

demarcation *The point at which the CPE ends and the local loop portion of the service begins. Often occurs at the POP of a building.*

demultiplexing *The separating of multiple input streams that have been multiplexed into a common physical signal back into multiple output streams. See also multiplexing.*

designated router *An OSPF router that generates LSAs for a multiaccess network and has other special responsibilities in running OSPF. Each multiaccess OSPF network that has at least two attached routers has a designated router that is elected by the OSPF Hello protocol. The designated router enables a reduction in the number of adjacencies required on a multiaccess network, which in turn reduces the amount of routing protocol traffic and the size of the topological database.*

destination address *An address of a network device that is receiving data. See also source address.*

destination service access point *See DSAP.*

DHCP *Dynamic Host Configuration Protocol. A protocol that provides a mechanism for allocating IP addresses dynamically so that addresses automatically can be reused when hosts no longer need them.*

dial-on-demand routing *See DDR.*

dialup line *A communications circuit that is established by a switched-circuit connection using the telephone company network.*

distance-vector routing protocol *A routing protocol that iterates on the number of hops in a route to find a shortest-path spanning tree. Distance-vector routing protocols call for each router to send its entire routing table in each update, but only to its neighbors. Distance-vector routing protocols can be prone to routing loops, but are computationally simpler than link-state routing protocols. Also called Bellman-Ford routing algorithm. Compare with balanced-hybrid routing protocol and link-state routing protocol.*

distribution layer *The layer in which the distribution of network services occurs to multiple LANs within a WAN environment. This layer is where the WAN backbone network is found, typically based on Fast Ethernet.*

DLCI (data-link connection identifier) *A value that specifies a PVC or an SVC in a Frame Relay network. In the basic Frame Relay specification, DLCIs are* *locally significant (that is, connected devices can use different values to specify the same connection). In the LMI extended specification, DLCIs are globally significant (that is, DLCIs specify individual end devices).*

DNS (Domain Name System) *A system used in the Internet for translating names of network nodes into addresses.*

DoD (Department of Defense) *The U.S. government organization that is responsible for national defense. The DoD has frequently funded communication protocol development.*

dotted-decimal notation *The common notation for IP addresses in the form* a.b.c.d, *where each number represents, in decimal, 1 byte of the 4-byte IP address. Also called dotted notation or four-part dotted notation.*

DRP (DECnet Routing Protocol) *A proprietary routing scheme introduced by Digital Equipment Corporation in DECnet Phase III. In DECnet Phase V, DECnet completed its transition to OSI routing protocols (ES-IS and IS-IS).*

DSAP (destination service access point) *The SAP of the network node designated in the Destination field of a packet. Compare with SSAP. See also SAP (service access point).*

DTE (data terminal equipment) *A device at the user end of a user-to-network interface that serves as a data source, destination, or both. A DTE connects to a data network through a DCE device (for example, a modem) and typically uses clocking signals generated by the DCE. DTEs includes such devices as computers, protocol translators, and multiplexers. Compare with DCE.*

dual attachment station *See DAS.*

dual counter-rotating rings *A network topology in which two signal paths, whose directions are opposite each other, exist in a token-passing network. FDDI and CDDI are based on this concept.*

dual-homed station *A device attached to multiple FDDI concentrators to provide redundancy.*

dual homing *A network topology in which a device is connected to the network by way of two independent access points (points of attachment). One access point is the primary connection, and the other is a standby connection that is activated in the event of a failure of the primary connection.*

dynamic routing *Routing that adjusts automatically to network topology or traffic changes. Also called adaptive routing. Compare with static routing.*

dynamic VLAN *A VLAN that is based on the MAC addresses, the logical addresses, or the protocol type of the data packets. Compare with static VLAN. See also LAN and VLAN.*

E

E1 *A wide-area digital transmission scheme used predominantly in Europe that carries data at a rate of 2.048 Mbps. E1 lines can be leased for private use from common carriers. Compare with T1.*

E3 *A wide-area digital transmission scheme used predominantly in Europe that carries data at a rate of 34.368 Mbps. E3 lines can be leased for private use from common carriers. Compare with T3.*

E channel (echo channel) *A 64-kbps ISDN circuit-switching control channel. The E channel was defined in the 1984 ITU-T ISDN specification, but was dropped in the 1988 specification. Compare with B channel, D channel, and H channel.*

echo channel *See E channel.*

EEPROM (electrically erasable programmable read-only memory) *EPROM that can be erased using electrical signals applied to specific pins.*

EIA (Electronic Industries Association) *A group that specifies electrical transmission standards. EIA and TIA have developed numerous well-known communications standards together, including EIA/TIA-232 and EIA/TIA-449.*

EIA/TIA 568 *A standard that describes the characteristics and applications for various grades of UTP cabling.*

Enhanced IGRP (Enhanced Interior Gateway Routing Protocol) *An advanced version of IGRP developed by Cisco. Provides superior convergence properties and operating efficiency, and combines the advantages of link-state protocols with those of distance-vector protocols. Compare with IGRP. See also OSPF and RIP.*

encapsulate *To wrap data in a particular protocol header. For example, Ethernet data is wrapped in a specific Ethernet header before network transit. Also,* *when bridging dissimilar networks, the entire frame from one network is simply placed in the header used by the data link layer protocol of the other network.*

encapsulation *Wrapping of data in a particular protocol header. For example, upper-layer data is wrapped in a specific Ethernet header before network transit. Also, when bridging dissimilar networks, the entire frame from one network can simply be placed in the header used by the data link layer protocol of the other network. See also tunneling.*

encoding *The process by which bits are represented by voltages.*

enterprise network *A corporation, agency, school, or other organization's network that ties together its data, communication, computing, and file servers.*

enterprise server *A server that supports all the users on a network, by offering services such as e-mail or Domain Name System (DNS). Compare with workgroup server.*

EPROM (erasable programmable read-only memory) *Nonvolatile memory chips that are programmed after they are manufactured and, if necessary, can be erased by some means and reprogrammed. Compare with EEPROM and PROM.*

ES-IS (End System-to-Intermediate System) *An OSI protocol that defines how end systems (hosts) announce themselves to intermediate systems (routers). See also IS-IS.*

Ethernet *A baseband LAN specification invented by Xerox Corporation and developed jointly by Xerox, Intel, and Digital Equipment Corporation. Ethernet networks use CSMA/CD and run over a variety of cable types at 10 Mbps. Ethernet is similar to the IEEE 802.3 series of standards. See also Fast Ethernet.*

excess rate *Traffic in excess of the insured rate for a given connection. Specifically, the excess rate equals the maximum rate minus the insured rate. Excess traffic is delivered only if network resources are available and can be discarded during periods of congestion. Compare with insured rate and maximum rate.*

extended ACL (extended access control list) *An ACL that checks for source address and destination address. Compare with standard ACL. See also ACL.*

exterior protocol *A protocol that is used to exchange routing information between networks that do not share a common administration. Compare with interior protocol.*

F

Fast Ethernet *Any of a number of 100-Mbps Ethernet specifications. Fast Ethernet offers a speed increase ten times that of the 10BaseT Ethernet specification, while preserving such qualities as frame format, MAC mechanisms, and MTU. Such similarities allow the use of existing 10BaseT applications and network management tools on Fast Ethernet networks. Based on an extension to the IEEE 802.3 specification. See also Ethernet.*

fast-forward switching *Switching that offers the lowest level of latency by immediately forwarding a packet after receiving the destination address.*

fault management *Five categories of network management— accounting management, configuration management, performance management, and security management—defined by ISO for management of OSI networks. Fault management attempts to ensure that network faults are detected and controlled.*

FDDI (Fiber Distributed Data Interface) *A LAN standard, defined by ANSI X3T9.5, specifying a 100-Mbps token-passing network using fiber-optic cable, with transmission distances of up to 2 km. FDDI uses a dual-ring architecture to provide redundancy. Compare with CDDI and FDDI II.*

FDDI II *An ANSI standard that enhances FDDI. FDDI II provides isochronous transmission for connectionless data circuits and connection-oriented voice and video circuits. Compare with FDDI.*

FECN (forward explicit congestion notification) *A bit set by a Frame Relay network to inform DTE devices receiving the frame that congestion was experienced in the path from source to destination. DTE devices receiving frames with the FECN bit set can request that higher-level protocols take flow-control action as appropriate. See also BECN.*

Fiber Distributed Data Interface *See FDDI.*

fiber-optic cable *A physical medium capable of conducting modulated light transmission. Compared with other transmission media, fiber-optic cable is more expensive, but is not susceptible to electromagnetic interference, and is capable of higher data rates. Sometimes called optical fiber.*

File Transfer Protocol   *See FTP.*

filter   *Generally, a process or device that screens network traffic for certain characteristics, such as source address, destination address, or protocol, and determines whether to forward or discard that traffic based on the established criteria.*

firewall   *A router or an access server, or several routers or access servers, designated as a buffer between any connected public networks and a private network. A firewall router uses access control lists and other methods to ensure the security of the private network.*

firmware   *Software instructions set permanently or semipermanently in ROM.*

Flash memory   *Nonvolatile storage that can be electrically erased and reprogrammed so that software images can be stored, booted, and rewritten as necessary. Flash memory was developed by Intel and is licensed to other semiconductor companies.*

flash update   *The process of the sending of an update sooner than the standard periodic update interval for notifying other routers of a metric change.*

flat addressing   *A scheme of addressing that does not use a logical hierarchy to determine location.*

flat network   *A network in which there are no routers placed between the switches, broadcasts and Layer 2 transmissions are sent to every switched port, and there is one broadcast domain across the entire network.*

flooding   *A traffic-passing technique used by switches and bridges in which traffic received on an interface is sent out all the interfaces of that device except the interface on which the information was originally received.*

flow   *A stream of data traveling between two endpoints across a network (for example, from one LAN station to another). Multiple flows can be transmitted on a single circuit.*

flow control   *A technique for ensuring that a transmitting entity does not overwhelm a receiving entity with data. When the buffers on the receiving device are full, a message is sent to the sending device to suspend the transmission until the data in the buffers has been processed. In IBM networks, this technique is called pacing.*

forwarding *A process of sending a frame toward its ultimate destination by way of an internetworking device.*

fragment *A piece of a larger packet that has been broken down into smaller units. In Ethernet networks, also sometimes referred to as a frame less than the legal limit of 64 bytes.*

fragment-free switching *A switching technique that filters out collision fragments, which are the majority of packet errors, before forwarding begins.*

fragmentation *The process of breaking a packet into smaller units when transmitting over a network medium that cannot support the original size of the packet.*

frame *A logical grouping of information sent as a data link-layer unit over a transmission medium. Often refers to the header and trailer, used for synchronization and error control, that surround the user data contained in the unit. The terms datagram, message, packet, and segment are also used to describe logical information groupings at various layers of the OSI reference model and in various technology circles.*

frame forwarding *A mechanism by which frame-based traffic, such as HDLC and SDLC, traverses an ATM network.*

Frame Relay *An industry-standard, switched data link-layer protocol that handles multiple virtual circuits using HDLC encapsulation between connected devices. Frame Relay is more efficient than X.25, the protocol for which it is generally considered a replacement.*

FTP (File Transfer Protocol) *An application protocol, part of the TCP/IP protocol stack, used for transferring files between network nodes. FTP is defined in RFC 959.*

full duplex *The capability for simultaneous data transmission between a sending station and a receiving station. Compare with half duplex and simplex.*

full-duplex Ethernet *A capability for simultaneous data transmission between a sending station and a receiving station. Compare with half-duplex Ethernet.*

fully meshed topology *A topology in which every Frame Relay network device has a PVC to every other device on the multipoint WAN.*

G

gateway *In the IP community, an older term referring to a routing device. Today, the term router is used to describe nodes that perform this function, and gateway refers to a special-purpose device that performs an application-layer conversion of information from one protocol stack to another. Compare with router.*

gateway of last resort *A router to which all unroutable packets are sent.*

Gb (gigabit) *Approximately 1,000,000,000 bits.*

Gbps (gigabytes per second) *A rate of transfer speed.*

Get Nearest Server *See GNS.*

gigabit *See Gb.*

GNS (Get Nearest Server) *A request packet sent by a client on an IPX network to locate the nearest active server of a particular type. An IPX network client issues a GNS request to solicit either a direct response from a connected server or a response from a router that tells it where on the internetwork the service can be located. GNS is part of IPX SAP.*

GUI (graphical user interface) *A user environment that uses pictorial as well as textual representations of the input and output of applications and the hierarchical or other data structure in which information is stored. Conventions such as buttons, icons, and windows are typical, and many actions are performed using a pointing device (such as a mouse). Microsoft Windows and the Apple Macintosh are prominent examples of platforms utilizing GUIs.*

H

half duplex *A capability for data transmission in only one direction at a time between a sending station and a receiving station. Compare with full duplex and simplex.*

half-duplex Ethernet *A capability for data transmission in only one direction at a time between a sending station and a receiving station. Compare with full-duplex Ethernet.*

handshake *A sequence of messages exchanged between two or more network devices to ensure transmission synchronization before sending user data.*

hardware address *See MAC address.*

H channel (high-speed channel) *A full-duplex ISDN primary rate channel operating at 384 kbps. Compare with B channel, D channel, and E channel.*

HCC (horizontal cross-connect) *A wiring closet where the horizontal cabling connects to a patch panel that is connected by backbone cabling to the MDF.*

HDLC (High-Level Data Link Control) *A bit-oriented synchronous data link-layer protocol developed by ISO. HDLC specifies a data encapsulation method on synchronous serial links by using frame characters and checksums.*

header *Control information placed before data when encapsulating that data for network transmission.*

hello packet *A multicast packet that is used by routers using certain routing protocols for neighbor discovery and recovery. Hello packets also indicate that a client is still operating and network ready.*

hexadecimal (base 16) *A number representation using the digits 0 through 9, with their usual meaning, plus the letters A through F, to represent hexadecimal digits with values 10 to 15. The rightmost digit counts ones, the next counts multiples of 16, the next is $16^2=256$, and so on.*

holddown *An IGRP feature that rejects new routes for the same destination for some period of time.*

hop *The passage of a data packet between two network nodes (for example, between two routers).*

hop count *A routing metric used to measure the distance between a source and a destination. RIP uses hop count as its sole metric.*

horizontal cross-connect *See HCC.*

host *A computer system on a network. Similar to node, except that host usually implies a computer system, whereas node generally applies to any networked system, including access servers and routers. See also node.*

host address *See host number.*

host number *The part of an IP address that designates which node on the subnetwork is being addressed. Also called a host address.*

HTML (Hypertext Markup Language) *A simple hypertext document formatting language that uses tags to indicate how a given part of a document should be interpreted by a viewing application, such as a Web browser.*

HTTP (Hypertext Transfer Protocol) *The protocol used by Web browsers and Web servers to transfer files, such as text and graphics files.*

hub *1. Generally, a device that serves as the center of a star-topology network. Also called a multiport repeater. 2. A hardware or software device that contains multiple independent but connected modules of network and internetwork equipment. Hubs can be active (where they repeat signals sent through them) or passive (where they do not repeat, but merely split, signals sent through them).*

hybrid network *An internetwork made up of more than one type of network technology, including LANs and WANs.*

Hypertext Markup Language *See HTML.*

Hypertext Transfer Protocol *See HTTP.*

I

IAB (Internet Architecture Board) *A board of internetwork researchers who discuss issues pertinent to Internet architecture. Responsible for appointing a variety of Internet-related groups such as the IANA, IESG, and IRSG. The IAB is appointed by the trustees of the ISOC. See also IANA, IESG, IRSG, and ISOC.*

IANA (Internet Assigned Numbers Authority) *An organization operated under the auspices of the ISOC as a part of the IAB. IANA delegates authority for IP address-space allocation and domain-name assignment to the InterNIC* *and other organizations. IANA also maintains a database of assigned protocol identifiers used in the TCP/IP stack, including autonomous system numbers.*

ICMP (Internet Control Message Protocol) *A network-layer Internet protocol that reports errors and provides other information relevant to IP packet processing. Documented in RFC 792.*

IDF (intermediate distribution facility) *A secondary communications room for a building using a star networking topology. The IDF is dependent on the MDF.*

IEC (International Electrotechnical Commission) *An industry group that writes and distributes standards for electrical products and components.*

IEEE (Institute of Electrical and Electronic Engineers) *A professional organization whose activities include the development of communications and network standards. IEEE LAN standards are the predominant LAN standards today.*

IEEE 802.2 *An IEEE LAN protocol that specifies an implementation of the LLC sublayer of the data link layer. IEEE 802.2 handles errors, framing, flow control, and the network layer (Layer 3) service interface. Used in IEEE 802.3 and IEEE 802.5 LANs. See also IEEE 802.3 and IEEE 802.5.*

IEEE 802.3 *An IEEE LAN protocol that specifies an implementation of the physical layer and the MAC sublayer of the data link layer. IEEE 802.3 uses CSMA/CD access at a variety of speeds over a variety of physical media. Extensions to the IEEE 802.3 standard specify implementations for Fast Ethernet. Physical variations of the original IEEE 802.3 specification include 10Base2, 10Base5, 10BaseF, 10BaseT, and 10Broad36. Physical variations for Fast Ethernet include 100BaseTX and 100BaseFX.*

IEEE 802.5 *An IEEE LAN protocol that specifies an implementation of the physical layer and MAC sublayer of the data link layer. IEEE 802.5 uses token passing access at 4 or 16 Mbps over STP or UTP cabling and is functionally and operationally equivalent to IBM Token Ring. See also Token Ring.*

IETF (Internet Engineering Task Force) *A task force consisting of more than 80 working groups responsible for developing Internet standards. The IETF operates under the auspices of ISOC.*

IGRP (Interior Gateway Routing Protocol) *A protocol developed by Cisco to address the problems associated with routing in large, heterogeneous networks.*

Institute of Electrical and Electronic Engineers *See IEEE.*

insured rate *The long-term data throughput, in bits or cells per second, that an ATM network commits to support under normal network conditions. The insured rate is 100 percent allocated; the entire amount is deducted from the total trunk bandwidth along the path of the circuit. Compare with excess rate and maximum rate.*

Integrated Services Digital Network *See ISDN.*

interior protocol *A protocol that is used for routing networks that are under a common network administration.*

intermediate distribution facility *See IDF.*

International Organization for Standardization *See ISO.*

interface *1. A connection between two systems or devices. 2. In routing terminology, a network connection. 3. In telephony, a shared boundary defined by common physical interconnection characteristics, signal characteristics, and meanings of interchanged signals.4. A boundary between adjacent layers of the OSI reference model.*

Internet *The largest global internetwork, connecting tens of thousands of networks worldwide and having a culture that focuses on research and standardization based on real-life use. Many leading-edge network technologies come from the Internet community. The Internet evolved in part from ARPANET. At one time called the DARPA Internet, not to be confused with the general term internet.*

internet *Short for internetwork. Not to be confused with the Internet. See internetwork.*

Internet Control Message Protocol *See ICMP.*

Internet protocol *Any protocol that is part of the TCP/IP protocol stack. See IP. See also TCP/IP.*

Internet Protocol *See IP.*

internetwork *A collection of networks interconnected by routers and other devices that functions (generally) as a single network*

internetworking *The industry devoted to connecting networks together. The term can refer to products, procedures, and technologies.*

Internetwork Packet Exchange *See IPX.*

InterNIC *An organization that serves the Internet community by supplying user assistance, documentation, training, registration service for Internet domain names, network addresses, and other services. Formerly called NIC.*

interoperability *The capability of computing equipment manufactured by different vendors to communicate with one another successfully over a network.*

intranet *An internal network that is to be accessed by users who have access to an organization's internal LAN.*

IOS (Internetwork Operating System) *See Cisco IOS software.*

IP (Internet Protocol) *A network-layer protocol in the TCP/IP stack offering a connectionless internetwork service. IP provides features for addressing, type-of-service specification, fragmentation and reassembly, and security. Defined in RFC 791. IPv4 (Internet Protocol version 4) is a connectionless, best-effort packet switching protocol. See also IPv6.*

IP address *A 32-bit address assigned to hosts by using TCP/IP. An IP address belongs to one of five classes (A, B, C, D, or E) and is written as 4 octets separated by periods (that is, dotted-decimal format). Each address consists of a network number, an optional subnetwork number, and a host number. The network and subnetwork numbers together are used for routing, and the host number is used to address an individual host within the network or subnetwork. A subnet mask is used to extract network and subnetwork information from the IP address. Also called an Internet address.*

IP datagram *A fundamental unit of information passed across the Internet. Contains source and destination addresses along with data and a number of fields that define such things as the length of the datagram, the header checksum, and flags to indicate whether the datagram can be (or was) fragmented.*

IPv6 (IP version 6) *A replacement for the current version of IP (version 4). IPv6 includes support for flow ID in the packet header, which can be used to identify flows. Formerly called IPng (IP next generation).*

IPX (Internetwork Packet Exchange) *A NetWare network-layer (Layer 3) protocol used for transferring data from servers to workstations. IPX is similar to IP and XNS.*

IPXWAN (IPX wide-area network) *A protocol that negotiates end-to-end options for new links. When a link comes up, the first IPX packets sent across are IPXWAN packets negotiating the options for the link. When the IPXWAN options are successfully determined, normal IPX transmission begins. Defined by RFC 1362.*

IS-IS (Intermediate System-to-Intermediate System) *An OSI link-state hierarchical routing protocol based on DECnet Phase V routing whereby ISs (routers) exchange routing information based on a single metric to determine network topology. See also ES-IS and OSPF.*

ISO (International Organization for Standardization) *An international organization that is responsible for a wide range of standards, including those relevant to networking. ISO developed the OSI reference model, a popular networking reference model.*

ISDN (Integrated Services Digital Network) *A communication protocol, offered by telephone companies, that permits telephone networks to carry data, voice, and other source traffic.*

ISOC (Internet Society) *An international nonprofit organization, founded in 1992, that coordinates the evolution and use of the Internet. In addition, ISOC delegates authority to other groups related to the Internet, such as the IAB. ISOC is headquartered in Reston, Virginia, U.S.A. See also IAB.*

ITU-T (International Telecommunication Union Telecommunication Standardization Sector) *Formerly the Committee for International Telegraph and Telephone (CCITT), an international organization that develops communication standards. See also CCITT.*

K

kb (kilobit) *Approximately 1,000 bits.*

kB (kilobyte) *Approximately 1,000 bytes.*

kbps (kilobits per second) *A rate of transfer speed.*

kBps (kilobytes per second) *A rate of transfer speed.*

keepalive *A message sent by one network device to inform another network device that the virtual circuit between the two is still active.*

keepalive interval *The period of time between each keepalive message sent by a network device.*

kilobit *See kb.*

kilobits per second *See kbps.*

kilobyte *See kB.*

kilobytes per second *See kBps.*

L

LAN (local-area network) *A high-speed, low-error data network covering a relatively small geographic area (up to a few thousand meters). LANs connect workstations, peripherals, terminals, and other devices in a single building or other geographically limited area. LAN standards specify cabling and signaling at the physical and data link layers of the OSI model. Ethernet, FDDI, and Token Ring are widely used LAN technologies. Compare with MAN and WAN. See also VLAN.*

LAN switch *A high-speed switch that forwards packets between data-link segments. Most LAN switches forward traffic based on MAC addresses. LAN switches are often categorized according to the method they use to forward traffic: cut-through packet switching or store-and-forward packet switching. An example of a LAN switch is the Cisco Catalyst 5000.*

LAPB (Link Access Procedure, Balanced) *A data link-layer protocol in the X.25 protocol stack. LAPB is a bit-oriented protocol derived from HDLC. See also HDLC and X.25.*

LAPD (Link Access Procedure on the D channel) *An ISDN data link-layer protocol for the D channel. LAPD was derived from LAPB and is designed primarily to satisfy the signaling requirements of ISDN basic access. Defined by ITU-T Recommendations Q.920 and Q.921.*

LAT (local-area transport) *A network virtual terminal protocol developed by Digital Equipment Corporation.*

latency *The delay between the time a device requests access to a network and the time it is granted permission to transmit.*

layering *The separation of networking functions used by the OSI reference model, which simplifies the tasks required for two computers to communicate with each other.*

LCP (Link Control Protocol) *A protocol that provides a method of establishing, configuring, maintaining, and terminating the point-to-point connection.*

leased line *A transmission line reserved by a communications carrier for the private use of a customer. A leased line is a type of dedicated line. See also dedicated link.*

link *A network communications channel consisting of a circuit or transmission path and all related equipment between a sender and a receiver. Most often used to refer to a WAN connection. Sometimes referred to as a line or a transmission link.*

Link Access Procedure, Balanced *See LAPB.*

Link Access Procedure on the D channel *See LAPD.*

Link Control Protocol *See LCP.*

link layer *See data link layer.*

link-layer address *See MAC address.*

link-state routing protocol *A routing protocol in which each router broadcasts or multicasts information regarding the cost of reaching each of its neighbors to all nodes in the internetwork. Link-state protocols create a consistent view of the network and are therefore not prone to routing loops, but they achieve this at the cost of relatively greater computational difficulty and more widespread traffic (compared with distance-vector routing protocols). Compare with balanced-hybrid routing protocol and distance-vector routing protocol.*

LLC (logical link control) *The higher of the two data link-layer sublayers defined by the IEEE. The LLC sublayer handles error control, flow control, framing, and MAC-sublayer addressing. The most prevalent LLC protocol is IEEE 802.2, which includes both connectionless and connection-oriented variants.*

LMI (Local Management Interface) *A set of enhancements to the basic Frame Relay specification. LMI includes support for a keepalive mechanism, which verifies that data is flowing; a multicast mechanism, which provides the network server with its local DLCI and the multicast DLCI; global addressing, which gives DLCIs global rather than local significance in Frame Relay networks; and a status mechanism, which provides an ongoing status report on the DLCIs known to the switch.*

load *The amount of activity on a network resource, such as a router or link.*

load balancing *In routing, the capability of a router to distribute traffic over all its network ports that are the same distance from the destination address. Good load-balancing algorithms use both line speed and reliability information. Load balancing increases the use of network segments, thus increasing effective network bandwidth.*

load sharing *The use of two or more paths to route packets to the same destination evenly among multiple routers to balance the work and improve network performance.*

local access rate *The clock speed (port speed) of the connection (local loop) to the Frame Relay cloud. It is the rate at which data travels into or out of the network.*

local-area network *See LAN.*

local loop *Cabling (usually copper wiring) that extends from the demarc into the WAN service provider's central office.*

Local Management Interface *See LMI.*

local traffic filtering *A process by which a bridge filters out (drops) frames whose source and destination MAC addresses are located on the same interface on the bridge, thus preventing unnecessary traffic from being forwarded across the bridge. Defined in the IEEE 802.1 standard.*

logical link control *See LLC.*

loop *A route where packets never reach their destination but simply cycle repeatedly through a constant series of network nodes.*

loopback test   *A test in which signals are sent and then directed back toward their source from some point along the communications path. Loopback tests are often used to test network interface usability.*

LSA (link-state advertisement)   *A broadcast packet used by link-state protocols that contains information about neighbors and path costs. LSAs are used by the receiving routers to maintain their routing tables. Sometimes called link-state packet (LSP).*

M

MAC (Media Access Control)   *The part of the data link layer that includes the 6-byte(48-bit) address of the source and destination, and the method of getting permission to transmit. See also data link layer and LLC.*

MAC (Media Access Control) address   *A standardized data link-layer address that is required for every port or device that connects to a LAN. Other devices in the network use these addresses to locate specific ports in the network and to create and update routing tables and data structures. MAC addresses are each 6 bytes long, and they are controlled by the IEEE. Also known as a hardware address, a MAC-layer address, or a physical address. Compare with network address.*

MAC address learning   *A service that characterizes a learning switch in which the source MAC address of each received packet is stored so that future packets destined for that address can be forwarded only to the switch interface on which that address is located. Packets destined for unrecognized broadcast or multicast addresses are forwarded out every switch interface except the originating one. This scheme helps minimize traffic on the attached LANs. MAC address learning is defined in the IEEE 802.1 standard.*

MAC-layer address   *See MAC address.*

MAN (metropolitan-area network)   *A network that spans a metropolitan area. Generally, a MAN spans a larger geographic area than a LAN, but a smaller geographic area than a WAN. Compare with LAN and WAN.*

Management Information Base   *See MIB.*

mask   *See address mask and subnet mask.*

MAU (media attachment unit) *A device used in Ethernet and IEEE 802.3 networks that provides the interface between the AUI port of a station and the common medium of the Ethernet. The MAU, which can be built into a station or can be a separate device, performs physical-layer functions including the conversion of digital data from the Ethernet interface, collision detection, and injection of bits onto the network. Sometimes referred to as a media access unit, also abbreviated MAU, or as a transceiver.*

maximum rate *The maximum total data throughput allowed on a given virtual circuit, equal to the sum of the insured and uninsured traffic from the traffic source. The uninsured data might be dropped if the network becomes congested. The maximum rate, which cannot exceed the media rate, represents the highest data throughput the virtual circuit will ever deliver, measured in bits or cells per second. Compare with excess rate and insured rate.*

Mb (megabit) *Approximately 1,000,000 bits.*

MB (megabyte) *Approximately 1,000,000 bytes.*

Mbps (megabits per second) *A rate of transfer speed.*

MDF (main distribution facility) *The primary communications room for a building. The central point of a star networking topology where patch panels, hub, and router are located.*

media *Plural of medium. The various physical environments through which transmission signals pass. Common network media include twisted-pair, coaxial, and fiber-optic cable, and the atmosphere (through which microwave, laser, and infrared transmission occurs). Sometimes called physical media.*

Media Access Control *See MAC.*

media access unit *See MAU.*

media attachment unit *See MAU.*

megabit *See Mb.*

megabits per second *See Mbps.*

megabyte *See MB.*

memory buffer *The area of memory where the switch stores the destination and transmission data.*

mesh *A network topology in which devices are organized in a manageable, segmented manner with many, often redundant, interconnections strategically placed between network nodes. See also full mesh and partial mesh.*

message *An application-layer logical grouping of information, often composed of a number of lower-layer logical groupings such as packets. The terms datagram, frame, packet, and segment are also used to describe logical information groupings at various layers of the OSI reference model and in various technology circles.*

metric *A standard of measurement (for example, path length) that is used by routing protocols to determine the optimal path to a destination.*

MIB (Management Information Base) *A database of network management information that is used and maintained by a network management protocol such as SNMP. The value of a MIB object can be changed or retrieved by using SNMP commands, usually through a GUI network management system. MIB objects are organized in a tree structure that includes public (standard) and private (proprietary) branches.*

microsegmentation *The division of a network into smaller segments, usually with the intention of increasing aggregate bandwidth to network devices.*

modem (modulator-demodulator) *A device that converts digital and analog signals. At the source, a modem converts digital signals to a form suitable for transmission over analog communication facilities. At the destination, the analog signals are returned to their digital form. Modems allow data to be transmitted over voice-grade telephone lines.*

MSAU (multistation access unit) *A wiring concentrator to which all end stations in a Token Ring network connect. The MSAU provides an interface between these devices and the Token Ring interface of a router. Sometimes abbreviated MAU.*

MTU (maximum transmission unit) *Maximum packet size, in bytes, that a particular interface can handle.*

multicast *Single packets copied by a network and sent out to a set of network addresses. These addresses are specified in the destination address field. Compare with broadcast and unicast.*

multicast address *A single address that refers to multiple network devices. Synonymous with group address. Compare with broadcast address and unicast address. See also multicast.*

multimode fiber *Optical fiber supporting propagation of multiple frequencies of light.*

multiplexing *A scheme that allows multiple logical signals to be transmitted simultaneously across a single physical channel. Compare with demultiplexing.*

multiprotocol routing *Routing in which a router delivers packets from several routed protocols, such as TCP/IP and IPX, over the same data links.*

multistation access unit *See MSAU.*

multivendor network *A network using equipment from more than one vendor. Multivendor networks pose many more compatibility problems than single-vendor networks. Compare with single-vendor network.*

N

NAK (negative acknowledgment) *A response sent from a receiving device to a sending device indicating that the information received contained errors. Compare with acknowledgment.*

name resolution *Generally, the process of associating a name with a network address.*

name server *A server connected to a network that resolves network names into network addresses.*

NAT (network address translation) *A mechanism for reducing the need for globally unique IP addresses. NAT allows an organization with addresses that are not globally unique to connect to the Internet by translating those addresses into globally routable address space. Also known as network address translator.*

NAUN (nearest active upstream neighbor) *In Token Ring or IEEE 802.5 networks, the closest upstream network device from any given device that is still active.*

NCP (Network Control Program) *A program that routes and controls the flow of data between a communications controller and other network resources.*

neighboring routers *In OSPF, two routers that have interfaces to a common network. On multiaccess networks, neighbors are dynamically discovered by the OSPF Hello protocol.*

NetBEUI (NetBIOS Extended User Interface) *An enhanced version of the NetBIOS protocol used by network operating systems such as LAN Manager, LAN Server, Windows for Workgroups, and Windows NT. NetBEUI formalizes the transport frame and adds additional functions. NetBEUI implements the OSI LLC2 protocol.*

NetBIOS (Network Basic Input/Output System) *An application programming interface used by applications on an IBM LAN to request services from lower-level network processes. These services might include session establishment and termination, and information transfer.*

NetWare *A popular distributed NOS developed by Novell. Provides transparent remote file access and numerous other distributed network services.*

NetWare Link Services Protocol *See NLSP.*

NetWare Loadable Module *See NLM.*

network *A collection of computers, printers, routers, switches, and other devices that are able to communicate with each other over some transmission medium.*

network address *A network-layer address referring to a logical, rather than a physical, network device. Also called a protocol address.*

network address translation *See NAT.*

network administrator *A person responsible for the operation, maintenance, and management of a network.*

network analyzer *A hardware or software device offering various network troubleshooting features, including protocol-specific packet decodes, specific preprogrammed troubleshooting tests, packet filtering, and packet transmission.*

Network Basic Input/Output System *See NetBIOS.*

network byte order *An Internet-standard ordering of the bytes corresponding to numeric values.*

Network Control Program *See NCP.*

Network File System *See NFS.*

network interface *The boundary between a carrier network and a privately owned installation.*

network interface card *See NIC.*

network layer *Layer 3 of the OSI reference model. This layer provides connectivity and path selection between two end systems. The network layer is the layer at which routing occurs. Corresponds roughly with the path control layer of the SNA model. See also OSI reference model.*

network management *Using systems or actions to maintain, characterize, or troubleshoot a network.*

network management system *See NMS.*

network number *The part of an IP address that specifies the network to which the host belongs.*

network operating system *See NOS.*

networking *The interconnection of workstations, peripherals such as printers, hard drives, scanners, CD-ROMs, and other devices.*

next-hop address *The IP address that is computed by the IP routing protocol and software.*

NFS (Network File System) *As commonly used, a distributed file system protocol suite developed by Sun Microsystems that allows remote file access across a network. In actuality, NFS is simply one protocol in the suite. NFS protocols include RPC and XDR. These protocols are part of a larger architecture that Sun refers to as ONC.*

NIC (Network Information Center) *An organization whose functions have been assumed by InterNIC. See InterNIC.*

NIC (network interface card) *A board that provides network communication capabilities to and from a computer system. Also called an adapter.*

NLM (NetWare Loadable Module) *An individual program that can be loaded into memory and function as part of the NetWare NOS.*

NLSP (NetWare Link Services Protocol) *A link-state routing protocol based on IS-IS. The Cisco implementation of NLSP also includes MIB variables and tools to redistribute routing and SAP information between NLSP and other IPX routing protocols.*

NMS (network management system) *A system responsible for managing at least part of a network. An NMS is generally a reasonably powerful and well-equipped computer such as an engineering workstation. NMSs communicate with agents to help keep track of network statistics and resources.*

node *An endpoint of a network connection or a junction common to two or more lines in a network. Nodes can be processors, controllers, or workstations. Nodes, which vary in routing and other functional capabilities, can be interconnected by links, and serve as control points in the network. Node is sometimes used generically to refer to any entity that can access a network, and is frequently used interchangeably with device.*

nonextended network *An AppleTalk Phase 2 network that supports addressing of up to 253 nodes and only 1 zone.*

nonseed router *In AppleTalk, a router that must first obtain, and then verify, its configuration with a seed router before it can begin operation. See also seed router.*

nonstub area *A resource-intensive OSPF area that carries a default route, static routes, intra-area routes, interarea routes, and external routes. Non-stub areas are the only OSPF areas that can have virtual links configured across them, and are the only areas that can contain an ASBR. Compare with stub area.*

NOS (network operating system) *The operating system used to run a network such Novell NetWare and Windows NT.*

Novell IPX *See IPX.*

NT1 (network termination type 1) *A device that connects four-wire ISDN subscriber wiring to the conventional two-wire local loop facility.*

NT2 (network termination type 2) *A device that directs traffic to and from different subscriber devices and the NT1. The NT2 is an intelligent device that performs switching and concentrating.*

NTP (Network Time Protocol) *A protocol built on top of TCP that assures accurate local time-keeping with reference to radio and atomic clocks located on the Internet. This protocol is capable of synchronizing distributed clocks within milliseconds over long time periods.*

NVRAM (nonvolatile RAM) *RAM that retains its contents when a unit is powered off.*

O

octet *8 bits. In networking, the term octet is often used (rather than byte) because some machine architectures employ bytes that are not 8 bits long.*

ODI (Open Data-Link Interface) *A Novell specification providing a standardized interface for network interface cards (NICs) that allows multiple protocols to use a single NIC.*

Open Shortest Path First *See OSPF.*

Open System Interconnection *See OSI.*

Open System Interconnection reference model *See OSI reference model.*

OSI (Open System Interconnection) *An international standardization program created by ISO and ITU-T to develop standards for data networking that facilitate multivendor equipment interoperability.*

OSI presentation address *An address used to locate an OSI application entity. It consists of an OSI network address and up to three selectors, one each for use by the transport, session, and presentation entities.*

OSI reference model (Open System Interconnection reference model) *A network architectural model developed by ISO and ITU-T. The model consists of seven layers, each of which specifies particular network functions such as addressing, flow control, error control, encapsulation, and reliable message transfer. The lowest layer (the physical layer) is closest to the media technology. The lower two layers are implemented in hardware and software, and the upper five layers are implemented only in software. The highest layer (the application layer) is closest to the user. The OSI reference model is used universally as a method for teaching and understanding network functionality. Similar in some respects to SNA. See application layer, data link layer, network layer, physical layer, presentation layer, session layer, and transport layer.*

OSPF (Open Shortest Path First) *A link-state, hierarchical routing protocol proposed as a successor to RIP in the Internet community. OSPF features include least-cost routing, multipath routing, and load balancing.*

OUI (organizational unique identifier) *3 octets assigned by the IEEE in a block of 48-bit LAN addresses.*

P

packet *A logical grouping of information that includes a header containing control information and (usually) user data. Packets are most often used to refer to network-layer units of data. The terms datagram, frame, message, and segment are also used to describe logical information groupings at various layers of the OSI reference model and in various technology circles.*

packet internet groper *See* **ping**.

packet switching *A networking method in which nodes share bandwidth with each other by sending packets.*

PAP (Password Authentication Protocol) *An authentication protocol that allows PPP peers to authenticate one another. The remote router attempting to connect to the local router is required to send an authentication request. Unlike CHAP, PAP passes the password and host name or username in cleartext (that is, unencrypted). PAP does not itself prevent unauthorized access, but it identifies the remote end; the router or access server then determines whether that user is allowed access. PAP is supported only on PPP lines. Compare with CHAP.*

parallel transmission *A method of data transmission in which the bits of a data character are transmitted simultaneously over a number of channels. Compare with serial transmission.*

partially meshed topology *A topology in which not every device on the Frame Relay cloud has a PVC to every other device.*

Password Authentication Protocol *See PAP.*

patch panel *An assembly of pin locations and ports that can be mounted on a rack or wall bracket in the wiring closet. Patch panels act like switchboards that connect workstations' cables to each other and to the outside.*

path control layer *Layer 3 in the SNA architectural model. This layer performs sequencing services related to proper data reassembly. The path control layer is also responsible for routing. Corresponds roughly with the network layer of the OSI reference model. See also data flow control layer, data link control layer, physical control layer, presentation services layer, transaction services layer, and transmission control layer.*

path determination *The decision of which path traffic should take through the network cloud. Path determination occurs at the network layer of the OSI reference model.*

payload *A portion of a cell, frame, or packet that contains upper-layer information (data).*

PBX (private branch exchange) *A digital or an analog telephone switchboard located on the subscriber premises and used to connect private and public telephone networks.*

PDN (public data network) *A network operated either by a government (as in Europe) or by a private concern to provide computer communications to the public, usually for a fee. PDNs enable small organizations to create a WAN without all the equipment costs of long-distance circuits.*

PDU (protocol data unit) *The OSI term for a packet.*

peer-to-peer computing *Peer-to-peer computing calls for each network device to run both client and server portions of an application. Also describes communication between implementations of the same OSI reference model layer in two different network devices. Compare with client/server computing.*

permanent virtual circuit *See PVC.*

PHY *1. physical sublayer. One of two sublayers of the FDDI physical layer. 2. physical layer. In ATM, the physical layer provides for the transmission of cells over a physical medium that connects two ATM devices. The PHY is composed of two sublayers: PMD and TC.*

physical address *See MAC address.*

physical control layer *Layer 1 in the SNA architectural model. This layer is responsible for the physical specifications for the physical links between end systems. Corresponds to the physical layer of the OSI reference model. See also data flow control layer, data link control layer, path control layer, presentation services layer, transaction services layer, and transmission control layer.*

physical layer *Layer 1 of the OSI reference model. This layer defines the electrical, mechanical, procedural, and functional specifications for activating, maintaining, and deactivating the physical link between end systems. Corresponds with the physical control layer in the SNA model. See also OSI reference model.*

ping (packet internet groper) *An ICMP echo message and its reply. Often used in IP networks to test the reachability of a network device.*

PLP (packet level protocol) *A network-layer protocol in the X.25 protocol stack. Sometimes called X.25 Level 3 and X.25 Protocol. See also X.25.*

point-to-multipoint connection *One of two fundamental connection types. In ATM, a point-to-multipoint connection is a unidirectional connection in which a single source end system (known as a root node) connects to multiple destination end systems (known as leaves). Compare with point-to-point connection.*

point-to-point connection *One of two fundamental connection types. In ATM, a point-to-point connection can be a unidirectional or bidirectional connection between two ATM end systems. Compare with point-to-multipoint connection.*

point-to-point link *A link that provides a single, preestablished WAN communications path from the customer premises through a carrier network, such as a telephone company, to a remote network. Also called a dedicated link or a leased line.*

Point-to-Point Protocol *See PPP.*

poison reverse update *An IGRP feature intended to defeat larger routing loops. Poison reverse updates explicitly indicate that a network or subnet is unreachable, rather than imply that a network is unreachable by not including it in updates.*

POP (point of presence) *The point of interconnection between the communication facilities provided by the telephone company and the building's main distribution facility.*

port *1. An interface on an internetworking device (such as a router). 2. A female plug on a patch panel that accepts the same size plug as an RJ-45 jack. Patch cords are used in these ports to cross connect computers wired to the patch panel. It is this cross-connection that allows the LAN to function. 3. In IP terminology, an upper-layer process that receives information from lower layers. Ports are numbered, and many are associated with a specific process. For example, SMTP is associated with port 25. A port number of this type is called a well-known address. 4. To rewrite software or microcode so that it will run on a different hardware platform or in a different software environment than that for which it was originally designed.*

port-centric VLAN *A VLAN in which all the nodes in the same VLAN are attached to the same switch port.*

POST (power-on self-test) *A set of hardware diagnostics that runs on a hardware device when that device is powered up.*

PPP (Point-to-Point Protocol) *A successor to SLIP, a protocol that provides router-to-router and host-to-network connections over synchronous and asynchronous circuits.*

presentation layer *Layer 6 of the OSI reference model. This layer provides data representation and code formatting, along with the negotiation of data transfer syntax. It ensures that the data that arrives from the network can be used by the application, and it ensures that information sent by the application can be transmitted on the network. See also OSI reference model.*

presentation services layer *Layer 6 of the SNA architectural model. This layer provides network resource management, session presentation services, and some application management. Corresponds roughly with the presentation layer of the OSI reference model.*

PRI (Primary Rate Interface) *An ISDN interface to primary rate access. Primary rate access consists of a single 64-kbps D channel plus 23 (T1) or 30 (E1) B channels for voice or data. Compare with BRI.*

priority queuing *A routing feature in which frames in an interface output queue are prioritized based on various characteristics such as protocol, packet size, and interface type.*

PROM (programmable read-only memory) ROM *that can be programmed using special equipment.* PROMs *can be programmed only once. Compare with* EPROM.

propagation delay *The time required for data to travel over a network, from its source to its ultimate destination. Also called latency.*

protocol *A formal description of a set of rules and conventions that govern how devices on a network exchange information.*

protocol address *See network address.*

protocol analyzer *See network analyzer.*

protocol stack *A set of related communications protocols that operate together and, as a group, address communication at some or all of the seven layers of the OSI reference model. Not every protocol stack covers each layer of the model, and often a single protocol in the stack will address a number of layers at once. TCP/IP is a typical protocol stack.*

proxy *An entity that, in the interest of efficiency, essentially stands in for another entity.*

proxy Address Resolution Protocol *See proxy ARP.*

proxy ARP (proxy Address Resolution Protocol) *A variation of the ARP protocol in which an intermediate device (for example, a router) sends an ARP response on behalf of an end node to the requesting host. Proxy ARP can lessen bandwidth use on slow-speed WAN links.*

PTT (post, telephone, and telegraph) *A government agency that provides telephone services. PTTs exist in most areas outside North America and provide both local and long-distance telephone services.*

punch tool *A spring-loaded tool used for cutting and connecting wire in a jack or on a patch panel.*

PVC (permanent virtual circuit) *A virtual circuit that is permanently established. PVCs save bandwidth associated with circuit establishment and tear-down in situations where certain virtual circuits must exist all the time. Compare with SVC.*

Q

Q.931 *A protocol that recommends a network layer between the terminal endpoint and the local ISDN switch. Q.931 does not impose an end-to-end recommendation. The various ISDN providers and switch types can and do use various implementations of Q.931.*

QoS (quality of service) *A measure of performance for a transmission system that reflects its transmission quality and service availability.*

queue *1. Generally, an ordered list of elements waiting to be processed. 2. In routing, a backlog of packets waiting to be forwarded over a router interface.*

queuing *A process in which ACLs can designate certain packets to be processed by a router before other traffic, on the basis of a protocol.*

queuing delay *The amount of time that data must wait before it can be transmitted onto a statistically multiplexed physical circuit.*

R

RAM (random-access memory) *Volatile memory that can be read and written by a microprocessor.*

random-access memory *See RAM.*

RARP (Reverse Address Resolution Protocol) *A protocol in the TCP/IP stack that provides a method for finding IP addresses based on MAC addresses. Compare with ARP.*

RBOC (regional Bell operating company) *A local or regional telephone company that owns and operates telephone lines and switches in one of seven U.S. regions. The RBOCs were created by the divestiture of AT&T.*

reassembly *The putting back together of an IP datagram at the destination after it has been fragmented either at the source or at an intermediate node.*

redirect *Part of the ICMP and ES-IS protocols that allows a router to tell a host that using another router would be more effective.*

redundancy *1. In internetworking, the duplication of devices, services, or connections so that, in the event of a failure, the redundant devices, services, or* *connections can perform the work of those that failed. 2. In telephony, the portion of the total information contained in a message that can be eliminated without loss of essential information or meaning.*

reference point   *A specification that defines the connection between specific devices, depending on their function in the end-to-end connection.*

Regional Bell operating company   *See RBOC.*

reliability   *The ratio of expected to received keepalives from a link. If the ratio is high, the line is reliable. Used as a routing metric.*

repeater   *A device that regenerates and propagates electrical signals between two network segments.*

Request for Comment   *See RFC.*

Reverse Address Resolution Protocol   *See RARP.*

RFC (Request for Comment)   *A document series used as the primary means for communicating information about the Internet. Some RFCs are designated by the IAB as Internet standards. Most RFCs document protocol specifications such as Telnet and FTP, but some are humorous or historical. RFCs are available online from numerous sources.*

ring   *A connection of two or more stations in a logically circular topology. Information is passed sequentially between active stations. Token Ring, FDDI, and CDDI are based on this topology.*

ring topology   *A network topology that consists of a series of repeaters connected to one another by unidirectional transmission links to form a single closed loop. Each station on the network connects to the network at a repeater. Although logically rings, ring topologies are most often organized in a closed-loop star. Compare with bus topology, star topology, and tree topology.*

RIP (Routing Information Protocol)   *A protocol supplied with UNIX BSD systems. The most common Interior Gateway Protocol (IGP) in the Internet. RIP uses hop count as a routing metric.*

RMON (remote monitoring)   *A MIB agent specification described in RFC 1271 that defines functions for the remote monitoring of networked devices.*

The RMON specification provides numerous monitoring, problem detection, and reporting capabilities.

ROM (read-only memory) *Nonvolatile memory that can be read, but not written, by the microprocessor.*

routed protocol *A protocol that can be routed by a router. A router must be able to interpret the logical internetwork as specified by that routed protocol. Examples of routed protocols include AppleTalk, DECnet, and IP. Compare with routing protocol.*

route map *A method of controlling the redistribution of routes between routing domains.*

route summarization *The consolidation of advertised network numbers in OSPF and IS-IS. In OSPF, this causes a single summary route to be advertised to other areas by an area border router.*

router *A network-layer device that uses one or more metrics to determine the optimal path along which network traffic should be forwarded. Routers forward packets from one network to another based on network layer information. Occasionally called a gateway (although this definition of gateway is becoming increasingly outdated).*

routing *The process of finding a path to a destination host. Routing is very complex in large networks because of the many potential intermediate destinations a packet might traverse before reaching its destination host.*

routing metric *A method by which a routing protocol determines that one route is better than another. This information is stored in routing tables. Metrics include bandwidth, communication cost, delay, hop count, load, MTU, path cost, and reliability. Sometimes referred to simply as a metric.*

routing protocol *A protocol that accomplishes routing through the implementation of a specific routing protocol. Examples of routing protocols include IGRP, OSPF, and RIP. Compare with routed protocol.*

routing table *A table stored in a router or some other internetworking device that keeps track of routes to particular network destinations and, in some cases, metrics associated with those routes.*

Routing Table Maintenance Protocol *See RTMP.*

routing update *A message sent from a router to indicate network reachability and associated cost information. Routing updates are typically sent at regular intervals and after a change in network topology. Compare with flash update.*

RPC (remote-procedure call) *The technological foundation of client/server computing. RPCs are procedure calls that are built or specified by clients and executed on servers, with the results returned over the network to the clients.*

RPF (Reverse Path Forwarding) *A multicasting technique in which a multicast datagram is forwarded out of all but the receiving interface if the receiving interface is the one used to forward unicast datagrams to the source of the multicast datagram.*

RSVP (Resource Reservation Protocol) *A protocol that supports the reservation of resources across an IP network. Applications running on IP end systems can use RSVP to indicate to other nodes the nature (bandwidth, jitter, maximum burst, and so forth) of the packet streams they want to receive. RSVP depends on IPv6. Also known as Resource Reservation Setup Protocol.*

RTMP (Routing Table Maintenance Protocol) *Apple Computer's proprietary routing protocol. RTMP establishes and maintains the routing information that is required to route datagrams from any source socket to any destination socket in an AppleTalk network. Using RTMP, routers dynamically maintain routing tables to reflect changes in topology. RTMP was derived from RIP.*

RTP (Routing Table Protocol) *A VINES routing protocol based on RIP. Distributes network topology information and aids VINES servers in finding neighboring clients, servers, and routers. Uses delay as a routing metric.*

RTP (Rapid Transport Protocol) *A protocol that provides pacing and error recovery for APPN data as it crosses the APPN network. With RTP, error recovery and flow control are done end-to-end rather than at every node. RTP prevents congestion rather than reacts to it.*

RTP (Real-Time Transport Protocol) *One of the IPv6 protocols. RTP is designed to provide end-to-end network transport functions for applications transmitting real-time data, such as audio, video, or simulation data, over multicast or unicast network services. RTP provides services such as payload type identification, sequence numbering, timestamping, and delivery monitoring to real-time applications.*

S

SAP (Service Advertising Protocol) *An IPX protocol that provides a means of informing network clients, via routers and servers, of available network resources and services.*

SAS (single attachment station) *A device attached only to the primary ring of an FDDI ring. Also known as a Class B station. Compare with DAS. See also FDDI.*

scalability *The ability of a network to grow, without any major changes to the overall design.*

SDLC (Synchronous Data Link Control) *An SNA data link-layer communications protocol. SDLC is a bit-oriented, full-duplex serial protocol that has spawned numerous similar protocols, including HDLC and LAPB.*

secondary station *In bit-synchronous data link-layer protocols such as HDLC, a station that responds to commands from a primary station. Sometimes referred to simply as a secondary.*

seed router *A router in an AppleTalk network that has the network number or cable range built in to its port descriptor. The seed router defines the network number or cable range for other routers in that network segment and responds to configuration queries from nonseed routers on its connected AppleTalk network, allowing those routers to confirm or modify their configurations accordingly. Each AppleTalk network must have at least one seed router.*

segment *1. A section of a network that is bounded by bridges, routers, or switches. 2. In a LAN using a bus topology, a continuous electrical circuit that is often connected to other such segments with repeaters. 3. In the TCP specification, a single transport-layer unit of information. The terms datagram, frame, message, and packet are also used to describe logical information groupings at various layers of the OSI reference model and in various technology circles.*

segmentation *The process of splitting a single collision domain into two or more collision domains in order to reduce collisions and network congestion.*

Sequenced Packet Exchange *See SPX.*

serial transmission *A method of data transmission in which the bits of a data character are transmitted sequentially over a single channel. Compare with parallel transmission.*

server *A node or software program that provides services to clients. See also client.*

service access point *A field defined by the IEEE 802.2 specification that is part of an address specification.*

Service Advertising Protocol *See SAP.*

session *1. A related set of connection-oriented communications transactions between two or more network devices. 2. In SNA, a logical connection enabling two network addressable units to communicate.*

session layer *Layer 5 of the OSI reference model. This layer establishes, maintains, and manages sessions between applications. See also OSI reference model.*

shortest-path routing *Routing that minimizes distance or path cost through application of an algorithm.*

signal reference ground *A reference point used by computing devices to measure and compare incoming digital signals to. The reference point used by computing devices to measure and compare incoming digital signals.*

signaling *In the ISDN context, the process of call setup used, such as call establishment, call termination, information, and miscellaneous messages, including setup, connect, release, user information, cancel, status, and disconnect.*

simplex *The capability for transmission in only one direction between a sending station and a receiving station. Broadcast television is an example of a simplex technology. Compare with full duplex and half duplex.*

single-vendor network *A network using equipment from only one vendor. Single-vendor networks rarely suffer compatibility problems. See also multivendor network.*

sliding window *A window whose size is negotiated dynamically during the TCP session.*

sliding window flow control *A method of flow control in which a receiver gives a transmitter permission to transmit data until a window is full. When the window is full, the transmitter must stop transmitting until the receiver advertises a larger window. TCP, other transport protocols, and several data link-layer protocols use this method of flow control.*

SLIP (Serial Line Internet Protocol) *A standard protocol for point-to-point serial connections using a variation of TCP/IP. The predecessor of PPP.*

small office/home office *See SOHO.*

SMI (Structure of Management Information) *A document (RFC 1155) specifying rules used to define managed objects in the MIB.*

SNA (Systems Network Architecture) *A large, complex, feature-rich network architecture developed in the 1970s by IBM. Similar in some respects to the OSI reference model, but with a number of differences. SNA is essentially composed of seven layers. See data flow control layer, data-link control layer, path control layer, physical control layer, presentation services layer, transaction services layer, and transmission control layer.*

SNMP (Simple Network Management Protocol) *A network management protocol used almost exclusively in TCP/IP networks. SNMP provides a means to monitor and control network devices, and to manage configurations, statistics collection, performance, and security.*

socket *1. A software structure operating as a communications endpoint within a network device (similar to a port). 2. An addressable entity within a node connected to an AppleTalk network; sockets are owned by software processes known as socket clients. AppleTalk sockets are divided into two groups: SASs, which are reserved for clients such as AppleTalk core protocols, and DASs, which are assigned dynamically by DDP upon request from clients in the node. An AppleTalk socket is similar in concept to a TCP/IP port.*

socket number *An 8-bit number that identifies a socket. A maximum of 254 socket numbers can be assigned in an AppleTalk node.*

SOHO (small office/home office) *A small office or home office consisting of a few users requiring a connection that provides faster, more reliable connectivity than an analog dialup connection.*

source address *An address of a network device that is sending data.*

spanning tree *A loop-free subset of a Layer 2 (switched) network topology.*

spanning-tree algorithm *An algorithm used by the Spanning-Tree Protocol to create a spanning tree. Sometimes abbreviated as STA.*

Spanning-Tree Protocol *A bridge protocol that utilizes the spanning-tree algorithm, enabling a learning bridge to dynamically work around loops in a network topology by creating a spanning tree. Bridges exchange BPDU messages with other bridges to detect loops, and then remove the loops by shutting down selected bridge interfaces. Refers to both the IEEE 802.1 Spanning-Tree Protocol standard and the earlier Digital Equipment Corporation Spanning-Tree Protocol on which it is based. The IEEE version supports bridge domains and allows the bridge to construct a loop-free topology across an extended LAN. The IEEE version is generally preferred over the Digital version.*

SPF (shortest path first) protocol *A routing protocol that iterates on length of path to determine a shortest-path spanning tree. Commonly used in link-state routing protocols. Sometimes called Dijkstra's algorithm.*

SPID (service profile identifier) *A number that some service providers use to define the services to which an ISDN device subscribes. The ISDN device uses the SPID when accessing the switch that initializes the connection to a service provider.*

split horizon *An IGRP feature designed to prevent routers from picking up erroneous routes. Split horizon prevents loops between adjacent routers and keeps down the size of update messages.*

split-horizon updates *A routing technique in which information about routes is prevented from exiting the router interface through which that information was received. Split-horizon updates are useful in preventing routing loops.*

spoofing *1. A scheme used by routers to cause a host to treat an interface as if it were up and supporting a session. The router spoofs replies to keepalive messages from the host in order to convince that host that the session still exists. Spoofing is useful in routing environments such as DDR, in which a circuit-switched link is taken down when there is no traffic to be sent across it in order to save toll charges. 2. The act of a packet illegally claiming to be from an address from which it was not actually sent. Spoofing is designed to foil network security mechanisms such as filters and ACLs.*

SPP (Sequenced Packet Protocol) *A protocol that provides reliable, connection-based, flow-controlled packet transmission on behalf of client processes. Part of the XNS protocol suite.*

SPX (Sequenced Packet Exchange) *A reliable, connection-oriented protocol that supplements the datagram service provided by network-layer protocols. Novell derived this commonly used NetWare transport protocol from the SPP of the XNS protocol suite.*

SQE (signal quality error) *In Ethernet, a transmission sent by a transceiver back to the controller to let the controller know whether the collision circuitry is functional. Also called heartbeat.*

SS7 (Signaling System 7) *A standard common channel signaling system developed by Bellcore, used in ISDN, that uses telephone control messages and signals between the transfer points along the way to the called destination.*

SSAP (source service access point) *The SAP of the network node designated in the Source field of a packet. Compare with DSAP. See also SAP.*

standard *A set of rules or procedures that are either widely used or officially specified.*

standard ACL (standard access control list) *An ACL that filters based on a source address and mask. Standard ACLs permit or deny the entire TCP/IP protocol suite. See also ACL, extended ACL.*

star topology *A LAN topology in which endpoints on a network are connected to a common central switch by point-to-point links. A ring topology that is organized as a star implements a unidirectional closed-loop star, instead of point-to-point links. Compare with bus topology, ring topology, and tree topology.*

static routing *Routing that is explicitly configured and entered into the routing table. Static routes take precedence over routes chosen by dynamic routing protocols. Compare with dynamic routing.*

static VLAN *A VLAN in which the ports on a switch are statically assigned. Compare with dynamic VLAN. See also LAN and VLAN.*

store-and-forward *A packet-switching technique in which frames are completely processed before being forwarded out the appropriate port. This processing includes calculating the CRC and checking the destination address. In* *addition, frames must be temporarily stored until network resources (such as an unused link) are available to forward the message.*

STP (shielded twisted-pair) *A two-pair wiring medium used in a variety of network implementations. STP cabling has a layer of shielded insulation to reduce EMI. Compare with UTP. See also twisted pair.*

stub area *An OSPF area that carries a default route, intra-area routes, and interarea routes, but does not carry external routes. Virtual links cannot be configured across a stub area, and they cannot contain an ASBR. Compare with nonstub area.*

stub network *A network that has only a single connection to a router.*

subinterface *One of a number of virtual interfaces on a single physical interface*

subnet *See subnetwork.*

subnet address *A portion of an IP address that is specified as the subnetwork by the subnet mask.*

subnet mask *A mask used to extract network and subnetwork information from the IP address.*

subnetwork *1. A network that is segmented into a series of smaller networks. 2. In IP networks, a network sharing a particular subnet address. Subnetworks are networks arbitrarily segmented by a network administrator in order to provide a multilevel, hierarchical routing structure while shielding the subnetwork from the addressing complexity of attached networks. Sometimes called a subnet. 3. In OSI networks, a collection of ESs and ISs under the control of a single administrative domain and using a single network access protocol.*

surge *Any voltage increase above 110% of the normal voltage carried by a power line.*

SVC (switched virtual circuit) *A virtual circuit that is dynamically established on demand and is torn down when transmission is complete. SVCs are used in situations in which data transmission is sporadic. Compare with PVC.*

switch *A network device that filters, forwards, and floods frames based on the destination address of each frame. The switch operates at the data link layer of the OSI reference model.*

switching *The process of taking an incoming frame from one interface and delivering it out through another interface.*

synchronous circuit *A signal that is transmitted with precise clocking. Such signals have the same frequency, with individual characters encapsulated in control bits (called start bits and stop bits) that designate the beginning and end of each character.*

Synchronous Data Link Control *See SDLC.*

T

T1 *A digital WAN carrier facility that transmits DS-1-formatted data at 1.544 Mbps through the telephone-switching network, using AMI or B8ZS coding. Compare with E1.*

T3 *A digital WAN carrier facility that transmits DS-3-formatted data at 44.736 Mbps through the telephone switching network. Compare with E3.*

TA (terminal adapter) *A device used to connect ISDN BRI connections to existing interfaces such as EIA/TIA-232. Essentially, an ISDN modem.*

TACACS (Terminal Access Controller Access Control System) *An authentication protocol, developed by the DDN community, that provides remote access authentication and related services, such as event logging. User passwords are administered in a central database rather than in individual routers, providing an easily scalable network security solution.*

TCP (Transmission Control Protocol) *A connection-oriented transport-layer protocol that provides reliable full-duplex data transmission. TCP is part of the TCP/IP protocol stack.*

TCP/IP (Transmission Control Protocol/Internet Protocol) *A common name for the suite of protocols developed by the U.S. DoD in the 1970s to support the construction of worldwide internetworks. TCP and IP are the two best-known protocols in the suite.*

TDM (time-division multiplexing) *A circuit-switching signal used to determine the call route, which is a dedicated path between the sender and the receiver.*

TE1 (terminal equipment type 1) *A device that is compatible with the ISDN network. A TE1 connects to a network termination of either Type 1 or Type 2.*

TE2 (terminal equipment type 2) *A device that is not compatible with ISDN and requires a terminal adapter.*

Telnet *A standard terminal emulation protocol in the TCP/IP protocol stack. Telnet is used for remote terminal connection, enabling users to log in to remote systems and use resources as if they were connected to a local system. Telnet is defined in RFC 854.*

TFTP (Trivial File Transfer Protocol) *A simplified version of FTP that allows files to be transferred from one computer to another over a network.*

throughput *The rate of information arriving at, and possibly passing through, a particular point in a network system.*

TIA (Telecommunications Industries Association) *An organization that develops standards relating to telecommunications technologies. Together, TIA and EIA have formalized standards, such as EIA/TIA-232, for the electrical characteristics of data transmission.*

tick *The delay on a data link using IBM PC clock ticks (approximately 55 milliseconds). One tick is a second.*

timeout *An event that occurs when one network device expects to hear from another network device within a specified period of time but does not. The resulting timeout usually results in a retransmission of information or the dissolving of the session between the two devices.*

Time To Live *See TTL.*

token *A frame that contains control information. Possession of the token allows a network device to transmit data onto the network.*

token bus *A LAN architecture using token passing access over a bus topology. This LAN architecture is the basis for the IEEE 802.4 LAN specification.*

token passing *An access method by which network devices access the physical medium in an orderly fashion based on possession of a small frame called a token. Compare with circuit switching and contention.*

Token Ring *A token-passing LAN developed and supported by IBM. Token Ring runs at 4 or 16 Mbps over a ring topology. Similar to IEEE 802.5.*

TokenTalk *Apple Computer's data-link product that allows an AppleTalk network to be connected by Token Ring cables.*

toll network *The collective switches and facilities (called trunks) inside the WAN provider's cloud.*

topology *A physical arrangement of network nodes and media within an enterprise networking structure.*

traceroute *A program available on many systems that traces the path a packet takes to a destination. It is mostly used to debug routing problems between hosts. There is also a* **traceroute** *protocol defined in RFC 1393.*

traffic management *Techniques for avoiding congestion and shaping and policing traffic. Allows links to operate at high levels of utilization by scaling back lower-priority, delay-tolerant traffic at the edge of the network when congestion begins to occur.*

trailer *Control information appended to data when encapsulating the data for network transmission. Compare with header.*

transaction services layer *Layer 7 in the SNA architectural model. Represents user application functions, such as spreadsheets, word processing, or electronic mail, by which users interact with the network. Corresponds roughly with the application layer of the OSI reference model. See also data flow control layer, data link control layer, path control layer, physical control layer, presentation services layer, and transmission control layer.*

transmission control layer *Layer 4 in the SNA architectural model. This layer is responsible for establishing, maintaining, and terminating SNA sessions, sequencing data messages, and controlling session level flow. Corresponds to the transport layer of the OSI reference model. See also data flow control layer, data link control layer, path control layer, physical control layer, presentation services layer, and transaction services layer.*

Transmission Control Protocol *See TCP.*

transport layer *Layer 4 of the OSI reference model. This layer segments and reassembles data into a data stream. The transport layer has the potential to guarantee a connection and offer reliable transport. See also OSI reference model.*

trap *A message sent by an SNMP agent to an NMS, a console, or a terminal to indicate the occurrence of a significant event, such as a specifically defined condition or a threshold that was reached.*

tree topology *A LAN topology similar to a bus topology, except that tree networks can contain branches with multiple nodes. Transmissions from a station propagate the length of the medium and are received by all other stations. Compare with bus topology, ring topology, and star topology.*

TTL (Time To Live) *A field in an IP header that indicates how long a packet is considered valid.*

tunneling *An architecture that is designed to provide the services necessary to implement any standard point-to-point encapsulation scheme.*

U

UDP (User Datagram Protocol) *A connectionless transport-layer protocol in the TCP/IP protocol stack. UDP is a simple protocol that exchanges datagrams without acknowledgments or guaranteed delivery, requiring that error processing and retransmission be handled by other protocols. UDP is defined in RFC 768.*

UNI (User-Network Interface) *A specification that defines an interoperability standard for the interface between products (a router or a switch) located in a private network and the switches located within the public carrier networks. Also used to describe similar connections in Frame Relay networks.*

unicast *A message sent to a single network destination.*

unicast address *An address specifying a single network device. Compare with broadcast address and multicast address.*

uniform resource locator *See URL.*

UPS (uninterruptable power supply) *A backup device designed to provide an uninterrupted power source in the event of a power failure. UPSs are commonly installed on file servers and wiring hubs.*

URL (uniform resource locator) *A standardized addressing scheme for accessing hypertext documents and other services using a browser.*

UTP (unshielded twisted-pair) *A four-pair wire medium used in a variety of networks. UTP does not require the fixed spacing between connections that is necessary with coaxial-type connections. There are five types of UTP cabling commonly used: Category 1 cabling, Category 2 cabling, Category 3 cabling, Category 4 cabling, and Category 5 cabling. Compare with STP.*

User Datagram Protocol *See UDP.*

User-Network Interface *See UNI.*

V

VCC (vertical cross-connect) *A connection that is used to interconnect the various IDFs to the central MDF.*

vertical cabling *Backbone cabling.*

vertical cross-connect *See VCC.*

VINES (Virtual Integrated Network Service) *A NOS developed and marketed by Banyan Systems.*

virtual circuit *A logical circuit created to ensure reliable communication between two network devices. A virtual circuit is defined by a VPI/VCI pair, and can be either permanent (a PVC) or switched (an SVC). Virtual circuits are used in Frame Relay and X.25. In ATM, a virtual circuit is called a virtual channel. Sometimes abbreviated VC.*

VLAN (virtual LAN) *A group of devices on a LAN that are configured (using management software) so that they can communicate as if they were attached to the same wire, when in fact they are located on a number of different LAN segments. Because VLANs are based on logical instead of physical connections, they are extremely flexible.*

W

WAN (wide-area network) *A data communications network that serves users across a broad geographic area and often uses transmission devices provided by common carriers. Frame Relay, SMDS, and X.25 are examples of WAN technologies. Compare with LAN and MAN.*

WAN link *A WAN communications channel consisting of a circuit or transmission path and all related equipment between a sender and a receiver.*

watchdog packet *A method used to ensure that a client is still connected to a NetWare server. If the server has not received a packet from a client for a certain period of time, it sends that client a series of watchdog packets. If the station fails to respond to a predefined number of watchdog packets, the server concludes that the station is no longer connected and clears the connection for that station.*

watchdog spoofing *A subset of spoofing that refers specifically to a router acting especially for a NetWare client by sending watchdog packets to a NetWare server to keep the session between client and server active. Useful when the client and server are separated by a DDR WAN link.*

watchdog timer *1. A hardware or software mechanism that is used to trigger an event or an escape from a process unless the timer is periodically reset. 2. In NetWare, a timer that indicates the maximum period of time that a server will wait for a client to respond to a watchdog packet. If the timer expires, the server sends another watchdog packet (up to a set maximum).*

wildcard mask *A 32-bit quantity used in conjunction with an IP address to determine which bits in an IP address should be ignored when comparing that address with another IP address. A wildcard mask is specified when setting up an ACL.*

window *The number of octets that the sender is willing to accept.*

window size *The number of messages that can be transmitted while awaiting an acknowledgment.*

workgroup server *A server that supports a specific set of users and offers services such as word processing and file sharing, which are services that only a few groups of people would need. Compare with enterprise server.*

X–Z

X.25 *An ITU-T standard that defines how connections between DTEs and DCEs are maintained for remote terminal access and computer communications in public data networks. Frame Relay has to some degree superseded X.25.*

XNS (Xerox Network Systems) *A protocol suite originally designed by PARC. Many PC networking companies, such as 3Com, Banyan, Novell, and UB Networks used or currently use a variation of XNS as their primary transport protocol.*

ZIP (Zone Information Protocol) *An AppleTalk session-layer protocol that maps network numbers to zone names. ZIP is used by NBP to determine which networks contain nodes that belong to a zone.*

zone *In AppleTalk, a logical group of network devices.*

zone multicast address *A data-link-dependent multicast address at which a node receives the NBP broadcasts directed to its zone.*

Numerics

Cisco Press

Staying Connected to Networkers

We want to hear from **you**! Help Cisco Press **stay connected** to the issues and challenges you face on a daily basis by registering your book and filling out our brief survey.

Complete and mail this form, or better yet, jump to **www.ciscopress.com** and do it online. Each complete entry will be eligible for our monthly drawing to **win a FREE book** from the Cisco Press Library.

Thank you for choosing Cisco Press to help you work the network.

Name _____

Address _____

City _____ State/Province _____

Country _____ Zip/Post code _____

E-mail address _____

May we contact you via e-mail for product updates and customer benefits?
❐ Yes   ❐ No

Where did you buy this product?
❐ Bookstore   ❐ Computer store   ❐ Electronics store
❐ Online retailer   ❐ Office supply store   ❐ Discount store
❐ Mail order   ❐ Class/Seminar
❐ Other _____

When did you buy this product? _____ Month _____ Year

What price did you pay for this product?
❐ Full retail price   ❐ Discounted price   ❐ Gift

How did you learn about this product?
❐ Friend   ❐ Store personnel   ❐ In-store ad
❐ Catalog   ❐ Postcard in the mail   ❐ Saw it on the shelf
❐ Magazine ad   ❐ Article or review   ❐ Used other products
❐ School   ❐ Professional Organization
❐ Other _____

What will this product be used for?
❐ Business use   ❐ Personal use   ❐ School/Education
❐ Other _____

How many years have you been employed in a computer-related industry?
❐ 2 years or less   ❐ 3-5 years   ❐ 5+ years

CISCO SYSTEMS

CISCO PRESS

www.ciscopress.com

Cisco Systems
CISCO PRESS

www.ciscopress.com

Which best describes your job function?
❏ Corporate Management ❏ Systems Engineering ❏ IS Management
❏ Network Design ❏ Network Support ❏ Webmaster
❏ Marketing/Sales ❏ Consultant ❏ Student
❏ Professor/Teacher

❏ Other _____

What is your formal education background?
❏ High school ❏ Vocational/Technical degree ❏ Some college
❏ College degree ❏ Masters degree ❏ Professional or Doctoral degree

Have you purchased a Cisco Press product before?
❏ Yes ❏ No

On what topics would you like to see more coverage?

_____

_____

Do you have any additional comments or suggestions?

_____

_____

Cisco Networking Academy Program: Second-Year Companion Guide
1-57870-169-4

Cisco Press
201 West 103rd Street
Indianapolis, IN 46290
www.ciscopress.com

Place
Stamp
Here

Cisco Press
Customer Registration
P.O. Box 189014
Battle Creek, MI 49018-9947